Rick Steves

PORTUGAL

CONTENTS

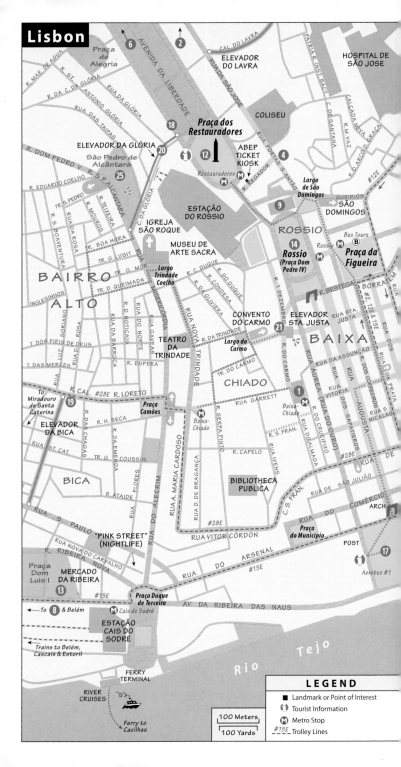

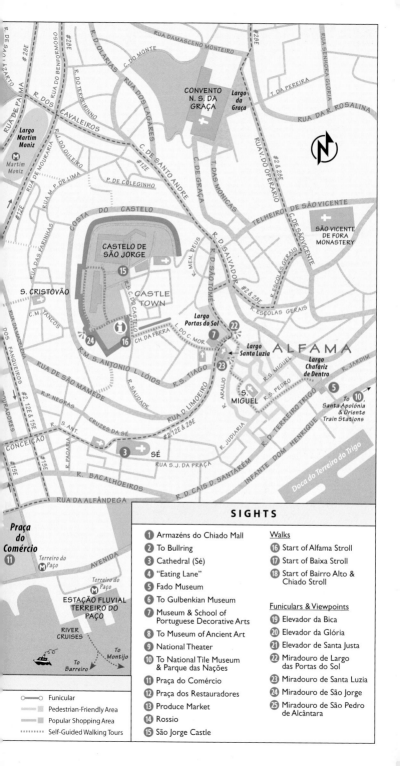

RUA DAMASCENO MONTEIRO

CONVENTO N. S. DA GRAÇA

Largo da Graça

RUA DA R. ROSALINA

Largo Martim Moniz

M Martim Moniz

CASTELO DE SÃO JORGE

S. CRISTOVÃO

CASTLE TOWN

Largo Portas do Sol

Largo Santa Luzia

ALFAMA

Largo Chafariz de Dentro

S. MIGUEL

To Santa Apolónia & Oriente Train Stations

SÉ

SÃO VICENTE DE FORA MONASTERY

Praça do Comércio

M Paço

Terreiro do Paço

Terreiro do Paço

ESTAÇÃO FLUVIAL TERREIRO DO PAÇO

RIVER CRUISES

To Montijo

To Barreiro

Doca do Terreiro do Trigo

SIGHTS

1. Armazéns do Chiado Mall
2. To Bullring
3. Cathedral (Sé)
4. "Eating Lane"
5. Fado Museum
6. To Gulbenkian Museum
7. Museum & School of Portuguese Decorative Arts
8. To Museum of Ancient Art
9. National Theater
10. To National Tile Museum & Parque das Nações
11. Praça do Comércio
12. Praça dos Restauradores
13. Produce Market
14. Rossio
15. São Jorge Castle

Walks

16. Start of Alfama Stroll
17. Start of Baixa Stroll
18. Start of Bairro Alto & Chiado Stroll

Funiculars & Viewpoints

19. Elevador da Bica
20. Elevador da Glória
21. Elevador de Santa Justa
22. Miradouro de Largo das Portas do Sol
23. Miradouro de Santa Luzia
24. Miradouro de São Jorge
25. Miradouro de São Pedro de Alcântara

○—○ Funicular

Pedestrian-Friendly Area

Popular Shopping Area

•••••••• Self-Guided Walking Tours

Lisbon at night

Market vendor

Futebol on Nazaré's beach

Terraced vineyards in the Douro Valley

Fado—songs of sadness and hope

Rick Steves.

PORTUGAL

Top Destinations in Portugal

PORTO

DOURO VALLEY

COIMBRA

Atlantic Ocean

NAZARÉ & NEARBY

SINTRA

LISBON

ÉVORA

THE ALGARVE

INTRODUCTION

Tucked into a far corner of the Continent, Portugal is Western Europe's least-touristed country. Its relative isolation preserves a traditional culture of widows in black and fishermen mending nets. Along with the old, you'll find the modern, especially in the culturally rich capital of Lisbon and in the resort towns that rival Spain's (but feel more authentic). If your idea of travel includes friendly locals (who speak a bit of English), exotic architecture, windswept castles, and fresh seafood with chilled wine on a beach at sunset... you've chosen the right destination.

In recent years, Portugal has experienced some economic success, thanks to its membership in the European Union. While Portugal is no longer a bargain basement for travelers, it's still a good budget option compared to the tourist-mobbed destinations of Northern Europe.

This book breaks Portugal into its top big-city, small-town, and rural destinations, giving you all the information and opinions necessary to wring the maximum value out of your limited time and money. Experiencing Portugal's culture, people, and natural wonders economically and hassle-free has been my goal for more than three decades of traveling, guiding tours, and travel writing. With this new edition, I pass on to you the lessons I've learned.

While including the predictable biggies, this book also mixes in a healthy dose of Back Door intimacy. You'll eat barnacles with green wine, recharge your solar cells in an Algarve fishing village, and wax nostalgic over bluesy fado singing. This book is selective. For example, while there are plenty of Algarve beach towns, I recommend only the top stops: Salema and Tavira.

The best is, of course, only my opinion. But after spending half my adult life exploring and researching Europe, I've developed a

Map Legend

↳	Viewpoint	✈	Airport	→→	One-way
↑	Entrance	Ⓣ	Taxi Stand		Pedestrian Zone
❶	Tourist Info	Ⓣ	Tram Stop	—·—·—	Railway
WC	Restroom	Ⓑ	Bus Stop	··········	Ferry/Boat Route
⛫	Castle	Ⓜ	Metro Stop	●—🚋—	Funicular
⛪	Church	Ⓟ	Parking	··········	Stairs
▪	Statue/Point of Interest	🚲	Bike Rental	· · · · · ·	Walk/Tour Route
⊠	Elevator		Park	- - - - - -	Trail

Use this legend to help you navigate many of the maps in this book.

sixth sense for what travelers enjoy. Just thinking about the places featured in this book makes me want to hang out in a fado bar.

ABOUT THIS BOOK

Rick Steves Portugal is a personal tour guide in your pocket. This book is organized by destinations. Each destination is a mini-vacation on its own, filled with exciting sights, strollable neighborhoods, affordable places to stay, and memorable places to eat. In the following chapters, you'll find these sections:

Planning Your Time suggests a schedule for how to best use your limited time.

Orientation includes specifics on public transportation, helpful hints, local tour options, easy-to-read maps, and tourist information.

Sights describes the top attractions and includes their cost and hours.

Self-Guided Walks take you through interesting neighborhoods, pointing out sights and fun stops.

Sleeping describes my favorite hotels, from good-value deals to cushy splurges.

Eating serves up a range of options, from inexpensive eateries to fancy restaurants.

Connections outlines your options for traveling to destinations by train, bus, or plane, plus route tips for drivers.

Portugal: Past and Present gives you a quick overview of Portugal, from its prehistoric beginnings to the issues it faces today.

Practicalities is a traveler's tool kit, with my best travel tips and advice about money, sightseeing, sleeping, eating, staying connected, and transportation (trains, buses, car rentals, driving, and flights). There's also a list of recommended books and films.

The **appendix** has nuts-and-bolts information, including use-

Key to This Book

Updates
This book is updated regularly—but things change. For the latest, visit www.ricksteves.com/update.

Abbreviations and Times
I use the following symbols and abbreviations in this book:
Sights are rated:

▲▲▲	**Don't miss**
▲▲	**Try hard to see**
▲	**Worthwhile if you can make it**
No rating	**Worth knowing about**

Tourist information offices are abbreviated as **TI,** and bathrooms are **WCs**. To categorize accommodations, I use a **Sleep Code** (described on page 357).

Like Portugal, this book uses the **24-hour clock** for schedules. It's the same through 12:00 noon, then keeps going: 13:00, 14:00, and so on. For anything over 12, subtract 12 and add p.m. (14:00 is 2:00 p.m.).

When giving **opening times,** I include both peak season and off-season hours if they differ. So, if a museum is listed as "May-Oct daily 9:00-16:00," it should be open from 9 a.m. until 4 p.m. from the first day of May until the last day of October (but expect exceptions).

For **transit** or **tour departures,** I first list the frequency, then the duration. So, a train connection listed as "2/hour, 1.5 hours" departs twice each hour, and the journey lasts an hour and a half.

ful phone numbers and websites, a festival list, a climate chart, a handy packing checklist, and Portuguese survival phrases.

Browse through this book, choose your favorite destinations, and link them up. Then have a great trip! Traveling like a temporary local, you'll get the absolute most of every mile, minute, and dollar. As you visit places I know and love, I'm happy that you'll be meeting some of my favorite Portuguese people.

Planning

This section will help you get started planning your trip—with advice on trip costs, when to go, and what you should know before you take off.

TRAVEL SMART
Your trip to Portugal is like a complex play—easier to follow and really appreciate on a second viewing. While no one does the same

Portugal's Best Two-Week Trip by Car

Day	Plan	Sleep in
1	Arrive in Lisbon	Lisbon
2	Lisbon	Lisbon
3	More time in Lisbon or side-trip to Sintra by train; pick up car and drive to Salema in evening	Salema
4	Salema	Salema
5	Salema, side-trip to Cape Sagres	Salema
6	To Tavira via Lagos	Tavira
7	To Évora	Évora
8	More time in Évora, then to Nazaré via Óbidos in the afternoon	Nazaré
9	Nazaré	Nazaré
10	Near Nazaré (Alcobaça, Batalha, and Fátima), continue to Coimbra	Coimbra
11	Coimbra	Coimbra
12	To Douro Valley	Douro Valley
13	Douro Valley, end in Porto (could drop off car)	Porto
14	Porto	Porto
15	Drive or take the train back to Lisbon; or drive north to Santiago, Spain	

Notes: Try to avoid being in Lisbon (or Porto) on a Monday, when many major sights are closed. If you're in Lisbon on a Monday, take a walking tour, a trolley ride, any of my self-guided neighborhood walks, or a side-trip to Sintra, where the major sights are open.

Lisbon is worth an extra day if you like big cities. But if you're a beach lover, leave Lisbon early and drive to Salema.

If, after touring Portugal, you're continuing to the Spanish destinations of Salamanca or Madrid, it's better to visit Porto and the Douro Valley before Coimbra.

By Train and Bus: While this itinerary is designed to be done by car, it can also be done by train and bus. If you're taking public transportation, stay three nights in Lisbon and catch a bus to Salema on the morning of the fourth day. Skip Tavira. From the

Algarve, take the bus to Évora (via Lagos) and spend a day and night, then take a bus to Nazaré (there's no direct service, so you have to go via Lisbon). See the sights near Nazaré by bus, using Nazaré as your home base. Take the bus to Coimbra. Catch the bus or train to Porto, and using Porto as a home base, see the Douro Valley on a combination boat/train tour (or, with extra time, spend the night).

trip twice to gain that advantage, reading this book in its entirety before your trip accomplishes much the same thing.

Design an itinerary that enables you to visit sights at the best possible times. Note holidays, festivals, specifics on sights, and days when sights are closed (all covered in this book). For example, many museums and sights close on Mondays. Hotels are most crowded on Fridays and Saturdays, especially in resort towns. To get between destinations smoothly, read the tips in Practicalities on taking trains and buses, and renting a car and driving. A smart trip is a puzzle—a fun, doable, and worthwhile challenge.

When you're plotting your itinerary, strive for a mix of intense and relaxed stretches. To maximize rootedness, minimize one-night stands. It's worth taking a long drive after dinner (or a train ride with a dinner picnic) to get settled in a town for two nights. Every trip—and every traveler—needs slack time (for laundry, picnics, people-watching, and so on). Pace yourself. Assume you will return.

Reread this book as you travel, and visit local tourist information offices (abbreviated as TI in this book). Upon arrival in a new town, lay the groundwork for a smooth departure; get the schedule for the train or bus that you'll take when you depart. Drivers can figure out the best route to their next destination.

Update your plans as you travel. You can carry a small mobile device (phone, tablet, laptop) to find out tourist information, learn the latest on sights (special events, tour schedules, etc.), book tickets and tours, make reservations, reconfirm hotels, research transportation connections, and keep in touch with your loved ones. If you don't want to bring a pricey device, you can use guest computers at hotels and make phone calls from landlines.

Enjoy the hospitality of the Portuguese people. Connect with the culture. Set up your own quest for the best cod dish, cloister, fado bar, or custard tart. Slow down and be open to unexpected experiences. Ask questions—most locals are eager to point you toward their idea of the right direction. Keep a notepad in your pocket for noting directions, organizing your thoughts, and confirming prices. Wear your money belt, learn the currency, and figure out how to estimate prices in dollars. Those who expect to travel smart, do.

TRIP COSTS

Five components make up your trip costs: airfare, surface transportation, room and board, sightseeing and entertainment, and shopping and miscellany.

Airfare: A basic round-trip flight from the US to Lisbon can cost, on average, about $1,000-2,000 total, depending on where you fly from and when (cheaper in winter). Smaller budget airlines

Portugal at a Glance

▲▲▲**Lisbon** Lively, hilly port and capital, with historic trolleys, grand squares, fado clubs, fine art, and a salty sailors' quarter topped by a castle.

▲▲**Sintra** A striking town, within easy day-tripping distance from Lisbon, known for its fairy-tale castles, verdant hills, and beautiful gardens.

▲▲▲**The Algarve** Portugal's sunny southern coast, strung with the simple fishing village of Salema, the historic "end of the road" of Cape Sagres, the beach-party town of Lagos, and the laid-back resort of Tavira.

▲▲**Évora** Whitewashed little college town with big Roman, Moorish, and Portuguese history encircled by its medieval wall.

▲▲**Nazaré and Nearby** Traditional fishing village turned small-town resort, and jumping-off point for day trips to the monastery at Batalha, the pilgrimage site of Fátima, Portugal's largest church in Alcobaça, and the photogenic walled town of Óbidos.

▲▲**Coimbra** Portugal's Oxford, home to an Arab-influenced old town and bustling with students from its prestigious university.

▲▲**Porto** Gritty, urban second city with picturesque riverfront, charming old town, and museums sporting modern architecture.

▲**Douro Valley** Terraced farming valley and birthplace of port wine, with home bases in modern Peso da Régua and workaday Pinhão.

provide bargain service from several European capitals to Lisbon (see "Flights" on page 388). Consider saving time and money in Europe by flying into one city and out of another; for instance, into Lisbon and out of Barcelona. Overall, Kayak.com is the best place to start searching for flights on a combination of mainstream and budget carriers.

Surface Transportation: For a two-week whirlwind trip of all of my recommended destinations by public transportation, allow $300 per person. If you'll be renting a car, allow $200 per week, not including tolls, gas, and supplemental insurance. If you'll be keeping the car for three weeks or more, look into leasing, which can save you money on insurance and taxes for trips of this length. Car rental and leases are cheapest if arranged from the US. Train passes normally must be purchased outside Europe but are a waste of money for a Portugal-only trip. It's more economical to buy bus and train tickets as you go. Buses are often more flexible and affordable than trains in Portugal. If combining Portugal with other European destinations, don't hesitate to consider flying, as budget airlines can be less expensive than taking the train (check www.skyscanner.com for intra-European flights). For more on public transportation and car rental, see "Transportation" in Practicalities.

Room and Board: You can thrive in Portugal on $100 a day per person for room and board (less in villages). This allows $15 for lunch, $5 for snacks, $30 for dinner, and $50 for lodging (based on two people splitting the cost of a $100 double room that includes breakfast). Students and tightwads can enjoy Portugal for as little as $60 a day ($30 for a bed, $30 for meals).

Sightseeing and Entertainment: You'll pay about $6-10 per major sight (museums, churches), $4-5 for minor ones (climbing towers), and $30-40 for splurge experiences (fado concerts, bullfights). An overall average of $15 a day works for most people. Don't skimp here. After all, this category is the driving force behind your trip—you came to sightsee, enjoy, and experience Portugal.

Shopping and Miscellany: Figure roughly $1-2 per postcard (including postage), coffee, beer, and ice-cream cone. Shopping can vary in cost from nearly nothing to a small fortune. Good budget travelers find that this category has little to do with assembling a trip full of lifelong and wonderful memories.

SIGHTSEEING PRIORITIES

So much to see, so little time. How to choose? Depending on the length of your trip, and taking geographic proximity into account, here are my recommended priorities.

3 days:	Lisbon, Sintra
6 days, add:	The Algarve (Salema and Tavira)
9 days, add:	Évora, Nazaré
11 days, add:	Sights near Nazaré, Coimbra
14 days, add:	Porto, Douro Valley

WHEN TO GO

In peak season, May through September, sightseeing attractions are wide open. While it's not nearly as hot in Portugal as it is in Spain (except in the Alentejo region), an air-conditioned room is worth the splurge in summer. Book ahead if your stay coincides with a holiday or festival (see the list in the appendix).

Spring and fall offer the best combination of good weather,

light crowds, long days, and plenty of tourist and cultural activities. In the off-season, roughly October through April, expect shorter hours, more lunchtime breaks at sights, and fewer activities. Confirm your sightseeing plans locally, especially when traveling off-season.

For weather specifics, see the climate chart in the appendix.

KNOW BEFORE YOU GO

Your trip is more likely to go smoothly if you plan ahead. Check this list of things to arrange while you're still at home.

You need a **passport**—but no visa or shots—to travel in Portugal. You may be denied entry into certain European countries if your passport is due to expire within three months of your ticketed date of return. Get it renewed if you'll be cutting it close. It can take up to six weeks to get or renew a passport (for more on passports, see www.travel.state.gov). Pack a photocopy of your passport in your luggage in case the original is lost or stolen.

Book rooms well in advance if you'll be traveling during peak season (May-Sept) or any major holidays (see page 396).

Call your **debit and credit card companies** to let them know the countries you'll be visiting, to ask about fees, request your PIN code (it will be mailed to you), and more. See page 350 for details.

Do your homework if you want to buy **travel insurance.** Compare the cost of the insurance to the likelihood of your using it and your potential loss if something goes wrong. Also, check whether your existing insurance (health, homeowners, or renters) covers you and your possessions overseas. For more information, see www.ricksteves.com/insurance.

If you're planning on **renting a car,** be aware that Portugal has one of the highest rates of automobile accidents in Europe—but also delightfully uncrowded highways outside major cities.

If you plan to hire a **local guide,** reserve ahead by email. Popular guides can get booked up.

If you're bringing a **mobile device,** download any apps you might want to use on the road, such as translators, maps, and transit schedules. Check out **Rick Steves Audio Europe,** featuring hours of travel interviews and other audio content about Portugal (via the Rick Steves Audio Europe free app, www.ricksteves.com/audioeurope, iTunes, or Google Play; for details, see page 389).

Check the **Rick Steves guidebook updates** page for any recent changes to this book (www.ricksteves.com/update).

Because **airline carry-on restrictions** are always changing, visit the Transportation Security Administration's website (www.tsa.gov) for an up-to-date list of what you can bring on the plane and for the latest security measures (including screening of electronic devices, which you may be asked to power up).

How Was Your Trip?

Were your travels fun, smooth, and meaningful? If you'd like to share your tips, concerns, and discoveries, please fill out the survey at www.ricksteves.com/feedback. To check out readers' hotel and restaurant reviews—or leave one yourself—visit my travel forum at www.ricksteves.com/travel-forum. I value your feedback. Thanks in advance—it helps a lot.

Traveling as a Temporary Local

We travel all the way to Europe to enjoy differences—to become temporary locals. You'll experience frustrations. Certain truths that

we find "God-given" or "self-evident," such as cold beer, ice in drinks, bottomless cups of coffee, and bigger being better, are suddenly not so true. One of the benefits of travel is the eye-opening realization that there are logical, civil, and even better alternatives. A willingness to go local ensures that you'll enjoy a full dose of Portuguese hospitality.

Europeans generally like Americans. But if there is a negative aspect to the European image of Americans, it's that we are loud, wasteful, ethnocentric, too informal (which can seem disrespectful), and a bit naive.

While the Portuguese look bemusedly at some of our Yankee excesses—and worriedly at others—they nearly always afford us individual travelers all the warmth we deserve.

Judging from all the happy feedback I receive from travelers who have used this book, it's safe to assume you'll enjoy a great, affordable vacation—with the finesse of an independent, experienced traveler.

Thanks, and *boa viagem!*

Rick Steves

Back Door Travel Philosophy

From *Rick Steves Europe Through the Back Door*

Travel is intensified living—maximum thrills per minute and one of the last great sources of legal adventure. Travel is freedom. It's recess, and we need it.

Experiencing the real Europe requires catching it by surprise, going casual..."through the Back Door."

Affording travel is a matter of priorities. (Make do with the old car.) You can eat and sleep—simply, safely, and enjoyably—anywhere in Europe for $125 a day plus transportation costs. In many ways, spending more money only builds a thicker wall between you and what you traveled so far to see. Europe is a cultural carnival, and time after time, you'll find that its best acts are free and the best seats are the cheap ones.

A tight budget forces you to travel close to the ground, meeting and communicating with the people. Never sacrifice sleep, nutrition, safety, or cleanliness to save money. Simply enjoy the local-style alternatives to expensive hotels and restaurants.

Connecting with people carbonates your experience. Extroverts have more fun. If your trip is low on magic moments, kick yourself and make things happen. If you don't enjoy a place, maybe you don't know enough about it. Seek the truth. Recognize tourist traps. Give a culture the benefit of your open mind. See things as different, but not better or worse. Any culture has plenty to share.

Of course, travel, like the world, is a series of hills and valleys. Be fanatically positive and militantly optimistic. If something's not to your liking, change your liking.

Travel can make you a happier American, as well as a citizen of the world. Our Earth is home to seven billion equally precious people. It's humbling to travel and find that other people don't have the "American Dream"—they have their own dreams. Europeans like us, but with all due respect, they wouldn't trade passports.

Thoughtful travel engages us with the world. In tough economic times, it reminds us what is truly important. By broadening perspectives, travel teaches new ways to measure quality of life.

Globetrotting destroys ethnocentricity, helping us understand and appreciate other cultures. Rather than fear the diversity on this planet, celebrate it. Among your most prized souvenirs will be the strands of different cultures you choose to knit into your own character. The world is a cultural yarn shop, and Back Door travelers are weaving the ultimate tapestry. Join in!

PORTUGAL

Portugal is underrated. The country seems somewhere just beyond Europe—prices are a bit cheaper, and the pace of life is noticeably slower than in Spain. While the unification of Europe is bringing sweeping changes to Portugal, the traditional economy is still based on fishing, cork, wine, and textiles.

Portugal has few major sights—even its coastal towns lack glitzy attractions. The beach and the sea are enough, as they have been for centuries. They were the source of Portugal's seafaring wealth long ago, and are the draw for tourists today.

The locals, not jaded by tourists, will meet you with warmth—especially if you learn at least a few words of Portuguese, instead of launching into Spanish (see "Portuguese Survival Phrases" in the appendix).

Over the centuries, Portugal and Spain have had a love-hate, on-again-off-again relationship, but they have almost always remained separate, each with their own distinct language and culture. The Portuguese seem humbler and friendlier than the Spanish. In Spain, if you ever feel like you can't do anything right, you'll find it's just the opposite in Portugal—you can't do anything wrong. Portugal is also more ethnically diverse than Spain, as it's inhabited by many people from its former colonies in Brazil, Africa, and Asia. The Portuguese continue to have a special affinity for their Brazilian cousins.

Portugal bucked the Moors before Spain did, establishing its present-day borders 800 years ago. A couple of centuries later, the Age of Discovery (1400-1600) made Portugal one of the world's richest nations.

Portugal's Prince Henry the Navigator sponsored the voyages of explorers who traveled to Africa seeking a trade route to India. Bartolomeu Dias and Vasco da Gama, building upon the knowledge of previous generations, actually found the way. Portuguese-

Portugal Almanac

Official Name: It's República Portuguesa, but locals just say "Portugal."

Population: Nearly 11 million people. Most Portuguese are Roman Catholic (81 percent), with indigenous Mediterranean roots; there are a few black Africans from former colonies and some Eastern Europeans.

Latitude and Longitude: 39°N and 8°W (similar latitude to Washington, D.C. or San Francisco).

Area: 35,000 square miles, which includes the Azores and Madeira, two island groups in the Atlantic.

Geography: Portugal is rectangular, 325 miles long and 125 miles wide. (It's roughly the size and shape of Indiana.) The half of the country north of Lisbon is more mountainous, cool, and rainy. The south consists of rolling plains, where it's hot and dry. Portugal has 350 miles of coastline, much of it sandy beaches.

Rivers: The major rivers, most notably the Tejo (or Tagus) River (600 miles long, spilling into the Atlantic at Lisbon) and the Douro (100 miles, flowing through wine country, ending at Porto), run east-west from Spain.

Mountains: Serra da Estrela, at 6,500 feet, is the highest point on the mainland, but Portugal's highest peak is Mt. Pico (7,713 feet) in the Azores.

Biggest Cities: Lisbon (the capital, 548,000 in the core, with more than 3 million in greater Lisbon), Porto (238,000 in the core, with 1.7 million total), and Coimbra (143,000 in the core).

Economy: The Gross Domestic Product is about $240 billion, and the GDP per capita is around $23,000 (comparable to Louisiana's). Some major money-makers for Portugal are fish (canned sardines), cork, budget clothes and shoes, port wine, and tourism. More than 20 percent of Portugal's foreign trade is with Spain. Portugal's outlook has improved

born Ferdinand Magellan, sailing under the auspices of Spain, was the first to undertake a voyage that successfully circumnavigated the globe (though he himself died en route).

A naval superpower for a century, Portugal established trading posts that eventually became colonies in Brazil and throughout Africa. The wealth that flowed into the country led to an explosion of the arts back home. The finest architecture from this era (now named the Manueline period, after King Manuel I)

considerably since joining the European Union in 1986 (then called the European Community), thanks to EU subsidies, but it's still struggling, with unemployment in 2013 hovering around 16 percent. One in 10 Portuguese works in agriculture, 60 percent work in service jobs, and 30 percent in industry.

Government: The prime minister—currently the center-right Social Democrat Pedro Passos Coelho—is the chief executive, having assumed power as the head of the leading vote-getting party in legislative elections. President Aníbal Cavaco Silva, re-elected in 2011 to a second five-year term, commands the military and can dissolve the Parliament when he sees fit (it's rarely done, but he has the power). There are 230 legislators, elected to four-year terms, making up the single-house Assembly. Regionally, Portugal is divided into 18 districts (Lisbon, Coimbra, Porto, etc.).

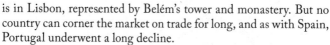

Flag: The flag is two-fifths green and three-fifths red, united by the Portuguese coat of arms—a shield atop a navigator's armillary sphere.

Soccer: The three most popular teams are Sporting CP Lisbon, Benfica (also from Lisbon), and FC Porto.

***Senhor* and *Senhora* Average:** The average Portuguese is 41 years old and will live 79 years. Two in five Portuguese live near either Lisbon or Porto, and slightly less than two in three own a car.

is in Lisbon, represented by Belém's tower and monastery. But no country can corner the market on trade for long, and as with Spain, Portugal underwent a long decline.

From 1932 to 1974, Portugal endured the repressive regime of António de Oliveira Salazar and his successor Marcello Caetano—the longest dictatorship in Western European history. Salazar pumped money into fighting wars to hang on to the last of the country's African colonies. When Portuguese military officers staged a coup in 1974, the locals were on their side (see sidebar on the Carnation Revolution, page 63). Portugal lost its colonies, but those former holdings—as well as the Portuguese people—won their freedom.

Once the poorest European Union country in Western Eu-

rope, Portugal has worked hard to meet EU standards...and has enjoyed heavy EU investment. The major issues facing the country are how to tame its rising national debt, repay EU loans, continue providing generous social services, keep taxes reasonable, and reduce unemployment. Poverty still exists in Portugal, particularly in rural areas, but overall, the country has become more prosperous since joining the EU. New products are on the market, the infrastructure has been improved, and Portugal is participating more in international politics.

With a rich culture, friendly people, affordable prices, and a salty setting on the edge of Europe, Portugal understandably remains a rewarding destination for travelers.

LISBON

Lisboa

Lisbon is a ramshackle but charming mix of now and then. Vintage trolleys shiver up and down its hills, bird-stained statues mark grand squares, taxis rattle and screech through cobbled lanes, and well-worn people sip coffee in Art Nouveau cafés. It's a city of faded iron-work balconies, multicolored tiles, and mosaic sidewalks, of bougainvillea and red-tiled roofs with antique TV antennas. Men in suits and billed caps offer to "plastify" your documents, and Africans in traditional garb sell gemstones from handkerchiefs spread on sidewalks.

Lisbon, Portugal's capital, is the country's banking and manufacturing center. Residents call their city Lisboa (leezh-BOH-ah), which comes from the Phoenician term *Alis Ubbo*, meaning "calm port." A port city on the yawning mouth of the Rio Tejo (Tagus River), Lisbon welcomes large ships to its waters and state-of-the-art dry docks. And it's becoming a popular stop with cruise ships.

Romans and Moors originally populated Lisbon, but the city's glory days were in the 15th and 16th centuries, when explorers such as Vasco da Gama opened new trade routes around Africa to India, making Lisbon one of Europe's richest cities. Portugal's Age of Discovery fueled rapid economic growth, which sparked the flamboyant art boom called the Manueline period—named after King Manuel I (r. 1495-1521). In the 17th and 18th centuries, the gold, diamonds, and sugarcane of Brazil (one of Portugal's colonies) made Lisbon even wealthier.

Then, on the morning of All Saints' Day in 1755, while most of the population was at church, a tremendous underwater earthquake occurred off the southern Portuguese coast. The violent series of tremors were felt throughout Europe—as far away as Fin-

LISBON

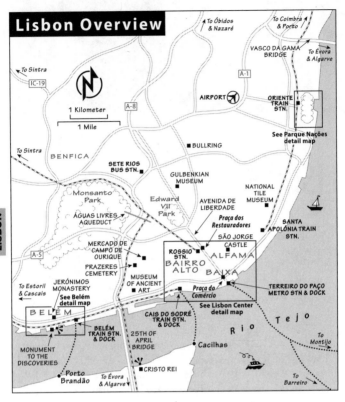

Lisbon Overview

To Óbidos & Nazaré

To Coimbra & Porto

VASCO DA GAMA BRIDGE

To Évora & Algarve

To Sintra

IC-19

A-1

AIRPORT

A-8

1 Kilometer

1 Mile

ORIENTE TRAIN STN.

See Parque Nações detail map

To Sintra

BENFICA

BULLRING

SETE RIOS BUS STN.

GULBENKIAN MUSEUM

NATIONAL TILE MUSEUM

Monsanto Park

Edward VII Park

AVENIDA DE LIBERDADE

ÁGUAS LIVRES AQUEDUCT

Praça dos Restauradores

SANTA APOLÓNIA TRAIN STN.

A-5

MERCADO DE CAMPO DE OURIQUE

PRAZERES CEMETERY

ROSSIO STN.

SÃO JORGE CASTLE

ALFAMA

BAIRRO ALTO

BAIXA

To Estoril & Cascais

JERÓNIMOS MONASTERY

See Belém detail map

MUSEUM OF ANCIENT ART

Praça do Comércio

TERREIRO DO PAÇO METRO STN & DOCK

BELÉM

See Lisbon Center detail map

BELÉM TRAIN STN. & DOCK

CAIS DO SODRÉ TRAIN STN. & DOCK

25TH OF APRIL BRIDGE

Rio Tejo

To Montijo

MONUMENT TO THE DISCOVERIES

Porto Brandão

To Évora & Algarve

Cacilhas

CRISTO REI

To Barreiro

land. Two-thirds of Lisbon was leveled. Fires—started by cooking flames and church candles—raged through the wooden city center, and a huge tsunami caused by the earthquake blasted the waterfront. Imagine a disaster similar to 2004's Indian Ocean earthquake and tsunami, devastating Portugal's capital city. (For more on this tragic event, see page 53.)

Under the energetic and eventually dictatorial leadership of Prime Minister Marquês de Pombal—who had the new city planned within a month of the quake—downtown Lisbon was rebuilt on a progressive grid plan, with broad boulevards and generous squares. Remnants of Lisbon's pre-earthquake charm survive in Belém, the Alfama, and the Bairro Alto district. The bulk of your sightseeing will likely be in these neighborhoods.

As the Paris of the Portuguese-speaking world, Lisbon (pop. 548,000 in the core) is the Old World capital of its former empire—for some 100 million people stretching from Europe to Brazil to Africa to China. Immigrants from former colonies such as Mozambique and Angola have added diversity and flavor to the

Pronunciation Guide to Lisbon

Lisboa	leezh-BOH-ah
Rossio (main square)	roh-SEE-oo
Praça da Figueira (major square)	PRAH-sah dah fee-GAY-rah
Baixa (lower town)	BYE-shah
Alfama (hilly neighborhood)	al-FAH-mah
Bairro Alto (high town)	BYE-roh AHL-too
Chiado (part of Bairro Alto)	shee-AH-doo
Belém (suburb with sights)	bay-LEHM
Rio Tejo (Tagus River)	REE-oo TAY-zhoo
rua (street)	ROO-ah

LISBON

city, making it as likely that you'll hear African music as Portuguese fado these days.

With its characteristic hills, trolleys, famous suspension bridge, and rolling fog, Lisbon has a San Francisco feel. And Lisbon's heritage survives. Enjoy all this world-class city has to offer, from its elegant outdoor cafés, exciting art, stunning vistas, and entertaining museums, to the salty sailors' quarter with its hill-capping castle.

PLANNING YOUR TIME

For a two-week tour of Portugal, Lisbon is worth three days, including perhaps a day for a side-trip to Sintra. If you have an extra day, there's plenty to do.

Note that many top sights are closed on Monday, particularly in Belém. That'd be a good day to choose among the following options: Take my self-guided neighborhood walks; day-trip to Sintra (where all of the major sights are open); go on a guided walking tour with Lisbon Walker or Inside Lisbon (see page 37); or head to Parque das Nações for a dose of modern Lisbon.

Day 1: See Lisbon's three downtown neighborhoods (following my self-guided "Three Neighborhoods" Walk): Alfama, Baixa, and Bairro Alto. Start where the city did, at its castle (hop a taxi to get there at 9:00 before the crowds hit). After surveying the city from the highest viewpoint in town, you'll take the walk downhill into the characteristic Alfama neighborhood and end at the Fado Museum. From there, zip over to the big main square (Praça do Comércio) to begin exploring the Baixa ("lower town"). That walk takes you through the major squares, Praça da Figueira and Rossio. Then ride up the Elevador da Glória funicular to begin the Bairro Alto and Chiado walk. Art lovers can then hop a taxi to the Gulbenkian Museum (open until 18:00, closed Mon). Consider dinner at a fado show in the Bairro Alto or the Alfama. For more evening options, see "Entertainment in Lisbon" (page 95) and "Shopping in Lisbon" (malls/cinemas are open late, page 94).

Day 2: Trolley to Belém and tour the monastery, tower, and National Coach Museum. Have lunch in Belém or across the river in Porto Brandão, then tour the Museum of Ancient Art on your way back to Lisbon.

Day 3: Side-trip to Sintra to tour the Pena Palace and explore the ruined Moorish castle.

Orientation to Lisbon

Downtown Lisbon fills a valley flanked by two hills along the banks of the Rio Tejo. At the heart sits the main square, **Rossio,** in the center of the valley (with Praça dos Restauradores and Praça da Figueira nearby). The **Baixa,** or lower town, stretches from Rossio to the waterfront. It's a flat, pleasant shopping area of grid-patterned streets and the pedestrian-only Rua Augusta. The **Alfama,** the hill to the east, is a colorful tangle of medieval streets, topped by São Jorge Castle. The **Bairro Alto** ("high town"), the hill to the west, has characteristic old lanes on the top and high-fashion stores along Rua Garrett (in the lower section called **Chiado**).

From Rossio, the **modern city** stretches north (sloping uphill) along wide Avenida da Liberdade and beyond (way beyond), where you find Edward VII Park, breezy botanical gardens, the bullring, and the airport. To the east is **Parque das Nações,** site of the 1998 World Expo and now a modern shopping complex and riverfront promenade. The suburb of Belém, home to several Age of Discovery sights, is three miles west of the city, along the waterfront.

Greater Lisbon has more than three million people and some frightening sprawl, but for the visitor, the old city center is your target—a delightful series of parks, boulevards, and squares in a crusty, well-preserved architectural shell. Focus on the three characteristic neighborhoods that line the downtown harborfront: the Alfama, Baixa, and Bairro Alto.

TOURIST INFORMATION

Lisbon has several tourist offices—all branded "ask me Lisboa"—and additional information kiosks sprout around town late each spring. The main TIs are: on **Praça dos Restauradores** at Palácio Foz (daily 9:00-20:00, tel. 213-463-314; TI for rest of Portugal in same office, tel. 218-494-323 or 213-463-658); on **Praça do Comércio** (daily 9:00-20:00, tel. 210-312-810); and at the **airport** (daily 7:00-24:00, especially helpful, tel. 218-450-660). Small TI kiosks are at the **Santa Apolónia train station** (Tue-Sat 7:30-9:30, closed Sun-Mon, toward the end of track 3) and in front of the monastery in **Belém** (Tue-Sat 10:00-13:00 & 14:00-18:00, closed Sun-Mon, tel. 213-658-435).

Each TI offers handy freebies including a Lisbon city map (with helpful inset of town center), an in-depth *Public Transport Guide* (showing bus, Metro, and trolley lines in detail), and the monthly *Follow Me Lisboa* magazine (monthly, mainly cultural and museum listings). If you want a LisboaCard (described next), buy it at a TI. Good websites for information are www.insidelisbon.com, www.visitlisboa.com (click on "Publications" to find the *Follow Me Lisboa* magazine as a free PDF), and www.visitportugal.com.

LisboaCard: This card covers all public transportation (as well as trains to Sintra and Cascais) and free entry to many museums (including the Museum of Ancient Art, National Tile Museum, National Coach Museum, Monastery of Jerónimos, and Bélem Tower, plus some Sintra sights). It also provides discounts on many museums, city tours, and river cruises.

You can buy the card at Lisbon's TIs (including the airport TI), but not at participating sights. If you plan to museum-hop, the card is a good value, particularly for a day in Belém (covers your transportation and most sightseeing). Don't get the card for Sunday, when many sights are free until 14:00, or for Monday, when many sights are closed. The card is also unnecessary if you're a student or senior, for whom most sights are free or half-price.

The LisboaCard is straightforward and can save you well over €25 if you do everything suggested in my three-day plan for Lisbon. Carry the LisboaCard booklet with you when you sightsee; some discounts require coupons contained inside, plus it serves as a proof of purchase (€19/24 hours, €32/48 hours, €39/72 hours, kids 5-11 half-price, includes excellent explanatory guidebook, www.askmelisboa.com).

ARRIVAL IN LISBON

Information on arriving in Lisbon by plane, train, bus, cruise ship, and car follows. A helpful website is www.golisbon.com/transport. If you have a little money and/or are traveling with a group, simply hop in a taxi upon arrival—they're plentiful and cheap (except at the cruise terminals; see warning later). You can get from the airport or train station to your hotel for under €10 by taxi.

By Plane

Lisbon's easy-to-manage Portela Airport is five miles northeast of downtown (airport code: LIS; for airport info, call 218-413-500 or TAP Portugal at tel. 707-205-700). While you're at the airport,

LISBON

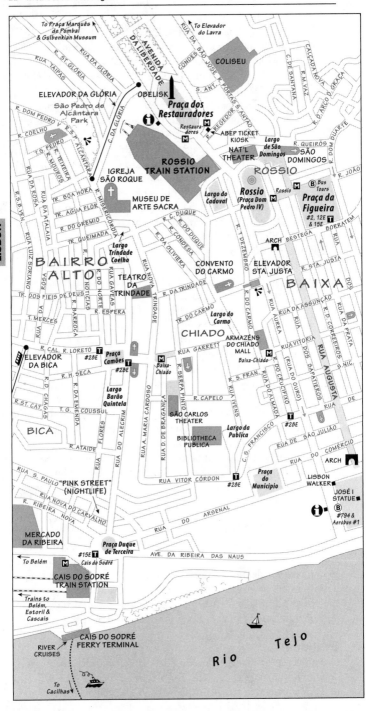

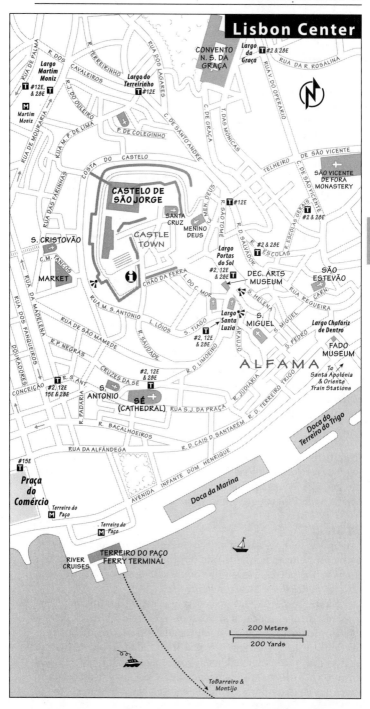

Lisbon Center

LISBON

CONVENTO N. S. DA GRAÇA

Largo da Graça 🚋 #2 & 28E

RUA DA R. ROSALINA

Largo Martim Moniz 🚋 #12E & 28E

RUA DE PALMA

R. DOS CAVALEIROS

TERREIRINHO

RUA DOS LAGARES

Largo do Terreirinho 🚋 #12E

R. J. DO OULEIRO

Ⓜ Martim Moniz

RUA DE MOURARIA

RUA M. P. DE LIMA

P. DE COLEGINHO

C. DE SANTO ANDRÉ

C. DE GRAÇA

T. DAS MÓNICAS

RUAY DO OPERARIO

DE SÃO VICENTE

TELHEIRO

C. DE SÃO VICENTE

SÃO VICENTE DE FORA MONASTERY

COSTA DO CASTELO

RUA DAS FARINHAS

CASTELO DE SÃO JORGE

SANTA CRUZ

R. SÃO DEUS

🚋 #12E

R. SÃO TOMÉ

CASTLE TOWN

MENINO DEUS

R. D. SALVADOR

🚋 #2 & 28E ESCOLAS

R. D. ESCOLAS GERAIS

🚋 #2 & 28E

S. CRISTOVÃO

C. M. FANCOS

Largo Portas do Sol 🚋 #2, 12E & 28E

DEC. ARTS MUSEUM

SÃO ESTEVÃO

RUA REGUEIRA

RUA M. S. ANTONIO

CHÃO DA FERA

L. DO C. MOR

S. HELENA

S. MIGUEL

R. CARN.

MARKET

RUA DA MADALENA

RUA DOS FANGUEIROS

R. P. NEGRAS

R. DE SÃO MAMEDE

L. LÓIOS

S. TIAGO

R. SAUDADE

Largo Santa Luzia 🚋 #2, 12E & 28E

S. BRAÚJO

S. PEDRO

S. MIGUEL

Largo Chafariz de Dentro

FADO MUSEUM

To Santa Apolónia & Oriente Train Stations

R. D. LIMOEIRO

ALFAMA

CRUZES DA SÉ

🚋 #2, 12E & 28E

DOURADORES

🚋 #2, 12E 15E & 28E

CONCEIÇÃO

R. S. ANT.

S. ANTONIO

R. PADARIA

SÉ (CATHEDRAL)

RUA S. J. DA PRAÇA

RUA DE SÃO MAMEDE

RUA JUDIARIA

R. D. TERREIRO TRIGO

R. BACALHOEIROS

R. D. CAIS D. SANTAREM

Doca do Terreiro do Trigo

RUA DA ALFÂNDEGA

🚋 #15E

Praça do Comércio

Terreiro do Paço Ⓜ

Terreiro do Paço Ⓜ

AVENIDA INFANTE DOM HENRIQUE

Doca da Marina

RIVER CRUISES

TERREIRO DO PAÇO FERRY TERMINAL

200 Meters

200 Yards

To Barreiro & Montijo

get info on Lisbon and all of Portugal at the helpful TI (daily 7:00-24:00, tel. 218-450-660). Next to the TI is a handy Vodafone shop that sells Portuguese SIM cards (daily 8:00-22:00).

Getting downtown from Lisbon's very central airport is a snap. There are three options: taxi, shuttle bus, and Metro.

Taxis line up on the curb (if there's a long line, go upstairs to the departure level where, across the street, there's another taxi rank with rarely a line). Rides into town cost about €10. There's a legitimate €1.60 fee for your luggage (not per bag, but to use the trunk). In the past it was tough to get cabbies to use their meter for airport pickups, but these days that rule is more strictly enforced. If the meter starts at €3.90 and is set to *Tarifa 1* (or *Tarifa 2* for nights, weekends, and holidays), relax—you should be fine. There is no "airport fee" supplement. To return to the airport by taxi from downtown to the airport is easy, fast, and cheap. Simply hail one on the street (€10). Skip the €23 taxi vouchers sold by the airport TI—these are for rides outside the center and double your cost.

While dirt-cheap **public buses** leave from the airport curb, these are not really intended for people with luggage. The **AeroBus** is faster and nearly as cheap. You likely want their city center route #1 (€3.50, 3/hour, runs 7:00-23:00, departs outside of arrival level at bus stop marked "AeroBus #1"—not #2), which stops at Marquês de Pombal, Avenida da Liberdade, Restauradores, Rossio, and Praça do Comércio. Route #2 avoids the downtown and ends in the financial district (of no interest to tourists), but makes a handy stop at the bus station at Sete Rios if you plan to go elsewhere immediately (see "By Bus," later). Aerobus tickets are sold at the airport TI or on the bus for the same price.

To take the **Metro**'s red line into Lisbon, exit the airport arrivals hall and turn right to find the Aeroporto stop. Before boarding, buy a reloadable Viva Viagem card at the ticket machine; you can get a 24-hour pass and have Lisbon by the tail for just €6 (see details under "Getting Around Lisbon," later).

By Train

Lisbon has four primary train stations—Santa Apolónia (to Spain and most points north), Oriente (for the Algarve, Évora, and fast trains to the north), Rossio (for Sintra, Óbidos, and Nazaré), and Cais do Sodré (for Cascais and Estoril).

Santa Apolónia Station covers international trains and nearly all of Portugal. Located just east of the Alfama, it has ATMs, a morning-only TI, baggage storage, and good Metro and bus connections to the town center. A taxi from Santa Apolónia Station to any of my recommended hotels costs roughly €8. Bus #794 goes downtown to Praça do Comércio. Bus #759 goes to Rossio and Praça dos Restauradores. From the station, here's how to get to the

bus stop: Look for the Metro sign, walk past the escalators to exit the station, and find the bus stop on your right along busy Avenida Infante Dom Henrique. Most trains using Santa Apolónia Station also stop at **Oriente Station** (Metro: Oriente; for more on this architecturally interesting station, see page 73).

Rossio Station, which handles trains to Sintra (direct, 4/hour, 40 minutes, buy tickets from machines at track level on second floor), is in the town center and an easy walk from most recommended hotels. It also handles trains to Óbidos and Nazaré, but since both destinations require a transfer at Cacém, the bus is a better option. Its all-Portugal ticket office on the ground floor (next to Starbucks) sells long-distance and international train tickets (Mon-Fri 7:00-20:00, closed Sat-Sun, cash only).

Cais do Sodré Station, near the waterfront just west of Praça do Comércio (Metro: Cais do Sodré), serves coastal towns Cascais and Estoril (30 minutes).

By Bus

Lisbon's efficient Sete Rios bus station is in the modern part of the city, several miles inland from the harbor. It has ATMs, a rack of schedules (near entrance), a nifty computer that displays routes and ticket prices, and two information offices—one for buses within Portugal, the other for international routes (Intercentro booth). While you can buy bus tickets up to a week in advance, you can almost always buy a ticket just a few minutes before departure. The EVA company covers the south of Portugal (www.eva-bus.com), while Rede Nacional de Expressos does the rest of the country (www.rede-expressos.pt; bus info for both companies—toll tel. 707-223-344).

The bus station is across the street from the large Sete Rios train station, which sits above the Jardim Zoológico Metro stop. To get from the bus station to downtown Lisbon, it's a €6 taxi ride or a short Metro trip on the blue line (from bus station, walk down and across to Sete Rios train station, then follow signs for *Metro: Jardim Zoológico*).

By Cruise Ship

Lisbon's port is the busiest on Europe's Atlantic coast, with most cruise ships docking at one of two terminals: Alcântara (about two miles west of downtown) or Santa Apolónia (near the train station of the same name, at the base of the Alfama).

Both terminals have ATMs, and WCs, public phones, and taxi stands. The taxis that wait at either terminal are notoriously dishonest. For a fair, metered rate, you might have better luck walking across the big street and hailing one as it drives by. Even better, choose among the following options:

Most cruise lines offer inexpensive shuttle service from either terminal to Praça do Comércio. If you're taking public transit from the Alcântara terminal, you can reach central Lisbon on trolley #15E (use pedestrian underpass to reach trolley stop, 5/hour, 15 minutes, €3, coins only) or on any bus (direction: Centro, €2, pay the driver). From the Santa Apolónia cruise-ship terminal, it's a short walk to the Santa Apolónia train station, described earlier under "By Train." From this terminal, bus #794 goes to Praça do Comércio. Transfer there via trolley #15E or bus #714 out to Belém.

By Car

It makes absolutely no sense to drive in Lisbon. If you're starting your trip in Lisbon, don't rent a car until you're on your way out of town.

If you enter Lisbon from the north, a series of boulevards takes you into the center. Navigate by following signs to *Centro, Avenida da República, Marquês de Pombal, Avenida da Liberdade, Praça dos Restauradores, Rossio,* and *Praça do Comércio.* If coming from the east over the Vasco da Gama Bridge and heading for the airport, take the first exit after the bridge.

If you're turning in your car in Lisbon, consider dropping it at the airport (rental-car turn-in clearly signposted, no extra expense to drop it here, very helpful TI open late) and riding a sweat-free taxi for €10 to your hotel. Or, if you must drive into town, consider hiring a taxi and following it to your hotel.

There are many safe underground pay parking lots in Lisbon (follow blue *P* signs), but they discourage anything but short stays by getting more expensive by the hour. They can cost a maximum €20 per day (at the most central Praça dos Restauradores).

HELPFUL HINTS

Theft Alert: Lisbon has piles of people doing illegal business on the street. While the city is generally safe, if you're looking for trouble—especially after dark—you may find it. Pickpockets target tourists on the trolleys (especially #12E, #15E, and #28E) and on the Metro.

Enjoy the sightseeing, but seriously be aware of your surroundings—wear your money belt and keep your pack zipped up. Many thieves pose as tourists by wearing cameras and toting maps. Be on guard whenever you're in a crush of people, or jostled as you enter or leave a tram or bus. If you carry valuables in your pockets, keep your hands on them when possible.

You'll see Gypsies begging on the street—some are scammers and pickpockets. They're generally Romanians who, with that country's membership in the European Union, are free to roam and take advantage of Europe's generous social security. Portugal has its poor, but they are generally too proud to work the system and are considered "the invisible poor."

Pedestrian Warning: Sidewalks can be narrow in certain neighborhoods, and drivers are daring; cross the street with care. The cobbles, while picturesque, can be very slippery. And trams can sneak up on you if you're not paying attention.

Calendar Concerns: National museums are free on Sunday (all day or until 14:00). Many major sights are closed on Monday, including Lisbon's Museum of Ancient Art, National Tile Museum, and Fado Museum, as well as Belém's Monastery of Jerónimos, Coach Museum, and Belém Tower. Tuesdays and Saturdays are flea- and food-market days in the Alfama's Campo de Santa Clara. Bullfights take place irregularly throughout the summer, mainly on Thursdays (see page 100).

Laundry: Drop off clothes at centrally located **5àSec Lavandaria** (€7.50/kilo, same-day wash-and-dry service, Mon-Fri 8:00-20:00, Sat-Sun 10:00-20:00, near Baixa-Chiado Metro stop at Rua do Crucifixo 99, tel. 213-479-599). Hostels and shopping malls generally have laundry services, or your hotelier can recommend a place nearby.

Internet Access: Praça da Figueira has downtown's most convenient Internet café (**Western Union,** on corner nearest the Church of São Domingos, Mon-Fri 8:15-20:15, Sat-Sun 9:00-19:15, longer hours in summer, €1.25/30 minutes). There are other cheap hole-in-the-wall shops catering to immigrants' need for low-cost Internet access.

Post Office and Telephones: The post offices *(correios)* at Praça dos Restauradores 58 (Mon-Fri 8:00-22:00, Sat 9:00-18:00) and on Rua da Santa Justa 15 (Mon-Fri 9:00-18:00) are modern and user-friendly. The **Western Union** office mentioned above in "Internet Access" also has metered phones.

Travel Agency: Agencies line the Avenida da Liberdade. For flights (and train tickets in Portugal only—same price as at station, no fee), **GeoStar** is handy and helpful (€15 booking fee for flights, Mon-Fri 9:30-18:30, closed Sat-Sun, Praça dos Restauradores 14, tel. 213-245-240).

Ticket Kiosk: The green **ABEP kiosk** at the bottom end of Praça dos Restauradores is a handy spot to buy a city transit pass, LisboaCard, and tickets to just about anything: bullfights, soccer games, concerts, and other events. They know what's on (daily 9:00-20:00, across from TI).

Updates to This Book: For updates to this book, check www.ricksteves.com/update.

GETTING AROUND LISBON

To use Lisbon's transit economically, either use your LisboaCard (see page 21) or take advantage of the reloadable Viva Viagem card (a paper card containing a magnetic strip). The card works on the Metro, funiculars, trolleys, buses, and some trains.

Viva Viagem cards are sold at smart machines at any Metro stop for a one-time €0.50 fee and loaded with your choice of options: single ride (€1.40, good for one hour of travel within Zone 1); 24-hour pass (€6, not valid for trains); or "Zapping" (pre-load the card with up to €15, and credit is deducted at the single-ride rate of €1.40 as you use it—you can "top it up" when the credit runs out; valid on trains). For intense users, the 24-hour pass is best. If using the system more sparingly, "Zapping" is better (www.carris.pt). Note, too, that the 24-hour pass cannot be used for trains, but "Zapping" cards can get you to Sintra, Cascais, or Estorial by train with no problem.

To buy or top up your Viva Viagem card at a smart machine, touch the screen to begin, press the British flag for English, then make your selection: "without a reusable card" for first-time users, or "with a reusable card" to top up. To buy a card without using the machine—or to get information on the system—drop by the Casa da Sorte office (see blue sign from Rossio and Praça da Figueira, Mon-Fri 8:00-20:00, closed Sat-Sun).

Hang onto your Viva Viagem card, as you'll need to place it on the magnetic pad when entering and leaving the system, and to avoid paying an extra €0.50 each time you buy a ticket.

By Metro

Lisbon's simple, fast, and color-coded subway system is a delight to use (runs daily 6:30-1:00 in the morning). Though it's not necessary for getting around the historic downtown, the Metro is handy for trips to or from Rossio (Metro: Rossio or Restauradores), Praça do Comércio (Metro: Terreiro do Paço), the Gulbenkian Museum (Metro: São Sebastião), the

Chiado neighborhood (Metro: Baixa-Chiado), Centro Colombo shopping mall (Metro: Colégio Militar/Luz), Parque das Nações and the Oriente train station (both at Metro: Oriente), Sete Rios

bus and train stations (Metro: Jardim Zoológico), and the airport (Metro: Aeroporto).

With the Viva Viagem card (described earlier), a Metro ride costs €1.40 within Zone 1 (which includes everything of interest to most tourists). Place the card flat on the magnetic scanner as you enter, and keep the card handy until your trip is over—you'll need it again to exit the sliding doors.

Metro stops are marked above ground with a red "M." *Saída* means exit. You can find a Metro map at any Metro stop, on most city maps, and on the Metro website (www.metrolisboa.pt/eng/).

By Trolley, Funicular, and Bus

Lisbon's buses are fine, but for fun and practical public transportation, use the trolleys and funiculars. Buy your ticket from the driver (bus-€2, trolley-€3, no transfers), or use your Viva Viagem card (€1.40/ride if "Zapping" or covered by €6 24-hour pass). Like San Francisco, Lisbon sees its trolleys as part of its heritage, and has kept a few in use. Trolleys #12E (circling the Alfama) and #28E (a scenic ride across the old town) use vintage cars; #15E (to Belém) uses a modern version. Buy a ticket, have a pass, or risk a big fine on the spot. Please be mindful of locals—especially little old Alfama ladies—who need a seat. Funiculars cost €3.60 round-trip if you don't have a pass. Also see "Trolley" under "Tours in Lisbon," later.

By Taxi

Lisbon is a great taxi town. Cabbies are good-humored and (except for crooked ones at the cruise terminals) willing to use their meters. Rides start at €3.90, and you can go anywhere in the center for around €6. Decals on the window clearly spell out all charges in English. The meter should start at €3.90 and be set to *Tarifa 1* (Mon-Fri 6:00-21:00, including the airport) or *Tarifa 2* (same drop rate, a little more per kilometer; for nights, weekends, and holidays). If the meter reads *Tarifa 3, 4,* or *5,* simply ask the cabbie to change it, unless you're going to Belém, which is considered outside the city limits of Lisbon.

Cabs are generally easy to hail on the street (green light means available, lit number on the roof indicates it's taken). If you're having a hard time flagging one down, ask a passerby for the location of the nearest taxi stand: *praça de taxi* (PRAH-sah duh taxi). They're all over the town center.

Especially if you're with a companion, Lisbon's cabs are a cheap time-saver. For an average trip, couples save only a few dollars each by taking public transportation, but spend an extra 15 minutes getting there—bad economics. If you're traveling with a companion and your time is limited, taxi everywhere.

LISBON

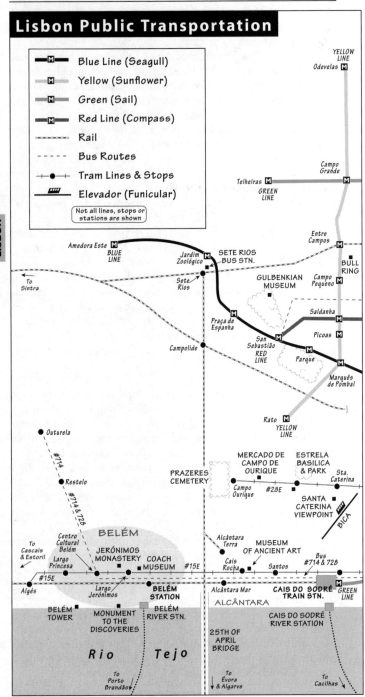

Lisbon Public Transportation

Legend:
- Ⓜ Blue Line (Seagull)
- Ⓜ Yellow (Sunflower)
- Ⓜ Green (Sail)
- Ⓜ Red Line (Compass)
- Rail
- Bus Routes
- Tram Lines & Stops
- Elevador (Funicular)

Not all lines, stops or stations are shown

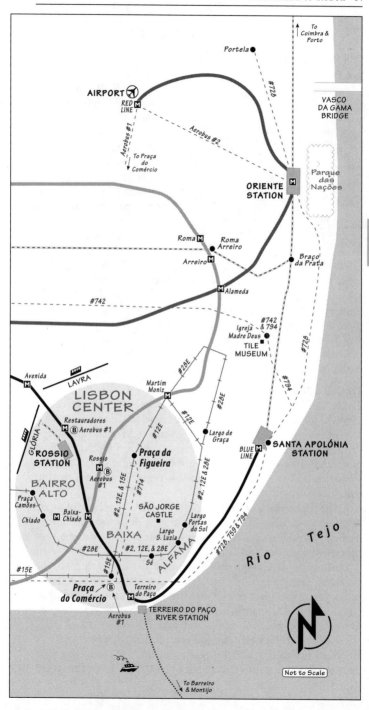

Tours in Lisbon

ON WHEELS
▲▲Trolleys

Lisbon's trolleys, many vintage models from the 1920s, shake and shiver through the old parts of town, somehow safely weaving

within inches of parked cars, climbing steep hills, and offering sightseers breezy views of the city (rubberneck out the window and you die). As you board, pay the driver (€3) or swipe your Viva Viagem card (much cheaper), take a seat, and watch the pensioners as they lurch by. Buses and trolleys usually share the same stops and routes. Signs for bus stops list the bus number, while signs for trolley stops include an E (for *eléctrico*) before or after the route number. Remember that most pickpocketing in Lisbon takes place on trolleys, so enjoy the ride, but keep an eye on your belongings. You can think of trolleys #28E and #12E as hop-on, hop-off do-it-yourself tours ("Zapping" tickets are good for an hour, and with a 24-hour pass, hopping on and off is essentially free).

Trolley #28E

Trolley #28E is a San Francisco-style Lisbon joyride. In the center of town, this trolley is often extremely crowded. To enjoy a seat for the entire scenic ride, consider taking a taxi to Mercado de Campo de Ourique for a meal or to the Prazeres Cemetery (both described next) and catching the #28E from there, where it starts its route across town. The following are notable trolley stops from west to east:

The Prazeres Cemetery, at the western terminus of route #28E, is a vast park-like necropolis dense with the mausoleums of leading Lisbon families and historic figures dating back to the 19th century (daily 9:00-17:00).

Mercado de Campo de Ourique, at the first stop after the Prazeres Cemetery (stop: Igreja Sto. Condestáovel), is a 19th-century iron-and-glass market that's now a trendy food circus (daily 10:00-23:00). The market is behind the big church on Campo de Ourique (for market description, see page 118).

At the **Estrela Basilica and Park,** you'll see the 18th-century, late Baroque basilica, with stairs winding up to the roof for a view both out and down into the church (for €4), and across the street,

Lisbon's Best Viewpoints
(*Miradouros* and *Belvederes*)

The first three viewpoints are included in the self-guided walks described in this chapter:

- Miradouro de São Pedro de Alcântara (view terrace in Bairro Alto, at top of Elevador da Glória funicular; see "The Bairro Alto and Chiado Stroll," page 57)
- São Jorge Castle (on top of the Alfama; see photo above and "The Alfama Stroll and the Castle," page 39)
- Miradouro de Largo das Portas do Sol (south slope of Alfama; see "The Alfama Stroll and the Castle," page 39)
- Elevador de Santa Justa (in the Baixa, page 62)
- Cristo Rei (statue on hillside across the Rio Tejo, page 79)
- Edward VII Park (at north end of Avenida da Liberdade)
- Bica Miradouro (atop the Elevador da Bica funicular)

the Estrela Park—a cozy neighborhood scene with pond-side café and a "garden library kiosk."

Bica is great for a stroll through the characteristic back side of the Bairro Alto over to the Miradouro de Santa Catarina (a great view terrace with inviting cafés and bars) and the top of the Elevador da Bica funicular (which drops steeply through a rough-and-tumble neighborhood to the riverfront).

Trolley #28E then laces together **Chiado** (at Chiado's main square, Lisbon's café and "Latin Quarter"); **Baixa** (on Rua da Conceição between Augusta and Prata); **Sé** (the cathedral); **Miradouro de Largo das Portas do Sol** (the Alfama viewpoint); **Campo de Santa Clara** (flea market on Tue and Sat); and the pleasant and untouristy **Graça** district (with another excellent viewpoint).

Trolley #12E

For a colorful, 20-minute loop around the castle and the Alfama, catch trolley #12E on Praça da Figueira (departs every few minutes from the stop at corner of square closest to castle). The driver can tell you when to get out for the Miradouro de Largo das Portas do Sol (viewpoint) near the castle (about three-quarters of the way up the hill), or stay on the trolley and you'll be dropped back where you started. Here's what you'll see on this loop ride:

Leaving Praça da Figueira, you enter **Largo de Martim Moniz**—named for a knight who died heroically while using his body as a doorjamb to leave the castle gate open, allowing his Christian Portuguese comrades to get in and capture Lisbon from the Moors in 1147. On the right is the picturesque Centro Comercial da Mouraria, a **marketplace** filled with a wide variety of products and aromas from around the world. The big, maroon-colored building capping the hill on the left was a Jesuit monastery until 1769, when the dictatorial Marquês de Pombal booted the pesky order out of Portugal and turned the building into the Hospital São Jose. Today, this is an immigrant neighborhood with lots of cheap import shops.

Turning right onto Rua de Cavaleiros, you climb through the atmospheric **Mouraria neighborhood** on a street so narrow that a single trolley track is all that fits. Notice how the colorful mix of neighbors who fill the trolley all seem to know each other. If the trolley's path is blocked and can't pass, lots of horn-honking and shouts from passengers ensue until your journey resumes. Look up the skinny side streets. Marvel at the creative parking and classic laundry scenes. This was the area given to the Moors after they were driven out of the castle and Alfama. Natives know it as the home of the legendary fado singer Maria Severa as well as modern-day singer Mariza. The majority of residents these days are immigrants from Asia, making this Lisbon's version of Chinatown and Bollywood wrapped up in one.

At the crest of the hill **(Largo Rodrigues de Freitas),** you can get out to explore, eat at a cheap restaurant (see "Eating in Lisbon," later), or follow Rua de Santa Marinha to the Campo de Santa Clara flea market (Tue and Sat).

When you see the river, you're at **Largo das Portas do Sol** (Gates of the Sun), where you'll also see the remains of one of the seven old Moorish gates of Lisbon. The driver usually announces *"castelo"* (cahzh-TAY-loo) at this point. Hop out here if you want to visit the Museum and School of Portuguese Decorative Arts (see page 46), enjoy the most scenic cup of coffee in town, explore the **Alfama,** or tour the **castle.**

The trolley continues downhill past the fortress-like **cathedral** (Sé, on left—see page 66) and into the **Baixa** (grid-planned Pombaline city—get off here to take my self-guided "Baixa Stroll"—see page 48). After a few blocks, you're back where you started—Praça da Figueira.

Trolley #2

A new hop-on, hop-off "tourist trolley," using green vintage cars marked "Lisbon Historical Route/Castle Line," runs from **Praça da Figueira** through the **Baixa,** past the **cathedral** (Sé), into the **Alfama** past **Miradouro de Largo das Portas do Sol** (the Alfama viewpoint), and up to **Largo da Graça,** where the line ends (€9 ticket valid for 24 hours, not covered by Viva Viagem cards, runs 10:00-17:40, 40 minutes, with audio commentary in English, Portuguese, and French).

By Bus and Tram
Yellow Bus Tours

Yellow Bus Tours offers three different downtown tours (all hop-on, hop-off). While uninspiring and not cheap, they're handy and run daily year-round. The tram and bus tours, which last about 1.5 hours, start and end at Praça da Figueira (look for yellow bus and tram signs at stops, buy tickets from driver). For more info, stop by the TI at Praça do Comércio or Praça dos Restauradores, or contact Yellow Bus (tel. 213-478-030, www.yellowbustours.com). Tickets for their hop-on, hop-off tours do double-duty as a 24-hour public transit pass, covering Lisbon's trolleys, buses, Elevador de Santa Justa, and funiculars (but not the Metro, which is owned by a different company).

Hop-on, Hop-off Bus Tours

Two tours on yellow, double-decker buses make overlapping loops around Lisbon, starting from Praça da Figueira (€15 apiece, includes audioguide). You can get off, tour a sight, and catch a later bus. The **Tagus Tour** covers north and west Lisbon, stopping at major sights such as the Museum of Ancient Art and Belém (runs every 15 minutes June-Sept 9:00-20:00, fewer in winter). The **Olisipo Tour** covers east Lisbon, with stops at Parque das Nações, the National Tile Museum, and more (runs every 30 minutes year-round 9:15-19:15, shorter hours in winter). You cannot hop on and hop off between the two different tours without buying a second ticket. You can combine a Tagus Tour with the Cruzeiros no Tejo boat tour (see "By Boat," later) for a discount.

Hills Tramcar Tour

This hop-on, hop-off tour takes you on a shiny red 1900s tramcar through the Alfama, Bairro Alto, and other Lisbon hills (€18, 1.5-hour tour with five stops, recorded narration available in English, runs every 20 minutes June-Sept 9:15-19:00, fewer off-season).

Gray Line/Cityrama Tours

Another option for hop-on, hop-off tours, the red Gray Line/Cityrama buses, offer four routes: The **Castle** line covers the Alfama and city center; the **Belém** line gets you to that district; the **Oriente** line includes Bairro Alto and Parque das Nações; and the **Cascais** line heads west along the coast past the charming beach towns of Estoril and Cascais to the scenic beaches near Guincho. Buses have free onboard Wi-Fi, making multitasking a snap (one line-€12, two lines-€18, four lines-€25, one-line ticket valid 24 hours, multi-line tickets valid 48 hours, recorded English narration available; Castle and Belém lines run 2/hour April-Oct 9:30-18:00, Oriente line runs every 45 minutes, Cascais line departs 6/day but last bus doesn't return to Lisbon).

The main info kiosk is at the north side of Marquês de Pombal roundabout, but you can purchase tickets at any TI or on board (tel. 800-208-513, www.cityrama.pt). Tickets also include discounts to certain sights.

BY BOAT
Rio Tejo Cruise
Cruzeiros no Tejo runs two river tour routes. Their longer tour does a big east-west loop to the Vasco da Gama Bridge and Parque das Nações, then to Belém and back (€20, daily at 15:00, 2.5 hours, departs from Terreiro do Paço dock off Praça do Comércio). Their shorter tour makes a loop downtown to Belém and back (€15, departs from Terreiro do Paço at 11:15, same boat departs from Cais do Sodré ferry terminal at 11:30, also an afternoon departure from Cais do Sodré at 16:15). Each operates April through October and comes with a four-language narration (free drinks and WC on board, tel. 210-422-417, www.transtejo.pt). An interesting way to visit Belém would be to take the 11:00 boat from either downtown terminal, see the Monastery of Jerónimos and related sights, then return in the afternoon from the Belém ferry terminal (departures approximately at 16:45, confirm hours when purchasing tickets).

Another outfit, **Lisboa Vista do Tejo,** runs tours from Cais do Sodré to the Belém Tower (at 11:45 and 15:15) and vice versa (at 14:00 and 16:30). Trips are narrated in Portuguese and English (€12 one-way, €16 round-trip, April-Oct, no Mon tours, one hour each way, book ahead, tel. 213-913-030, www.lvt.pt).

Cheap River Ferry Ride to Cacilhas
For a quick, cheap trip across the river with great city and bridge views in the company of Lisbon commuters rather than tourists, hop the ferry to Cacilhas (kah-SEE-lahsh) from the Cais do Sodré Station (a 10-minute walk from Praça do Comércio). At the terminal, follow signs to *Cacilhas,* not *Montijo* (€1.20 each way, 4/hour weekdays, fewer on weekends, signs say *partida*—departure—and *destino*). Either hop out for a look at the rough little industrial port, or stay on for a 25-minute round-trip.

Ways to Get from the Baixa Up to the Bairro Alto and Chiado

- Ride the Elevador da Glória funicular (a few blocks north of Rossio on Avenida da Liberdade, opposite the Hard Rock Café), or hike alongside the tracks if the funicular isn't running.
- Walk up lots of stairs from Rossio (due west of the central column).
- Taxi to the Miradouro de São Pedro de Alcântara.
- Take the escalator at the Baixa-Chiado Metro stop.
- Catch trolley #28E from Rua da Conceição.
- Hike up Rua do Carmo from Rossio to Rua Garrett.
- Take escalators or elevators from the Armazéns mall to Rua Garrett.
- Take the Elevador de Santa Justa, which goes right by the Convento do Carmo and the Chiado.

ON FOOT
Walking Tours

Two walking-tour companies—Lisbon Walker and Inside Lisbon—offer excellent, affordable tours led by young, top-notch guides with a passion for sharing insights to their hometown. Well-priced to start with, both companies give my readers their discounted student prices. Tour groups are small (generally 2-12 people) and given in English only. Each company has a helpful website explaining their tours and has an easygoing style. With either company, you'll likely feel you've made a friend in your guide (a great way to get to know a local). Especially with the substantial discount given to readers of this book, these tours are time and money very well spent.

Lisbon Walker

Standard tours include: "Revelation" (best 3-hour overview with good coverage of the Baixa and the main squares, a quick look at the Bairro Alto, and a trolley ride across town to the Graça viewpoint); "Old Town" (2-hour walk through Alfama that examines the origins of Lisbon—Romans, Moors, and its castle); and "Downtown" (2-3 hours, covers the 1755 earthquake and the rebirth of Lisbon). Other more-focused tours are "Legends & Mysteries," "City of Spies," and "Castle Hill," which includes the tangled, multi-ethnic Mouraria neighborhood (€15/person; €10 for youth, seniors, and those with this book; daily year-round at 10:00, meet at northwest corner of Praça do Comércio near Rua do Arsenal, in front of the TI—see map on page 105, tel. 218-861-840, www.lisbonwalker.com).

Inside Lisbon

Tours include the "Best of Lisbon Walk" (a good highlights tour of the main squares, the Chiado, and the Alfama; €18, daily year-round at 10:00) and food and wine tours (see "Food Tours," next). Most tours meet at the statue of Dom Pedro IV in the center of Rossio and last about three to four hours. A €5 discount is offered to anyone with this book (reserve by the day before the tour via website or phone, tel. 968-412-612, www.insidelisbon.com). They also offer private tours and day trips by minivan to Sintra/Cascais and Obidos/Fátima. You can organize a private city tour with them, or use their helpful website as a resource for seeing Lisbon on your own.

Food Tours

Guided food tours are trendy these days. Several companies offer three- to four-hour multi-stop tours that introduce you to lots of local food culture while filling your stomach at the same time (search the Web for the latest).

I've enjoyed tours by several good outfits. In each case, the groups are small, the teaching is great, and—when you figure into it the cost of the meal—the tours are a solid value.

Inside Lisbon offers a €35 "Food and Wine Walk," which makes five to six short, tasty, and memorable stand-up stops, as well as a €35 "Lisbon Experience Walk," a walking-and-eating tour from Praça dos Restauradores to Mouraria, ending with a ferry to Cacilhas for seafood (www.insidelisbon.com).

Two different companies, **Eat Portugal** and **Eat Drink Walk,** offer similar slower-paced, more top-end, and substantial tours. Their €66 tapas walks have five to six stops, and their €85 gourmet walks stop at finer places, with lots of food and local wines (www.eatportugal.com, Celia; www.eatdrinkinlisbon.com, Filomena).

Local Guides

Hiring a private local guide in Lisbon can be a wonderful luxury. They'll meet you at your hotel and tailor a tour to your interests. Especially with a small group, this can be a fine value. Audioguides are rare in Lisbon, so having your own guide can really help. Guides charge roughly the same rates (Mon-Fri €100-125/half-day, €195/day). Delightful **Alex Almeida** runs **Your Friend in Lisbon** tours (mobile 919-292-151, alex@yourfriendinlisbon.com). **Cristina Duarte** leads tours for my company and knows Lisbon well (mobile 919-316-242, acrismduarte@gmail.com). **Claudia da Costa,** whom you may have seen on my Lisbon TV show, is also excellent (mobile 965-560-216, claudiadacosta@hotmail.com).

Cristina Quental is another fine local guide (mobile 919-922-480, anacristinaquental@hotmail.com).

The "Three Neighborhoods" Walk

The essential Lisbon is easily and enjoyably covered in three self-guided walking tours (described next). You can explore Lisbon's three downtown neighborhoods—the Alfama, Baixa, and Bairro Alto—either as individual walks or by lacing them together into a single walk (which would take a minimum of five hours, but could be done as a more leisurely all-day experience). While it's easy to do these walks in any order you like, starting with the Alfama lets you get to the castle before the crowds hit (avoiding the need to line up for a ticket) and kick things off with the grand city view from Lisbon's fortified birthplace. Doing the walks in this order makes connecting them convenient as well. And you'll finish in the liveliest quarter for evening fun—the Bairro Alto/Chiado.

LISBON

▲▲▲THE ALFAMA STROLL AND THE CASTLE

Explore the Alfama, the colorful sailors' quarter that dates back to the age of Visigoth occupation, from the sixth to eighth centuries A.D. This was a bustling district during the Moorish period, and eventually became the home of Lisbon's fishermen and mariners (and of the poet Luís de Camões, who wrote, "Our lips meet easily, high across the narrow street"). The Alfama's tangled street plan is one of the few features of Lisbon to survive the 1755 earthquake. It helps make the neighborhood a cobbled playground of Old World color. Visit at the best time, during the busy mid-morning market, or in the cooler hours in the late afternoon or early evening, when the streets teem with residents. While much of its grittiness has been cleaned up in recent years (as traditional residents have been replaced by immigrant laborers), the Alfama remains one of Europe's most photogenic neighborhoods.

• *Start your walk at the highest point in town, São Jorge Castle. Get to the castle gate by taxi (€5) or by minibus #737 from Praça da Figueira. (Trolleys #28E and #12E go to Largo Santa Luzia and Largo das Portas do Sol, respectively, a few blocks below.)*

❶ São Jorge Castle Gate and Fortified Castle Town

The formidable gate to the castle is part of a fortification that, these days, surrounds three things: the view terrace, the small town that stood within the walls, and the castle itself. The ticket office is in the small town, and the turnstile is situated so that those without a ticket are kept away from the view terrace and castle proper (castle entry-€7.50, daily March-Oct 9:00-21:00, Nov-Feb 9:00-18:00).

Just inside the castle gate (on left) is a little statue of George,

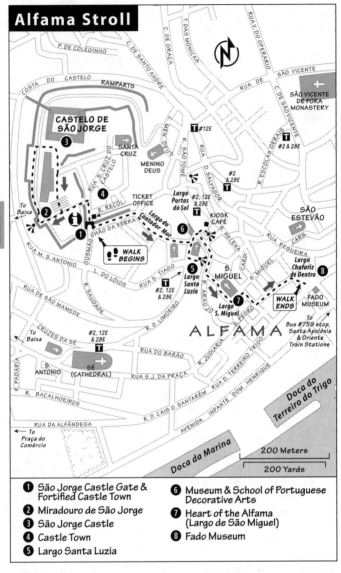

Alfama Stroll

1 São Jorge Castle Gate & Fortified Castle Town

2 Miradouro de São Jorge

3 São Jorge Castle

4 Castle Town

5 Largo Santa Luzia

6 Museum & School of Portuguese Decorative Arts

7 Heart of the Alfama (Largo de São Miguel)

8 Fado Museum

named for a popular saint in the 14th century. St. George (São Jorge; pronounced "sow ZHOR-zh") hailed from Turkey and was known for fighting valiantly (he's often portrayed slaying a dragon). When the Christian noble Afonso Henriques called for help to eliminate the Moors from his newly founded country of Portugal, the Crusaders who helped him prayed to St. George...and won.

(If money is tight, the castle and view are skippable—the

castle is just stark, rebuilt ruins from the Salazar era, and while the hill-capping park has a commanding view, there are other fine views coming up...just jump ahead to stop #4 on this walk.)

• *If you decide to go in, pick up your ticket and then follow the cobbles uphill past the first lanes of old Lisbon into the Miradouro de São Jorge.*

❷ Miradouro de São Jorge (View Terrace)

Enjoy the grand view. The Rio Tejo is one of five main rivers in Portugal, four of which come from Spain. (Only the Mondego River, which passes by Coimbra, originates inside Portuguese territory, in the Serra de Estrela.) While Portugal and Spain generally have very good relations, a major sore point is the control of all this water. From here, you have a good view of the 25th of April Bridge, which leads south to the Cristo Rei statue (described on page 79). Past the bridge, you can barely see the Monument to the Discoveries and the Belém Tower on a clear day.

Look up at the statue marking the center of this terrace. Afonso Henriques, a warlord with a strong personal army, was the founder of Portugal. In 1147 he besieged this former Moorish castle until the hungry, thirsty residents gave in. Every Portuguese schoolkid knows the story of this man—a Reconquista hero and their country's first king.

Stroll inland along the **ramparts** for a more extensive view of Pombal's Lisbon, described in a circa-1963 tile-panorama chart (which lacks the big 25th of April Bridge—it was built in 1969). From Praça do Comércio on the water, the grid streets of the Baixa lead up to the tree-lined Avenida da Liberdade and the big Edward VII Park, often capped with a large Portuguese flag on the far right. Locate city landmarks, such as the Elevador de Santa Justa (the Eiffel-style elevator in front of the ruined Convento do Carmo) and the sloping white roof of Rossio Station.

After walking farther inland under the second arch, take a right and then a left to wander the grounds. Then enter the inner castle (which usually only offers a chance to climb up for more views). The strolling peacocks remind visitors that exotic birds like these came to Lisbon originally as trophies of the great 16th-century voyages and discoveries.

❸ São Jorge Castle

While the first settlements here go back to the 7th century B.C., this castle dates to the 11th century when Moors built it to house their army and provide a safe haven where their elites could retreat

Lisbon at a Glance

In Lisbon

▲▲▲Alfama Stroll and the Castle Tangled medieval streets topped by São Jorge Castle. See page 39.

▲▲▲Baixa Stroll: Lisbon's Historic Downtown The lower town, gridded with streets and dotted with major squares. See page 48.

▲▲▲Bairro Alto and Chiado Stroll The high town's views, churches, and Chiado fashion district. See page 57.

▲▲▲Gulbenkian Museum Lisbon's best museum, featuring an art collection spanning 5,000 years, from ancient Egyptian to Impressionist to Art Nouveau. **Hours:** Wed-Mon 10:00-18:00, closed Tue. See page 67.

▲▲Museum of Ancient Art Portuguese paintings from the 15th- and 16th-century glory days. **Hours:** Tue 14:00-18:00, Wed-Sun 10:00-18:00, closed Mon. See page 71.

▲▲Parque das Nações Inviting waterfront park with a long promenade (and rental bikes), modern mall, aquarium, and the Expo '98 fairgrounds. **Hours:** Park always open. See page 73.

▲Fado Museum The story of Portuguese folk music. **Hours:** Tue-Sun 10:00-18:00, closed Mon. See page 48.

▲National Tile Museum Tons of artistic tiles, including a panorama of pre-earthquake Lisbon. **Hours:** Tue-Sun 10:00-18:00, closed Mon. See page 77.

▲São Roque Church and Museum Fine 16th-century Jesuit church with false dome ceiling, chapel made of precious stones, and a less-interesting museum. **Hours:** Tue-Sun 9:00-18:00, Mon 14:00-18:00. See page 60.

Port Wine Institute Plush place selling tastes of the world's greatest selection of ports. **Hours:** Mon-Sat 11:00-24:00, closed Sun. See page 58.

São Jorge Castle Originally an eighth-century bastion, first built by the Moors, with kingly views at the highest point in town.

Hours: Daily March-Oct 9:00-21:00, Nov-Feb 9:00-18:00. See page 41.

Museum and School of Portuguese Decorative Arts A stroll through aristocratic households richly decorated in 16th- to 19th-century styles. **Hours:** Wed-Mon 10:00-17:00, closed Tue. See page 46.

Elevador de Santa Justa A 150-foot-tall iron elevator offering a glittering city vista. **Hours:** Daily 7:00-21:30. See page 62.

Cathedral (Sé) From the outside, an impressive Romanesque fortress of God; inside, not much. **Hours:** Church—daily Tue-Sat 9:00-19:00, Sun-Mon 9:00-17:00; cloister—Tue-Sat 10:00-18:30, Mon 10:00-17:00, closed Sun. See page 66.

In Belém

Note that all of these sights—except the Monument to the Discoveries—are closed on Monday year-round.

▲▲▲**Monastery of Jerónimos** King Manuel's giant 16th-century, white limestone church and monastery, with remarkable cloister and the explorer Vasco da Gama's tomb. **Hours:** May-Sept Tue-Sun 10:00-18:30, off-season until 17:30, closed Mon. See page 83.

▲▲**National Coach Museum** Dozens of carriages, from simple to opulent, displaying the evolution of coaches from 1600 on. **Hours:** Tue-Sun 10:00-18:00, closed Mon. See page 82.

▲**Maritime Museum** A salty selection of exhibits on the ships and navigational tools of the Age of Discovery. **Hours:** May-Sept daily 10:00-18:00, off-season until 17:00. See page 88.

▲**Monument to the Discoveries** Giant riverside monument honoring the explorers who brought Portugal great power and riches centuries ago. **Hours:** May-Sept daily 10:00-19:00; Oct-April Tue-Sun 10:00-18:00, closed Mon. See page 89.

▲**Belém Tower** Consummate Manueline building with a worthwhile view up 120 steps. **Hours:** May-Sept Tue-Sun 10:00-18:30, off-season until 17:30, closed Mon. See page 92.

LISBON

in times of siege. After Afonso Henriques took the castle in 1147, Portugal's royalty lived here for several
centuries. The sloping walls—typical of castles from this period—were
designed to withstand 14th-century
cannonballs. In the 16th century, the
kings moved to their palace on Praça
do Comércio and the castle became

a military garrison. Despite suffering major damage in the 1755
earthquake, the castle later served another stint as a military garrison. In the 20th century, it became a national monument.

As you explore the castle's inner sanctum, imagine it lined
with simple wooden huts. The imposing part of the castle is the exterior. The builders' strategy was to focus on making the castle appear so formidable that its very existence was enough to discourage
any attack. If you know where to look, you can still see stones laid
by ancient Romans, Visigoths, and Moors. The Portuguese made
the most substantial contribution, with a wall reaching all the way
to the river to withstand anticipated Spanish attacks.

The humble museum (between the castle and the view terrace)
houses archaeological finds from the 7th century B.C. to the 18th
century, with emphasis on the Moorish period in the 11th and 12th
centuries. You'll also see 18th-century tiles from an age when Portugal was flush with money from its colony, Brazil. While simple,
the museum has nice displays and descriptions.

➍ Castle Town

Just outside the castle turnstile is the tiny neighborhood within
the castle walls built to give Moorish elites refuge from sieges and,
later, for Portuguese nobles to live close to their king. While it's
partly taken over by cute shops and cafés, if you wander up Rua
de Santa Cruz do Castelo and stroll into its back lanes, you can
enjoy a peaceful bit of Portugal's past. Most of the houses date from
the Middle Ages. Poking around, go on a cultural scavenger hunt.
Look for: 1) clever, space-efficient, triangular contraptions for drying clothes (hint: see the bottle cap in the wall used to prop the
sticks out when in use); 2) Benfica soccer team flag (that's the team
favored by Lisbon's working class—an indication that the upper
class no longer chooses to live here); 3) short doors that were tall
enough for people back when these houses were built; and 4) noble
family crests over doors—dating to when important families wanted to be close to the king.

• Leave the castle. Across the ramp from the castle entrance (just outside
the turnstile 20 yards ahead, on the left) is a tidy little castle district
with cute shops and cafés, worth a wander for its peaceful lanes and a

Pombal's Lisbon

In 1750, lazy King José I (r. 1750-1777) turned the government over to a minor noble, the Marquês de Pombal (1699-1782). Talented, ambitious, and handsome, Pombal was praised as a reformer, but reviled for his ruthless tactics. Having learned modern ways as the ambassador to Britain, he battled Church repression and promoted the democratic ideals of the Enlightenment, but enforced his policies with arrests, torture, and executions. He expelled the Jesuits to keep them from monopolizing the education system, put the bishop of Coimbra in prison, and broke off relations with the pope. When the earthquake of 1755 leveled the city, within a month Pombal had kicked off major rebuilding in much of today's historic downtown—featuring a grid plan for the world's first quakeproof buildings. In 1777, the king died and the controversial Pombal was dismissed.

chance to enjoy the Manueline architecture. When you finally leave the castle complex grounds (at the little statue of St. George), jog to the left 30 yards past the gate, turn right on Travessa de São Bartolomeu, which becomes Travessa do Chão da Feira, and follow the striped lane downhill through Largo do Contador Mor (a small, car-clogged square with a Parisian ambience that has two handy outdoor restaurants, with grilled sardines as their specialty. Continue downhill 50 yards farther, pass the trolley tracks, circle right around the little church, to reach a superb Alfama viewpoint at...

❺ Largo Santa Luzia

From this square (a stop for trolleys #12E and #28E), admire the panoramic view from the small terrace, Miradouro de Santa Luzia, where old-timers play cards amid lots of tiles.

In the distance to the left, the **Vasco da Gama Bridge** (opened in 1998, described on page 76) connects Lisbon with new, modern bedroom communities south of the river. Below, the purple building with the green shades marks the square called Largo de São Miguel—the center of the Alfama. Where the Alfama neighborhood hits the river, notice the recently built embankment. It reclaimed 100 yards of land from the river to make a modern port, used these days to accommodate Lisbon's growing cruise ship industry.

On the wall of the church (facing the little view park) find two 18th-century tiles. One (on the left) shows Praça do Comércio before the 1755 earthquake. The 16th-century royal palace (shown on the left of the tilework, where the king went after abandoning the castle) was completely destroyed in the quake. The other tile (on the right) depicts the reconquest of Lisbon from the Moors by Afonso Henriques, described earlier. You can see the Portuguese hero, Martim Moniz, who let himself be crushed in the castle door to hold it open for his comrades. Notice the panicky Moors inside realizing that their castle is about to be breeched by invading Crusaders. It was a bad day for the Moors.

For an even better city view, hike back around the church and walk out to the seaside end of the Miradouro de Largo das Portas do Sol catwalk. The huge building dominating the neighborhood on the far left is the Monastery of São Vicente, constructed around 1600 by the Spanish king, Philip II, who wanted to leave his mark with this tribute to St. Vincent. A few steps away, under a statue of St. Vincent, is a kiosk café where you can enjoy perhaps the most scenic cup of coffee in town (daily 10:00-18:00).

• *Across the street from the café, you'll find the...*

❻ Museum and School of Portuguese Decorative Arts

The Museum and School of Portuguese Decorative Arts (Museu Escola de Artes Decorativas Portuguesas) offers a unique stroll through an aristocratic household, richly decorated in 16th- to 19th-century styles. In 1947, Ricardo do Espírito Santo Silva restored this Azurura Palace to house his collection of 15th- to 18th-century fine art, and then willed it to the state. He created perhaps the best chance for visitors to experience what an aristocratic home looked like during Lisbon's glory days. The coach at the ground level is "Berlin style," with a state-of-the-art suspension system. The grand stairway leads past 18th-century glazed tiles (Chinese-style blue-and-white was in vogue) upstairs into a world rich in colonial riches. Portuguese aristocrats had a flair for "Indo-Portuguese" decorative arts: exotic woods, shells, and Oriental porcelain (€4, Wed-Mon 10:00-17:00, closed Tue, Largo das Portas do Sol 2, tel. 218-814-640, www.fress.pt).

• *From here, it's downhill all the way. From Largo das Portas do Sol (the plaza with the statue of local patron St. Vincent, near the kiosk café on the terrace), go down the stairs (Rua Norberto de Araújo, between the church and the catwalk). The massive eighth-century fortified wall (on the right) once marked the boundary of Moorish Lisbon. Consider that the great stones on your right were stacked here over a thousand years ago. At the bottom of the wall, continue downhill, then turn left at the railing...and go down more stairs. Explore downhill from here.*

The main thoroughfare, a concrete stepped lane called Escadinhas de São Miguel, leads to the Alfama's main square, and...

❼ The Heart of the Alfama

This square, Largo de São Miguel, is the best place to observe a slice of Alfama life. While city leaders rebuilt the rest of Lisbon after the 1755 quake, this neighborhood was left out and consequently retains its tangled medieval street plan.

If you've got the time, explore the Alfama from this central square. Its urban-jungle roads are squeezed into confusing alleys—the labyrinthine street plan was designed to frustrate invaders and guidebook researchers trying to get up to the castle. What was defensive then is atmospheric now. Bent houses comfort each other in their romantic shabbiness, and the air drips with laundry and the smell of clams. Get lost. Poke aimlessly, peek through windows, buy a fish. Locals hang plastic water bags from windows in the summer to try to keep away the flies. Favorite saints decorate doors to protect families. St. Peter, protector of fishermen, is big in the Alfama. Churches are generally closed, since they share a priest. As children have very little usable land for a good soccer game, goalposts are painted onto the stairs. The tiny balconies were limited to "one-and-a-half hands" in width. A strictly enforced health initiative kept the town open and well-ventilated. If you see carpets hanging out to dry, it means a laundry is nearby. Because few homes have their own, every neighborhood has a public laundry and bathroom. Until recently, in the early morning hours, the streets were busy with residents in pajamas, heading for these public baths. Today, many are choosing to live elsewhere, lured by modern conveniences unavailable here, and the old flats became congested with immigrant laborers (mostly Ukrainian and Brazilian) who came during the construction boom a decade ago. Today, with the bad economy, they are moving on in search of employment. In just a couple of generations, the demographics have changed—from fishermen's families to immigrants to young bohemians.

Traditionally the neighborhood here was tightly knit, with families routinely sitting down to communal dinners in the streets. Feuds, friendships, and gossip were all intense. Historically, when a woman's husband died, she wore black for the rest of her life—a tradition that's just about gone.

The Alfama hosts Lisbon's most popular outdoor party on St. Anthony's Day (June 13). Imagine tables set up everywhere, bands playing, bright plastic flowers strung across the squares, and

LISBON

all the grilled sardines *(sardinhas grelhadas)* you can eat. The rustic paintings of festive characters (with hints of Moorish style) remind locals of past parties, and strings and wires overhead await future festival dates when the neighborhood will again be festooned with colorful streamers.

While there are plenty of traditional festivals here, the most action on the Alfama calendar is the insane, annual mountain-bike street race from the castle to the sea (which you can see hurtle by in under two minutes on YouTube; search "Lisboa downtown race").

• *Continue exploring downhill from here. You'll see a trendy little restaurant (the recommended Restaurante Santo Antonio de Álfama) and the recommended amateur fado restaurant (A Baiuca). Then, a few steps below the square, you'll hit the cobbled pedestrian lane, Rua São Pedro. This darkest of the Alfama's streets, in nearly perpetual shade, was the logical choice for the neighborhood's fish market. Modern hygiene requirements (which forbid outdoor stalls) killed the market, but it's still a characteristic lane to explore. Turn left and follow Rua São Pedro out of the Alfama to the square called Largo do Chafariz de Dentro and, across the street, the...*

❽ Fado Museum

This museum, rated ▲, tells the story of fado in English—with a great chance to hear these wailing fisherwomen's blues. Three levels of wall murals show three generations of local fado stars, and the audioguide lets you hear the Billie Holidays of Portugal (€5, includes audioguide, Tue-Sun 10:00-18:00, closed Mon, last entry 30 minutes before closing, Largo do Chafariz de Dentro, tel. 218-823-470, www.museudofado.pt).

• *This walk is over. To get back downtown (or to Praça do Comércio, where the next walk starts) from the Fado Museum, walk a block to the main waterfront drag and cruise-ship harbor (facing museum, go left around it) where busy Avenida Infante Dom Henrique leads back to Praça do Comércio downtown. While it's a 15-minute walk or quick taxi ride to Praça do Comércio, just to the left is a bus stop. Ride any bus for two stops and you're there in moments. (Also, bus #759 goes on to Praça dos Restauradores; #9, #90, and #746 continue up Avenida da Liberdade.)*

▲▲▲THE BAIXA STROLL: LISBON'S HISTORIC DOWNTOWN

This walk covers the highlights of Lisbon's downtown, the Baixa, which fills the flat valley between two hills, sloping gently from the waterfront up to the Rossio, Praça dos Restauradores, Avenida da Liberdade, and the newer town. The walk starts at Praça do Comércio and ends at Praça dos Restauradores.

After the disastrous 1755 earthquake, the Baixa district was

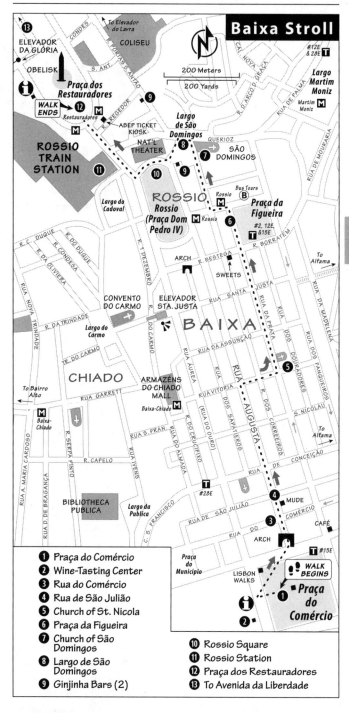

Baixa Stroll

To Elevador
do Lavra

❶❸ ELEVADOR
DA GLÓRIA

CONDES

COLISEU

N

200 Meters

200 Yards

OBELISK

Praça dos
Restauradores

S. ANT

R. PORTAS S ANTÃO

CAL. NOVA DE

R. D'ARCO P. GRAÇA

#12E
& 28E

Largo
Martim
Moniz

RUA DE PALMA

Martim
Moniz

WALK
ENDS

❶❷

Restauradores

R. REGEDOR

❾

Largo
de São
Domingos

QUERIOZ

ROSSIO
TRAIN
STATION

ABEP TICKET
KIOSK

NAT'L
THEATER

❽

❼

SÃO
DOMINGOS

❶❶

❶❶

Largo do
Cadoval

❶⓪

❾

ROSSIO
Rossio
(Praça Dom
Pedro IV)

Rossio

Rossio

❻

RUA DE MOURARIA

Bus Tours

Praça da
Figueira

B

#2, 12E,
&15E

LISBON

R. C DUQUE

R. DO DUQUE

R. CONDESA

RUA DA OLIVIERA

RUA NOVA TRINDADE

R. DA TRINDADE

Largo do
Carmo

TR. DO CARMO

CHIADO

Baixa-
Chiado

RUA A. MARIA CARDOSO

RUA D. D. BRAGANÇA

CONVENTO
DO CARMO

R. DO CARMO

ARCH

R. BESTEGA

SWEETS

ELEVADOR
STA. JUSTA

RUA SANTA JUSTA

BAIXA

RUA DA ASSUNÇÃO

RUA AUREA

ARMAZÉNS
DO CHIADO
MALL

Baixa-Chiado

RUA GARRETT

R. SERPA PINTO

R. CAPELO

RUA IVENS

BIBLIOTHECA
PUBLICA

RUA S. FRAN.

RUA DO CARMO

RUA DO ORO

RUA VITORIA

RUA DOS SAPATEIROS

(RUA DO OURO)

R. DO CRUCIFIXO

RUA DA PRATA

RUA DOS CORREEIROS

RUA DOS DOURADORES

RUA DA MADELENA

RUA DOS FANQUEIROS

S. NICOLAU

RUA DO COMÉRCIO

RUA DE CONCEIÇÃO

Largo da
Publica

C. S. FRANCISCO

RUA DE SÃO JULIÃO

#28E

MUDE

❹

❺

To
Alfama

To
Alfama

To Bairro
Alto

To Bairro
Alto

RUA DE

RUA DO

CAFÉ

ARCH

❸

Praça
do
Municipio

LISBON
WALKS

#15E

WALK
BEGINS

❶

Praça
do
Comércio

❷

❶ Praça do Comércio
❷ Wine-Tasting Center
❸ Rua do Comércio
❹ Rua de São Julião
❺ Church of St. Nicola
❻ Praça da Figueira
❼ Church of São
    Domingos
❽ Largo de São
    Domingos
❾ Ginjinha Bars (2)

⓾ Rossio Square
⓫ Rossio Station
⓬ Praça dos Restauradores
⓭ To Avenida da Liberdade

rebuilt on a grid street plan. The uniform and utilitarian Pombaline architecture (named after the Marquês
de Pombal, the prime minister who
rebuilt the city—see sidebar, earlier)
feels almost military. That's because
it is. The Baixa was built by military
engineers who had experience build-

ing garrison towns overseas. The new Lisbon featured the architecture of conquest—simple to assemble, economical, with all the
pieces easy to ship. The 18th-century buildings you'd see in Mozambique and Brazil are interchangeable with those in Lisbon.

The buildings are all uniform, with the same number of floors
and standard facades. They were designed to survive the next
earthquake, with stone firewalls and wooden frameworks featuring crisscross beams that flexed. The priorities were to rebuild fast,
cheap, and earthquake-proof.

If it were left up to the people, who believed the earthquake
was a punishment from God, they would have rebuilt their churches bigger and more impressive than ever. But Pombal was a practical military man with a budget, a timeline, and an awareness of his
society's limits. He didn't want church-building to compromise the
needs of the people. In those austere post-earthquake days, Pombal
got his way.

The Baixa has three squares: two pre-earthquake (Comércio
and Rossio) and one added later (Figueira), and three main streets:
Prata (silver), Aurea (gold), and Augusta (relating the Portuguese
king to a Roman emperor). The former maze of the Jewish Quarter
was eliminated, but the area has many streets named for the crafts
and shops once found there.

The Baixa's pedestrian streets, inviting cafés, bustling shops,
and elegant old storefronts give the district a certain charm. City-
government subsidies make sure the old businesses stay around,
but modern ones find a way to creep in. I find myself doing laps up
and down Rua Augusta in a people-watching stupor. Its delightful
ambience is perfect for strolling and reminiscent of the Ramblas in
Barcelona.

• *Start your walk under the statue of King José I in the center of Praça
do Comércio.*

❶ Praça do Comércio ("Trade Square")

At this riverfront square bordering the Baixa—long the gateway
to Lisbon—ships used to dock and sell their goods. Nicknamed
"Palace Square" by locals, it was the site of Portugal's royal palace
for 200 pre-earthquake years. After the 1755 earthquake/tsunami/

fire, the jittery king fled to more-stable
Belém, never to return. These days, government ministries ring Praça do Comércio. It's also the departure point for
city bus and tram tours, and boats that
cruise along the Rio Tejo. The area opposite the harbor was conceived as a residential neighborhood for the upper class,
but they chose the suburbs. Today, the
square has two names ("Palace Square"
and "Commercial Square") and little real
life. Locals consider it just a big place to
pass through.

The statue is of King José I, the man who gave control of the
government to Pombal, who rebuilt the city after the earthquake.
Built 20 years after the quake, it shows the king on his horse, with
Pombal (on the medallion), looking at their port. The horse (symbolic of triumph) stomps on snakes (symbolic of evil—perhaps
Protestants...or troublemaking noble families), while the elephant
represents the Portuguese empire's colonies in India and Africa. In
its glory days, this city was where east met west.

The big arch marking the inland side of the square is Lisbon's
Arch of Triumph (with Vasco da Gama on the left and Pombal on
the right). Disregarding his usual austerity, Pombal restored some
of the city's Parisian-style grandeur at this central approach into
downtown.

Note there are two tourist sights on the square, neither worth
your time nor money. The much-promoted "Lisbon Story Center"
is a childish exhibit with no artifacts—you pay €7 to stand for an
hour looking at animated history on computer screens. The towering Rua Augusta Arch is open to climb (€2.50, elevator plus 74
steps), but affords only a mediocre view from its empty rooftop.

• *With your back to the harbor (facing the Arch of Triumph), the TI, Vini
Portugal wine-tasting center, and meeting point for walking tours are
on your left; and the Terriero do Paço Metro stop is behind you on the
right (in the southeast corner of the square).*

❼ Wine-Tasting Center

At the **Wines of Portugal Tasting Room**, the country's vintners
sponsor a nonprofit wine-appreciation venue. Sixteen local wines
are offered with English descriptions above each tap, with a helpful
attendant happy to explain things. To taste, you buy a chip card (€2
minimum), are given a glass, and serve yourself various samples
of eight whites and eight reds from €0.50 and up (Tue-Sat 11:00-
19:00, closed Sun-Mon, next to TI).

Martinho da Arcada, a fine option for a coffee, pastry, or snack, is under the arcades on Praça do Comércio. It was founded in 1782—when the wealthy would come here to savor early ice cream made with mountain snow, lemon, and spices. While it has a fancy restaurant, I'd enjoy just coffee and pastry in its café bar. This place was one of poet Fernando Pessoa's old haunts (they display a few Pessoa artifacts). In the early 20th century, painters, writers, and dreamers shared revolutionary ideas here over coffee (Praça do Comércio 8, at the corner of Rua da Prata).

• *Pass through the big arch and walk down Rua Augusta into the Baixa district. The next two stops along this walk take you straight down Rua Augusta, pausing at three cross streets.*

❸ Rua do Comércio

Look right to see the old cathedral with its Romanesque fortress-like crenellations (described on page 66). Notice that many of the surrounding buildings are austere, with no tiles—this was the architectural style adopted immediately after the earthquake, when only the interiors of buildings were tiled. In the Portuguese colony of Brazil, people found that tiles protected against humidity, and eventually (by the 19th century), tilework was adopted as a form of exterior decoration here in Lisbon.

The characteristic black-and-white cobbled sidewalk *(calçada)* is uniquely Portuguese. These mosaic limestone and basalt cobbles were first cut and laid by 19th-century prison laborers. To this day patterns are chosen from a book of acceptable designs. As the stones are slippery and expensive to maintain, the city government is talking about replacing them with modern pavement. And locals are crying out to keep the tradition.

Across the street, on the right, you'll pass the Museum la Mode, Lisbon's museum of design (a.k.a. MUDE; free, Tue-Sun 10:00-18:00, closed Mon). Filling the Art Deco ground floor of a former bank, it offers a quick, one-floor stroll through 20th-century fashion. Special exhibits are on other floors, and a huge bank vault in the basement is often part of the show.

• *At Rua de São Julião, look left about 30 yards and try to find the church—it's hiding.*

❹ Rua de São Julião

Churches are scarce in the post-earthquake Baixa. Only a few of the churches destroyed by the quake were permitted to be rebuilt. The replacement churches were incorporated into the no-nonsense military style, with facades that match the rest of the street. You'll notice that the Baixa district is struggling to stay vital, with the upper floors of many buildings now mostly empty. Look up for evidence of how downtown Lisbon's population is shrinking, as more people move to the suburbs.

The Lisbon Earthquake of 1755

At 9:40 in the morning on Sunday, November 1—All Saints' Day—an earthquake estimated to be close to 9.0 in magnitude

rumbled through the city, punctuated by three main jolts. Its arrival came midway through Mass. Ten minutes later, thousands lay dead under the rubble.

Along the waterfront, shaken survivors scrambled aboard boats to sail to safety. They were met by a 20-foot wall of water, the first wave of a tsunami that rushed up the Rio Tejo. The ravaging water capsized ships, swept people off the docks, crested over the seawall, and crashed 800 feet inland.

After the quake, the city turned into an inferno, as overturned cooking fires and fallen candles ignited raging fires. The fires blazed for five days, ravaging the downtown from the Bairro Alto across Rossio to the castle atop the Alfama.

Of Lisbon's 270,000 citizens, over 10,000 may have perished. Besides leveling the city, the quake shook conservative Portugal's moral and spiritual underpinnings. Had God punished Lisbon for the Inquisition killings carried out on nearby Praça do Comércio?

King José I was so affected by the earthquake that he moved his entire court to an elaborate complex of tents in the foothills of Belém and resisted living indoors for the rest of his life.

LISBON

At the next block, the handy trolley #28E stops at Rua da Conceição. Ahead on the right (in the windows of the Millennium Bank) are Roman artifacts—a reminder that Lisbon's history goes way back.

• *At Rua da Vitoria, turn right and walk to Rua da Prata, where you'll see the camouflaged...*

❺ Church of St. Nicola (Igreja de São Nicolau)
Notice how its church-like facade was allowed, but the entire green-tiled side is disguised as just another stretch of post-earthquake Baixa architecture.

• *Head left down Rua da Prata toward the statue marking Praça da Figueira. At Rua de Santa Justa, look left for a good view of Elevador de Santa Justa before continuing straight to the square.*

❻ Praça da Figueira ("Fig Tree Square")
This was the site of a huge hospital destroyed in the earthquake. With no money to replace the hospital, the space was left open

until the late 1880s, when it was filled with a big iron-framed market (similar to Barcelona's La Boqueria). That structure was torn down decades ago, leaving the square you see today. The big building on the left is run-down—after 50 years of rent control, many landowners are demoralized and do nothing to fix up their property. Buildings like this are often either vacant or occupied by old pensioners living out their lives amid increasingly decrepit conditions. By contrast, the right side (under the castle) is more lived-in and vibrant.

The nearby **Confeitaria Nacional** shop (on the corner of the square, 20 yards to your left) is a venerable palace of sweets little changed since the 19th century. In the window is a display of *"conventuel* sweets"—special nun-made treats often consisting of sugar and egg yolks (historically, the nuns, who used the egg whites to starch their laundry, had an abundance of yolks). Consider a light lunch here in the upstairs dining room (see page 116 for details).

The square is a transportation hub, with stops for the minibus #737 and the old trolley #12E going to the castle (see page 33 for a self-guided trolley tour), the modern trolley #15E and bus #714 heading out to Belém, and the touristic hop-on, hop-off buses.

• *Walk to the far-left corner of the square, past skateboarders oblivious to its historical statue—Portugal's King John I on a horse. Leave the square down the Rua Dom Antão de Almada. This lane has several characteristic shops. Pop into the classic cod shop (on the left at #1C—you'll smell it). Cod is part of Portugal's heritage as a nation of seafaring explorers: It was salted and could keep for a year on a ship. Just soak in water to rinse out the salt and enjoy. The adjacent ham counter serves pata negra (presunto ibérico) from acorn-fed pigs—the very best. The non-pork alheira sausage is made with game and was a favorite among Lisbon's Jews back when they needed to fake being Christians. At the end of the lane stands a big church facing another square.*

❼ Church of São Domingos

A center of the Inquisition in the 1600s, this is now one of Lisbon's most active churches (daily 7:30-19:00). The evocative interior—more or less rebuilt from the ruins left by the 1755 earthquake—reminds visitors of that horrible All Saints' Day Sunday, when most of the city was at Mass and the earth rolled. Across the city, heavy stone church walls like these collapsed on their congregations. Standing at the back of the nave, you can see which parts of the pre-1755 stone walls remained standing afterward. The black soot on the walls and the charred stonework at the altar recalls the horrible fires that followed the earthquake. Our Lady of Fátima is Portugal's most popular saint. Her chapel (in the left rear of the church) always has the most candles. She's accompanied by two of the three children who saw the miraculous apparition (the third was still alive when this chapel was made and so is not shown in heaven with the saint).

• *Step into the square just beyond the church.*

❽ Largo de São Domingos

This area was just outside of the old town walls—long a place where people gathered to keep watering holes busy and enjoy bohemian entertainment. Today the square is home to classic old bars (a *ginjinha* bar is described next) and a busy "eating lane," Rua das Portas de Santo Antão (kitty-corner from where you entered the square, to the right of the National Theater on the far side of the square).

The square once held a palace that functioned as the head-quarters of the Inquisition. It was demolished, and in an attempt to erase its memory, the National Theater was built in its place. The city massacred the town's Jews on this square in 1506. A stone monument, unveiled in 2008, remembers this sad event.

Once the site of Lisbon's 16th-century slave market, this square is now a meeting point for the city's African immigrant community—people from former Portuguese colonies such as Angola, Mozambique, and Portuguese Guinea. They hang out, trade news from home, and watch the tourists go by.

• *Find the colorful little hole-in-the-wall tavern facing the square and serving the traditional cherry brandy.*

❾ Liquid Sightseeing

Ginjinha (zheen-ZHEEN-yah) is a favorite Lisbon drink. While nuns baked sweets, the monks took care of quenching thirsts with this sweet liquor, made from the sour cherry-like *ginja* berry, sugar, cinna-mon, and brandy. It's now sold for €1.10 a shot in funky old shops throughout downtown. Buy it with or without berries (*com elas* or *sem elas*—that's "with them" or "without them") and *gelada* (if you want it poured from a chilled bottle). In Portugal, when people are impressed by the taste of something, they say, *"Sabe que nem ginjas"*—literally "It tastes like *ginja*," but meaning "finger-lickin' good." The oldest *ginjinha* joint in town is a colorful hole-in-the-wall at Largo de São Domingos 8. If you hang around the bar long enough, you'll see them refill the bottle from an enormous vat. (Another *ginjinha* bar, named for Eduardino the clown and con-sidered the most authentic, is a block away on the restaurant row, Rua das Portas de Santo Antão, next to #59; daily 7:00-24:00.)

• *The big square around the corner (fronting the National Theater) is Rossio.*

⓾ Rossio

Lisbon's historic center, Rossio, is still the city's bustling cultural heart. Given its elongated shape, historians believe it was a Roman racetrack 2,000 years ago; these days, cars circle the loop instead of chariots. It's home to the colonnaded National Theater, a McDonald's, and street vendors who can shine your shoes, laminate your documents, and sell you cheap watches, autumn chestnuts, and lottery tickets. The column in the square's center honors Pedro IV—king of Portugal and emperor of Brazil. (Many maps refer to the square as Praça Dom Pedro IV, but residents always just call it Rossio, referring to the train station at one corner.)

From here you can see the Elevador de Santa Justa and the ruined convent breaking the city skyline. Notice the fine stone patterns in the pavement—evoking waves encountered by the great explorers—which once upon a time made locals seasick.

• *Crossing the square in front of the National Theater, you see Rossio Station.*

⓫ Rossio Station

The circa-1900 facade of Rossio Station is Neo-Manueline. You can read the words *Central Station* printed on its striking horseshoe arches. Find the statue of King Sebastian in the center of two arches. This romantic, dashing, and young soldier king was lost in 1580 in an ill-fated crusade in Africa. As Sebastian left no direct

heir, the crown ended up with Philip II of Spain, who became Philip I of Portugal. The Spanish king promised to give back the throne if Sebastian ever turned up—and ever since, the Portuguese have dreamed that Sebastian will return, restoring their national greatness. Even today, in a crisis, the Portuguese like to think that their Sebastian will save the day—he's the symbol of being ridiculously hopeful.

• *Just uphill from Rossio Station is Praça dos Restauradores, at the bottom of Lisbon's long and grand Avenida da Liberdade.*

⓬ Praça dos Restauradores

This monumental square connects Rossio with Avenida da Liberdade (described next). Its centerpiece, an obelisk, celebrates the restoration of Portuguese independence from Spain in 1640 (without any help from the still-missing Sebastian mentioned earlier).

Just off the square is Lisbon's oldest hotel (the Hotel Avenida Palace, built as a terminus hotel at the same time as Rossio Station), the 1920s Art Deco facade of the Eden Theater, a TI, a green ABEP kiosk (selling tickets for concerts, movies, bullfights, and sports events) at the southern end, the Elevador da Glória funicular that climbs to the Bairro Alto (a bit up the street, opposite the Hard Rock Café), and a Metro station. A block to the east is Lisbon's "eating lane" (Rua das Portas de Santo Antão), the restaurant-lined street mentioned earlier.

• *While this walk ends here, stroll up Avenida da Liberdade for a good look at another facet of this fine city.*

LISBON

⓭ Avenida da Liberdade

This tree-lined grand boulevard, running north from Rossio, connects the old town (where most of the sightseeing action is) with the newer upper town. Before the great earthquake, this was the city's royal promenade. After 1755, it was the grand boulevard of Pombal's new Lisbon—originally limited to the aristocracy. The present street, built in the 1880s and inspired by Paris' Champs-Elysées, is lined with banks, airline offices, nondescript office buildings...and eight noisy lanes of traffic. The grand "rotunda"—as the roundabout formally known as Marquês de Pombal is called—tops off the Avenida da Liberdade with a commanding statue of Pombal. Allegorical symbols of his impressive accomplishments decorate the statue. (A single-minded dictator can do a lot in 27 years.) Beyond that lies the fine Edward VII Park. From the Rotunda (Metro: Marquês de Pombal), it's an enjoyable 20-minute downhill walk along the mile-long avenue back to the Baixa.

▲▲▲THE BAIRRO ALTO AND CHIADO STROLL

Rise above the Baixa on the funicular, Elevador da Glória, located near the obelisk at Praça dos Restauradores (opposite the Hard Rock Café, €3.60 if you pay driver, cheaper with Viva Viagem card, 6/hour); you can also hike up alongside the tracks.

• *Leaving the funicular on top, turn right (go 100 yards, up into a park) to enjoy the city view from the...*

❶ Miradouro de São Pedro de Alcântara (San Pedro Belvedere)

The tile map guides you through the view, stretching from the twin towers of the cathedral (Sé, on far right behind trees), to the ramparts of the castle birthplace of Lisbon (capping the hill, on right), to another quaint, tree-topped viewpoint in Graça (directly across, end of trolley #28E), to the skyscraper towers of the new city in the distance (on far left). Note that whenever you see a big old building in Lisbon, it's often a former convent or monastery, nationalized by the state, and now occupied by a hospital, school, or the military.

In the park, a bust honors a 19th-century local journalist (founder of Lisbon's first daily newspaper) and a charming, bare-footed delivery boy. This district is famous for its writers, poets, publishers, and bohemians. (The walk continues downhill from here.)

• *Directly across the street from where you got off the Elevador da Glória is the...*

❷ Port Wine Institute

If you're into port (the fortified wine that takes its name from the city of Porto, covered later in this book), you'll find the world's greatest selection at **Solar do Vinho do Porto,** run by the Port Wine Institute (Mon-Sat 11:00-24:00, closed Sun, WCs, Rua São Pedro de Alcântara 45, tel. 213-475-707). You're welcome to go in to simply browse even if you're not drinking. The plush, air-conditioned, Old World living room is furnished with leather chairs (this is not a shorts-and-T-shirt kind of place). You can order from a selection of more than 150 different ports (€1.50-22 per glass), generally poured by an English-speaking bartender. Read the instructive menu for an education in port. Fans of port describe it as "a liquid symphony playing on the palate." Browse through the easy menu. Start white and sweet (cheapest), taste your way through spicy and ruby, and finish mellow and tawny. A *colheita* (single harvest) is particularly good. Appetizers *(aperitivos)* are listed in the menu with small photographs. Seated service can be slow and disinterested when it's busy. As these are government employees and their jobs are secure, smiles are unnecessary. To be served without a long wait, go to the bar. Enjoy the Douro Valley photos, maps, and models of traditional boats that add to the port-industry ambience of the place. For more on port, see page 300.

• *Next, side-trip directly across from the top of the funicular into the old grid-plan streets of the Bairro Alto. While it's fun to wander, follow this route for a good sampling: Go three blocks uphill, turn left on Rua da Atalaia, continue three blocks, and then head left down Travessa da Queimada until you cross the big street (leaving the Bairro Alto) and reach the small square, Largo Trindade Coelho.*

❸ Bairro Alto Detour

The "High Town," or Bairro Alto, is one of the most characteristic and charming districts in Lisbon. While the Baixa (lower town) has a grid plan because it was rebuilt after the 1755 earthquake, the Bairro Alto was designed in the 16th century with a very modern (at the time) grid-plan layout. The district housed ship work-

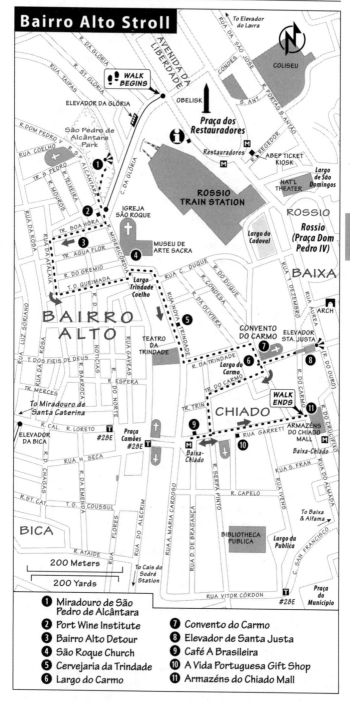

Bairro Alto Stroll

LISBON

WALK BEGINS

To Elevador do Lavra

ELEVADOR DA GLÓRIA

São Pedro de Alcântara Park

OBELISK

Praça dos Restauradores

Restauradores

ABEP TICKET KIOSK

COLISEU

NAT'L THEATER

Largo de São Domingos

IGREJA SÃO ROQUE

MUSEU DE ARTE SACRA

ROSSIO TRAIN STATION

Largo do Cadoval

ROSSIO

Rossio (Praça Dom Pedro IV)

BAIXA

Largo Trindade Coelho

BAIRRO ALTO

TEATRO DA TRINDADE

CONVENTO DO CARMO

ELEVADOR STA. JUSTA

Largo do Carmo

ARCH

To Miradouro de Santa Caterina

WALK ENDS

ELEVADOR DA BICA

Praça Camões
#28E

CHIADO

Café A Brasileira

RUA GARRETT

ARMAZÉNS DO CHIADO MALL

Baixa-Chiado

Baixa-Chiado

BICA

BIBLIOTHECA PUBLICA

Largo da Publica

To Baixa & Alfama

200 Meters

200 Yards

To Cais do Sodré Station

#28E

Praça do Municipio

❶ Miradouro de São Pedro de Alcântara
❷ Port Wine Institute
❸ Bairro Alto Detour
❹ São Roque Church
❺ Cervejaria da Trindade
❻ Largo do Carmo

❼ Convento do Carmo
❽ Elevador de Santa Justa
❾ Café A Brasileira
❿ A Vida Portuguesa Gift Shop
⓫ Armazéns do Chiado Mall

Lisbon's Kiosks

The kiosk—that's *quiosque* in Portuguese—has become a standard feature of squares and viewpoints all over town. Many originated a century ago as the city's first phone terminals. Later they became newsstands, lottery sales points, and now outdoor cafés turning parks and squares into neighborhood hangouts and meeting points. New ones are being built all the time and can be quite trendy. If you see a group of people talking, you'll likely notice a newsstand kiosk nearby—kiosks sell three daily newspapers devoted to football (soccer). With tough economic times, and what many consider a corrupt elite colluding with the government to keep the populace down, working-class people are conveniently distracted by sports.

ers back when Portugal was a world power and its ships planted the Portuguese flag all around the globe. Today, the Bairro Alto is quiet in the morning, but buzzes with a thriving restaurant scene in the evening.

• *On the square, Largo Trindade Coelho, is the...*

❹ São Roque Church

Step inside, and then sit on a pew in the middle to take it all in (free, Mon 14:00-18:00, Tue-Sun 9:00-18:00). Built in the 16th century, the church of St. Roque, worth ▲, is one of Portugal's first Jesuit churches. The painted wood, false-domed ceiling is perfectly flat. The acoustics here are top-notch, important in a Jesuit church, where the emphasis is on the sermon (given from twin pulpits mid-nave). The numbered panels on the floor were tombs, nameless because they were for lots of people. They're empty now—the practice was stopped in the 19th century when parishioners didn't want plague victims rotting under their feet.

Survey the rich side chapels. The highlight is the Chapel of St. John the Baptist (left of altar, gold and blue lapis lazuli columns). It looks like it came right out of the Vatican—and that's because it did. Made in Rome out of the most precious materials, the chapel was the site of one papal Mass; then it was disassembled and shipped to Lisbon. Per square inch, it was the most costly chapel ever constructed in Portugal. Notice the mosaic floor (with the spherical symbol of Portugal) and the three "paintings" that are actually intricate, beautiful mosaics—a Vatican specialty, designed to avoid damage from candle smoke that would darken real paintings. Notice also the delicate "sliced marble" symmetry and imagine the labor involved in so artfully cutting that stone five centuries ago. To the right, a glass case is filled with relics trying to grab your attention. The next chapel to the left features a riot of babies. Individual chapels—each for a different noble family—seem to be in competition. Keep in mind that the tiles are considered as extravagant as the gold leaf and silver.

To the right of the altar is the sacristy where, along with huge chests of drawers for vestments, you can see a series of 17th-century paintings illustrating scenes from the life of St. Frances Xavier—co-founder of the Jesuit order with St.Ignatius of Loyola.

The São Roque Museum (outside the church, to the left as you leave) is more interesting than your typical small church museum. It's filled with perhaps the best-presented collection of 16th- and 17th-century church art in town, and is well described in English. The church and this art, rare survivors of the 1755 earthquake, illustrate the religious passion that accompanied Portugal's Age of Discovery, with themes including: the mission of the Jesuits and their response to the Reformation; devotion to relics; and devotion to the Virgin (€2.50, same hours as the church).

• *Back outside in the church square (charming WC underground), visit the statue of a friendly lottery-ticket salesman. Two lottery kiosks are nearby. Locals who buy into the* totoloto *(which, like national lotteries everywhere, is a form of taxation on gamblers that helps fund government social programs) rub the statue's ticket for good luck. Continue (kitty-corner across the square) downhill along Rua Nova da Trindade. At #20, pop into...*

❺ Cervejaria da Trindade

The famous "oldest beer hall in Lisbon" is worth a visit for a look at its 19th-century tiles. The beautifully tiled main room, once a refectory (monks' dining hall), still holds the pulpit from which the Bible was read as the monks ate. After the monastery was abolished in 1836 it became a brewery—you'll notice that while the oldest tiles have Christian themes, the later ones (from around 1860) are all about the beer. They have five Portuguese beers on tap—Sagres is the standard lager, Sagres Preta is a good dark beer (like a porter), and Bohemia is sweet, with more alcohol. At the bar in front you can get a snack and beer, while more expensive dining is in the back (see page 114).

When you're done, continue downhill to Livraria Barateira at #16, Lisbon's biggest used bookstore, where you can sell this book.

• *Continue down the hill, where at the next intersection, signs point left to the ruined Convento do Carmo. Follow the inside trolley tracks downhill and to the left to the next square...*

❻ Largo do Carmo

On this square decorated with an old fountain, lots of pigeons, and jacaranda trees from South America (with purple blossoms in June), police officers guard the headquarters of the National Guard.

Famous among residents, this was the last refuge of the fascist dictator António Salazar's successor. The Portuguese people won their revolution in 1974, in a peaceful uprising called the Carnation Revolution. The name came when revolutionaries placed flowers in the guns of the soldiers, making it clear it was time for democracy here. For more history, see the sidebar.

• *On Largo do Carmo, check out the ruins of...*

❼ Convento do Carmo

After the convent was destroyed by the 1755 earthquake, the Marquês de Pombal directed that the delicate Gothic arches of its church be left standing—supporting nothing but open sky—as a permanent reminder of that disastrous event. If you pay to enter, you'll see a fine memorial park in what was the nave, and a simple museum with Bronze Age and Roman artifacts, medieval royal sarcophagi, and a couple of Peruvian mummies—all explained in English (€3.50—cheapskates can do a deep knee-bend at the ticket desk, sneak a peek, and then crawl away; June-Sept Mon-Sat 10:00-19:00, Oct-May until 18:00, closed Sun year-round).

• *Just past the convent (to the right as you face it), a lane leads out and around to a fine city viewpoint from the top of the Elevador de Santa Justa.*

❽ Elevador de Santa Justa

In 1902, an architect—who studied under Gustav Eiffel—completed this 150-foot-tall iron elevator, connecting the lower and upper parts of town. The elevator's Neo-Gothic motifs are an attempt to match the ruined church near its top. While you'll need to pay extra to go to the top-floor lookout for a fine city view, the view from the entry-ramp level is nearly as good—and free (€5 round-trip ticket, free with Via Viagem card loaded with 24-hour pass—if "Zapping," it'll cost your card €1.40, daily 7:00-21:30).

Stroll around this celebration of the Industrial Age, enjoy the view, and retrace your steps to the square in front of the convent. (The nearby Leitaria Académica, a venerable little working-class eatery with tables spilling onto the delightful square, can be handy for a snack or drink.)

• *Leave Largo do Carmo, walking a block slightly uphill on Travessa do Carmo. At the next square, take a left on Rua Serpa Pinto, walking downhill to Rua Garrett, where—in the little pedestrian zone 50 yards uphill on the right—you'll find a famous old café across from the Baixa-Chiado Metro stop.*

❾ Café A Brasileira

Reeking of smoke and slinky with Art Nouveau decor, this café is a 100-year-old institution for coffeehouse junkies. Drop in for

The Carnation Revolution

António Salazar, who ruled Portugal from 1926 to 1968, was modern Europe's longest-ruling dictator (he died in 1970).

Salazar's authoritarian regime, the Estado Novo, continued in power under Prime Minister Marcelo Caetano until 1974.

By the 1970s, all the fighting in Portugal's far-flung colonies over the past decade had demoralized much of Salazar's military, and at home, there was a growing appetite for a modern democracy. On April 25, 1974, several prominent members of the military reluctantly sided with a growing popular movement to oust the government. Their withdrawal of support spelled the end of the Salazar era. Five people died that April day, in a well-planned, relatively bloodless coup. Citizens spilled into the streets to cheer and put flowers in soldiers' rifle barrels, giving the event its name: the Carnation Revolution. Suddenly, people were free to speak aloud what they formerly could only whisper in private.

In the revolution's aftermath, the country struggled to get the hang of modern democracy. Its economy suffered as overseas colonies fell to nationalist uprisings, flooding the country with some 800,000 emigrants. For colonial overlords, life went from "shrimp day and night" to a sudden collapse of the empire; for their own safety, they fled back to Portugal. A good number of these "returnees" didn't fit into their newly democratic old country—feeling like people without a homeland, many ultimately left Portugal (joining Salazar's henchmen, who took refuge in Brazil). Even those who stayed were generally pro-dictator and angry about the revolution, contributing to a polarization of modern Portuguese society that exists to this day.

In 1976, the Portuguese adopted a constitution that separated church and state. These changes helped to break down the almost-medieval class system and establish parliamentary law. Mario Soares, a former enemy of the Salazar regime, became the new prime minister, ruling as a stabilizing presence through much of the next two decades. Today, Portugal is enthusiastically democratic.

LISBON

a *bica* (Lisbon slang for an espresso, €0.70 at the bar) and a €1.30 *pastel de nata* custard tart—a Lisbon specialty. (WCs are down the stairs near the entrance.) This café was the literary and creative soul of Lisbon in the 1920s and 1930s, when the country's avant-garde poets, writers, and painters would hang out here. The statue outside is of the poet Fernando Pessoa (see sidebar), making him a perpetual regular at this café. A Brasileira was originally a shop

Portugal's Two Greatest Poets

The Portuguese are justifiably proud of their two most famous poets, whose names, works, and memorials you may encounter in your travels.

Portugal's most important poet, **Luís de Camões** (1524-1580), was a Renaissance-age equivalent of the ancient Greek poet, Homer. Camões' masterpiece, *The Lusiads (Os Lusíadas)*, tells the story of an explorer far from home. But instead of Odysseus, this epic poem describes the journey of Vasco da Gama, the man who found the route from Europe to India. Camões—who had sailed to Morocco to fight the Moors (where he lost an eye), to Goa (where he was imprisoned for debt), and to China (where he was shipwrecked)—was uniquely qualified to write about Portugal's pursuit of empire on the high seas. For more on Camões, see page 85.

Fernando Pessoa (1888-1935) used multiple personas in his poetry. He'd take on the voice of a simple countryman and

express his love of nature in free verse. Or he'd write as an erudite scholar, sharing philosophical thoughts in a more formal style. By varying his voice, he was able to more easily explore different viewpoints and truths. While Pessoa loved the classics—reading Milton, Byron, Shelley, and Poe—he was a true 20th-century bohemian at heart. Café A Brasileira, where he'd often meet with friends, has a statue of Pessoa outside. Today, fado musicians still remember Pessoa, paying homage to him by putting his poetry into the Portuguese version of the blues.

selling Brazilian products, a reminder that this has long been the city's shopping zone.

At the neighboring Baixa-Chiado (shee-AH-doo) Metro stop, a slick series of escalators whisks people effortlessly between Chiado Square and the Baixa (the lower town). It's a free and fun way to survey a long, long line of Portuguese—but for now, we'll stay in the Chiado neighborhood. (If you'll be coming for fado in the evening—recommended places are nearby—consider getting here by zipping up the escalator.)

The Chiado District is popular for its shopping and theaters. Browse downhill on Rua Garrett and notice its mosaic sidewalks, ironwork balconies, and fine shops. Peek into classy stores, such as the fabric-lover's paradise Paris em Lisboa—imagine how this would have been the ultimate in oo-la-la fashion in the 19th century (at #77). The venerable Bertrand bookstore (at #73) sells English books and has a good guidebook selection in Room 5. My favorite shop for traditional and retro Portuguese gifts is behind the bookstore: ❿ **A Vida Portuguesa** (daily 10:00-20:00, Rua Anchieta 11). The street lamps you see are decorated with the symbol of Lisbon: a ship, carrying the remains of St. Vincent, guarded by two ravens. In 1988, much of this area was destroyed in a fire.

• *Rua Garrett ends abruptly at the entrance of the big vertical mall. For Italian-style gelato, locals like Santini em Casa, a few steps downhill to the left (at #9, 30 yards below mall entry). Step into the fancy...*

⓫ **Armazéns do Chiado Mall:** This grand, six-floor shopping center connects Lisbon's lower and upper towns with a world of ways to spend money (daily 10:00-22:00, lively food court on sixth floor open daily about 12:00-23:00—see page 116).

• *This walk is over. Whether you leave the Bairro Alto or stay to explore, directions are below.*

Leaving the Bairro Alto: *To get from the mall to the Baixa—the lower town—take the elevator (press 1) or the escalators down (to exit on the ground level, you'll pass through the Sports Zone shop). To get from the mall to the Metro, exit through the lowest floor of the mall, turn right, and walk 50 yards to the Baixa-Chiado Metro stop.*

Exploring More of the Bairro Alto: *A short walk from the mall gives you a more complete look at this high-altitude neighborhood and a scenic viewpoint. Get out your map and backtrack (heading west) up Rua Garrett (which becomes Rua do Loreto), passing the picturesque Elevador da Bica funicular, then turn left on Rua Marechal Saldanha to reach the Miradouro de Santa Catarina (a.k.a. the "Bica mirador"), a terrace—flanked by bars—that overlooks the city's harbor and river. You'll see a monument to the Cape of Good Hope (a.k.a. the Cape of Torment) that personifies the cape as a monster. This mythic treatment was popularized by poet Camões' The Lusiads, which celebrated and nearly deified the great explorers of Portugal's Age of Discovery (such as Vasco da Gama, portrayed as Ulysses), who had to overcome such demons in their conquest of the sea.*

LISBON

Sights in Lisbon

CENTRAL LISBON

To get a full picture of the best of central Lisbon, take the "Three Neighborhoods" walk (the Bairro Alto, Alfama, and Baixa) covered earlier.

Cathedral (Sé)

The cathedral, just a few blocks east of Praça do Comércio, is not much on the inside, but its fortress-like exterior—solid enough to survive the 1755 earthquake—is a textbook example of the stark and powerful Romanesque "fortress of God" so typical of its age. Twin, castle-like, crenellated towers solidly frame an impressive rose window.

Cost and Hours: Church—free, Tue-Sat 9:00-19:00, Sun-Mon 9:00-17:00; cloister—€2.50, Tue-Sat 10:00-18:30, Mon 10:00-17:00, closed Sun; treasury—€2.50, €4 combo-ticket includes cloister; on Largo da Sé, several blocks east of Baixa—take Rua da Conceição east, which turns into Rua de Santo António da Sé.

Visiting the Church: Started in 1150, this was the first place of worship that Christians built after they retook Lisbon from the Moors. Located on the former site of a mosque, it made a powerful statement: The Reconquista was here to stay. The church is also the site of the 1195 baptism of St. Anthony—a favorite saint of Portugal (locals appeal to him for help in finding a parking spot, true love, and lost objects). Naturally for Portugal, tile panels around the baptismal font portray St. Anthony preaching to the fish. Also, some of St. Vincent is buried here—legend has it that in the 12th century, his remains were brought to Lisbon on a ship guarded by two sacred black ravens, the symbol of the city.

The **cloister** at the right side of the church is peaceful and an archaeological work-in-progress—they're currently uncovering Roman ruins. The humble **treasury** is worth its fee only if you want to support the church and climb some stairs.

Elevador de Santa Justa

This 150-foot-tall iron tower, built in 1902, connects the flat Baixa district with the Bairro Alto/Chiado districts up above. You can ride the elevator for a fine city view, while getting a sweat-free connection to the upper town (€5 round-trip tickets only; covered by Viva Viagem card—a great value with 24-hour card which makes it free, if "Zapping," it'll cost your card €1.40; departures every 10 minutes, daily 7:00-23:00, until 22:00 in winter).

NORTH LISBON
▲▲▲Gulbenkian Museum

This is the best of Lisbon's 40 museums. It's two miles north of the city center, and worth the trip for art lovers. Calouste Gulbenkian (1869-1955), an Armenian oil tycoon, gave Portugal his art collection (or "harem," as he called it). His gift was an act of gratitude for the hospitable asylum granted him during World War II (he lived in Lisbon from 1942 until he died in 1955). The Portuguese consider Gulbenkian—whose billion-dollar estate is still a growing and vital arts foundation promoting culture in Portugal—an inspirational model of how to be thoughtfully wealthy. (He made a habit of "tithing for art," spending 10 percent of his income on things of beauty.) The foundation, with its building set in a delightful garden, often hosts classical music concerts in the museum's auditoriums.

Gulbenkian's collection, spanning 5,000 years and housed in a classy modern building, offers the most purely enjoyable museum experience in Iberia—it's both educational and just plain beautiful. The museum is cool, uncrowded, gorgeously lit, and easy to grasp, displaying only a few select and exquisite works from each epoch. Walk through five millennia of human history, appreciating our ancestors by seeing objects they treasured.

Cost and Hours: €5, free on Sun; open Wed-Mon 10:00-18:00, closed Tue, last entry 30 minutes before closing; terse 1.5-hour audioguide-€4, pleasant gardens, good air-conditioned cafeteria, Berna 45, tel. 217-823-000, www.museu.gulbenkian.pt.

Getting There: From downtown, hop a cab (€7) or take the Metro from Restauradores to the São Sebastião stop, get off, and leave the platform by following the *Avenida de Aguiar (norte)* signs. Then, to leave the station, follow signs to *Avenida de Aguiar (nascente)*. Once at street level, walk a long block downhill on Avenida de Aguiar with the massive El Corte Inglés department store behind you. Just before the roundabout (across from the funky, pink Spanish embassy on the left), you'll see a small sign pointing right to the *fundação*—the museum entrance is straight ahead through this park, past a long concrete office building, about 100 yards away.

Nearby: A fine modern art gallery (CAMJAP) is next door. And Belém is a quick €8 taxi ride away.

❷ Self-Guided Tour: From the entrance lobby, there are two

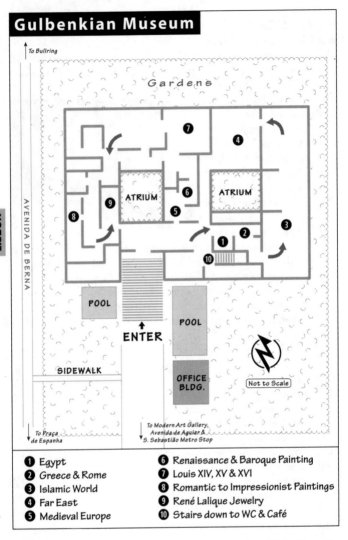

Gulbenkian Museum

To Bullring

Gardens

To Bulllring

AVENIDA DE BERNA

LISBON

ATRIUM

ATRIUM

7

4

9

8

6

5

1

2

3

10

POOL

POOL

ENTER

SIDEWALK

OFFICE BLDG.

Not to Scale

To Praça de Espanha

To Modern Art Gallery, Avenida de Aguiar & S. Sebastião Metro Stop

❶ Egypt
❷ Greece & Rome
❸ Islamic World
❹ Far East
❺ Medieval Europe
❻ Renaissance & Baroque Painting
❼ Louis XIV, XV & XVI
❽ Romantic to Impressionist Paintings
❾ René Lalique Jewelry
❿ Stairs down to WC & Café

wings, covering roughly pre-1500 and post-1500. Following the museum's layout, you'll see...

❶ **Egypt (2,500-500 B.C.):** Ancient Egyptians, believing that life really began after death, carved statues to preserve the memory of the deceased, whether it be a prince (Statue of the Courtier Bes, 664-610 B.C., with an inscription calling him "the king's friend") or a likeness of the family pet. The cat statue nurses her kittens atop a coffin that once held the cat's mummy, preserved for the afterlife. Egyptians honored cats—even giving them gold earrings like those on the statue. They believed cats helped the goddess

Bastet keep watch over the household. Now, more than 2,500 years later, we remember the Egyptians for these sturdy, dignified statues, built for eternity.

❷ Greece and Rome (500 B.C.-A.D. 500): The black-and-red Greek vase (calyx-crater), decorated with scenes of half-human satyrs chasing human women, reminds us of the rational Greeks' struggle to overcome their barbarian, animal-like urges as they invented Western civilization. Alexander the Great (r. 336-323 B.C., seen on a coin) used war to spread Greek culture throughout the Mediterranean, creating a cultural empire that would soon be taken over by Roman emperors (seen on medallions).

Journey even further back in time to the very roots of civilization: Mesopotamia (modern Iraq), where writing was invented. Five thousand years ago, the cylinder seals were used to roll an impression in sealing wax or clay.

❸ Islamic World (700-1500): The Muslims who lived in Portugal—as far west of Mecca as you could get back then—might have decorated their homes with furnishings from all over the Islamic world. Imagine a Moorish sultan, dressed in a shirt from Syria, sitting on a carpet from Persia in a courtyard with Moroccan tiles. By a bubbling fountain, he puffs on a hookah.

The culture of Moorish Iberia (711-1492) was among Europe's most sophisticated after the Fall of Rome. The intricate patterns on the glass lanterns are not only beautiful...they're actually quotes (in Arabic) from the Quran, such as "Allah (God) is the light of the world, shining like a flame in a glass lamp, as bright as a star."

❹ Far East (1368-1644): For almost 300 years, the Ming dynasty ruled China, having reclaimed the country from Genghis Khan and his sons. When Portuguese traders reached the Orient, they brought back blue-and-white ceramics such as these. They became all the rage, inspiring the creation of both Portuguese tiles and Dutch Delftware. Writing utensils fill elaborately decorated boxes from Japan. Another type of box was the ultimate picnic basket—*bento* was the best way to enjoy the Japanese countryside.

In the other wing, look for the art of...

❺ Medieval Europe (500-1500): While China was thriving and inventing, Europe was stuck in a thousand-year medieval funk (with the exception of Muslim Arab-ruled Iberia). Most Europeans from the "Age of Faith" channeled their spirituality into objects of Christian devotion. A priest on a business trip could pack a portable altarpiece in his backpack, travel to a remote village that had no church, and deliver a sermon carved in ivory. In monasteries,

LISBON

the monks with the best penmanship laboriously copied books (illuminated manuscripts) and decorated them with scenes from the text—and wacky doodles in the margins. These books were virtual time capsules, preserving the knowledge of Greece and Rome until it could emerge again, a thousand years later, in the Renaissance.

❻ **Renaissance and Baroque Painting (1500-1700):** Around 1500, a cultural revolution was taking place—the birth of humanism. Painters saw God in the faces of ordinary people, whether in Domenico Ghirlandaio's fresh-faced maiden, Frans Hals' wrinkled old woman, or Rembrandt's portrait of an old man, whose crease-lined hands tell the story of his life.

❼ **Louis XIV, XV, XVI (1700-1800):** After the Italian-born Renaissance, Europe's focus shifted northward to the luxurious court of France, where a new secular culture was blossoming. In one tapestry, love is in the air (see cupids flying overhead) as Venus frolics in a landscaped garden. Powder-wigged nobles in their palaces enjoyed the luxury of viewing art like this pagan scene, while relaxing in chairs like the kind you see here. This furniture, once owned by French kings (and Marie-Antoinette and Madame de Pompadour), is a royal home show. Anything heavy, ornate, and gilded (or that includes curved legs and animal-clawed feet) is from the time of Louis XIV. The Louis XV style is lighter and daintier, with Oriental motifs, while furniture from the Louis XVI era is stripped-down, straight-legged, tapered, and more modern. Listen to find out which clocks still work.

❽ **Romantic to Impressionist Paintings (1700-2000):** Europe ruled the world, and art became increasingly refined. Young British aristocrats (Thomas Gainsborough portrait) traveled Europe on the Grand Tour to see great sights like Venice (Guardi landscape). Follow the progression in styles from stormy Romanticism (J. M. W. Turner's tumultuous shipwreck) to Pre-Raphaelite dreamscapes *(Mirror of Venus)* to Realism's breath-of-fresh-air simplicity (Manet's bubble-blower) to the glinting, shimmering Impressionism of Monet... Renoir...and John Singer Sargent.

❾ **René Lalique Jewelry:** Finish your visit with the stunning, sumptuous Art Nouveau glasswork and jewelry of French designer René Lalique (1860-1945). Fragile beauty like this, from the elegant turn-of-the-century belle époque, was about to be shattered by the tumultuous 20th century. Art Nouveau emphasized forms from nature and valued the organic and artisan over cold, calculated mass production. Ordinary dragonflies, orchids, and beetles become breathtaking when transformed into jewelry. The work of Lalique—just another of Gulbenkian's circle of friends—is a fitting finale to a museum that features both history and beauty.

WEST LISBON
▲▲Museum of Ancient Art
(Museu Nacional de Arte Antiga)

This is Portugal's finest museum for paintings from its glory days, the 15th and 16th centuries. (Most of these works were gathered from Lisbon's abbeys and convents after their dissolution in 1834.) You'll also find a rich collection of furniture, as well as art by renowned European masters such as Hieronymus Bosch, Jan van Eyck, and Raphael—all in a grand palace. Pick up the free informative pamphlet at the entrance.

Cost and Hours: €6, free first Sun of every month; open Tue 14:00-18:00, Wed-Sun 10:00-18:00, closed Mon; tel. 213-912-800.

Getting There: It's about a mile west of downtown Lisbon at Rua das Janeles Verdes 9. From Praça da Figueira, take trolley #15E to Cais Rocha, cross the street, and walk up a lot of steps. Or take bus #714 from either Praça da Figueira or Praça do Comércio. The same bus and trolley continue to the sights in Belém.

Services: The museum has a good cafeteria with outdoor seating in a shaded garden overlooking the river.

Visiting the Museum: Here are some of the museum's highlights, starting on the top floor.

Third Floor—Portuguese Painting and Sculpture: The *Adoration of St. Vincent* in Room 12 is a multi-paneled altarpiece by the late-15th-century master Nuno Gonçalves. A gang of 60 real people—everyone from royalty to sailors and beggars—surrounds Lisbon's patron saint. Of note is the only recognized portrait of Prince Henry, responsible for setting Portugal on the path to exploration. Find him in the middle—an elder gentleman dressed in black with a wide-brimmed hat, hands together almost in prayer. In Room 3, if you've visited the sights in Belém, you'll recognize the Monastery of Jerónimos before it was fully

decorated (painting by Felipe Lobo in 1657). Find an exceptional portrait of young King Sebastian in Room 9. The armor is typical of Iberia for the era, as is the royal jaw and pursed lips due to Habsburg inbreeding. Considering Sebastian died so young, we are fortunate to have this wonderful portrait.

Second Floor—Japanese Screen and Jewels: Find the enchanting Namban screen paintings in Room 14 (*Namban* means "barbarians from the south"). It shows the Portuguese from a 16th-century Japanese perspective—with long noses as well as great skill at climbing rigging, like acrobats. The Portuguese, the first Europeans to make contact with Japan, gave the Japanese guns, Catholicism (Nagasaki was founded by Portuguese Jesuits), and a new deep-frying technique we now know as tempura.

On the same floor, have a quick look at the impressive jewelry collection decorated with the red cross of the Order of Christ, responsible for funding Portuguese explorations. Make your way to a freestanding glass case in Room 29 to see the Monstrance of Belém, made for Manuel I from the first gold brought back by Vasco da Gama. Restored in 2008, squint at the fine enamel creatures filling a tide pool on the base, the 12 apostles gathered around the glass case for the Communion wafer (the fancy top pops off), and the white dove hanging like a mobile under the all-powerful God bidding us peace on earth. Another notable monstrance is nearby in Room 27—a bejeweled Rococo masterpiece made for Lisbon's Bemposta Palace, with its carrying case displayed just behind it. More jewels and fine porcelain complete the rest of this floor; of note are tiles from Damascus—a gift from Calouste Gulbenkian. Before continuing downstairs, stop to admire a 17th-century painting of Lisbon before the 1755 earthquake.

First Floor—European Paintings: Pass through the gift shop and veer left (follow the numbering on the museum plan). Note the collection of the larger-than-life *Twelve Apostles* by the Spanish master Zurburán. Continue to the end of the hall, then go right into Room 61 for Bosch's *Temptations of St. Anthony* (a three-paneled altarpiece fantasy, c. 1500) and Albrecht Dürer's *St. Jerome*. St. Jerome is all-important to Lisbon as the primary figure behind the Monastery of Jerónimos in Belém. Finally, exit through the few remnants of the palace. Note the Pombal coat-of-arms that decorates the elaborate, Baroque doorway (find the star); the palace was originally purchased by the brother of the powerful Marquês de Pombal.

MODERN LISBON: ORIENTE, PARQUE DAS NAÇÕES, AND MORE

To get out of the quaint, Pombal-esque old town and enjoy a peek at the modern side of Lisbon, ride the Metro east to Oriente Station. Nearby you can stroll through a light and airy shopping mall, bike across the sprawling site of the 1998 World Expo, and promenade with locals along the Rio Tejo riverfront park. It's worth a visit any day, especially on Monday (when most museums in town are closed). It's a particularly vibrant scene when the people are out early on summer evenings.

Oriente Station (Gare do Oriente)

Oriente means "facing east." This impressive hub ties together trains (to the Algarve and Évora), the Metro, and buses under a swooping concrete roof designed by the Spanish architect Santiago Calatrava. From the Oriente Station, you'll notice right away that the theme here is the sea. That was the theme of the 1998 Expo. And just about everything in this area is named for the great Portuguese explorer Vasco da Gama.

Vasco da Gama Mall

Facing Oriente Station is the inviting, soaring glass facade of Lisbon's top shopping mall, also designed by Calatrava (daily 9:00-24:00). Originally the grand entrance to the 1998 World Expo, the city has done a good job of turning the remains of that fair into useful infrastructure. Stepping into the mall, you'll see that its design seems to have been inspired by the main shopping hall of a luxury cruise ship. Notice the water cascading down the glass roof—a clever and fun-to-look-at way to keep things cool and avoid any greenhouse effect. From the mall's entrance, climb the stairs to a small outdoor terrace for a good view back at the train station. Then stroll through the upper level of the mall to the opposite end, where you can step out to another outdoor terrace—giving you yet again the feeling that you're vacationing on a cruise ship. Survey the scene. With your back to the river, look up at the two skyscraping luxury condo buildings. With fine transportation connections and modern office space, this area holds lots of promise, both for residences and businesses. Microsoft set up its Portuguese headquarters here, and the Portuguese national court is in contemporary new buildings nearby. From here you can also look toward the river and survey Parque das Nações—the grounds of Portugal's 1998 World Expo (described next).

▲▲Parque das Nações

Lisbon celebrated the 500th anniversary of Vasco da Gama's voyage to India by hosting Expo '98 here at Parque das Nações. The theme was "The Ocean and the Seas," emphasizing the global importance of healthy, clean waters.

To get the lay of the land, climb to the outdoor terrace at the Vasco de Gama Mall (see previous listing), or look out over the Grand Esplanade (Rossio Olivais). Ahead of you, lining the espla-

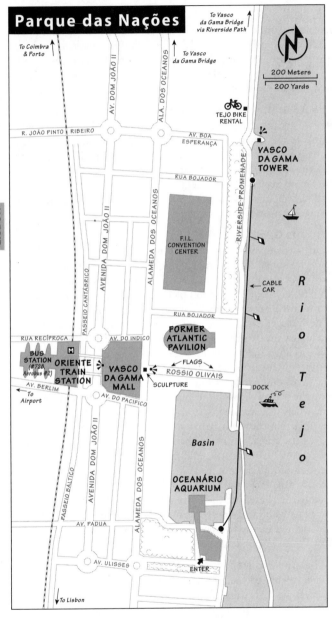

Parque das Nações

To Coimbra & Porto

To Vasco da Gama Bridge via Riverside Path

To Vasco da Gama Bridge

200 Meters
200 Yards

LISBON

AV. DOM JOÃO II
ALA. DOS OCEANOS

R. JOÃO PINTO RIBEIRO

AV. BOA ESPERANÇA

TEJO BIKE RENTAL

VASCO DA GAMA TOWER

RUA BOJADOR

AVENIDA DOM JOÃO II

ALAMEDA DOS OCEANOS

RIVERSIDE PROMENADE

F.I.L. CONVENTION CENTER

PASSEIO CANTÁBRICO

CABLE CAR

R i o

RUA BOJADOR

FORMER ATLANTIC PAVILION

RUA RECÍPROCA

AV. DO ÍNDICO

BUS STATION (#728, Aerobus #2)

ORIENTE TRAIN STATION

VASCO DA GAMA MALL

FLAGS

ROSSIO OLIVAIS

SCULPTURE

DOCK

T e j o

AV. BERLIM

To Airport

AV. DO PACÍFICO

AVENIDA DOM JOÃO II

ALAMEDA DOS OCEANOS

Basin

PASSEIO BÁLTICO

OCEANÁRIO AQUARIUM

AV. PÁDUA

AV. ULISSES

ENTER

To Lisbon

nade, are 155 flags—one for each country represented at the fair. The flags are arranged in alphabetical order, so the first ones are South Africa (Africa dul Sul), Albania, and Germany (Alemanha). In the middle you'll find the US (Estados Unidos), Spain (Espanha), and Estonia side by side. The striped oval dome to the left, once the Atlantic Pavilion (Pavilhão Atlântico), is now an 18,000-seat concert hall. The oil refinery tower far to the right marks the west end of the park and stands as a reminder of the industrial wasteland that was here before the fair.

The basin in front of you pre-dates the fair. Back before World War II it was a watery "parking lot" (just 1.5 yards deep) for seaplanes. Across the basin to your right, the blocky building that resembles an aircraft carrier with a spiky rooftop is the Oceanário aquarium (described later)—the big hit of the fair and still the park's major attraction. From behind that the cable car (€4

one-way, €6 round-trip, nothing special) drifts east to the Vasco da Gama Tower, which marks that end of the park. Two miles away, built as part of the 1998 celebrations, is the Vasco da Gama Bridge (described later). A delightful promenade (Caminho dos Pinheiros; "The Way of the Pine Trees") runs along the riverfront from the marina all the way to a park at the base of the Vasco de Gama Bridge.

Parque das Nações Bike Ride

The most enjoyable way to explore the sprawling park is by bike. Simply enjoy a big loop pedaling around modern art, under fancy eaves, along the riverside promenade, and past local lovers enjoying a little *"marmalade"* (local slang for heavy petting). **Tejo Bike Rental,** which operates out of a red shipping container on the Grand Esplanade (*Esplanando,* north of the Vasco da Gama Tower), rents simple one-speed bikes (€3/30 minutes, €5/hour, daily in summer 10:00-20:00, off-season 12:00-18:00, no locks).

Oceanário

Europe's largest aquarium simulates four different oceanic underwater and shoreline environments. Built in a modern version of a ship at sea, the aquarium's enormous centerpiece is a central tank with lots of fish and the occasional hungry shark. Penguins, sea otters, and weekday-morning school groups are all happily on display.

Cost and Hours: €16, daily April-Oct 10:00-20:00, off-season until 19:00, last entry one hour before closing, tel. 218-917-000, www.oceanario.pt.

Azulejos

During visits to neighboring Spain, King Manuel I not only acquired wives, but he also obtained several thousand tiles to decorate palaces throughout Portugal. Vibrant colors must have attracted the king's attention, and some examples from his visits can still be seen in the National Palace in Sintra. It wasn't long before Portuguese artists began producing for local clients, and tiles became synonymous with the seafaring empire.

The biggest challenge for early artisans was how to keep colors separate during the firing process. A number of techniques developed to solve this problem: *Alicatados* are mosaic pieces, cut after firing, to form intricate geometric patterns; *corda seca* fills thick outlines of manganese oxide with different colors, like a children's coloring book; and *aresta* sculpts color wells directly into the tile. The biggest breakthrough came with the development of *majólica*, or *faiança*—the undecorated clay tile is baked first, then covered with an opaque glaze that makes a canvas for the painted design, which is set by a second firing.

Brazilians loved tilework, too, and after the return of the Portuguese king to European shores, factories began producing tilework for the masses. But tilework began to fall out of fashion by the early 20th century. Then Lisbon's 1959 Metro system gave tile artists a new playground. While not originally in the budget, artist Maria Keil could not bear to see the walls vacant. Her original designs are still on display, and future artists continue to make the Metro an underground art museum.

Unfortunately, others have noticed the beauty (and profitability) of historic tilework panels. Theft is common—often for resale on the black market—and many of Lisbon's older panels are at risk. In the past decade, local watch groups have documented several hundred cases of missing panels and helped recover several of them. Think twice before purchasing tilework at the Feira da Ladra flea market.

To go on your own *azulejo* scavenger hunt, check out Endless Mile's tile guide to Lisbon that lists nearly 100 of the city's best tile panels (www.endlessmile.com).

Vasco da Gama Bridge

Europe's longest bridge (10.7 miles) was opened in 1998 to connect the Expo grounds with the south side of the Rio Tejo, and to alleviate the traffic jams on Lisbon's only other bridge over the river, the 25th of April Bridge. The Vasco de Gama Bridge helped connect north and south Portugal, back when a freeway was a big deal in this late-to-develop European nation. Built low to the water, the bridge's towers and cables are meant to suggest the sails of a caravel ship.

EAST LISBON
▲National Tile Museum (Museu Nacional do Azulejo)
Filling the Convento da Madre de Deus, the museum features piles of tiles, which, as you've probably noticed, are an art form in Portu-

gal. They've tried to show-case the tiles as they would have originally appeared (note the diamond-shaped staircase tiles). While the presentation is low-tech, the church is sumptuous, and the tile panorama of pre-earthquake Lisbon (upstairs) is fascinating.

LISBON

Cost and Hours: €5, free first Sun of every month; open Tue-Sun 10:00-18:00, closed Mon; last entry 30 minutes before closing; located about a mile east of Praça do Comércio—15 minutes on bus #794 from Praça do Comércio or bus #742 from São Sebastião Metro station (near Gulbenkian Museum), buses stop at museum entrance on Rua da Madre de Deus 4, tel. 218-100-340, mnazulejo.imc-ip.pt.

SOUTH OF LISBON, ACROSS THE RIVER
▲25th of April Bridge (25 de Abril)
At 1.5 miles (3,280 feet between the towers), this is one of the longest suspension bridges in the world. The foundations are sunk

260 feet below the surface into the riverbed, making it the world's deepest bridge. It was built in 1966 by the same company that made its famous San Francisco cousin (but notice the lower deck for train tracks). Originally named for the dictator Salazar, the bridge was renamed for the date of Portugal's 1974 revolution and liberation. For a generation, natives would show their political colors by choosing which name to use. While conser-

vative Portuguese called it the "Salazar Bridge," liberals referred to it as the "25th of April Bridge" (just as Washington, D.C.'s airport is called "National" by some and "Reagan" by others). Imagine that before 1966, there was no way across the Rio Tejo except by ferry.

António Salazar

Q: What do you get when you cross a lawyer, an economist, and a dictator?

A: António Salazar, who was all three—a dictator who ruled Portugal through harsh laws and a strict budget that hurt the poor.

Shortly after a 1926 military coup "saved" Portugal's floundering democracy from itself, General Oscar Carmona appointed António de Oliveira Salazar (1889-1970) as finance minister. A former professor of economics and law at the University of Coimbra, Salazar balanced the budget and the interests of the country's often-warring factions. His skill and his reputation as a clean-living, fair-minded patriot earned him a promotion. In 1932, he became prime minister, and he set about creating his New State *(Estado Novo)*.

For nearly four decades, Salazar ruled a stable but isolated nation based on harmony between the traditional power blocs of the ruling class—the military, big business, large landowners, and the Catholic Church. This Christian fascism, backed by the military and secret police, was ratified repeatedly in elections by the country's voters—the richest 20 percent of the populace.

As a person, Salazar was respected, but not loved. The son of a farm manager, he originally studied to be a priest before going on to become a scholar and writer. He never married. Quiet, low-key, and unassuming, he attended church regularly and lived a nonmaterialistic existence. But when faced with opposition, he was ruthless, and his secret police became an object of fear and hatred.

Salazar steered Portugal through the turmoil of Spain's Civil War (1936-1939), remaining officially neutral while secretly supporting Franco's fascists. He detested Nazi Germany's "pagan" leaders, but respected Mussolini for reconciling with the pope. In World War II, Portugal was officially neutral, but was often friendly with longtime ally Britain and used as a base for espionage. After the war, it benefited greatly from the United States' Marshall Plan for economic recovery (which Spain missed out on during Franco's rule), and the country joined NATO in 1949.

Salazar distracted his poor and isolated masses with a cynical credo: *"Fado, Fátima, and Futebol"* (the three "Fs"). Salazar's regime was undone by two factors: the liberal 1960s and the unpopular, draining wars Portugal fought abroad to try to keep its colonial empire intact. When Salazar died in 1970, the regime that followed became increasingly less credible, leading to the liberating events of the Carnation Revolution in 1974.

Cristo Rei (Christ of Majesty)

A huge, 330-foot concrete statue of Christ (à la Rio de Janeiro, in the former Portuguese colony of Brazil) overlooks Lisbon from

across the Rio Tejo, stretching its arms wide to symbolically bless the city (or as less reverent Portuguese say, "to dive into the river"). Lisbon's cardinal, inspired by a visit to Rio de Janeiro in 1936, wanted a replica built back home. Increased support came after an appeal was made to Our Lady of Fátima in 1940 to keep Portugal out of World War II. Portugal survived the war relatively unscathed, and funds were collected to build this statue in appreciation. After 10 years of construction, it opened to the public in 1959. It's now a sanctuary and pilgrimage site, and the chapel inside holds regular Sunday Mass. The statue was designed to be seen from a distance, and there's little reason to go to the trouble of actually visiting it. If you do visit, an elevator will take you to the top for a panoramic view: From left to right, see Belém, the 25th of April Bridge, downtown Lisbon (Praça do Comércio and the green Alfama hilltop with the castle), and the long Vasco da Gama Bridge.

Cost and Hours: €5, daily 9:30-18:00, until 19:00 in summer, last elevator ride 15 minutes before closing, tel. 212-751-000.

Getting There: To get to Cristo Rei, catch the 10-minute ferry from downtown Lisbon to Cacilhas (€2, 4/hour, more during rush hour, from Cais do Sodré Metro/train station follow signs to *Terminal Fluvial*, which serves many destinations). The bus marked *101 Cristo Rei* takes you to the base of the statue in 15 minutes (3/hour, exit ferry dock left into the maze of bus stops to find the #20 stop with the "101 Cristo Rei" schedule under the awning). Because of bridge tolls to enter Lisbon, taxis from the site are expensive. Consider taking a late-morning ferry to Cristo Rei; catch a taxi from the statue to Porto Brandão and have lunch there (see page 93); and ferry direct to Belém and see the sights. For drivers, the most efficient visit is a quick stop on your way to or from Évora or the Algarve.

BELÉM

Three miles west of downtown Lisbon, the Belém district is a stately pincushion of important sights from Portugal's Golden Age, when Vasco da Gama and company turned the country into Europe's richest power. Belém was the send-off point for voyages in the Age of Discovery. Sailors would stay and pray here before embarking. The tower welcomed them home. The grand buildings of Belém survived the great 1755 earthquake, so this is the best

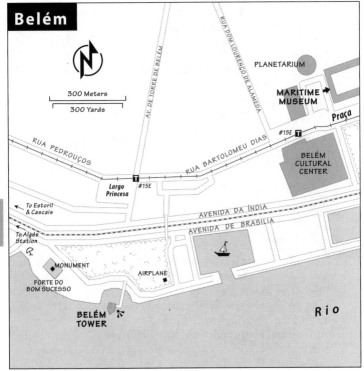

place to experience the grandeur of pre-earthquake Lisbon. After the earthquake, safety-conscious (and rattled) royalty chose to live here—in wooden rather than stone buildings. The modern-day president of Portugal calls Belém home.

To celebrate the 300th anniversary of independence from Spain, a grand exhibition was held here in 1940, resulting in the fine parks, fountains, and monuments. Nearly all of Belém's museums are closed on Monday (though the Monument to the Discoveries is open Mon May-Sept).

Getting to Belém

You'll get here quickest by taxi (€15 from downtown). Buses #714 and #728 serve Belém, but I prefer riding the slower trolley #15E (30-40 minutes, catch at Praça da Figueira or Praça do Comércio). In Belém, the first trolley stop is at the National Coach Museum, the second is at the Monastery of Jerónimos, and another is two blocks inland from the Belém Tower. Even if you miss the first stop, you can't miss the second stop at the massive monastery.

Consider doing Belém in this order: the National Coach Museum, pastry and coffee break, Monastery of Jerónimos, Maritime

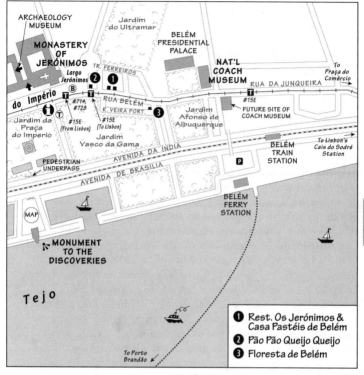

ARCHAEOLOGY MUSEUM
Jardim do Ultramar
BELÉM PRESIDENTIAL PALACE
MONASTERY OF JERÓNIMOS
TR. FERREIROS
NAT'L COACH MUSEUM
To Praça do Comércio
Largo Jerónimos
RUA DA JUNQUEIRA
do Império
RUA BELÉM
R. VEIRA PORT.
#714, #728
#15E (From Lisbon)
#15E (To Lisbon)
#15E
FUTURE SITE OF COACH MUSEUM
Jardim da Praça do Imperio
Jardim Afonso de Albuquerque
Jardim Vasco da Gama
AVENIDA DA INDIA
BELÉM TRAIN STATION
To Lisbon's Cais do Sodré Station
PEDESTRIAN UNDERPASS
AVENIDA DE BRASILIA
P
MAP
BELÉM FERRY STATION
MONUMENT TO THE DISCOVERIES
Tejo
To Porto Brandão

❶ Rest. Os Jerónimos & Casa Pastéis de Belém
❷ Pão Pão Queijo Queijo
❸ Floresta de Belém

LISBON

Museum (if interested) and/or lunch at its cafeteria (public access, museum entry not required), Monument to the Discoveries, and Belém Tower. If arriving by taxi, start at Belém Tower, the farthest point, and do the recommended lineup in reverse, ending at the National Coach Museum. Belém also has a cultural center, a children's museum, and a planetarium—not priorities for a quick visit. For recommended eateries in this area, see page 93.

When you're through, hop on trolley #15E or bus #714 to return to Praça da Figueira or Praça do Comércio. Bus #728 takes you to Santa Apolónia Station, and continues to Parque das Nações and Oriente Station.

Tourist Information

The little TI kiosk is directly across the street from the entrance to the monastery (Tue-Sat 10:00-13:00 & 14:00-18:00, closed Sun-Mon, tel. 213-658-437).

A little **Yellow Bus Tour** minibus offers a handy hop-on, hop-off tour around the Belém sights—which can feel far-flung if you're tired—departing every hour from the monastery entrance. You can get off to explore a sight and catch the next minibus (€5, daily, departs every 30 minutes, June-Sept 10:00-13:00 & 14:00-18:30).

Between the Coach Museum and Monastery
▲▲National Coach Museum

In 1905, the last Queen of Portugal saw that cars would soon obliterate horse-drawn carriages as a form of transportation. She decided to use the palace's riding-school building to preserve her fine collection of royal coaches, which became today's National Coach Museum (Museu dos Coches). A new, larger museum is being built kitty-corner from the present location. The following description is based on the current configuration; if you visit after the new building opens, request a map as you enter.

Cost and Hours: €6, free first Sun of every month, Tue-Sun 10:00-18:00, closed Mon, last entry 30 minutes before closing, tel. 213-610-850, www.museudoscoches.pt.

Visiting the Museum: The collection is impressive, with more than 70 dazzling carriages (described in English) lining the elegant old riding room. Check out the ceiling, which is as remarkable as the carriages, and look for coach #1 (from around 1600). This crude and simple coach was once used by Philip II, king of Spain and Portugal, to shuttle between Madrid and Lisbon. Notice that the coach has no driver's seat—its drivers would actually ride the horses. You'll have to trust me on this, but if you lift up the cushion from the passengers' seat, you'll find a potty hole—also handy for road sickness. Imagine how slow and rough the ride would be with bad roads and a crude leather-strap suspension.

Study the evolution of suspension technology, starting with the first coach, or "Kotze," made in the 15th century in a Hungarian town of that name. Trace the improvement of coaches through the next century, noticing that as the decoration increases, so does the comfort. A Portuguese coat of arms indicates that a carriage was part of the royal fleet. Ornamentation often includes a folk festival of exotic faces from Portugal's distant colonies. Examples of period riding costumes are displayed in cases between many of the coaches.

At the far end of the first room, the lumbering Ocean Coach, as ornate as it is long, stands shining. At the stern, gold figures symbolize the Atlantic and Indian Oceans holding hands, a reminder of Portugal's mastery of the sea. The Ocean Coach is flanked by two equally stunning coaches with similar symbols of ocean exploration.

The second room shows sedan chairs and traces the development of carriages as a common means of transportation. They got lighter and faster, culminating in a sporty, horse-drawn Lisbon taxi.

Wander upstairs to get a glimpse of velvet-covered saddles and special riding gear designed for the royal kids. A spectacular view of the entire building interior is picture-perfect (no flash). The portrait gallery of most Portuguese royalty is handy for putting a face to all the movers and shakers you've read about so far.

▲Casa Pastéis de Belém

The Casa Pastéis de Belém café is the birthplace of the wonderful custard tart that's called *pastel de nata* throughout Portugal, but here is dubbed *pastel de Belém*. Since 1837, residents have come to this café to get their tarts warm out of the oven. This place's popularity stems mainly from the fact that their recipe is a closely guarded secret—supposedly only three people know the exact proportions of ingredients. While the recipe is fine, my hunch is that the explanation for their undeniable goodness is simply that, because they crank out 20,000 or so a day, you get them fresh and crunchy, literally hot out of the oven. (Take one back to your hotel and eat it tonight and it'll taste just like any other in town.) Sit down and enjoy one with a *café com leite*. Sprinkle on as much cinnamon and powdered sugar as you like. If the to-go line is too long, there's plenty of seating in the café and perhaps faster service (if you need a WC, this is an easy choice). You can also often save time by lining up not at the front counter but on the back side of the counter (tarts €1.05 each, daily 8:00-24:00, Rua de Belém 84, tel. 213-637-423).

▲▲▲Monastery of Jerónimos

King Manuel (who ruled from 1495) erected this giant, white limestone church and monastery—which stretches 300 yards

along the Lisbon waterfront—as a "thank you" for the discoveries made by early Portuguese explorers. It was financed in part with "pepper money," a 5 percent tax on spices brought back from India. Manuel built the church on the site of a humble chapel where sailors spent their last night ashore in prayer before embarking on frightening voyages. What is the style of Manuel's church? Manueline.

Cost and Hours: The church is free, but the cloister costs €10. A €12 combo-ticket saves you €2 if you also visit the Tower of Belém (both the cloister and tower are free on first Sun of every month; hours for monastery: May-Sept Tue-Sun 10:00-18:30, off-season until 17:30, closed Mon, last entry 30 minutes before closing, www.mosteirojeronimos.pt; can purchase tickets online at bilhetes.igespar.pt). There's often a long line to visit the cloister, but you can cut through it to get to the church entrance.

LISBON

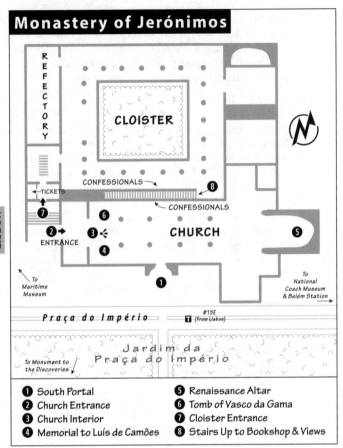

Monastery of Jerónimos

REFECTORY

CLOISTER

CONFESSIONALS →

← TICKETS

7

2 → ENTRANCE

6

3 ⟵

CONFESSIONALS

8

CHURCH

5

4

1

To Maritime Museum

To National Coach Museum & Belém Station →

Praça do Império

T #15E (From Lisbon)

Jardim da Praça do Império

To Monument to the Discoveries ↓

1 South Portal
2 Church Entrance
3 Church Interior
4 Memorial to Luís de Camões

5 Renaissance Altar
6 Tomb of Vasco da Gama
7 Cloister Entrance
8 Stairs Up to Bookshop & Views

○ **Self-Guided Tour:** Here's a tour, starting outside the monastery:

1 **South Portal:** The fancy portal, facing the street, is textbook Manueline. Henry the Navigator stands between the doors with the king's patron saint, St. Jerome (above on the left, with the lion). Henry (Manuel's uncle) built the original sailors' chapel on this site. This door is only used when Mass lets out or for Saturday weddings. (The electronic snapping sound you hear is designed to keep the pigeons away.)

2 **Church Entrance:** As you approach the main entrance, the church is on your right and the cloister is straight ahead. Flanking the church door are kneeling statues of King Manuel I, the Fortunate (left of door, with St. Jerome), and his Spanish wife, María (right, with John the Baptist).

3 **Church Interior:** The Manueline style is on the cusp of

the Renaissance. The space is more open than earlier medieval churches. Slender, palm tree-like columns don't break the interior space (as Gothic columns would), and the ceiling is all one height. Motifs from the sea hide in the decor. The sea brought Portugal 16th-century wealth and power, making this art possible. You'll see rope-like arches, ships, and monsters that evoke the mystery of undiscovered lands. Artichokes, eaten for their vitamin C to fend off scurvy, remind us of the hardships sailors faced at sea.

❹ Memorial to Luís de Camões: Camões (kah-MOISH, 1524-1580) is Portugal's Shakespeare and Casanova rolled into one, an adventurer and writer whose heroic poems glorifying the nation's sailing exploits live on today. It was Camões who described Portugal as the place "where land ends and the sea begins."

After college at Coimbra, Camões was banished from the court (1546) for flirting with the noble lady Dona Caterina. He lost an eye soldiering in Morocco (he's always portrayed squinting), served jail time for brawling with a bureaucrat, and then caught a ship to India and China, surviving a shipwreck on the way. While serving as a colonial administrator in India, he plugged away at the epic poem that would become his masterpiece. Returning to Portugal, he published *The Lusiads* (*Os Lusíadas*, 1572), winning minor recognition and a small pension.

The long poem describes Vasco da Gama's first voyage to India in heroic terms, on the scale of Homer's *Odyssey*. *The Lusiads* begins:

> *Arms and the heroes, from Lisbon's shore,*
> *sailed through seas never dared before,*
> *with awesome courage, forging their way*
> *to the glorious kingdoms of the rising day.*

The poem goes on to recite many events in Portuguese history, from the time of the Lusiads (the original pre-Roman natives) onward. Even today, Camões' words are quoted by modern Portuguese politicians in search of a heroic sound bite. And Portugal's national holiday, June 10, is known as Camões Day, remembering the day in 1580 when the great poet died. The stone monument here—with literary rather than maritime motifs—is a cenotaph (his actual burial spot is unknown).

❺ Renaissance Altar: Nearly everything here survived the 1755 earthquake, except for the stained glass (the replacement glass is from 1940). In the main altar, elephants—the Oriental symbol of power, which dethroned lions as the most powerful and kingly of beasts—support two kings and two queens (King Manuel I is front-left). Many Portuguese churches (such as the cathedrals in downtown Lisbon and Évora) were renovated in Renaissance and Baroque times, resulting in an odd mix of dark, older naves and pretty pastel altars. Walk back on the side with the seven wooden confessional doors (on your right). Notice the ornamental carving around the second one: a festival of faces from newly discovered corners of the world. Head back toward the entry. Under a ceiling that's a veritable *Boy Scout's Handbook* of rope and knots) is the...

❻ Tomb of Vasco da Gama: On the night of July 7, 1497, in the small chapel that stood here before the current church was

built, da Gama (1460-1524) prayed for a safe voyage. The next day, he set sail from Belém with four ships (see the caravel carved in the middle of the tomb's side) and 150 men. He was armed with state-of-the-art maps and sailing technology, such as the carved armillary sphere, a globe surrounded by movable rings de-signed to determine the positions of the sun or other stars to help sailors track their location on earth. (Some say its diagonal slash is symbolic of the unwritten pact and ambition of Spain and Portugal to split the world evenly, but it actually represents the path of the planets as they move across the heavens.)

Da Gama's mission? To confirm what earlier navigators had hypothesized—that the ocean recently discovered when Bartolomeu Dias rounded Africa was the same one seen by overland travelers to India. Hopefully, da Gama would find a direct sea route to the vast, untapped wealth of Asia. The symbols on the tomb show the icons of the period—the cross (symbolizing the religious military order of the soldier monks who funded these voyages), the caravel (representing the method of travel), and Portugal's trading power around the globe (the result).

By Christmas, da Gama rounded the Cape of Good Hope. After battling hostile Arabs in Mozambique, he hired an Arab guide to pilot the ships to India, arriving on the southwest coast in Calicut (from which we get the word "calico") in May of 1498. He traded for spices, networked with the locals for future outposts, battled belligerent chiefs, and then headed back home. Da Gama and his crew arrived home to Lisbon in September of 1499 (after two years and two months on the seas) and were greeted with all-out Vasco-mania. The few spices he'd returned with (many were lost in transit) were worth a staggering fortune. Portugal's Golden Age was launched.

Manueline Architecture (c. 1480-1580)

Portugal's unique style (from its peak of power under King Manuel I, the Fortunate, r. 1495-1521) reflects the wealth of the times and the many cultural influences of the Age of Discovery. The purpose is decorative, not structural. Whether the building uses pointed Gothic or round Renaissance arches, it can be embellished with elaborate Manueline carved stonework, particularly around windows and doors.

Manueline aesthetic is ornate, elaborate, and intertwined, often featuring symbols from a family's coat of arms (shields with castles, crosses, lions, banners, and crowns) or motifs from the sea (rope-like columns or borders, knots, shells, coral, anchors, and nets). Manuel's personal symbol was the armillary sphere—a globe of the earth surrounded by movable rings—which was an indispensable navigational aid for sailors. You'll also see imports of the age, from opium poppies to strange animals.

Architecture students will recognize elements from Gothic's elaborate tracery, the abstract designs of Moorish culture, similarities to Spain's intricate Plateresque style (which dates from the same time), and the elongated excesses of Italian Mannerism.

King Manuel dubbed da Gama "Admiral of the Sea of India" and sent him out again, this time to subdue the Indian people, establish more trade outposts, and again return home to wealth and honor. Da Gama died on Christmas Eve 1524, in India. His memory lives on due to the tribute of two men: Manuel, who built this large church, and Luís de Camões (honored opposite Vasco), who turned da Gama's history-making voyage into an epic poem.

❼ Cloister: Leave the church (turn right), purchase your ticket, and enter the cloister. The restored cloister is the architectural highlight of Belém. The lacy arcade is Manueline; the simpler diamond and decorative rose frieze above the top floor is Renaissance. Study the carvings, especially the gargoyles above the lower set of arches. Among these functioning rainspouts, find a monkey, a kitten, and a cricket. The small basin in the corner (where the monks

washed up before meals) marks the entrance to the refectory, or dining hall—today an occasional concert venue lined with fine 18th-century tiles. The tiles are considered textbook Rococo (from the French word for "shell," as you can see). Rococo ignores the parameters set by the architecture, unlike Baroque, which works within the structure.

To the left of the refectory is the burial spot of Portugal's most revered modern poet, Fernando Pessoa (see sidebar on page 64). Continuing around, a large room contains an exhibit of the lengthy restoration process, as well as the tomb of Alexandre Herculano, a Romantic 19th-century historian and poet. Quotes from Herculano adorn his tomb: "Sleep? Only the cold cadaver that doesn't feel sleeps. The soul flies and wraps itself around the feet of the All-Powerful."

Heads of state are often received in the cloister with a warm welcome. This is also the site of many important treaty signings, such as Portugal's admittance to the European Union in 1986.

❽ Upstairs: You'll find a bookshop, WCs (women's downstairs, men's upstairs), and better views of the church and the cloister, along with exhibits about the monastery's history.

Monks often accompanied the sailor-pirates on their trading/pillaging trips, hoping to convert the heathens to Christianity. Many expeditions were financed by the Knights of Christ, a brotherhood of soldier monks. (The monks who inhabited this cloister were Hieronymites—followers of St. Jerome, hence the monastery name of Jerónimos.)

King Manuel, who did so much to promote exploration, was also the man who forcibly expelled all Jews from the country. (In 1497, the Spanish *Reyes Católicos*—Ferdinand and Isabel—agreed to allow him to marry one of their daughters on the condition that he deport the Jews.) Francis Xavier, a Spanish Jesuit, did much of his missionary work traveling in Asia in the service of Portugal.

It was a time of extreme Christian faith. The sheer size of this religious complex is a testament to the zealous motivation that—along with money—propelled the Age of Discovery.

Age of Discovery Sights
▲Maritime Museum (Museu de Marinha)
If you're interested in Portugal's historic ships and navigational tools, this museum, which fills the west wing of the Monastery of Jerónimos (listed earlier) and has good English descriptions, is worth a look. Sailors love it.

Cost and Hours: €5, free Sun 10:00-14:00; open daily May-Sept 10:00-18:00, off-season until 17:00; facing the planetarium from the square, a cafeteria—open to the public—is to your left and the museum entrance is to your right.

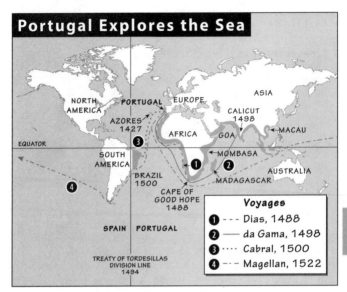

Portugal Explores the Sea

Voyages
1. - - - Dias, 1488
2. ——— da Gama, 1498
3. ···· Cabral, 1500
4. - - - Magellan, 1522

▲Monument to the Discoveries (Padrão dos Descobrimentos)

In 1960, the city honored the 500th anniversary of the death of Prince Henry the Navigator by rebuilding this giant riverside mon-

ument, which had originally been constructed for the 1940 World Expo (reached from the monastery via a pedestrian tunnel under the busy boulevard). The elevator inside takes you up to a tingly view.

Cost and Hours: €3; May-Sept daily 10:00-19:00; Oct-April Tue-Sun 10:00-18:00, closed Mon; last entry 30 minutes before closing, tel. 213-031-950.

Visiting the Monument: Walk around the huge monument. The 170-foot concrete structure shows that exploring the world was a team effort. The men who braved the unknown stand on the pointed, raised prow of a caravel, about to be launched into the Rio Tejo.

Leading the charge is Prince Henry the Navigator (for more about him, see page 154), holding a model of a caravel and a map, followed by kneeling kings and soldiers who Christianized foreign lands with the sword. Behind Henry (on the west side, away from bridge), find the men who financed the voyages (King Manuel I, holding an armillary sphere, his personal symbol), those who glorified it in poems and paintings (like Luís de Camões, holding his

Caravels

These easily maneuverable trading ships were fast, small (80 feet), and light (100 tons), with few guns and three triangular-shaped sails (called lateen-rigged sails) that could pivot quickly to catch the wind. They were ideal for sailing along coastlines. Many oceangoing caravels were also rigged with a square foresail to make them more stable. (This photo shows the model held by Prince Henry on Belém's Monument to the Discoveries.) Columbus' *Niña* and *Pinta* were re-rigged caravels.

famous poem *Os Lusíadas* on a scroll), and at the very end, the only woman, Philippa of Lancaster, Henry's British mother.

On the east side (closest to bridge—as you walk, notice the optical illusion of waves on the flat cobbled surface), Vasco da Gama stands with his eyes on the horizon and his hand on his sword. Magellan holds a circle, representing the round earth his ship circumnavigated, while in front of him, Pedro Cabral puts his hand to his heart, thankful to have (perhaps accidentally) discovered Brazil. Various monks, navigators with maps, and crusaders with flags complete the crew. Check out the pillory, decorated with the Portuguese coat of arms and a cross, erected in each place discovered by the Portuguese—leaving no doubt as to who was in charge.

In the **marble map in the pavement** (a gift from South Africa) in front of the Monument to the Discoveries, follow Portugal's explorers as they inched out into monster-infested waters at the edge of the world. From their tiny, isolated nation in Europe, the Portuguese first headed south to the coast of Morocco, conquering the Muslims of Ceuta in God's name (1415), and gaining strategic control of the mouth of the Mediterranean. They braved the open Atlantic to the west and southwest, stumbling on the Madeiras (1420), which Prince Henry planted with vineyards, and the remote Azore Islands (1427).

Meanwhile, the Portuguese slowly moved southward, hugging the African coast, each voyage building on the knowledge from previous expeditions. They cleared the biggest psychological hump when Gil Eanes sailed around Cape Bojador (Western Sahara, 1434)—the border of the known world—and into the equatorial seas where it was thought that sea monsters lurked, no winds blew, and ships would be incinerated in the hot sun. Eanes survived, returning home with 200 Africans in chains, the first of what would

The Age of Discovery

In 1560, you could sail from Lisbon to China without ever losing sight of land explored by Portugal. The riches of the  world poured into the tiny nation—spices from India and Java (black pepper, cinnamon, and curry powder); ivory, diamonds, and slaves (sold to New World plantations) from Africa; sugarcane, gold, and diamonds from Brazil; and, from everywhere, knowledge of new plants, animals, and customs. How did tiny Portugal pull this off?

First, its people were motivated by greed, hoping to break the Arab and Venetian monopoly on Eastern luxury goods (the price of pepper was jacked up 1,000 percent by the time it reached European dinner tables). They were also driven by a crusading Christian spirit, a love of science, and a spirit of adventure. An entire 15th-century generation was obsessed with finding the legendary kingdom of the fabulously wealthy Christian named "Prester John," supposedly located in either India or Africa. (The legend may be based on a historical figure from around 1120 who visited the pope in Rome as "patriarch of India.")

Portugal also had certain natural advantages. Its Atlantic location led to a strong maritime tradition. A unified nation-state (one of Europe's first) financed and coordinated expeditions. And a core of technology-savvy men used and developed their expansive knowledge of navigational devices, astronomy, maps, shipbuilding, and languages.

become a lucrative, abhorrent commodity. Two generations later, Bartolomeu Dias rounded the southern tip of Africa (1488), discovering the sea route to Asia that Vasco da Gama (1498) and others would exploit to colonize India, Indonesia, Japan, and China (Macao in 1557, on the south coast).

In 1500, Pedro Cabral (along with Dias and 1,200 men) took a wi-i-i-ide right turn on the way down the African coast, hoping to avoid windless seas, and landed on the tip of Brazil. Brazil proved to be an agricultural goldmine for Portugal, which profited from sugar plantations worked by African slaves. Two hundred years later, gold and gemstones were discovered in Brazil, jumpstarting the Portuguese economy again.

In 1520, Portuguese Ferdinand Magellan, employed by Spain, sailed west with five ships and 270 men, broke for R&R in Rio, continued through the Straits of Magellan (tip of South America), and suffered through mutinies, scurvy, and dinners of sawdust and ship rats before touching land in Guam. Magellan was killed in battle in the Philippines, but one remaining ship continued west and arrived back in Europe, having circumnavigated the globe after 30 months at sea.

By 1560, Portugal's global empire had peaked. Tiny-but-filthy-rich Portugal claimed (though they didn't actually occupy) the entire coastline of Africa, Arabia, India, the Philippines, and south China—a continuous stretch from Lisbon to Macao—plus Brazil. The Treaty of Tordesillas (1494) with Spain divvied up the colonial world between the two nations, split at 45 degrees west longitude (bisecting South America—and explaining why Brazil speaks Portuguese and the rest of the continent speaks Spanish) and 135 degrees east longitude (bisecting the Philippines and Australia).

But all of the wealth was wasted on Portugal's ruling class, who neglected to reinvest it in the future. Easy money ruined the traditional economy and stunted industry, hurting the poor. Over the next four centuries, one by one, Portugal's colonies were lost to other European nations or to local revolutions. Today, only the (largely autonomous) islands of the Azores and Madeiras remain from the once-global empire.

▲Belém Tower

Perhaps the purest Manueline building in Portugal (built 1515-1520), this white tower protected Lisbon's harbor. Today it symbolizes the voyages that made Lisbon powerful, with carved stone representing ropes, Manuel's coat of arms, armillary spheres, and shields with the cross of Manuel's military, called the Order of the Cross.

Cost and Hours: €6, €12 combo-ticket saves you €2 if you also visit the cloister at the Monastery of Jerónimos, free first Sun of every month, May-Sept Tue-Sun 10:00-18:30, off-season until 17:30, closed Mon, last entry 30 minutes before closing, tel. 213-620-034.

Visiting the Tower: This was the last sight sailors saw as they left, and the first as they returned, loaded with gold, spices, and social diseases. When the tower was built, the river went nearly to the walls of the monastery, and the tower was mid-river. Its interior is pretty bare, but the views of the bridge, river, and Cristo Rei statue are worth the 120 steps.

The floatplane on the grassy lawn is a monument to the first flight across the

Eating in Belém

You'll find snack bars at Belém Tower, a cafeteria at the Maritime Museum, and fun little restaurants along Rua de Belém, between the National Coach Museum and the monastery. Here are a few other eateries worth checking out:

Restaurante Os Jerónimos is a busy little place good for fresh fish, where hardworking Carlos treats his customers well and serves fine €10 meals (Sun-Fri 12:00-22:30, closed Sat, Rua de Belém 74, tel. 213-638-423, next to renowned Casa Pastéis de Belém pastry café, see page 83).

Pão Pão Queijo Queijo ("Bread Bread Cheese Cheese") serves quick and tasty sandwiches, salads, kebabs, and shawarma sandwiches for less than €5. Place your order at the bar, then eat at tables outside, in the crowded upstairs dining room, or get it to go and picnic in the park across the street (€8 combo plates, Tue-Sat 10:00-24:00, Sun 10:00-20:00, closed Mon, Rua de Belém 124, tel. 213-626-369).

Restaurant Row: Many more fine places with outdoor seating are in the restaurant row behind the McDonald's that faces the park, including **Floresta de Belém,** the local favorite for their home-style Portuguese cooking, such as tasty grilled sardines and *feijoada* bean stew. They have minimal seating inside, but two cozy terraces outside (daily 11:00-23:00 but closed Sept, Praça Afonso de Albuquerque 1A, tel. 213-636-307).

South Atlantic (Portugal to Brazil) in 1922. The original plane (which beat Charles Lindbergh's *Spirit of Saint Louis* across the North Atlantic by five years) is in Belém's Maritime Museum.

If you're choosing between towers, the Monument to the Discoveries is probably the better choice, because it offers a better view of the monastery. Both towers are interesting to see from the outside, whether or not you go up.

Ferry from Belém to Porto Brandão

For a delightfully untouristy little adventure, consider having lunch across the river in **Porto Brandão.** The ferry terminal is immediately in front of the National Coach Museum, across a busy road and train tracks (€1.65 each way, 8-minute cruise, ferries depart on the hour and half hour except hourly from 13:30-15:30, last ferry departs 23:00 weekdays and 22:00 weekends; for a memorable Tejo experience, tall men can use the urinal while sticking their head out the porthole). Boats continue to Trafaria before returning to Belém via Porto Brandão. Upon arrival, carefully confirm return times.

Porto Brandão is a tiny (and dead) three-street town whose harborfront square has several good fish restaurants. I like cozy, blue-and-white-tiled **Restaurante Porto Brandão** (€10-20 fish meals, daily 12:00-15:00 & 18:00-23:00, Rua Bento Jesus Caraça 25, tel. 212-959-145). Their *bacalhau à lagareiro* is for garlic lovers. The *cataplana* (a traditional fish-and-veggie stew) and seafood fondue meals are made for two but stuff three (€15-20/person).

Shopping in Lisbon

Lisbon—Portugal's capital city—has shopping opportunities that run the gamut from flea markets to the country's biggest shopping mall.

Market
The market closest to downtown is Mercado da Ribeira. The recently renovated western section highlights Portuguese gastronomy. Local chefs have adopted famous recipes for sampling, and the casual vibe makes for a fun, on-the-move lunch (produce section Mon-Sat 6:00-14:00, dining section daily 10:00-24:00, Metro: Cais do Sodré).

Flea Markets
On Tuesdays and Saturdays, the Feira da Ladra flea market attracts bargain hunters to Campo de Santa Clara in the Alfama (8:00-15:00, best in morning). A coin market jingles at Mercado da Ribeira, listed above, on Cais do Sodré (Sun 9:00-13:00).

Vasco da Gama Mall
The finest shopping mall in town fills the grand entryway to the 1998 World Expo site at the Oriente train/Metro station. It's well worth a trip out here to feel the pulse of today's Portuguese society, enjoy Parque das Nações, and take in the modern architecture (daily 9:00-24:00, mall described on page 73).

Centro Colombo Shopping Mall
This is the largest shopping center in Spain or Portugal. More than 400 shops—including FNAC's biggest department store, 10 movie screens, 60 restaurants, and a health club—sit atop what they claim is Europe's biggest underground parking lot and under a vast, entertaining play center. There's plenty to amuse children here, and the place offers a fine look at workaday Lisbon (shops open daily 10:00-22:00, food court and cinemas remain open until 24:00, pick up a map at info desk, Metro: Colégio Militar/Luz takes you right there, tel. 217-113-636).

Armazéns do Chiado
This shopping center's six surprisingly modern floors connect Lisbon's lower and upper towns. It's a stop on "The Bairro Alto and Chiado Stroll" described earlier in this chapter, and has a lively food court on the sixth floor. The FNAC department store hides

behind an old facade and is known for its helpful English-speaking staff. The mall is open daily from 10:00 to 22:00 (eateries about 12:00-23:00, www.armazensdochiado.com).

Here's how to find the mall: If you approach from Chiado, take Rua Garrett, which dead-ends at the main entrance. If coming from the Baixa, head up Rua da Assunção toward the mall, where you'll find three subtle entrances on Rua do Crucifixo—through the Sports Zone store (take their escalators up into the mall), at #113, or at #89 (where small, simple, unmarked doorways lead to elevators).

Lisbon Shop

If you need a souvenir with Lisbon's trademarks—sardines, fado, or trolleys—look no further than this large and inviting store run by the city TI. Music, books, T-shirts, and trinkets are more affordable here than in other shops in the Baixa (daily 9:30-19:30, Rua do Arsenal 13, tel. 210-312-802, www.askmelisboa.com).

A Vida Portuguesa

Located just two blocks from the Armazéns do Chiado shopping center, this is the best shop I found for genuine traditional Portuguese products, from stationery and toiletries to toys and jewelry (Mon-Sat 10:00-20:00, closed Sun, Rua Anchieta 11, tel. 213-465-073, www.avidaportuguesa.com).

El Corte Inglés

The Spanish mega-department store has arrived in Lisbon with a huge store at the top of Edward VII Park, offering an enormous supermarket with great picnic supplies, a food court, a cinema, and much more (Mon-Sat 10:00-22:00, Sun 10:00-20:00, Avenida António Augusto de Aguiar 31, Metro: São Sebastião, near Gulbenkian Museum, tel. 213-711-700).

Entertainment in Lisbon

NIGHTLIFE

Nightlife in the Baixa seems to be little more than loitering prostitutes and litter stirred by the wind. Head instead up to the Bairro Alto for fado halls, bars, and the Miradouro de São Pedro de Alcântara (view terrace), a pleasant place to hang out. Nearby Rua Diario de Noticias is lined with busy bars and fun crowds spilling onto the street.

The Docas

The trendy hot spot for Lisbon's young people is the dock district under the 25th of April Bridge. The Docas (DOH-kash) is a 400-yard-long strip of warehouses turned into pricey restaurants and nightclubs (particularly Doca de Alcântara and Doca de Santo

Amaro). Popular places include Hawaii, Buddha, Havana, and Doca 6 (catch a taxi or trolley #15E from Praça da Figueira to the Avenida Infante Santo stop, take overpass, then a 10-minute walk toward bridge; or bus #714 from Praça da Figueira, ask driver for *"Paragem Docas"*). If you're returning late, night bus #201 starts at 1:00 in the morning and runs every 30 minutes to Cais do Sodré, where you can walk 15 minutes or connect with night bus #205 or #207 to Rossio.

Pink Street

This happening, crazy street (much easier to get to than the Docas) is a short walk downhill from Chiado and a block inland from Praça Duque da Terceira in the Cais do Sodré neighborhood. Rua Nova do Carvalho, otherwise known as "Pink Street," was once notorious as the sailors' red-light zone. Now the prostitutes are just painted onto the walls, and the made-over street is painted a bright pink. After the bars in other neighborhoods close, late-night revelers hike 10 minutes from Chiado down Rua do Alecrim to reach Pink Street. Surrounded by largely uninhabited Pombaline buildings, Pink Street's four bars are allowed to make noise—and they do—until late in the night.

Pensão Amor ("House of Love") is a velvety place for a cocktail. Wallpapered with sexy memories of the days when it was a brothel, it's a grungy tangle of corners to hang out in and enjoy a drink (or just stare at the wallpaper), often against a backdrop of live jazz (no food, Rua Nova do Carvalho 38, also possible to enter from top at Rua do Alecrim 19, tel. 213-143-399).

Sol e Pesca Bar, a nostalgic reminder of the sailor-and-fisherman heritage of this street, sells drinks and preserved food in tins. Just browse the shelves of classic €1-6 tinned seafood—from pâté and sardines to caviar (€1 extra to eat from a tin at a table)—and wash down your salty seafood tapas with a glass of wine amid the lures and nets (Rua Nova do Carvalho 44, tel. 213-467-203).

Bar de Velha Senhora ("The Old Lady") is a dark bar with live music most nights starting at 23:00 on its cozy little stage (burlesque Thu-Sat, jazz and other music on other nights, no cover, Rua Nova do Carvalho 38, tel. 213-468-479).

Povo Lisboa is a trendy little bar serving delightful Portuguese tapas (from 18:00) and enlivening things with fado later on (Sun and Tue-Thu 21:30, no cover, just buy a drink, light food, Rua Nova do Carvalho 32, tel. 213-473-403).

Evening Stroll

While not as big a deal as in Spain, the people of Lisbon enjoy an early evening stroll after work and before dinner when the weather is balmy. When it comes to weather, Lisboners are pretty spoiled. If it's even a little blustery, they'll likely stay in. But when it's nice, in the summer, you'll find lots of people out strolling. Four good places: Rua Augusta through the heart of the Baixa district; along the seaside promenade near the Belém Tower; along the fine riverfront promenade at Parque das Nações; and the river walk at Ribeira das Naus (from the water at Praça do Comércio to Cais do Sodré).

▲▲FADO

Fado is the folk music of Lisbon's back streets. Since the mid-1800s, it's been the Lisbon blues—mournfully beautiful and haunting ballads about lost sailors, broken hearts, and bittersweet romance. While generally sad, fado can also be jaunty—in a nostalgic way— and captivating. A stout 60-year-old widow singing fado can be invitingly sexy.

Fado has become one of Lisbon's favorite late-night tourist traps, but it's easy to find a convivial and rustic bar without the high prices and tour groups. Both the Bairro Alto and the Alfama have small, informal fado restaurants. Go either for a late dinner (after 21:00) or an even later evening of drinks and music. Homemade "fado tonight" *(fado esta noite)* signs in Portuguese are good news, but even a restaurant filled with tourists can come with good food and fine fado. I like "fado vadio," a kind of open-mic fado evening when amateurs line up at the door of neighborhood dives for their chance to warble.

Prices for a fado performance vary greatly. Many have a steep cover charge, while others just expect you to buy a meal. Appetizers, bread, or cheese that appear on your table aren't free—if you nibble, you'll pay. Send them back if you don't want to be charged. Assume any place recommended by a hotel is a tourist trap with prices bloated by €15 kickbacks (don't even let the hotel call to confirm your reservation—or they'll take that kickback). Both elegant, high-end places and holes-in-the-wall generally let non-diners in late for the cost of a drink or a small cover charge.

Fado in the Bairro Alto

In the Bairro Alto, wander around Rua Diario de Noticias and neighboring streets. **Canto do Camões,** run by friendly, English-speaking Gabriel, is easy to reserve and has good music and tasty food. Call ahead to assure a seat (open at 20:00, music from 20:30 until after midnight; €27 meal required—includes appetizer, 3 courses, water, and wine; after 22:00 €12 minimum for two drinks; from Rua da Misericordia, go 2 blocks uphill on Travessa da Espera to #38, see map on page 113; tel. 213-465-464). When it's busy, the room feels like a stage show, with 25 or 30 tables filled mostly with tourists, all enjoying classic fado. Relax, spend some time, and close your eyes, or make eye contact with the singer. Let the music and wine collaborate.

Fado

Fado songs reflect Portugal's bittersweet relationship with the sea. Fado means "fate"—how fate deals with Portugal's adventurers...and the women they leave behind. These are songs of both sadness and hope, a bittersweet emotion called *saudade* (meaning yearning or nostalgia). The lyrics reflect the pining for a loved one across the water, hopes for a future reunion, remembrances of a rosy past or dreams of a better future, and the yearning for what might have been if fate had not intervened. (Fado can also be bright and happy when the song is about the virtues of cities such as Lisbon or Coimbra, or of the warmth of a typical *casa portuguesa*.)

The songs are often in a minor key. The singer *(fadista)* is accompanied by a 12-string Portuguese *guitarra* (with a round body like a mandolin) or other stringed instruments unique to Portugal. Many singers crescendo into the first word of the verse, like a moan emerging from deep inside. Though the songs are often sad, the singers rarely overact—they plant themselves firmly and sing stoically in the face of fate.

A verse from a typical fado song goes:

O waves of the salty sea,
where do you get your salt?
From the tears shed by the women in black
on the beaches of Portugal.

Restaurante Adega do Ribatejo is a homey place crowded with locals and tourists nightly (except Sun) from around 20:30 to 24:00. Just around the corner from Canto do Camões and less touristy (almost anti-touristy), you can sit down here and just pay for whatever you want to eat or drink with no required minimum (€15 meals, Mon-Sat from 19:00, closed Sun, Rua Diario de Noticias 23, see map on page 113, tel. 213-468-343). After 22:30 you're welcome to just buy a drink and enjoy the music for free.

Fado in Chiado, a sterile 50-minute performance in a small modern theater, is for tourists who don't want to stay out late or mess with a restaurant. Sitting with other tourists and without food or drink, you'll enjoy four musicians: a man and a woman singing, a guitarist, and a man on the Portuguese guitar, which gives fado its balalaika charm (€17, daily at 19:00 except Sun, conveniently located in Chiado at Rua da Misericordia 14, on second floor of in Cine Theatro Gymnasio, tel. 961-717-778).

Fado in the Alfama

While often pretty lonely and dead after dark, the Alfama has several bars offering fado with their meals—just head uphill from the Fado Museum. Some bars are geared for tourists and tour groups, but others feel organic, spontaneous, and part of the neighborhood culture. While schedules at any particular place can be inconsistent, if you hike up Rua São Pedro de Alcântara to the Church of São Miguel, you'll hear the music wafting out from hole-in-the-wall eateries and be greeted by men hustling business for their fado restaurants. Generally, you simply pay for the meal and enjoy the music as included entertainment. If it's late and there's room, you can just buy a drink.

A Baiuca, a tiny fun-loving restaurant, offers my favorite Alfama fado experience. A Baiuca—the name means a very rough tavern—packs people in and serves up spirited "fado vadio" (open mic for amateurs) with traditional home-cooking and lots of wine. As the English-speaking manager, Isabel, likes to say, "Fado needs wine." This intimate place is a neighborhood affair and has surround sound—as everyone seems to get into the music (€25 minimum, unless you come very late when you can just buy a drink, best singing Thu-Mon 20:00-24:00; reservations smart, in the heart of the Alfama, just off Rua São Pedro up the hill from Fado Museum, at Rua de São Miguel 20, see map on page 113, tel. 218-867-284). When the door is closed, they're full, but you can peek at the action through the window around to the left.

Clube de Fado is much classier—one of the best places in town to hear quality fado. While a bit pricey, there's not a bad seat in the house. Music plays nightly in this formal yet intimate setting. When busy, the musicians switch between two adjacent halls, giving waiters time to serve between sets, and diners get music about half the time (plan on €50 for dinner with wine, plus a €7.50 cover charge, meals from 20:00, dinner reservations required, music 21:30 until after midnight; after 23:00, pay just a €10 cover charge plus cost of your drink; around corner from cathedral at Rua São João da Praça 94, see map on page 113, tel. 218-852-704).

Casa de Linhares, a block downhill from Clube de Fado, offers similar quality fado and an even nicer space, with dinner served under the stone vaults of a 16th-century palace (plan about €40 for dinner, €15 cover for music, nightly from 20:00, after 22:00 €15 with drink purchase, Beco dos Armazéns Do Linho 2, tel. 218-865-088).

BULLFIGHTS, SOCCER, CONCERTS, AND MOVIES

Tickets to all bullfights, soccer games, concerts, and other events are sold at the green **ABEP kiosk** at the southern end of Praça dos Restauradores (daily 9:00-20:00, also sells city transit pass and LisboaCard, across the street from TI).

▲▲▲Portuguese Bullfight

If you always felt sorry for the bull, this is Toro's Revenge: In a Portuguese bullfight, the matador is brutalized along with the bull. Lisbon hosts only about a dozen fights a year, but if you're in town for one, it's an unforgettable experience.

In Act I, the horseman *(cavaleiro)* skillfully plants four beribboned barbs in the bull's back while trying to avoid the

leather-padded horns. The horses are the short, stocky Lusitano breed, with excellent balance. In Act II, a colorfully clad eight-man suicide squad (called *forçados*) enters the ring and lines up single file facing the bull. With testosterone sloshing everywhere, the leader taunts the bull—slapping his knees and yelling, *"touro!"*— then braces himself for a collision that can be heard all the way up in the cheap seats. As he hangs onto the bull's head, his buddies pile on, trying to wrestle the bull to a standstill. Finally, one guy hangs on to *o touro*'s tail and "water-skis" behind him. (In Act III, the *ambulância* arrives.)

Unlike the Spanish *corrida de toros,* the bull is not killed in front of the crowd at the Portuguese *tourada*...but it is killed later. (Some brave bulls with only superficial wounds are spared to fight another day.) Spanish aficionados insist that Portuguese fights are actually crueler, since they humiliate the bull, rather than fight him as a fellow warrior. Animal-rights groups enliven the scene before each fight.

The ring is small, so there are no bad seats. To sit nearly at ringside, try the cheapest *bancada* seats, on the generally half-empty and unmonitored main floor (Metro: Campo Pequeno). The ring is a spectacular, Moorish-domed brick structure that bears a resemblance to Madrid's bullring. After five years of remodeling, it reopened with a shopping mall underneath and a retractable roof overhead for concerts. It hosts a variety of restaurants inside, oddly including an Argentine steak restaurant. Maybe the beef served was in the ring earlier?

Fights are generally held on Thursday at 20:00 and on Sunday afternoons from Easter through September. Important note: Half the fights are simply Spanish-type *corridas* without the killing. For the real slam-bam Portuguese-style fight, confirm that there will be *grupo de forçados* ("bull grabbers"). Tickets are always available at the door (€20-50, no surcharge, tel. 217-932-143 to confirm; tickets sold at the ABEP kiosk on Praça dos Restauradores add a 10 percent surcharge).

Soccer

Lisbon is home to two *futebol* teams, Benfica and Sporting CP, which means there are lots of games (1-2/week Aug-May, tickets €20 and up) and lots of team spirit. Benfica, with the red jerseys, plays at the 65,400-seat Stadium of Light near the Centro Colombo mall (Estádio da Luz; Metro: Colegio Militar/Luz, www.slbenfica.pt). Sporting CP, with the green-and-white jerseys, plays at the 50,000-seat Estádio José Alvalade to the north of Lisbon's center (Metro: Campo Grande, www.sporting.pt). Tickets are generally available at the stadium or at the ABEP kiosk on Praça dos Restauradores.

Concerts

You can hear classical music by national and city orchestras at the Gulbenkian Museum (see page 67) and at the cultural center in Belém (www.ccb.pt). Traditional Portuguese theater plays in the National Theater on Rossio and in theaters along Rua das Portas de Santo Antão (the "eating lane"—see page 117) stretching north from Rossio. For popular music, these days you're more likely to find rock, jazz, Brazilian, and African music than traditional fado. The monthly *Agenda Cultural* provides the most up-to-date listing of world music, arts, and entertainment (free at TI, €0.50 at newsstands, online at www.agendalx.pt, in Portuguese only).

Movies

In Lisbon, unlike in Spain, most films are shown in the original language with subtitles. (That's one reason the Portuguese speak better English than the Spanish.) Many of Lisbon's theaters are classy, complete with assigned seats, ushers, and intermissions. Check the newspaper to see what's playing, or drop by the ABEP kiosk at Praça dos Restauradores, where a list of all the movies playing in town is taped to a side window (on the left). São Jorge Theater, located midway up Avenida da Liberdade, is a grand old Art Deco movie palace showing festival treats; it's run by the same cultural organization in charge of the São Jorge Castle and the Monument to the Discoveries. More modern options are in malls like Colombo, El Corte Inglés, or at the Monumental complex in the ritzy Saldanha neighborhood (Metro: Saldanha).

LISBON

Sleeping in Lisbon

With a few exceptions, cheaper hotels downtown feel tired and well-worn. Singles cost nearly the same as doubles. If you're on a tight budget and want to stay in the center, consider Lisbon's famously classy hostels, which welcome travelers of all ages. Addresses such as 26-3 stand for building #26, third floor (which is the fourth floor in American terms). For locations of accommodations, see the map on page 105.

Be sure to book in advance if you'll be in Lisbon during its festival—Festas de Lisboa—the last three weeks of June, when parades, street parties, concerts, and fireworks draw crowds to the city. Conventions can clog Lisbon at any time.

IN THE CENTER

Central as can be, the Baixa district bustles with lots of shops, traffic, people, street musicians, pedestrian areas, and urban intensity.

On Rossio

$$$ Internacional Design Hotel has 55 hip, ultra-modern double rooms centrally located at the southeast corner of Rossio. Each of its four floors has a different theme—pop, Zen, tribal, and urban. Having coffee in their expansive breakfast room overlooking Rossio is a fantastic way to start the day. I've listed its expensive rack rates, but you can often get a room for a 10 to 20 percent discount by booking ahead online (Db-€120-400 depending on size, Db with pull-out child's bed-€500, buffet breakfast in bright room overlooking Rossio, air-con, elevator, Wi-Fi, underground parking nearby-€15/day, Rua da Betesga 3, tel. 213-240-990, www.idesignhotel.com, book@idesignhotel.com).

$$$ Hotel Métropole keeps its elegant 1920s style throughout 36 carefully appointed but slightly worn rooms. It's overpriced, but you're paying for the prime location. The quieter back rooms are smaller, but cost the same unless you ask for a break. Prices drop by a third in slow times. Don't be shy; ask for a 10 percent Rick Steves discount when you reserve (Sb-€110-200, Db-€130-200, extra bed-€50, check website for discounts, buffet breakfast, air-con, elevator, free Wi-Fi in lobby, Rossio 30, tel. 213-219-030, www.metropole-lisbon.com, metropole@themahotels.com).

On Praça dos Restauradores

$$$ Hotel Avenida Palace, the most characteristic five-star splurge in town, was built with Rossio Station in 1892 to greet big-shot travelers. Back then, trains were new, and Rossio was the only station in town. The lounges are sumptuous, dripping with chandeliers, and the 82 rooms mix elegance with 21st-century comforts

---

LISBON

> ## Sleep Code
>
> **Abbreviations**   **(€1 = about $1.40, country code: 351)**
> **S** = Single, **D** = Double/Twin, **T** = Triple, **Q** = Quad, **b** = bathroom, **s** = shower only.
> **Price Rankings**
> **$$$** **Higher Priced**—Most rooms €115 or more.
>   **$$** **Moderately Priced**—Most rooms between €65-115.
>   **$** **Lower Priced**—Most rooms €65 or less.
> Unless otherwise noted, credit cards are accepted, tax is included in the price, English is spoken, breakfast is included, and Wi-Fi is generally free. Prices can change without notice; verify the hotel's current rates online or by email. For the best prices, always book directly with the hotel.

(Sb-€194, Db-€228, more expensive suites available, reserve on website for substantial discounts, air-con, elevator, Wi-Fi, laundry service, free parking, hotel's sign is on Praça dos Restauradores but entrance is at Rua 1 de Dezembro 123, down a small alleyway next to Starbucks, tel. 213-218-121, www.hotelavenidapalace.pt, reservas@hotelavenidapalace.pt).

$$$ VIP Executive Suites Eden rents 134 slick and contemporary compact apartments (with small kitchens). It has a rooftop

swimming pool and breakfast terrace with commanding city, castle, and river views. The building used to be a 1930s cinema, hence the Art Deco architecture and the slightly pie-shaped rooms. Perfectly located at the Rossio end of Avenida da Liberdade, this is a clean, quiet pool of modernity amid the ramshackle charm of Lisbon. It's also an intriguing option for groups or families of four (Db studio-€95-129, 2-bedroom apartment with bed-and-sofa combo that can sleep 4 people-€139-189, breakfast-€9, check website for deals, air-con, elevator, Praça dos Restauradores 24, tel. 213-216-600, www.viphotels.com, res.eden@viphotels.com).

Near Praça da Figueira
$$$ Hotel Lisboa Tejo (leezh-BOH-ah TAY-zhoo) is an oasis of 58 comfy ocean-blue rooms with hardwood floors (Sb-€60-113, Db-€70-131, 10 percent discount with this book only when reserved direct through hotel, crowded breakfast buffet, air-con, elevator, Wi-Fi; from southeast corner of Praça da Figueira, walk one block down Rua dos Condes de Monsanto and turn left to

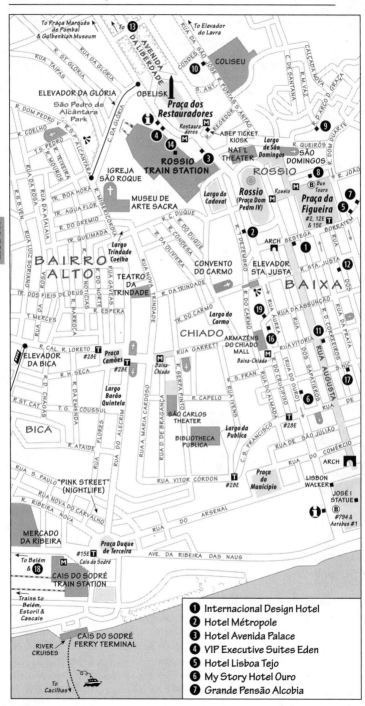

1 Internacional Design Hotel
2 Hotel Métropole
3 Hotel Avenida Palace
4 VIP Executive Suites Eden
5 Hotel Lisboa Tejo
6 My Story Hotel Ouro
7 Grande Pensão Alcobia

Lisbon Center Hotels

LISBON

- ⑧ Pensão Praça da Figueira
- ⑨ Pensão Residencial Gerês
- ⑩ Residencial Florescente
- ⑪ Hotel Duas Nações
- ⑫ Norte Guest House
- ⑬ To Avenida da Liberdade Area Hotels & Ibis Hotels
- ⑭ Lisbon Destination Hostel
- ⑮ Home Lisbon Hostel
- ⑯ Living Lounge Hostel
- ⑰ Lisbon Lounge Hostel
- ⑱ To Hotel As Janelas Verdes
- ⑲ Laundry

Condes de Monsanto 2; tel. 218-866-182, www.lisboatejohotel.com, reservas@lisboatejohotel.com).

$$ My Story Hotel Ouro has 51 rooms decorated in gold tones—*ouro* in Portuguese. Outside-facing rooms have interesting views, but ask for an inside room for a quiet night's sleep (Sb-€90, Db-€100-110, substantially less off-season, air-con, elevator, Wi-Fi, Rua Áurea 100, tel. 213-400-340, www.mystoryhotels.com, ouro@mystoryhotels.com).

$$ Grande Pensão Alcobia has 42 simple, worn rooms but offers an alternative to higher-priced hotels located in the same part of town. Some upper-floor rooms have views of São Jorge Castle (Sb-€45-60, Db-€50-80, Tb-€90-105, 10 percent discount with this book when reserved direct through hotel, air-con, small elevator, guest computer and Wi-Fi, Poço do Borratem 15, tel. 218-844-150, www.pensaoalcobia.com, reservasalcobia@sapo.pt).

$ Pensão Praça da Figueira is a backpacker place on a quiet back street with youth-hostel prices, a kitchen on every floor, and 37 clean, basic rooms (D-€35-45, Ds-€45-53, Db-€53-63, singles-€7 less, extra bed-€20, breakfast included, 2 flights up with no elevator, Wi-Fi, entrance is at Travessa Nova de São Domingos 9, behind Praça da Figueira, tel. 213-426-757, www.pensaopracadafigueira.com, pensaofigueira@clix.pt).

Near Rossio

$$ Pensão Residencial Gerês rents 20 bright, basic, cozy rooms with older plumbing but without the dingy smokiness that pervades Lisbon's cheaper hotels. Double-paned windows keep out much of the street noise (S-€45, Sb-€55, Db-€60, Tb-€85-100, 10 percent discount only Nov-March with cash and this book, no breakfast, pay Wi-Fi, uphill a block off northeast corner of Rossio, Calçada do Garcia 6, tel. 218-810-497, www.pensaogeres.net, info@pensaogeres.net). The super-sweet Nogueira family speaks some English.

$ Residencial Florescente rents 68 rooms on the "eating lane," a thriving pedestrian street a block off Praça dos Restauradores (Sb-€45-50, Db-€75, bigger twin Db-€75-85, Tb-€85-95, higher prices apply July-Sept, air-con, Wi-Fi, Rua das Portas de Santo Antão 99, tel. 213-426-609, www.residencialflorescente.com, geral@residencialflorescente.com).

$ Hotel Duas Nações offers 73 small, modern rooms in a great location (Db-€65, air-con, pay Wi-Fi, staff can be indifferent, Rua Augusta and Rua da Victoria 41, tel. 213-460-710, www.duasnacoes.com, reservas@duasnacoes.com).

$ Norte Guest House rents 34 small, linoleum-floored rooms. Although a bit dark, it beats a youth hostel—barely (Ds-€29-32, Db-€39-44, Tb/Qb-€44-49, higher prices apply July-Sept, no breakfast, a bit smoky, Wi-Fi, Rua dos Douradores 161, tel. 218-878-941, www.norteguesthouse.com, info@norteguesthouse.com).

Along Avenida da Liberdade

These listings are a 10-minute walk or short Metro ride from the center.

Near Metro: Avenida

$$$ Hotel Lisboa Plaza, a large, plush four-star gem, mixes traditional style with bright-pastel classiness. With 112 rooms, it offers snappy and polite service, all the amenities, and a free glass of port when you check in (Sb-€120-190, Db-€130-200, extra bed-€47, higher prices apply March-June and Sept-Oct, larger "superior" rooms cost 25 percent more, buffet breakfast-€14, air-con, one allergen-free floor, Wi-Fi, parking-€10/day; well-located on a quiet street off busy Avenida da Liberdade, a block from Metro: Avenida, Travessa do Salitre 7; tel. 213-218-218, www.heritage.pt, plaza@heritage.pt). Hotel Lisboa Plaza and its sister, Hotel Britania (listed later), offer a deal in July and August: free entrance to Lisbon's museums for guests who stay at least three nights.

$$ Hotel Botânico, in a blocky, modern building on a characteristic street a steep five-minute walk above Avenida da Liberdade, is quiet—unless there's a demonstration at the Planned Parenthood clinic across the street. The hotel rents 30 modern, business-class rooms; street-side rooms on the top floor have a view of São Jorge Castle (Sb-€45-90, Db-€50-95, Tb-€60-95, air-con, elevator, Wi-Fi, parking, Rua Mãe d'Água 16, tel. 213-420-392, www.hotelbotanico.pt, hotelbotanico@netcabo.pt).

$$ Residêncial Roma, a stark little place, rents 40 simple rooms. It's tucked away on a side street, 50 yards off the big Avenida da Liberdade (Sb-€35-50, Db-€45-70, extra bed-€10-15, air-con, no elevator, Travessa da Glória 22, tel. 213-460-558, www.residenciaroma.com, res.roma@cyclopnet.pt). They also rent apartments (Db-€75-120, €10/extra person).

$$ Hotel Alegria, a fine old establishment with 35 rooms, faces a quiet, inviting park in a peaceful neighborhood 200 yards from the Avenida Metro station. Varnished like a ship, it has sloping hardwood floors and solid furniture (Db-€60-85, third person-€15 extra, breakfast-€6, air-con, elevator, Praça da Alegria 12, tel. 213-220-670, www.alegrianet.com, mail@alegrianet.com).

Others near Avenida da Liberdade

$$$ Hotel Britania maintains its 1940s Art Deco charm throughout its 33 spacious rooms, offering a clean and professional haven on a tranquil street one block off Avenida da Liberdade. Three top-floor suites are decorated in a luxurious Mod Deco style. Run by the Hotel Lisboa Plaza folks (listed earlier), it offers the same four-star standards for the same prices (air-con, elevator, laundry service, Wi-Fi, free street parking or €15/day in next-door garage; from Metro: Avenida stop, walk uphill on boulevard, turn right on Rua Manuel de Jesus Coelho and take first left to Rua Rodrigues Sampaio 17; tel. 213-155-016, www.heritage.pt, britania.hotel@ heritage.pt).

$ Lisbon Dreams Guesthouse has 18 fresh, relaxing, Ikea-like rooms, occupying three apartments and sharing seven bathrooms (S-€50, D-€60, T-€80, discounts often available on website, Wi-Fi and free loaner laptops, laundry service-€6, two shared terraces, kitchen for guest use; Metro: Marquês de Pombal, then take Rua Alexandre Herculano uphill and turn left on Rua Rodrigo da Fonesca, or Metro: Rato, take Rua Alexandre Herculano downhill, then right to reach Rua Rodrigo da Fonesca 29, tel. 213-872-393, www.lisbondreams.com, info@lisbondreams.com).

$ Lisbon Centre Hostel has 31 dorm rooms and some private rooms in a 19th-century building (bed in 3- to 6-bed dorm-€18, D-€68, includes sheets, 24-hour access, elevator, Wi-Fi, café and bar, laundry, luggage storage, Rua Andrade Corvo 46 near Avenida da Liberdade, Metro: Picoas, tel. 213-532-696, www.hihostels. com, lisboa@movijovem.pt).

Boutique Hostels in the Baixa

Among hostel aficionados, Lisbon is famous for having the best hostels anywhere. They welcome travelers of any age and come with an artistic flair and plenty of double rooms. Here are four that are conveniently located in the center of town.

$ Lisbon Destination Hostel feels designed for backpackers—young and old—who appreciate style, peace, and quiet. Located upstairs in the Rossio train station, it provides a wonderful value and experience (85 beds, 23 rooms, €20/bed in 4-10-bed dorms, S-€35, D-€60, Db-€70, Wi-Fi, lockers, movie night in lounge, tel. 213-466-457, www.destinationhostels.com, lisbon@ destinationhostels.com).

$ Home Lisbon Hostel is a little more rough and homey, with free laundry, movies, and friendly management (91 beds, €15/bed in 4- to 8-bed dorms, Rua de São Nicolau 13-2, near corner of Rua dos Fanqueiros, Metro: Baixa-Chiado, tel. 218-885-312, www. mylisbonhome.com, info@mylisbonhome.com).

$ Living Lounge Hostel is clean, modern, and in a very central location near the Baixa-Chiado Metro stop. Each room is uniquely decorated (€18-24/bed in 4- to 8-bed mixed dorms, S-€30-37, D-€26-32; includes sheets and towels; air-con, elevator, lockers, laundry service, bike rentals, free tours and excursions, free guest computer and Wi-Fi, Rua Crucifixo 116, second floor, tel. 213-

461-078, www.livingloungehostel.com, info@livingloungehostel.com).

$ Lisbon Lounge Hostel, run by the same folks as the Living Lounge Hostel above, offers the same amenities, style and prices, but no singles. It's in the Baixa, roughly midway between Praça da Figueira and Praça do Comércio (€18-24/bed in 4- to 8-bed mixed dorms, D-€24-32, Rua de São Nicolau 41, tel. 213-462-061, www.lisbonloungehostel.com, info@lisbonloungehostel.com).

AWAY FROM THE CENTER
$$$ Hotel As Janelas Verdes, next door to the Museum of Ancient Art, is another of Hotel Lisboa Plaza's sister properties. An 18th-century mansion that's now a boutique hotel, it has 29 cushy rooms and comfortably elegant public spaces. The third-floor library overlooks the river (Sb/Db-€160-300, check website for specials, air-con, elevator, Wi-Fi, Rua das Janeles Verdes 7, bus #714 stops nearby, tel. 213-968-143, www.heritage.pt, janelas.verdes@heritage.pt).

$$ *Ibis Hotels:* Ibis hotels offer no-stress, no-character rooms for a good price in soulless areas away from the center—but near handy Metro stations. Each has air-conditioning and €5 breakfasts. One child under 12 stays for free and a third adult is €10 (www.ibishotel.com). **Ibis Liberdade** has the best location (70 rooms, Sb/Db-€80, 2 blocks uphill from Avenida da Liberdade's Hotel Tivoli, Metro: Avenida, Rua Barata Salgueiro 53, tel. 213-300-630), followed by **Ibis Saldanha** (116 rooms, Sb/Db-€70, 2-minute walk from Metro: Saldanha, Avenida Casal Ribeiro 23, tel. 213-191-690).

APARTMENTS
Cross-Pollinate is an online booking agency representing B&Bs and apartments in a handful of European cities, including Lisbon. Unlike huge aggregator websites like HomeAway or VRBO, Cross-Pollinate handpicks its listings. Search their website for a listing you like, then submit your reservation online. If the place is available, you'll be charged a small deposit and emailed the location and check-in details. Policies vary from owner to owner, but in most cases you'll pay the balance on arrival in cash. Lisbon listings range from a Rossio guesthouse room for two for €70 per night to a two-bedroom Alfama apartment sleeping four for €100 per night. Minimum stays vary from one to three nights (US tel. 800-270-1190, www.cross-pollinate.com, info@cross-pollinate.com).

LISBON

Eating in Lisbon

Each district of the city comes with fun and characteristic restaurants. (Good eateries in Belém are described on page 93.) Ideally, have one dinner with a fado performance—several good options for music with your meal are listed in this section, with more fado options described earlier, under "Entertainment in Lisbon."

Food Tours in Lisbon: To simultaneously eat good food, learn about Portuguese cuisine, and meet a knowledgeable local guide, consider taking one of the food tours offered by Inside Lisbon, Eat Portugal, or Eat Drink Walk. Their tours are a good value—informative and tasty—filling you in while filling you up (see page 38).

SNACK BARS

Lisbon seems enthusiastic about serving quick, light meals at characteristic bars. On just about any street, you can belly up to a bar, observe, and order what looks good for a tasty, memorable, and extremely cheap meal. You'll see lots of *pastel de bacalhau* (€1), Lisbon's ubiquitous and delicious cod cake. Strangely, this national dish of Portugal comes from Norway—salted cod. It's never fresh, always salty. Another good standby is a *bifana,* a pork sandwich made with a secret sauce to give it character.

Below the Castle and Above the Alfama

Farol de Santa Luzia, which offers a nice seafood feast with a delicate and delightful dining area, is a favorite of mine for lunch or dinner at the top of the Alfama. A family-run place with a local clientele, they offer the Algarve *cataplana* style of cooking (€7-8 daily specials; €26 big *cataplana* of meat, fish, or shellfish for two; indoor seating only, Mon-Sat 12:00-15:00 & 18:30-23:00, closed Sun, Largo Santa Luzia 5, across from Santa Luzia viewpoint terrace, tiny sign, tel. 218-863-884, Andre and family).

Lunch on Largo do Contador Mor: Two basic restaurants—**A Tasquinha Restaurante** and **Comidas de Santiago**—feed hungry tourists on this leafy square just below the castle. Both specialize in plates of grilled sardines *(sardinhas grelhadas)* and are handy for a simple lunch.

Near Largo Rodrigues de Freitas: For more of an adventure with your meal, walk past Largo das Portas do Sol and follow the trolley tracks along Rua de São Tomé to a square called Largo Rodrigues de Freitas—if riding trolley #12E, it's the first stop over the big hill. **Restaurante Frei Papinhas** is a classic, family-run, hole-in-the-wall where you can feast on fresh seafood for €10 a plate with the neighborhood crowd. Dine inside or on rickety tables across the street in a charming square, where you can watch the trolleys rattle by (daily, Rua de São Tome 13, tel. 218-866-471).

Appetizers Aren't Free

In Portugal, there's no such thing as a free munch. Appetizers brought to your table before you order (such as olives, bread, and fancy pâtés) are not free. So if you don't want to pay for them, just push them aside or wave them away when the waiter brings them. Don't eat any of it—not even one olive—or you'll be charged (only €1-2 for the simpler appetizers, but it's disturbing if you don't expect it).

RESTAURANTS DEEP IN THE ALFAMA

While the Bairro Alto is far livelier at night and has a better energy, the Alfama still has a unique charm. My favorite places for dinner with fado (the funky, characteristic **A Baiuca** and the more formal and classy **Clube de Fado**) are described earlier under "Entertainment in Lisbon."

Restaurante Santo Antonio de Alfama, buried scenically in the Alfama, is bohemian yet dressy and intimate (notice the classic cinema theme) and serves a global cuisine with creative €9 tapas and €15-20 main courses. While it's tempting to cobble together a tapas meal, I liked the main dishes better. On a balmy evening, the small courtyard seating overlooking the classic Alfama square offers a romantic setting (Wed-Sun 12:30-16:30 & 19:30-24:00, Beco de São Miguel 7, tel. 218-881-328).

BAIRRO ALTO, LISBON'S "HIGH TOWN"

The Bairro Alto is hopping lately with plenty of energy and fun eateries opening up all the time. For a characteristic meal in Old World surroundings, it's hard to beat. When considering the Bairro Alto listings, remember that the Chiado listings (which follow) are just a few minutes' walk away.

Fado with Dinner in Bairro Alto: For a most memorable dining experience with live fado music in the Bairro Alto, consider **Canto do Camões** (more formal and subdued, Travessa da Espera 38) or **Restaurante Adega do Ribatejo** (more rough and casual, Rua Diario de Noticias 23). Both are described under "Entertainment in Lisbon" on page 95.

Restaurante Bota Alta ("The Old Boot") is a classic—if a bit touristy—little eatery with a timeless Portuguese ambience, tight seating, and reliably good food. Portions are big, reservations are smart, and Paulo offers a fun dessert sampler plate (€10-15 main dishes, Mon-Sat 12:00-14:30, 19:00-23:00, closed Sun, straight up from lottery kiosk in front of São Roque Church, at corner of Travessa da Queimada and Rua da Atalaia, tel. 213-427-959).

A Primavera do Jerónimo is a quintessential Bairro Alto joint

LISBON

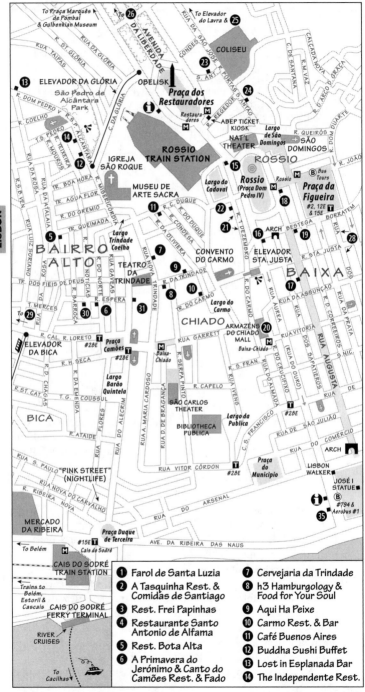

1 Farol de Santa Luzia
2 A Tasquinha Rest. & Comidas de Santiago
3 Rest. Frei Papinhas
4 Restaurante Santo Antonio de Alfama
5 Rest. Bota Alta
6 A Primavera do Jerónimo & Canto do Camões Rest. & Fado
7 Cervejaria da Trindade
8 h3 Hamburgology & Food for Your Soul
9 Aqui Ha Peixe
10 Carmo Rest. & Bar
11 Café Buenos Aires
12 Buddha Sushi Buffet
13 Lost in Esplanada Bar
14 The Independent Rest.

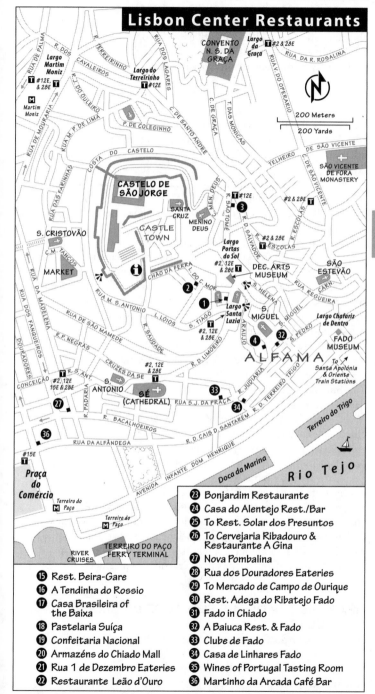

Lisbon Center Restaurants

LISBON

⑮ Rest. Beira-Gare
⑯ A Tendinha do Rossio
⑰ Casa Brasileira of the Baixa
⑱ Pastelaria Suíça
⑲ Confeitaria Nacional
⑳ Armazéns do Chiado Mall
㉑ Rua 1 de Dezembro Eateries
㉒ Restaurante Leão d'Ouro

㉓ Bonjardim Restaurante
㉔ Casa do Alentejo Rest./Bar
㉕ To Rest. Solar dos Presuntos
㉖ To Cervejaria Ribadouro & Restaurante A Gina
㉗ Nova Pombalina
㉘ Rua dos Douradores Eateries
㉙ To Mercado de Campo de Ourique
㉚ Rest. Adega do Ribatejo Fado
㉛ Fado in Chiado
㉜ A Baiuca Rest. & Fado
㉝ Clube de Fado
㉞ Casa de Linhares Fado
㉟ Wines of Portugal Tasting Room
㊱ Martinho da Arcada Café Bar

serving traditional home-style plates in a jam-packed, joyfully characteristic scene (€10-12 meals, Mon-Sat opens at 19:30, closed Sun; reserve, come early, or wait; at Travessa da Espera 38, a few steps below recommended fado place Canto do Camões, tel. 213-420-477).

IN CHIADO

Cervejaria da Trindade, a bright, boisterous, Portuguese-style beer hall, is full of historic tiles, seafood, and tourists. While over-priced and in all the guidebooks, people enjoy its atmosphere (€15-20 meals, confirm prices—especially since seafood is charged by weight, daily 12:00-24:00, liveliest 20:00-22:00, closed holidays, air-con, courtyard, a block down from São Roque Church at Rua Nova da Trindade 20-C, tel. 213-423-506). For a description, see page 61).

h3 Hamburgology is a modern and trendy joint serving fancy hamburgers. Thinking out of the box, they've invented dozens of creative hamburger patties, all displayed with photos on the menu wall. The *menu* price includes chips, rice, and a drink for €7 (self-serve from cafeteria line, daily 12:00-23:00, Rua da Trindade 13, tel. 213-803-110). Downstairs is **Food for Your Soul,** a Wagama-ma-style pan-Asian eatery, handy if your soul is craving noodles.

Aqui Ha Peixe, well-lit and innovative, serves quality fish dishes under antique arches. Owner Miguel Reino insists on serv-ing only the freshest fish (€10 lunch plates, €15-22 dinner plates, Tue-Sun 12:00-15:00 & 19:00-23:00, closed Mon, Rua da Trin-dade 18A, tel. 213-432-154).

Carmo Restaurante and Bar offers tasty, light lunches in a chic but homey setting. Try a tempting dessert in one of the se-cluded back patios far away from the crowds (daily 12:00-23:00, €7 *petiscos*—snacks, Largo do Carmo 11, tel. 213-460-088).

Café Buenos Aires is a friendly place serving Argentinian cuisine (lots of red meat, €15-25 plates), hearty dinner salads, veg-etarian homemade pasta, and famous chocolate cake. Dine in the charming and intimate woody interior or at fun tables outside on a characteristic, stepped pedestrian lane (Mon-Sat 18:00-24:00, closed Sun, Rua do Duque 22, tel. 213-420-739). Above this place and on the same stepped lane are several other typically Portuguese eateries.

NEAR THE TOP OF THE ELEVADOR DA GLÓRIA FUNICULAR

Buddha Sushi Buffet has a great formula, fun energy, and handy location. While the Portuguese say *obrigado* and the Japanese say *arigato,* sushi doesn't exactly come to mind when you think about Lisbon. Still, this place serves a hearty sushi buffet for a painless price—especially if you get it to go (€8 at lunch, €11 at dinner, €4 to-go box, delightful picnic-friendly park across street, long hours daily, Rua São Pedro de Alcântara 65, mobile 964-396-927).

Lost in Esplanada Bar is understandably popular, with a Zen-like terrace, a mellow teahouse interior, a splash of Pakistan, and a view patio. The hippies who run this place brag they have the third-best view in Lisbon. They offer tasty light meals, soup, salads, and ommmm-my-goodness cocktails (closed Sun, a few blocks uphill from the funicular, at Rua D. Pedro V 56, mobile 917-759-282).

The Independente Restaurant, youthful and classy, serves modern Portuguese dishes from a creative, accessible menu to an in-the-know crowd in one big woody, candlelit ground-floor dining hall. While a bit of a splurge, it's run by a hostel (reservations smart, daily from 20:00, across from view terrace at Rua São Pedro de Alcântara 81, tel. 213-461-381).

NEAR ROSSIO
Snacks and Light Meals
The area around Rossio Station and Rossio seems designed to cater to busy locals commuting in and out by train. You'll find plenty of practical, inexpensive eateries within a block or so of the station.

Restaurante Beira-Gare is my choice for a quick, cheap meal immediately across the street from the Rossio Station. A classic greasy-spoon diner, it dishes out cod and vegetables prepared faster than a Big Mac and served with more energy than a soccer team. The house specialty is a pork sandwich *(bifana no pão)*. Consider their soup-and-sandwich special (Mon-Sat 6:00-24:00, closed Sun, stand at the bar or grab a table, Rua 1 de Dezembro, tel. 213-420-405).

A Tendinha do Rossio, established in 1840 and run by Calheiros and Carmo, is a classic cherry brandy bar that also sells soups, sandwiches, and fishy snacks. Prices are dirt-cheap and the same whether you sit with the drunks at the bar, grab a tiny table inside, or serve yourself and sit outside overlooking Rossio (Mon-Sat 7:00-21:00, closed Sun, Praça Dom Pedro IV 6, tel. 213-468-156).

Casa Brasileira of the Baixa offers a characteristic budget snack or meal in a classic local scene (daily 7:00-24:00, 100 yards from Rossio at Rua Augusta 265). Fast, cheap lunch deals are served only at the bar, or choose the sidewalk tables with a higher-priced menu. And their *pastel de nata* (custard tart), made downstairs, is as tasty as those that people line up for in Belém.

Pastelaria Suíça (SWEE-sah) provides a serviceable, air-conditioned, and comfortable place for a no-stress meal. It's popular despite its surly wait staff and relatively high prices. Along with pastry, they serve light meals, sandwiches, salads, and fruit cups (daily 7:00-21:00, least expensive at the bar, reasonable at inside tables, pricey at outside tables overlooking Rossio or Praça da Figueira, located between the two squares with entrances and terraces on each—choose sun or shade, tel. 213-214-090).

Confeitaria Nacional has been proudly satisfying sweet-tooths for 180 years, and was once the favorite of Portuguese royalty. Stop in for a tasty pastry downstairs. Or, for a peaceful and inexpensive three-course lunch, go upstairs, where you'll choose between a cheaper meal in the cafeteria or pay a little extra for service and Old World sophistication in the elegant dining room (Mon-Sat 8:00-20:00, closed Sun, Praça da Figueira 18, tel. 213-424-470 or 213-243-000).

Between Rossio and Chiado

Armazéns do Chiado Mall: This shopping center, between the Bairro Alto and the Baixa, has a sixth-floor food court offering a selection of fun eateries—mostly fast food and chain restaurants you'd find in any modern mall (daily 12:00-23:00, between Rua Garrett and Rua da Assunção; from the lower town, find the inconspicuous elevator at Rua do Crucifixo 89 or 113, next to the Baixa-Chiado Metro entrance). Some of the mall's eateries are actual restaurants with castle views. But most are fast-food joints sharing common plastic tables. **Loja das Sopas** offers hearty soups with €5 fixed-price meals and **Companhia das Sandes** offers up healthy, big-bowl pasta salads topped with tropical fruits. **Restaurant Chimarrão** serves Brazilian cuisine and offers an impressive €11 *Rodizio:* an all-you-can-eat buffet of salad, veggies, and endless beef, ham, pork, sausage, and chicken. They also have daily €7 specials, desserts, and tropical juices and fruits (tel. 213-479-444).

Rua 1 de Dezembro: This street, which is busy during the workday and dead after hours, is lined with cheap restaurants. Walk the street from Rossio Station to the Elevador de Santa Justa to determine the prevailing menu of the day. Most options are self-service, with speed being the priority for the busy office workers who eat here. The **Companhia das Sandes** sandwich shop offers salads and healthy sandwiches that you design Subway-style (daily 9:00-20:00). **Tasquinha do Celeiro** is a self-service vegetarian joint at #53. **Pingo Doce supermarket** is the only grocery store in the area (daily 8:30-21:30, at #73).

Restaurantes Leão d'Ouro is actually two restaurants set side-by-side. The basic one, with old tiles on the walls and hams hanging from the ceiling, serves decent food at fair prices. Next door its hardworking cafeteria cousin offers a cheap-and-hearty buffet with an inviting Brazilian grill all day (€7 at lunch, €9 at dinner, long hours daily, next to Rossio Station at Rua 1 de Dezembro 105, tel. 213-342-6195).

Lisbon's "Eating Lane" (North of Rossio)

Rua das Portas de Santo Antão is Lisbon's "eating lane"—a galaxy of eateries, many specializing in seafood (off the northeast corner of Rossio). While the waiters are pushy and it's all very touristy, the lane—lively with happy eaters—is enjoyable to browse. This is a fine spot to down a beer, snack on some snails, and watch people go by.

Bonjardim, a family-friendly diner on the small side street, Travessa de Santo Antão, is known for its tasty roasted chicken (paint on some spicy African *piri-piri* sauce) and fries (€10-15 per meal, daily 12:00-23:00, Travessa do Santo Antão 7 or 10, both branches run by same owner, tel. 213-427-424).

Casa do Alentejo Restaurante specializes in Alentejo cuisine and fills an old, second-floor dining hall. The Moorish-looking building is a cultural and social center for people from the traditional southern province of Portugal living in Lisbon. While the food is mainly hearty and simple, the ambience is fabulous. It's a good place to try regional specialties such as pork with clams, or the super-sweet, eggy almond dessert called *charcada*. The full-bodied Alentejo red wine is cheap and solid (€10 two-course daily lunch special, €10-15 main dishes at dinner, daily 12:00-15:00 & 19:00-22:30, slip into the closed-looking building at Rua das Portas de Santo Antão 58 and climb stairs to the right, tel. 213-469-231). They host folk dancing in the grand ballroom (often on Sat from 15:00) and ballroom dancing (on many Sun from 15:00), except in summer when it's too hot (mid-June-mid-Sept).

The **Casa do Alentejo Bar,** in the same building, serves cheap bar food and wine (same hours as restaurant, spicy meat plates, hearty cheese, other tapas; to the right of the stairs, look for Taberna sign on ground floor).

Restaurante Solar dos Presuntos keeps the theater crowd happily fed with meat and seafood specialties. Its upstairs is more elegant, while the downstairs—with a colorful, open kitchen—is higher energy. Photos of Lisbon's celebrities and politicians who eat here enliven the walls. Reservations are smart. This place can take advantage of its popularity and bulldoze tourists into spending a lot—order cautiously and know what you're paying for (€25 plates, €35-40 meals, big splittable portions, good wine list presented on an iPad, Mon-Sat 12:00-15:30 & 19:00-23:00, closed Sun, at the top end of Rua das Portas de Santo Antão at #150, tel. 213-424-253).

On Avenida da Liberdade (North of Rossio)

Cervejaria Ribadouro is a favorite splurge for locals because of its quality meat and shellfish (€15-25 meals, daily 12:00-24:00, Avenida da Liberdade 155, at intersection with Rua do Salitre, Metro:

Avenida, tel. 213-549-411). Note that seafood prices are listed by weight; the waiter will help you determine the cost of a portion. To limit the cost, write down the number of grams you want. For a fun, quick €12 per-person meal, order a small draught beer *(uma imperial)*, 100 grams (about a quarter of a pound) of *percebes* (barnacles), and *pão torrado com manteiga* (toasted bread with butter).

Restaurante A Gina, glowing like a mirage in a vacant lot that used to be a fairground, is one of my favorite places for a fine dinner in Lisbon. The cloth bibs embroidered with Gina's name indicate it's a lunchtime hit with local office workers, who appreciate the tasty traditional Portuguese grilled meat and fish. Gina and her men scramble to give this wonderful place a genuine friendliness. Two minutes off of Avenida da Liberdade (directly behind recommended Hotel Lisboa Plaza) in Parque Mayer, it feels worlds away from the tourist crowds (€10-15 plates, daily 12:00-15:00 & 18:00-24:00, reservations recommended, tel. 213-420-296). The son, Rui, speaks English. Diners with this book get a free dessert port.

Near Praça do Comércio (South of Rossio)

Nova Pombalina is a busy little joint that serves quick-fire sandwiches (€3.50), soups, and exotic fresh-squeezed juices. It's famous among office workers for its suckling pig sandwich *(sandes de leitão)*. From Praça do Comércio, it's five blocks toward the castle, on the corner of Rua do Comércio and Rua da Madalena (Rua do Comércio 2, tel. 218-874-360).

Rua dos Douradores: This street, cutting from Praça da Figueira through the Baixa, is lined with very competitive little eateries. It's fun to browse down this lane on an empty stomach. If you're craving Indian food, stop at **Restaurante Gandhi Palace,** which has a friendly Punjabi staff and nonstop Bollywood musicals on TV (€10 plates, open daily, Rua dos Douradores 214, tel. 218-873-839). They also serve Italian dishes.

MEMORABLE MARKET DINING

Mercado de Campo de Ourique is a 19th-century iron-and-glass market that has morphed into a trendy food circus (with long hours). Produce stalls, fishmongers, and bakeries (many of which close for the evening) sell everything from pigs' ears to designer cupcakes while local diners jam the place, picking up meals from whichever counter appeals and finding a place to sit in the thriving center (daily 10:00-23:00, short taxi ride or take trolley #28E to second-to-last stop: Igreja Sto. Condestável). The market is behind the big church on Campo de Ourique. (Lisbon's most interesting cemetery is one stop farther, at the end of the trolley line.)

Lisbon Connections

BY TRAIN

If leaving Lisbon by train, check to see if your train requires an advance reservation (look for a boxed "R" in the timetable). All train stations are connected to the Metro system, making departure a breeze. For snacks or train picnics, Santa Apolónia has a tightly packed Pingo Doce supermarket inside the station just past the Metro (Mon-Sat 7:30-22:00, Sun 8:30-22:00). The Vasco da Gama shopping mall (see page 73) next to Oriente Station has an enormous Continente supermarket below street level (Mon-Sat 9:00-24:00, Sun 9:00-13:00).

From Lisbon by Train to: **Madrid** (1/day, "Lusitânia" overnight 21:15-8:00, 11 hours, departs from Santa Apolónia Station, arrives at Madrid's Chamartín Station), **Paris** (1/day, overnight 21:15-18:30, 20 hours, departs Santa Apolónia, no stop in Madrid, change at Hendaye at 11:30, arrives at Paris' Gare Montparnasse), **Évora** (4/day, 1.5 hours), **Lagos** (5/day, 4 hours, departs Oriente, transfer in Tunes or Faro), **Tavira** (5/day, 4-5 hours, departs Oriente, change at Faro), **Coimbra** (almost hourly, 2 hours, departs Santa Apolónia), **Nazaré/Valado** (3-5/day, 3.5-4 hours, involves 2-3 transfers; bus is better—see below), **Óbidos** (3/day, 2.25-3 hours, transfer in Mira Sintra-Melecas or Cacém, departs Oriente), **Porto** (almost hourly, 3 hours, departs Oriente), **Sintra** (4/hour, 40 minutes, departs Rossio; for suggested day-trip connections, see page 134). For train info, call tel. 808-208-208, visit www.cp.pt, or check Germany's excellent all-Europe website, www.bahn.com. Note: Any train leaving from Santa Apolónia passes through Oriente Station a few minutes later.

To Salema: To reach Salema, you'll first need to get to **Lagos,** which is about 4 hours from Lisbon by train (see above) or bus (see

below). Trains from Lisbon to the Algarve leave from Oriente Station on the Lisboa-Faro line. At Tunes, there is a transfer to a local train that takes you as far as Lagos. From there, it's a cheap bus ride or a pricier taxi ride to Salema (see page 168 for details).

BY BUS

Bus tickets to Spain are sold by InterCentro Lines in Lisbon, but the service is run by Alsa (www.alsa.es). All buses leave from Lisbon's Sete Rios bus station (Metro: Jardim Zoológico, toll tel. 707-223-344).

LISBON

From Lisbon by Bus to: **Coimbra** (hourly, 2.5 hours), **Nazaré** (6/day, 2 hours), **Fátima** (hourly, 1.5-2.5 hours), **Batalha** (5/day, 2 hours), **Alcobaça** (6/day, 2 hours, some transfer in Caldas da Rainha), **Óbidos** (hourly, 1.25 hours, transfer in Caldas da Rainha), **Porto** (at least hourly, 3 hours), **Évora** (almost hourly, 1.5 hours), **Lagos** (5/day, 4 hours, some transfer in Albufeira, easier than train, must book ahead, get details at TI), **Tavira** (5/day direct, 4.25 hours), **Madrid** (2/day, 8-9 hours, www.avanzabus.com), **Sevilla** (2/day, 7 hours, may be less off-season; you can also get to Sevilla by taking the overnight train to Madrid, then the hourly AVE train, but the bus is your better, faster, and cheaper option).

BY PLANE

You can generally buy a plane ticket from Lisbon to Madrid on short notice for as little as €30 or as much as €300, depending on the time of year. Shop around to get the best deal. Vueling (www.vueling.com), EasyJet (www.easyjet.com), and Ryanair (www.ryanair.com) have the cheapest flights. For more information, see "Flights" on page 388.

SINTRA

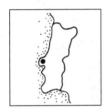

For centuries, Portugal's aristocracy considered Sintra the perfect place to escape from Lisbon. Now tourists do, too. Sintra (SEEN-trah) is a mix of natural and man-made beauty: fantasy castles set amid exotic tropical plants, lush green valleys, and craggy hilltops with hazy views of the Atlantic and Lisbon. For centuries, Sintra—just 15 miles northwest of Lisbon—was the summer escape of Portugal's kings. Those with money and a desire to be close to royalty built their palaces amid luxuriant gardens in the same neighborhood. Lord Byron called this bundle of royal fancies and aristocratic dreams a "glorious Eden," and even though it's mobbed with tourists today, it's still magnificent. Also consider checking out Europe's westernmost tip (at Cabo da Roca) and nearby resort towns.

PLANNING YOUR TIME

Sintra makes a great day trip from Lisbon, especially on Monday, when many museums in Lisbon are closed, but all major Sintra sights are open. Here you can romp along the ruined ramparts of a deserted Moorish castle, and climb through the Versailles of Portugal—the Pena Palace—on a neighboring hilltop.

Due to its concentration of popular sights and limited public transportation, a trip to Sintra requires patience and a flexible schedule—especially when it's most crowded, from July through September. To save money, bring a picnic lunch from Lisbon and plan to eat it at the Moorish Castle or the gardens of the Pena Palace.

Try to leave Lisbon around 8:30 to arrive in Sintra by 9:15, because most major sights open between 9:30 and 9:45. Pick up a

Near Lisbon

Major Train Stations
1. Santa Apolónia
2. Oriente
3. Rossio
4. Cais do Sodré

SINTRA

map at the TI in Sintra's train station, and catch Scotturb bus #434 to the Moorish Castle ruins. Then catch the bus up to the Pena Palace. After touring the palace and gardens, you could catch the bus back to town (bus leaves from either castle), or you could hike 30 minutes down a steep, wooded path into town (hiking instructions marked on TI's *Parques e Palácios* map; fork in path leads down from within the castle grounds). Have lunch (unless you already had a picnic, or lunched at the Pena Palace's café), explore the town, and visit the National Palace. Then catch the train back to Lisbon in time for dinner. This general plan also works well for drivers, who ideally should leave their car in Lisbon (or at least park in Sintra) and take advantage of public transportation.

With extra time, explore the rugged and picturesque westernmost tip of Portugal at Cabo da Roca. You can also mix and mingle with the jet set—or at least press your nose against their windows—at the resort towns of Cascais or Estoril (for information on how to reach these destinations, see "Near Sintra," at the end of the chapter).

GETTING TO SINTRA

Catch the **train** to Sintra from Lisbon's central Rossio Station (direct, 4/hour, 40 minutes). The easiest way to avoid early-morning lines is to use a LisboaCard or a Viva Viagem "Zapping" card (see page 28) that you've charged the night before or at the nearby Restauradores Metro station. If you don't have either card, buy your ticket at Rossio Station (upstairs—at track level) from the ticket window or an automated machine (select English, then "Buy Ticket + Card," then "Stations," select "Sintra" from the list of destinations, hit "+" for return ticket, then pop in coins or small bills; €2.15 each way, no discount for round-trip, add €0.50 fee for reusable Viva Viagem card; TV monitors list departure times). Pass your card over the scanner at the turnstile to enter. Your card may eventually be checked by someone on board, and you'll need to scan it again when you leave the station in Sintra. During your ride, take in the views of the 18th-century aqueduct (on the left) and the workaday Lisbon suburbs. Relax...Sintra is at the end of the line.

Sintra is far easier by train than by **car** from Lisbon. Consider waiting until after you visit Sintra to pick up your rental car. If you do drive to Sintra, see "Route Tips for Drivers" on page 134.

Orientation to Sintra

Sintra is small. The town itself sprawls at the foot of a hill, a 10-minute walk (or quick bus ride) from the train station. The National

Palace, with its unmistakable pair of cone-shaped chimneys, is in the center of the town, a block from the TI. But the other two main sights are a steep, long, uphill walk from town; most prefer to take the bus. If you're trying to decide, look up from the train station or center of town to see the Moorish Castle wall on top of the hill—it's quite a hike even for the physically fit. The Pena Palace is beyond that.

TOURIST INFORMATION

Sintra has two TIs: a small one in the train station (tel. 219-241-623) and a larger one a block off the main square in the Museu Regional building (both open daily 10:00-18:00, until 19:00 in Aug, tel. 219-231-157, www.askmelisboa.com). Pick up a free map with information on sights and a Scotturb bus schedule. Hikers should download walking routes from the city website before arrival; the TI no longer offers printed copies (www.cm-sintra.pt). The TI can arrange *quartos* (rooms in private homes, Db-€35-80) for overnighters.

ARRIVAL IN SINTRA

By Train: Upon arrival, stop at the TI in the station. To **bus** to the town center or palace, hop on Scotturb #434 (exit station to the right to reach the nearest stop, €5 ticket valid all day, schedules posted at stop; for more bus info, see "Getting Around Sintra," later). The bus stops in town first (across from the main TI) before heading up to the Pena Palace. You can also reach the town center easily on **foot** (exit station and go left; it's about a 10-minute walk filled with modern "art" and hippies selling handmade trinkets).

By Car: For tips on driving into Sintra, see "Route Tips for Drivers" on page 134.

HELPFUL HINTS

LisboaCard: This sightseeing pass gets you discounts on the Pena Palace, Moorish Castle, National Palace, Toy Museum, and the Monserrate gardens. It also covers the train ride from Lisbon to Sintra (buy it at a Lisbon TI before you visit Sintra—see page 20). Be sure to bring the LisboaCard booklet, which contains coupons required for some of the discounts.

Festivals: The Festival de Sintra music and dance festival from late May to early July keeps the town lively and fun (www.festivaldesintra.pt).

Money: ATMs are rare in Sintra. You'll find one at the train station, another inside the main TI, and one on Rua das Padarias, just up the hill from the recommended Casa Piriquita.

WCs: The only free WC in town—other than at restaurants—is located near the small, central parking lot where horse carriages also wait (Calçada do Pelourinho).

Bring a Picnic: If saving a few euros is important, buy picnic items in Lisbon. Sintra's reputation as a tourist destination means high prices for restaurant meals.

Local Guide: Christina Quental works mainly in Lisbon, but lives near Sintra and can meet you at the station (Mon-Fri €125/half-day, €195/day; mobile 919-922-480, anacristinaquental@hotmail.com).

GETTING AROUND SINTRA

Scotturb Bus #434 loops together all the important stops—the train station, the town center/TI/National Palace (stop is at TI), the Moorish Castle ruins, and the Pena Palace—before heading back to town and the train station (4/hour; schedule subject to traffic conditions; €5 ticket good all day for one loop with stops, buy

Sintra

Ⓣ Taxi Stand　Ⓑ Bus Stop
Ⓟ Parking　→ One-Way

See Central Sintra Map

N-247
To Cabo da Roca

Casa Miradouro Hotel

Estrada Carval-heiro

Casa do Valle Guesthouse

To Monserrate & Cabo da Roca

#434 Ⓑ Ⓣ

Quinta da Regaleira

Town Hall

National Palace

Main Square

Costa

#403 & #434 Ⓑ Ⓣ

Train Station

Ⓟ

To Lisbon

Rio do Porto

Volta do Duche

Liberdade Park

Rua

Mar. Saldanha

Ribeiro

To Lisbon
N-375

Old Town

Moorish Fountain

Estrada da Pena

Great View!

Moorish Castle

Ticket Booth

Trail

Santa Maria

Rua

Trin.
To Lisbon

Ticket Booth
Moorish Castle Parking
Ⓟ Ⓑ #434

Estrada de Pena

#434 Ⓑ

Lower Park Gate

Pena Park

Pena Palace

To Train Stn.

Main Entrance
Ⓑ #434
Ticket Booth
Pena Shuttle Tourist Bus

DCH

100 YARDS
100 METERS

N

To High Cross

from driver or Scotturb bus representative at stop near TI in town; first bus departs at 9:15 from train station; last bus leaves station at 19:50; entire circuit takes 30 minutes without traffic). On your way to the top of the hill, the bus will stop at the entrance to the Moorish Castle. Purchase a combo-ticket here, visiting the Moorish Castle first (because it has substantially shorter lines), then walk another 10-15 minutes—mainly uphill—to the Pena Palace (or take the bus). You can also take a **taxi** from the town center or

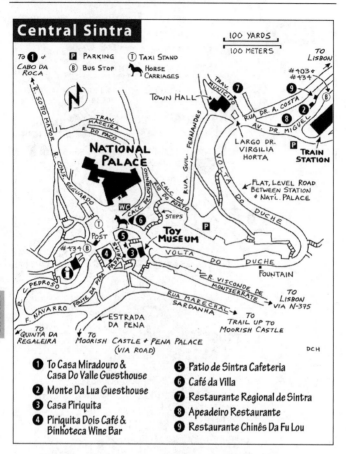

Central Sintra

100 YARDS
100 METERS

To ① & CABO DA ROCA

P PARKING
B BUS STOP

T TAXI STAND
🐎 HORSE CARRIAGES

TO LISBON

#403 & #434

TOWN HALL

NATIONAL PALACE

TRAV. MACEIRA
R. DO PACO
R. CONS. REGUARDO
R. SOTTO MAYOR

TRAV. MUNICIPIO

RUA DR. A. COSTA
AV. DR. MIGUEL

LARGO DR. VIRGILIA HORTA

TRAIN STATION

FLAT, LEVEL ROAD BETWEEN STATION & NAT'L. PALACE

RUA GUIL. FERNANDES

CALC. PELOURINHO
CALC. DO PORTO

VOLTA DO DUCHE

WC
STEPS

CALC. PATRIA
FONTE DA PIPA

TOY MUSEUM

P

POST

VOLTA   DO   DUCHE

FOUNTAIN

#434 B

R. VISCONDE DE MONTSERRATE

RUA MARECHAL SARDANHA

TO LISBON VIA N-375

R. C. PEDROSO
R. NAVARRO
F. SILVA

ESTRADA DA PENA

TO QUINTA DA REGALEIRA

TO MOORISH CASTLE & PENA PALACE (VIA ROAD)

TO TRAIL UP TO MOORISH CASTLE

DCH

① To Casa Miradouro & Casa Do Valle Guesthouse
② Monte Da Lua Guesthouse
③ Casa Piriquita
④ Piriquita Dois Café & Binhoteca Wine Bar
⑤ Patio de Sintra Cafeteria
⑥ Café da Villa
⑦ Restaurante Regional de Sintra
⑧ Apeadeiro Restaurante
⑨ Restaurante Chinês Da Fu Lou

the train station to the Moorish Castle or the Pena Palace (but it won't get you any closer to the palace entrance than the bus). From the Pena Palace, wait for a bus returning to town. If there are too many people in line, backtrack downhill to the Moorish Castle for practically no wait (return to the bus-and-taxi stop, then follow signs down road to the *Moorish Castle* or walk through the forest following *Canopy Sintra* signs).

The clip-clop **horse carriages** cost about €30 for 25 minutes (rates posted). They can take you anywhere; you'll likely see them waiting by the parking lot just in front of the National Palace.

Sights in Sintra

▲Moorish Castle (Castelo dos Mouros)

Sintra's thousand-year-old ruins of a Moorish castle are lost in an enchanted forest and alive with winds of the past. They're a castle lover's dream come true, and a great place for a picnic with a panoramic Atlantic view. Though built by the Moors, the castle was taken by Christian forces in 1147. What you'll climb on today—while dramatic—was significantly restored in the 19th century. The Moorish Castle, with its own bus #434 stop, is a steep 30-minute hike from town, and a 10- to 15-minute hike from the Pena Palace's main entrance.

Cost and Hours: Castle-€7.50, combo-ticket with Pena Palace and gardens-€18, daily 9:30-20:00, last entry one hour before closing, free map includes English info and detailed map, tel. 219-237-300, www.parquesdesintra.pt.

Getting In: If the ticket booth near the bus stop is crowded, head to the ticket booth inside the castle at the innermost gate, which typically has little or no wait (see map on page 125). Purchase your combo-ticket here to save time at the Pena Palace.

▲▲Pena Palace (Palácio de Pena)

This magical hilltop palace sits high above Sintra, above the Moorish Castle ruins. In the 19th century, Portugal had a very

romantic prince, German-born Prince Ferdinand. A contemporary and cousin of Bavaria's "Mad" King Ludwig (of Disneyesque Neuschwanstein Castle fame), Ferdinand was also a cousin of England's Prince Albert (Queen Victoria's husband). Flamboyant Ferdinand hired a German architect to build a fantasy castle, mixing elements of German and Portuguese style. He ended up with a crazy Neo-fortified casserole of Gothic towers, Renaissance domes, Moorish minarets, Manueline carvings, Disney playfulness, and an *azulejo* (tile) toilet for his wife.

Cost and Hours: Palace and gardens-€14, combo-ticket with Moorish Castle-€18, daily May-mid-Sept 9:45-19:00, last entry 45 minutes before closing, tel. 219-105-340, www.parquesdesintra.pt.

Getting In: Purchase your ticket at the small hut next to the gated main entrance. To avoid the 10-minute uphill climb from the entrance to the palace (and enjoy a lift back down), catch the green shuttle bus just inside the gate at the *paragem* sign (€3 round-trip, purchase ticket inside gift shop—*not* from driver, departs about every 10 minutes).

SINTRA

Information: English descriptions throughout the palace give meaning to the rooms. Your ticket also comes with a map showing a circular, 1.5-hour walking route of the park. Be sure to grab the English version of this map if you intend to explore the park after touring the palace.

Eating: The palace has a view café. If you brought your lunch with you, enjoy it in the picnic-perfect gardens either before or after your visit. Wander in, find a spot of shade, and enjoy views fit for a king.

❍ Visiting the Palace: The palace, built in the mid- to late 1800s, is so well-preserved that it feels as if it's the day after the royal family fled Portugal in 1910 (during a popular revolt that eventually made way for today's modern republic). This gives the place a charming intimacy rarely seen in palaces. Here are the highlights.

Entry: After you hop off the green shuttle bus, walk up through the Moorish archway with alligator decor. Keep your ticket handy because it will be checked several times during the visit. Cross the drawbridge that doesn't draw, and join an onion-domed world of tourists frozen in deep knee-bends with their cameras cocked. At the base of the stairs, you'll see King Ferdinand, who built this castle from 1840 until 1885, when he died. Though German, he was a romantic proponent of his adopted culture and did much to preserve Portugal's architectural and artistic heritage.

Courtyard: The palace was built on the site of a 16th-century monastery; the courtyard was the former location of the cloister. In spite of its plushness, the palace retains the monkish coziness of several small rooms gathered in two levels around the cloister.

Like its big brother in Belém, the monastery housed followers of St. Jerome, the hermit monk. Like their namesake, the monks wanted to be isolated, and this was about as isolated as you could be around here 500 years ago. The spot was also a popular pilgrimage destination for its statue of "Our Lady of the Feathers" (*pena* means feather—hence the palace's name). In 1498 King Manuel was up here enjoying the view when he spied Vasco da Gama sailing up the river, returning safely from his great voyage. To celebrate and give thanks, the king turned what was a humble wooden monastery into a fine stone palace.

Dining Room and Pantry: Stuck into a cozy corner, the monastery's original refectory was decked out with the royal family's finest tableware and ceiling tiles.

Workshop of King Charles (Carlos I): With a shaky empire crumbling around him, King Charles found refuge in art—specifically the latest style, Art Nouveau. Unfinished paintings and sketches eerily predict the king's unfinished rule.

King's Bedroom: The king enjoyed cutting-edge comforts, including the shower/tub imported from England, and even a telephone to listen to the opera when he couldn't face the Lisbon commute. The bedroom is decorated in classic Romantic style—dark, heavy, and crowded with knickknacks.

Queen's Bedroom and Dressing Room: Study the melancholy photos of Queen Amelia (Amélie of Orléans), King Charles, and their family in this room. The early 1900s were a rocky time for Portugal's royal family. The king and his eldest son were assassinated in 1908. His youngest son, Manuel II, became king until he, his mother the queen, and other members of the royal family fled Portugal during the 1910 revolution. The palm frond on the headboard of the queen's bed was from her last Palm Sunday Mass in Portugal. Poke around. Throughout the palace, you'll see state-of-the-art conveniences (the first flush toilets and hot shower in Portugal). The whole place is lovingly cluttered, typical of the Victorian horror of empty spaces.

Queen's View Balcony: On the upper floor, enjoy a sweeping view from Lisbon to the mouth of the Rio Tejo. Find the Cristo Rei statue and the 25th of April Bridge. The statue on the distant ridge honors the palace's architect.

The New Wing: This spacious addition to the original series of rooms around the cloister includes the apartments of the last king and the fantastically furnished Noble's Room.

End of Palace Tour: Your tour ends at the abundant kitchen; just after, a view café conveniently welcomes us peasants. After touring the palace, you can return directly to the main entrance (walk 10 minutes or catch the green shuttle bus—your ticket covers the round-trip), or you can detour for a self-guided tour of the park.

Chapel: Wander through the inner patio to find a pointed dome covered in green and white tiles. Climb the steps to visit the royal family's sumptuous private chapel decorated in a variety of styles. The structure is Manueline, reminiscent of the Monastery of Jerónimos in Belém.

Pena Palace Park: The lush, captivating, and sprawling palace grounds, rated ▲, are dotted with romantic surprises, including the High Cross (highest point around, with commanding views), chapels, a temple, lakes, giant sequoia trees, and exotic plants. If you want to walk through the park after you tour the palace, take a 30- to 40-minute stroll downhill (following the *Parques e Palácios* map that came with your palace admission) to the lower park gate, where you'll find a bus stop and the Estrada de Pena loop road.

From here, it's a five-minute hike uphill to the Moorish Castle, or a ten-minute hike up to the Pena Palace's main entrance.

▲▲National Palace (Palácio Nacional)

While the palace dates back to Moorish times, most of what you'll see is from the 15th-century reign of King John (João) I, with later Manueline architectural ornamentation from the 16th century.

This oldest surviving royal palace in Portugal is still used for official receptions. Having housed royalty for 500 years (until 1910), it's fragrant with history.

Cost and Hours: €9.50, daily 9:30-19:00, last entry 18:30; look for white, Madonna-bra building in town center, 10-minute walk from train station, photos allowed, tel. 219-237-300, www.parquesdesintra.pt.

❷ **Visiting the Palace:** The palace is a one-way romp with little information provided. As you tour the place, stop in these notable parts of the palace:

Swan Room: This first room is the palace's banquet room. A king's daughter—who loved swans—married into a royal house in Belgium. The king missed the princess so much that he decorated the ceiling with her favorite animal. These aren't the only creatures in the room, though. Check out the ceramic soup tureens designed in the shape of your favorite barnyard animal.

Courtyard: This was a fortified medieval palace, so rather than having fancy gardens outside, it has a stay-awhile courtyard within its protective walls. Notice the unique chimneys. They provide powerful suction that removes the smoke from the kitchen and also create a marvelous open-domed feeling (as you'll see at the end of your tour).

Magpie Room: King John I was caught kissing a lady-in-waiting by his queen. Frustrated by his court—abuzz with gossip—John had this ceiling painted with magpies. But to show what a good-spirited guy he was, around each magpie is the king's slogan—*Por bem,* "For good." The 15th-century Moorish tiles are from Spain, brought in before the development of the famous, ubiquitous Portuguese tiles, and are considered some of the finest Moorish-Spanish tiles in all of Iberia.

King's Bedroom: The king portrayed on the wall where you enter the room is King Sebastian (Dom Sebastião), a gung-ho, medieval-type monarch who went to battle in Africa, following the Moors even after they were chased out of Europe. He disappeared in 1578 at age 24 (although he was almost certainly killed in Morocco, "Sebastianists" awaited his mythical return into the 19th century). With the king missing, Portugal was left in unstable times with only Sebastian's great uncle (King Henrique) as heir. The new king died within two years, and the throne passed to his great uncle, King Philip II of Spain, leading to 60 years of Spanish rule (1580-1640).

Note the ebony, silver, and painted copper headboard of the Italian Renaissance bed. The tiles in this room are considered the first Portuguese tiles—from the time of Manuel I. The corn-on-the-cob motif topping the tilework is a reminder of American discoveries. Wander through more rooms upstairs, and through more quarters to the blue-and-gold...

Stag Room: The most striking room in the palace honors Portugal's loyal nobility. Study the richly decorated ceiling. The king's coat of arms at the top is surrounded by the coats of arms of his children, and below that, the coats of arms of all but one of Portugal's noble families (the omitted family had schemed a revolt, so received only a blank niche). The Latin phrase circling the room reads, "Honoring all the noble families who've been loyal to the king." The 18th-century tiles hang from the walls like tapestries. Enjoy the view: a garden-like countryside dotted with mansions of nobility who clamored to be near their king, the hill-capping castle, and the wide-open Atlantic. You're in the westernmost room of the westernmost palace on the European continent.

Kitchen: With all the latest in cooking technology, the palace chef could roast an entire cow on the spit, keep the king's plates warm in the iron dish warmer (with drawers below for the charcoal), and get really dizzy by looking up and spinning around three times. OK, you can go now.

▲Quinta da Regaleira

This Neo-everything (Manueline/Gothic/Renaissance) 1912 mansion and garden has mystical and Masonic twists. It was designed by an Italian opera-set designer for a wealthy but disgruntled monarchist two years after the royal family was deposed. The two-hour English tour is mostly in the garden (as the palace is quite small) and can be longish unless you're into quirky Masonic esoterica. If you like fantastic caves, bring a flashlight and follow the shaded black lines on the provided maps. Ask a local to pronounce "Regaleira" for you, and just try to repeat it.

Cost and Hours: €6 self-guided tour, €10 guided tour by reservation only, 7 tours daily April-Sept, fewer off-season; open daily 10:00-20:00, closes earlier off-season, last entry one hour before closing; 10-minute walk from downtown Sintra, café; book tours online at www.regaleira.pt or by calling 219-106-650.

Toy Museum (Museu do Brinquedo)

Just for giggles, you can wander through a collection of several thousand old-time toys, from small soldiers, planes, cars, trucks, and old tricycles to a dolls' attic upstairs. The 20th-century owner, João Arbués Moreira, started collecting toys when he was 14 and never quit. The collection is displayed in chronological order and comes with no English descriptions. Moreira typically hangs around the museum in his wheelchair, and loves to explain to visitors how he acquired each item.

Cost and Hours: €5, €3 for those under 19, Tue-Sun 10:00-18:00, closed Mon, last entry 30 minutes before closing, kids' play zone, one block in front of National Palace on Rua Visconde de Monserrate 26, tel. 219-242-171, www.museu-do-brinquedo.pt.

Monserrate

About 2.5 miles outside of Sintra are the wonderful gardens of Monserrate. If you like tropical plants and exotic landscaping, a visit is time well-spent, though many find that the Pena Palace's gardens are just as good as these more famous grounds.

Cost and Hours: €7.50, €5 extra for guided visit by reservation only, daily 9:30-20:00 last entry one hour before closing, no buses run here—allow about €10 for taxi, tel. 219-237-300, www.parquesdesintra.pt.

Sleeping in Sintra

$$ Casa Miradouro is a beautifully restored mansion from 1893. With eight spacious, stylish rooms, an elegant lounge, castle and sea views, and a wonderful garden, it's a worthy splurge (Db-€95-135, less Nov-March, includes buffet breakfast, Wi-Fi, street parking, Rua Sotto Major 55; from National Palace, go past Hotel Tivoli Sintra and 400 yards downhill, note that it's a stiff uphill hike to return to center; mobile 914-292-203, www.casa-miradouro.com, mail@casa-miradouro.com, Charlotte Lambregts).

$$ Casa Do Valle Guesthouse offers seven comfortable, modern rooms in a peaceful location. They have a lovely garden and large deck with valley and castle views (Db-€80-120, less Nov-March, breakfast-€4-6, guest computer, Wi-Fi, pool, street parking, behind Casa Miradouro on Rua da Paderna LT-2, tel. 219-244-699, www.casadovalle.com, info@casadovalle.com).

$ Monte Da Lua Guesthouse has seven clean, simple, fine rooms with shiny hardwood floors, facing the train station (one D-€55-60, six Db-€55-70, highest price is for July-Aug, 5 percent discount if you pay cash and mention this book, no breakfast, Wi-Fi, Avenida Dr. Miguel Bombarda 51, tel. 219-241-029, www.montedalua.org, montedalua51@gmail.com, Silvia).

Sleep Code

Abbreviations **(€1 = about $1.40, country code: 351)**
S = Single, **D** = Double/Twin, **T** = Triple, **Q** = Quad, **b** = bathroom, **s** = shower only.
Price Rankings
$$ Higher Priced—Most rooms €80 or more.
$ Lower Priced—Most rooms less than €80.
Unless otherwise noted, credit cards are accepted, English is spoken, breakfast is included, and Wi-Fi is generally free. Prices change; verify current rates online or by email. For the best prices, always book directly with the hotel.

Eating in Sintra

LIGHT MEALS

On Rua das Padarias

This touristy little cobbled lane is lined with charming shops and eateries. While there are plenty of appealing options, here are three notable choices:

Casa Piriquita bills itself as "the" *antiga fabrica de queijadas*—historic maker of tiny, tasty tarts with a cheesy filling. It's good for a sweet and a coffee or a simple lunch, such as toasted sandwiches. Take a seat in the café (up a few steps) to avoid groups who rush in to get pastries to go, or do battle and grab a half-dozen for €4.40 (daily 8:30-22:00, Rua das Padarias 1 at the base of the street, tel. 219-230-626).

Piriquita Dois, sister to Casa Piriquita, is a block farther up the lane and may have less commotion. It has a more extensive menu and a view terrace (same hours and phone as Casa Piriquita, Rua das Padarias 18).

Binhoteca, a welcoming little *enoteca,* provides wine-lovers with an astonishing array of Portuguese wines and ports available by the glass (€2-6 and way up), along with tasty meat-and-cheese plates and a knowledgeable staff happy to explain what you're enjoying (daily 12:00-22:00, Rua das Padarias 16, tel. 219-240-849).

More Light Choices

Patio de Sintra Cafeteria is a practical lunch stop just a block off Rua das Padarias (Rua Arco do Teixeira 15).

Café da Villa, a favorite of bus drivers and tour guides, offers generous portions of homemade-style soups and salads in a homey pub-like setting. It's good for a quiet, inexpensive lunch (€8 fixed-price meals, daily 12:00-24:00, down the road past horse-drawn carriages at Calçada do Pelourinho 2, tel. 219-241-174).

Pizza Hut, at the #434 bus stop outside the train station, has a salad bar and to-go boxes for a cheap meal to munch in the Pena Palace Park, on the grounds of the Moorish Castle, or on the train ride back to Lisbon (daily 12:00-23:00, Avenida Dr. Miguel Bombarda, Edifício Grande Velocidade, tel. 707-211-122).

DINING
While there are plenty of tourist eateries in Sintra's old center, I'd head a couple of blocks away to the station area for a serious meal.

Restaurante Regional de Sintra, which feeds locals and tourists very well, is my favorite place for dinner in Sintra. Gentle Paulo speaks English and serves huge, splittable portions (€15 *doses*, daily 12:00-16:00 & 19:00-22:30, 200 yards from train station at Travessa do Municipio 2; exit train station left, go downhill to the first square and to the far-right corner; tel. 219-234-444).

Apeadeiro Restaurante, named for the platform along the track at the train station just a block away, is a quality eatery serving good food at good prices. Their daily specials can be split, allowing two to eat for €15 (Fri-Wed 9:00-24:00, closed Thu, Avenida Dr. Miguel Bombarda 3, tel. 219-231-804).

Restaurante Chinês Da Fu Lou, across the street from the train station, offers decent, affordable Chinese food and an alternative to *bacalhau* and sandwiches (€5-10 entrées, daily 11:00-15:00 & 17:00-23:00, Avenida Dr. Miguel Bombarda 53, tel. 219-242-653).

Sintra Connections

From Sintra by Train and Bus to: Lisbon (4 trains/hour, 40 minutes), **Cascais** (8 buses/day, fewer on weekends, bus #403 also stops at Cabo da Roca and the Cascais train station, 45-60 minutes, catch bus at the Sintra train station).

ROUTE TIPS FOR DRIVERS
Sintra Day Trip from Lisbon: If you insist on taking a car to Sintra, take the IC-19 freeway out of Lisbon (allow 30 minutes). When you arrive in Sintra, follow *Centro Histórico* signs. Cars are the curse of Sintra—traffic can be terrible and parking difficult. Park your car and use bus #434 to get around. There's a strip of parking along Volta do Duche, near the town center (€0.50/hour, 4-hour maximum), and a small lot next to the train station. The most central free parking lot is on Rua do Porto in the valley just below and northeast of town (after parking, climb the long set of steps to get up to the main square). If you decide (probably regrettably) to drive to the sights, you'll take a one-way winding loop—park as soon as you can, or you'll risk having to drive the huge loop again (because

you can't backtrack). Large monitors can be found near every lot describing the current parking situation—most likely *completo*.

Loop Trip: It's possible to make a 70-mile circular trip and drive to all the destinations near Lisbon within a day (Lisbon–Belém–Sintra–Cabo da Roca–Cascais–Lisbon), but traffic congestion around Sintra, especially on weekends and during rush hour, can mess up your schedule.

Continuing to the Algarve: Drivers eager for beach time can leave Lisbon, visit Sintra, then head back south to drive directly to the Algarve that evening (4 hours from Lisbon). To get to the Algarve from Sintra/Cascais, get on the freeway heading for Lisbon and exit at the *Sul Ponte A-2* sign, which takes you over the 25th of April Bridge and south on A-2.

Near Sintra

The following sights are worth considering if you have extra time. They're tourable by car or by public transportation (bus and train).

If you're bent on seeing sights west of Lisbon (Sintra, Cabo da Roca, Cascais, and/or Estoril) in a long day using public transportation, consider this slam-bam swing around the peninsula: Start at the Sintra train station and buy a day pass for the Scotturb **bus** (€12). Use the pass to take bus #434 to Sintra's sights, then go to Cabo da Roca on bus #403 (see next). Next, catch the next bus #403 for the jaunt to Cascais and a seafood dinner on the waterfront.

From Cascais, returning to Lisbon is a snap—just buy a one-way **train** ticket to Lisbon at the train station. You'll get off at the last stop on the line (Cais de Sodré Station), a five-minute walk from Praça do Comércio in downtown Lisbon.

Estoril is a short train ride away on the same line to Lisbon, but seeing both Cascais and Estoril is probably redundant, and Cascais is more appealing.

Cabo da Roca

Wind-beaten, tourist-infested Cabo da Roca is the westernmost point in Europe, perhaps the inspiration for the Portuguese poet Luís de Camões' line, *"Onde a terra se acaba e o mar começa"* ("Where land ends and the sea begins"). It has a little shop, a café, and a tiny **TI** that sells an expensive €11 "proof of being here" certificate. Take a photo instead (daily May-Sept 9:00-20:00, until 19:00 off-

season, tel. 219-280-801). Nearby, on the road to Cascais, you'll pass a good beach for wind, waves, sand, and the chance to be the last person in Europe to see the sun set. For a remote beach, drive to Praia Adraga (north of Cabo da Roca).

Cascais and Estoril

Before the rise of the Algarve, these towns were the haunt of Portugal's rich and beautiful. Today, they are quietly elegant, with

noble old buildings, beachfront promenades, a bullring, a casino, and more fame than they deserve. Cascais (kahsh-KAH-eesh; see photo) is the more enjoyable of the two; it's not as rich and stuffy, and it has the cozy touch of a fishing village, great seafood, and a younger, less pretentious atmosphere. The TIs share the same hours (Mon-Fri 10:00-18:00, Sat-Sun 14:00-18:00; Cascais TI at Visconde de Luz 14, tel. 214-822-327, www. cm-cascais.pt; Estoril TI at Areada do Parque, tel. 214-663-813). Bullfight fans could enjoy a bullfight—if one is scheduled—in either city (ask at the TI).

Both towns are a simple day trip from Lisbon (4 trains/hour, 30 minutes from Lisbon's Cais do Sodré Station).

THE ALGARVE

Salema • Cape Sagres • Lagos • Tavira

The Algarve was once known as Europe's last undiscovered tourist frontier. But it's well-discovered now, and if you go to the places featured in tour brochures, you'll find it much like Spain's Costa del Sol—paved, packed, and pretty stressful. Still, there are a few great beach towns left, mostly on the western tip, and this part of the Algarve, the south coast, is part of any sun-worshipper's dream.

Portugal's warm and dry south coast, stretching for some 100 miles, has beach resorts along the water's edge and rolling green hills dotted with orchards farther inland. The coastline varies from lagoon estuaries in the east (Tavira), to sandy beach resorts in the center (from Faro to Lagos), to rugged cliffs in the west (Sagres).

The Moors (Muslims from North Africa who ruled Portugal for five centuries) chose not to live in the rainy north, but rather along the warm, dry south coast, in the land they dubbed Al-Gharb Al-Andalus ("to the west of Andalucía"—the westernmost edge of the huge Islamic world at the time). Today, the Algarve still holds elements introduced by the Muslims—groves of almond and orange trees, and white-domed buildings with blue trim, traditional *azulejos* (tiles), and pointy chimneys—reflecting the region's minaret heritage.

For some rigorous rest and intensive relaxation, make sunny Salema your Algarve hideaway. Here the tourists and fishermen sport the same stubble. It's just you, a beach with weathered fishing boats, no

must-see attractions, and a few other globetrotting experts in lethargy. Nearby sights include Cape Sagres (Europe's "Land's End" and home of Henry the Navigator's famous navigation school) and the beach-party/jet-ski resort of Lagos. Or you could just work on a tan and see how slow your pulse can get in sleepy Salema. If not now, when? If not you, who?

PLANNING YOUR TIME

The Algarve is your vacation from your vacation. How much time does it deserve? It depends upon how much time you have, and how much time you need to recharge your solar batteries. On a two-week trip of Portugal, I'd give it three nights and two days. After a full day of sightseeing in Lisbon (or Sevilla, if you're arriving from Spain), I'd push it by driving four hours around dinnertime to gain an entirely free beach day. With two days, I'd spend one enjoying side trips to Cape Sagres and Lagos, and another just lingering in Salema. The only other Algarve stop to consider is Tavira. (If you're visiting in winter, Tavira—which is lively year-round—makes a better stop than tiny Salema, which slows down.)

GETTING AROUND THE ALGARVE

Trains and buses connect the main towns along the south coast (skimpy service on weekends and off-season). Buses take you west from Lagos, where trains don't go. The freeway crossing the Algarve from Lagos to the Spanish border (and on to Sevilla, Spain) makes driving quick and easy. (See "Route Tips for Drivers in the Algarve," at the end of this chapter.)

Salema

One bit of old Algarve magic still glitters quietly in the sun—Salema. Fronting a fine sandy beach, it's at the end of a small road just off the main drag between the big city of Lagos and the rugged southwest tip of Europe, Cape Sagres.

Salema is changing but is still charming. The fishermen are fading into the past, the younger generation is moving to the big city, and the economy is evolving. Salema now draws visitors from nearby gated resorts and golfing clubs seeking local character and atmospheric restaurants. Yet Salema is still a place that will reward you with a great beach-town experience.

This simple fishing village has three beachside streets, a dozen or so restaurants, a few hotels, time-share condos up the road, a couple of bars, a classic beach with a paved promenade, and endless summer sun.

Orientation to Salema

TOURIST INFORMATION

Salema lacks an official TI, but people in the bars, restaurants, and pensions have heard all the questions and are happy to provide answers. There's a little information online at www.salema4u.com, but Romeu at the Salema Market is my man when I need to know something (see "Helpful Hints," later).

ARRIVAL IN SALEMA

By Train and Bus: To get to Salema, you'll arrive first at Lagos (with the closest train and bus stations), the western Algarve's transportation hub. From there, buses go every hour or two between Lagos and Sagres, with Salema about halfway between the two (30-minute ride, 10 miles, last bus departs Lagos at 20:30, fewer buses on weekends, €2.60, www.algarvebus.info and www. eva-bus.com). Catch the bus at either the Lagos bus station (see "Arrival in Lagos," page 160) or at one of the stops along the waterfront of the historic town.

About half the buses conveniently go right into the village of Salema (these are usually marked *Salema Village*). You should

confirm with the driver by asking: "*Você vai à praia de Salema?*" (voh-say vie ah pry-ah deh Salema).

The rest of the buses—marked with a cross ("X") in the schedule—stop at the top of the road, a 20-minute downhill walk into town. (If you're on one of these buses, it's better to stay on and get off at the next stop—Figueira—from there you can backtrack 20 yards, then follow the sign for *Salema*. It's the same distance as the first downhill walk, but there's a sidewalk, so it's safer and easier.)

By Car: If you're driving from Spain on the A-22 freeway, take the Lagos exit (marked *Lagos/Vila do Bispo/Sagres*) and follow *Sagres/Vila do Bispo* signs. Turn left at the sign for *Salema*. To stop in Lagos before continuing to Salema, take the exit marked *Lagos/Vila do Bispo/Sagres*, but follow signs to *Lagos centro*. Leave Lagos via the street Avenida dos Descobrimentos, and follow signs to *Sagres/Vila do Bispo*. In Salema, parking is free just about everywhere.

By Taxi: A cab from Lagos to Salema takes 20 minutes and costs about €25-30 (metered, but ask for an estimate first; see "Helpful Hints," next).

THE ALGARVE

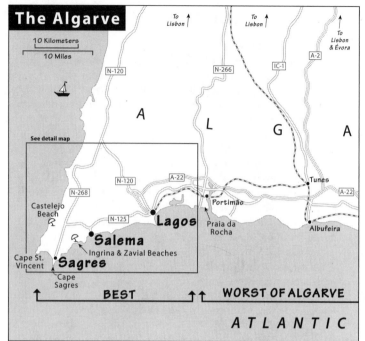

The Algarve

10 Kilometers
10 Miles

To Lisbon
To Lisbon
To Lisbon & Évora

N-120
N-266
IC-1
A-2

A   L   G   A

See detail map

N-120
N-268
A-22
Tunes
A-22

Castelejo Beach
N-125
Portimão
Lagos
Praia da Rocha
Albufeira

Salema
Ingrina & Zavial Beaches

Cape St. Vincent
Sagres
Cape Sagres

BEST   ↑↑   WORST OF ALGARVE

ATLANTIC

HELPFUL HINTS

Market: Romeu's Salema Market is handy for more than just shopping. Helpful Romeu also changes money and gives travel tips and advice on rooms or *quartos* to rent (daily July-Sept 8:30-22:00, Oct-June 9:00-13:00 & 15:00-19:30, Rua dos Pescadores).

Money: Stock up on cash before coming to Salema. Many places accept only cash and there's just one ATM in town (on the main square by the public WC). The next nearest ATMs are at the **Parque da Floresta** golf resort (about two miles inland), or at the **Intermarché** supermarket in Budens (the town just before Salema).

Internet Access: You can generally get online where you're sleeping. Otherwise you get free Wi-Fi with a drink at **Café Pastelaria Solmar** during the day (Margerita and Gregorio serve the best coffee in town, see "Breakfast in Salema," later) or at either bar (**A Aventura** or **A Tabua**) at night (see "Nightlife in Salema," later).

Taxi: Your hotel can arrange a taxi, or call José direct: He and his wife Isabel have a car and a black-and-green taxi minivan. Their rates: about €25 to Lagos; about €300 to Sevilla, Évora, or Lisbon). Both speak English and are happy to answer your

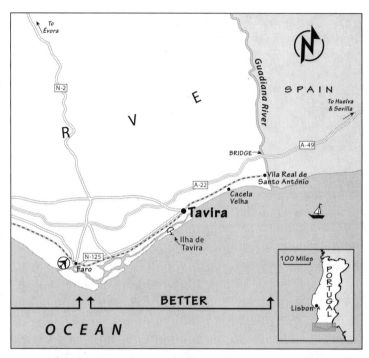

THE ALGARVE

questions about the area; Isabel is a former tour guide (mobile 919-385-139 or 919-422-061, www.vibeltaxisairporttransfers.com, info@vibeltaxisairporttransfers.com).

Taxi Tour with José or Isabel: If you're without wheels, hiring José or Isabel for a €50, two-hour guided tour of Cape Sagres can be a great value—especially if you can split the cost (their van takes up to six, add €10 for wait time if you want to explore more). You'll make all the stops, get out as you like, and enjoy a running commentary. They can also take you to desolate beaches. Call or email in advance to reserve longer trips (see previous listing).

Sights in Salema

Salema has a split personality: The whitewashed old town is for locals, and the other half was built for tourists—both groups pursue a policy of peaceful coexistence. Tourists laze in the sun, while locals grab the shade.

It's a small town where everyone seems connected in own way or another. (As the saying goes, "When you kick one person, everyone limps.") A good percentage of the population has the surname Duarte, and people have nicknames like Cucumber Ze and

Salema Area

5 Kilometers
5 Miles

N-268
N-120

To Lisbon via
Slow Coastal
Road

Carrapateira

Bensafrim

To
Portimão,
Tavira &
Lisbon →

A-22
N-125

To
Portimão

Castelejo
Beach

N-268

M-535

TRAIN
STN.

Meia
Praia

Vila do
Bispo

Raposeira   Budens

N-125

Lagos

Luz

Cape
St. Vincent
& LIGHTHOUSE

N-268

Ingrina &
Zavial Beaches

Burgau

Salema

100 Miles

PORTUGAL

Sagres Town

**Atlantic
Ocean**

Lisbon

Cape Sagres
& SAGRES FORT

Bread Roll Paulo. Several of the local
men married German women visiting back in the 1980s, showing the
town has a knack for making tourists
feel welcome.

Fishing Scene

Salema is still a fishing village—but
just barely. There are six or eight
working boats, but it's a far cry from
the days—just a generation ago—when the town's main drag, Rua
dos Pescadores, was, as its name suggests, literally the street of the
fishermen. While the fishermen's hut no longer hosts a fish auction,
you'll still see the old-timers enjoying its shade, oblivious to the
tourists, while mending their nets and reminiscing about the old
days when life was "only fish and hunger." To get permission before
taking their photo, ask *"Posso tirar uma foto, por favor?"* (paw-soo
teer-ar oo-mah foh-too poor fah-vor).

In the calm of the summer, boats are left out on buoys. In the
winter, the community-subsidized tractor earns its keep by haul-
ing the boats ashore. (In pre-tractor days, such boat-hauling was a
10-person chore.)

At night you'll see lights bobbing on the horizon, evenly
spaced, as fishermen are out catching squid, sardines, and the main
catch—octopi. The pottery jars stacked everywhere are traps; own-

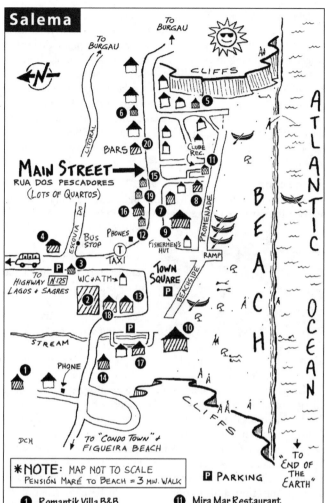

Salema

To BURGAU

To BURGAU

To BURGAU

CLIFFS

6

5

BARS **20**

MAIN STREET ←

RUA DOS PESCADORES
(LOTS OF QUARTOS)

CLUBE REC.

11

15

19

4

ESCOVIA DO

BUS STOP

PHONES

16

12

7

8

9

FISHERMEN'S HUT

PROMENADE

3

To HIGHWAY N 125 LAGOS & SAGRES

WC & ATM

2

13

18

TAXI

TOWN SQUARE

RAMP

BEACHSIDE

10

P

STREAM

PHONE

1

17

14

DCH

To "CONDO TOWN" & FIGUEIRA BEACH

CLIFFS

ATLANTIC OCEAN

BEACH

To "END OF THE EARTH"

✳NOTE: MAP NOT TO SCALE
PENSIÓN MARÉ TO BEACH = 3 MIN. WALK

P PARKING

1 Romantik Villa B&B
2 Hotel Residencial Salema
3 Casa Praiamar
4 Pensión Maré
5 Casa Hermínia
6 Afonso Houses
7 Ribeiro Rooms
8 Acacio Rooms
9 Boia Bar & Rest.
10 Atlântico Restaurant

11 Mira Mar Restaurant
12 Casa Pizza
13 Bistro Central
14 Restaurante O Lourençot
15 Agua Na Boca Restaurant
16 Romeu's Salema Market
17 Café Pastelaria Solmar
18 Corsario's Restaurant
19 A Tabúa Bar
20 A Aventura Bar

THE ALGARVE

ers take care to keep them clean because octopi prefer smooth, barnacle-free pots. Unwritten tradition allocates different chunks of undersea territory to each Salema family. The traps are tied about 15 feet apart in long lines and dropped offshore. Octopi, thinking these jars would make a cozy place to set an ambush, climb in and get ambushed themselves. (They also take refuge in pots during a storm.) When the fishermen hoist them in, they hang on—unaware they've made their final mistake. The fishermen mace them out of their pots with a squirt of bleach. The octopi flop angrily into the boat bound for the market and, who knows...maybe onto your dinner plate.

Beach Scene

Sunbathers enjoy the beach May through early October. Knowing their tourist-based economy sits on a foundation of sand, locals

hope and pray that the sand returns after being washed away each winter (some winters leave the beach just a pile of rocks).

A walk the length of the beach tracing the edge of the wet sand from the rocks in the west to the rocks in the east is a peaceful experience. Doing it early or late is a fine way to start or finish your day.

Locals claim the beach is safe for swimming, and in summer a lifeguard is often on duty, but the water is rarely really warm. The flag indicates the swimming conditions: Green is good, yellow means the current merits extra caution, and red means no swimming. You can rent beach items from Pedro (lounge chair-€5/day, 2 lounge chairs and bamboo sunshade-€10/day) at the Atlântico restaurant, and one- and two-person canoes (€5-7/30 minutes in July and Aug) from a little concession on the beach in front of the Balneario Municipal building (off parking lot, with WC). The fountain in front of the building is a reminder of the old days. When water to the village was cut off, this was always running.

On the west end, at low tide, you may be able to climb over the rocks past tiny tide pools to secluded Figueira Beach. (But be aware of when the tide comes in, or your route back will have to be over land.) While the old days of black-clad widows chasing topless Nordic women off the beach are gone, topless bathing is still risqué today: Northern European sun worshippers do so with discretion at the end of the beach among the rocks.

Hiking

There are several beautiful hikes from Salema along the beach and through the countryside out to neighboring villages such as Figueira. For routes, ask at your hotel, or see the walks and hikes described at www.salema4u.com/tours.

Community Development

The whole peninsula (west of Lagos) has been declared a natural park, and further development close to the beach is forbidden. But the village of Salema is becoming less and less ramshackle as it's gradually bought up by northern Europeans for vacation or retirement homes. Salema will live with past mistakes, such as the huge hotel in the town center that pulled some mysterious strings to go two stories over code. Up the street is a sprawling community of condos and Club Med-type vacationers who rarely leave their air-conditioned bars and swimming pools.

Across the highway and two miles inland is a big golfing resort, Quinta da Floresta, where several well-known European soccer players have snapped up holiday homes (main reception open 24 hours, golf reception open daily 8:00-20:00; €21 daily visitor pass for spa, gym, and outdoor pool—spa treatments extra; around €100 to golf, tennis courts available, spa tel. 282-690-007, golf tel. 282-690-054, www.quintadafloresta.sw-hotelguide.com).

Sleeping in Salema

Salema is crowded July through mid-September (and August is horribly packed). Prices jump in July and August, and the place is partially closed down in winter (when just a couple of restaurants stay open).

For maximum comfort, it's Pensión Maré. There's also the basic, utilitarian high-rise hotel in the center of town. And for economy, the experience, and an opportunity to practice your Portuguese, stay in a *quarto* (room). *Quartos* are primarily located along the main road that parallels the waterfront (Rua dos Pescadores). Because of new government regulations (to enforce the payment of taxes), running a B&B has become dishearteningly complex and now only a few remain in business. Still, you can ask around or check with Romeu at the Salema Market and generally find someone renting a private room.

PENSIÓNES AND HOTELS

$$$ Romantik Villa B&B, strictly run by Lisa from Brazil, is a chic, artsy house on top of the hill with three rooms, an apartment,

THE ALGARVE

Sleep Code

Abbreviations   **(€1 = about $1.40, country code: 351)**
S = Single, **D** = Double/Twin, **T** = Triple, **Q** = Quad, **b** = bathroom, **s** = shower only.
Price Rankings
$$$ **Higher Priced**—Most rooms €80 or more.
$$ **Moderately Priced**—Most rooms between €45-80.
$ **Lower Priced**—Most rooms €45 or less.
Credit cards are accepted only at Pensión Maré and Hotel Residencial Salema. Wi-Fi is generally free, and English is spoken unless otherwise noted. Prices change; verify current rates online or by email. For the best prices, always book directly with the hotel.

a garden, and a swimming pool. It's tastefully decorated and a good spot for people who want quiet—no children or teens are accepted (Db-€80-90, includes breakfast; apartment-€100-120, no breakfast; cash only, towels changed and room cleaned every two days, extra charge for daily service, next-day laundry service-€5/kilo, Praia de Salema, tel. 282-695-670, mobile 967-059-806, www.romantikvilla.com, romantikvilla@sapo.pt). The villa is a steep, 10-minute uphill walk—head up from the beach past Restaurante O Lourenço, take a right at the phone booth just after the *Salema Beach Club* sign, go up into Urbanização Beach Villas, and look for the *Romantik Villa* sign on the right. Drivers should take the first left past Restaurante O Lourenço (because of the one-way street, you'll need to go around the block), turn right at the stop sign, head back downhill for a few yards, then take the first left at the phone booth. Go up the steep hill and look for the *Romantik Villa M5* sign (on your right).

$$$ **Hotel Residencial Salema** rents basic, comfortable rooms handy to the beach. Their 32 rooms all have air-conditioning, balconies, and partial views (Sb-€81, Db-€94 mid-July-mid-Sept; Sb-€65, Db-€72 June-mid-July and mid-late Sept; Sb-€53, Db-€65 Easter-May and Oct; usually closed Nov-Easter, 10 percent discount with this book only with direct booking and when no specials in effect, includes breakfast and Wi-Fi, elevator, bar, tel. 282-695-328, www.hotelsalema.com, info@hotelsalema.com, Andrea).

$$$ **Casa Praiamar** is a new, sterile building just off the main square, with a pool and Astroturf. It rents 10 modern rooms, half with sea views and balconies (Sb-€57, Db-€85-120, less without a kitchen, triples and quads without sea views, Assildo promises 15 percent Rick Steves discount if you ask and book directly with

hotel, no breakfast, tel. 962-619-037, www.casapraiamar.com, casapraiamar@gmail.com).

$$ Pensión Maré, a blue-and-white building overlooking the village above the main road into town, is the best hotel value in Salema. It's run by friendly Bettina, who offers six comfortable rooms (Sb-€48-64, Db-€60-80, includes wonderful breakfast) and three fully equipped apartments (Db-€70-90) in a tidy paradise (10 percent discount with this book and cash if booked ahead via email, Wi-Fi, next-day laundry service-€3.50/kilo, Praia de Salema, tel. 282-695-165, bettina@the-mare.com, www.the-mare.com).

HOUSES AND APARTMENTS

Renting a house or apartment is a popular option that falls comfortably between staying in a hotel and spending the night in someone's home (see information on *quartos,* next).

Jorn and Sigrun, a Danish couple, manage **Casa Hermínia**—a house with sweeping views of Salema and the beach that sleeps up to six people—and an apartment near the beach (2-person apartment-€55, Casa Hermínia-€70-150, minimum 2-night stay, cash only, Wi-Fi, mobile 963-609-205, www.salema4u.com, jorn@salma4u.com).

José Afonso rents two simple houses—Anica and Patacas—that share the same address. Rentable only in summer, the two houses have some double rooms (Db-€35-40 in July-Aug, €30 in June and Sept) and several apartments that sleep 4-8 people (figure roughly €80/night July-Aug, €65/night June and Sept). Some rooms have ocean views, kitchenettes, or shared kitchens (Rua dos Pescadores 24, tel. 966-654-113, www.salema-house.com, salemahouse@gmail.com).

QUARTOS AND CAMPING

Quartos provide a great way to connect with locals. You'll find rooms for rent along the main street, Rua dos Pescadores ("Fishermen's Street").

To find a room, ask one of the locals at the waterfront, or check with Romeu at the Salema Market. Prices vary with the season, plumbing, and view, and if you're only staying one night in high season, you're bad news. It can be difficult to find a room for less than three nights, especially in July and August. Doubles cost about €25-60 (cash only, no breakfast). *Quarto* landladies generally speak only a little English, but they're used to dealing with visitors. Some will do your laundry for about €4 or so. Except for August weekends, there are always rooms available for drop-ins. Prices can be soft, especially outside of July and August.

$ Maria Helena and Jorge Ribeiro, a helpful young couple, rent two small, simple doubles (S or D-€35 all year, one has a tiny

THE ALGARVE

view) and a charming treehouse-type suite with a kitchen, a view terrace, and a view toilet for Db-€40-50 (Rua dos Pescadores 83, tel. 282-695-289).

$ The **Acacio family** rents a humble ground-floor double (D-€25-30) and a fine upstairs apartment with a kitchenette, a balcony over the beach, and a great ocean view for up to five people (minimum two nights, Db-€50, Tb-€70, Qb-€80, generally €15-20 more July-Aug, Rua dos Pescadores 91, tel. 282-695-473). Silvina doesn't speak English.

Campers who don't underestimate the high tides sleep free and easy on the **beach** or at a well-run **campground** with bungalows a half-mile inland, back toward the main road.

Eating in Salema

Eat fresh seafood here. The local specialty is *cataplana*—fish, tomatoes, potatoes, onions, and whatever else is available—cooked a long time in a traditional copper pot (somewhere between a pressure cooker and a steamer). Costing around €20, it's big enough for two or three. Also look for grilled golden bream *(dourada grelhada)* and giant prawns *(camarões)*. For wine, try *vinho verde* (a young white wine, a Portuguese specialty with a refreshing taste).

Salema has seven or so places that all serve fine €11 meals. Happily, those that face the beach (the first three listed here) are the most fun and have the best service, food, and atmosphere. The Boia Bar and the Atlântico have modern glass fronts so you can be both comfortable and seaside in cold weather. The Mira Mar is right on the beach, but it has no glassed-in area and can be chilly at dinnertime.

For a memorable last course at any of these places, consider taking your fine port, *moscatel* (dessert wine), *caipirinha* (Brazilian sugarcane liquor mixed with lime), or coffee to the beach for some stardust on the side.

The **Boia Bar and Restaurant,** at the base of the residential street, has a classy beachfront setting, noteworthy service by a friendly gang, and a knack for doing whitefish just right (always with free seconds on vegetables). Their vegetarian lasagna (€10.50) and salads are popular, as are their €8 breakfasts (daily 10:00-24:00, tel. 282-695-382, Anibal, Rui, and Carla).

The **Atlântico**—big, busy, and right on the beach—has long dominated the Salema scene and comes with a fun energy. It's known for tasty fish (see the daily board), friendly service, and a wonderful beachside terrace (daily 12:00-22:00, also rents lounge chairs and bamboo sunshades, tel. 282-695-142, Cristiano and his sister Sandra run the place).

Mira Mar, easily accessed from the promenade, is the only place actually on the beach—a last vestige of old Salema. Dieter (a German who adopted Salema as his hometown decades ago) offers a creative rotating menu for those venturing away from seafood. He serves hearty salads for lunch and always has a vegetarian entrée (Sun-Fri 12:30-16:00 & 18:30-22:30, closed Sat, cash only). As tables are outside on a covered patio facing the beach, it can be cool, but they have blankets.

Casa Pizza, across the street from the Boia Bar, isn't on the beach, but its upper deck has a great view. Run by Stelios and family, it serves a variety of tasty €7-10 pizzas, salads, and fresh fish, as well as €8-15 meat and pasta dishes (daily 12:00-24:00, Rua dos Pescadores 100, tel. 282-697-968). You can get a pizza to go, and eat it on the beach for the best view in town.

Bistro Central, on the town square (with no sea view), is run by Bertrand, who's French and artfully mixes Portuguese and French cuisine traditions. Along with Luisa and Natalia, he cooks up a variety of fish, meat, pasta, and vegetarian dishes (€17-20 plates, good wine list, homemade desserts, Tue-Sun 12:00-24:00, closed Mon, mobile 934-194-215).

Restaurante O Lourenço, a block up the hill, has no ambience or view but offers good-value meals, has a local clientele, and is the best value in town for lunch, with hearty €7 plates. Paulo fishes and serves what he catches, while his mother Aldina cooks. A fish dinner for two here will cost around €35; Paulo can knowledgeably explain the story and cost of each fish (Mon-Sat from noon and from 18:00, closed Sun, cash only; from Hotel Residencial Salema cross the bridge, restaurant is a half-block uphill; tel. 282-698-622).

Agua Na Boca ("Mouth Watering"), a sophisticated, atmospheric, and noisy eatery run by Paulo and his wife-and-chef Irene, serves up-market local cuisine complemented by an extensive wine list. It's always busy, especially with the fancy golf-club crowd, so reserve ahead. Dishes are innovative—more than the standard grilled fish—and their special plates (around €17) are huge and perfectly splittable. For about €60 you can enjoy a three-course meal for two people with wine (April-Sept daily from 18:00, Oct-May closed Sun, on Rua dos Pescadores 82, tel. 282-695-651).

Picnics: **Romeu's Salema Market** has all the fixings for a great picnic to take with you to a secluded beach or Cape Sagres. Look for fresh fruits, veggies, bread, sheep's cheese, sausage, and the white wine, *vinho verde.* Helpful Romeu also changes money and gives travel and *quarto* advice (daily July-Sept 9:00-20:00, Oct-June 9:00-13:00 & 15:00-20:00, on Rua dos Pescadores).

For drivers: Drivers who want a classy meal outside of town should consider the elegant **Vila Velha Restaurante** in Sagres or the more rustic **Castelejo Restaurante** at the surreal Praia do Castelejo (both described later).

Breakfast in Salema

Quartos don't serve breakfast, and breakfast at hotels isn't until 8:30 (after the bread guy arrives at Salema). You have a couple of options in this tiny town: **Café Pastelaria Solmar** (in the strip facing Hotel Residencial Salema) serves coffee and pastries from 7:00 until 21:00. **Corsario's** serves a hearty €7 English breakfast from 8:00 (Rosa is a kick, and proud of her homemade cakes; her son is a motorcycle racer). And the **Boia Bar** serves a big €8 breakfast all day from 10:00.

Nightlife in Salema

Salema has two late-night bars, each worth a visit to sample the local drinks. *Armarguinha* (ar-mar-GWEEN-yah) is a sweet, likeable almond liqueur. *Licor beirão* (LIK-kor bay-ROW; "row" rhymes with "cow") is Portuguese amaretto, a "double distillation of diverse plants and aromatic seeds in accordance with a secret old formula." *Caipirinha* (kay-peer-EEN-yah), tasty and powerful, is made of fermented Brazilian sugarcane with lime, sugar, and crushed ice. And *moscatel* is the local sweet dessert wine.

The two bars stand within a few steps of each other on the main street. **A Tabúa Bar** serves a popular sangria and feels a bit younger and more local. Just up the street, **A Aventura Bar** offers an intimate atmosphere for sipping drinks whipped up by Karl and Zoe, an English couple who prefer the Eagles to hip-hop. Both bars are open nightly from about 18:00 until very late and offer free Wi-Fi to guests.

I enjoy capping my dinner by taking a drink from any beachside restaurant and grabbing a bench on the promenade or a place on the beach to peacefully ponder the moon and the waves.

Cape Sagres

In the days before Columbus, when the world was presumed to be flat, this rugged southwestern tip of Portugal was the spot closest to the edge of the Earth. Prince Henry the Navigator (Henrique o Navegador), determined to broaden Europe's horizons and spread

Catholicism, founded his navigators' school here and sent sailors ever farther into the unknown. Shipwrecked and frustrated explorers were carefully debriefed as they washed ashore.

Orientation to Cape Sagres

Portugal's "end of the road" is two distinct capes. Windy **Cape St. Vincent** is actually the most southwestern tip. It has a desolate lighthouse that marks what was thought of even in prehistoric times as "the end of the world." **Cape Sagres,** with its old fort and Henry the Navigator lore, is the more historic cape of the two. At either cape, look for daredevil windsurfers and fishermen casting from the cliffs.

Lashed tightly to the windswept landscape is the salty **town of Sagres,** above a harbor of fishing boats.

Tourist Information: The TI is on the main street, Avenida Comandante Matoso (Tue-Sat 9:30-13:30 & 14:30-17:30, closed Sun-Mon, tel. 282-624-873).

Sights in Cape Sagres

The town of Sagres, which feels like the last town in Europe, is basically a main street with plenty of places to eat and sleep, a park, bus stop, and a TI. It sits on a bluff high above the shoreline. On one side is a fishing port with an auction (Docapesca, described next), and on the other side is a fine crescent beach, with a good beachside restaurant. Tourism here is all about surfing. When the surf's up, things are busy and there's a hip and youthful vibe. In low season, it feels pretty dead.

Docapesca
Sagres harbor hosts the biggest fish auction west of Lagos (Mon-Fri at 7:30 and 15:00). Snack Bar A Sereia is perched above the action, and from its big windows you can watch the fishy action as restaurateurs fill the two dozen chairs above the conveyor belt and bid against each other for the best fish.

Cape Sagres Fort and Navigators' School
The former "end of the world" is a craggy, windswept, wedge-shaped point that juts into the Atlantic (a short drive or 15-minute walk from Sagres). In 1420, Prince Henry the Navigator used his order's funds to establish a school here for navigators. It was devastated by the 1755 earthquake (which also destroyed Lisbon), the center of which was 50 miles offshore from here. Today, little remains of Henry's school, except the site of buildings replaced by a few more modern structures. An 18th-century fortress, built on the

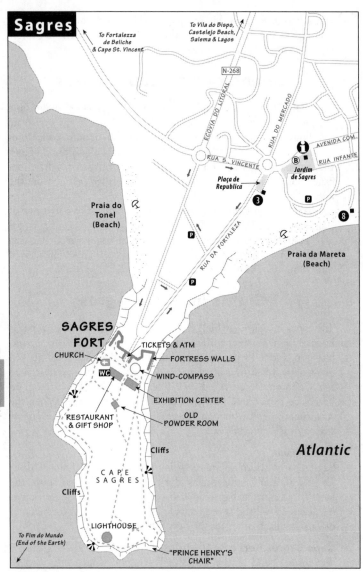

Sagres

To Fortalezza de Beliche & Cape St. Vincent

To Vila do Bispo, Castelejo Beach, Salema & Lagos

N-268

ECOVIA DO LITORAL

RUA DO MERCADO

RUA S. VINCENTE

AVENIDA COM.

RUA INFANTE

B

Jardim de Sagres

Plaça de Republica

3

P

P

8

Praia do Tonel (Beach)

RUA DA FORTALEZA

Praia da Mareta (Beach)

P

P

SAGRES FORT

TICKETS & ATM

CHURCH

FORTRESS WALLS

WC

WIND-COMPASS

EXHIBITION CENTER

OLD POWDER ROOM

RESTAURANT & GIFT SHOP

Cliffs

Atlantic

CAPE SAGRES

Cliffs

LIGHTHOUSE

To Fim do Mundo (End of the Earth)

"PRINCE HENRY'S CHAIR"

THE ALGARVE

school's original battlements and whitewashed in the 20th century, dominates the entrance to the point.

Cost and Hours: €3, daily May-Sept 9:30-20:00, Oct-April 9:30-17:30, last entry 30 minutes before closing, tel. 282-620-140.

◐ Visiting the Fort: After entering through the 18th-century battlements, look above the entry arch. Find the carved **stone plaque** that honors Henry. The ship in the plaque is a caravel,

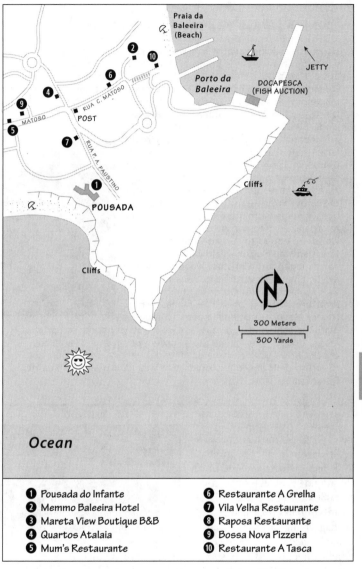

1 Pousada do Infante
2 Memmo Baleeira Hotel
3 Mareta View Boutique B&B
4 Quartos Atalaia
5 Mum's Restaurante
6 Restaurante A Grelha
7 Vila Velha Restaurante
8 Raposa Restaurante
9 Bossa Nova Pizzeria
10 Restaurante A Tasca

THE ALGARVE

one of the small, light craft that was constantly being reinvented by Sagres' shipbuilding grad students. The astrolabe, a compact instrument that uses the stars for navigation, emphasizes Henry's role in the exploration process. The stone column nearby honors Henry, who died here in 1460 (erected on 500th anniversary of his death). The top is a replica of the stone used by Portugal's great mariners to claim new territory.

Prince Henry the Navigator (1394-1460)

No swashbuckling sailor, Henry was a quiet scholar, an organizer, a religious man, and the brains behind Portugal's daring sea voyages. The middle child of King John (João) I of Portugal and Queen Philippa of England, he was one of what was dubbed "The Marvelous Generation" *(Ínclita Geração)* that drove the Age of Discovery. While his brothers and nephews became Portugal's kings, he worked behind the scenes.

At age 21, he planned the logistics for the large-scale ship invasion of the Muslim city of Ceuta (1415) on the north coast of Morocco, taking the city and winning knightly honors. Awed by the wealth of the city—a terminus of the caravan route—and intrigued by the high-quality maps he found there, Henry decided to organize expeditions to explore the Muslim world. He hoped to spread Christianity, contain Islam, tap Muslim wealth, and find Prester John's legendary Christian kingdom, said to exist somewhere in Africa or Asia.

As head of the Order of Christ—a powerful brotherhood of soldier-monks—Grand Master Henry used their money to found a maritime school at Sagres. While Henry stayed home to update maps, debrief returning sailors, order supplies, and sign paychecks, brave seamen traveled off under Henry's strict orders not to return until they'd explored what was known as the "Sea of Darkness."

There's little to actually see here. Sagres' most impressive sight—a circle on the ground, 100 feet across and outlined by round pebbles—is a mystery. Some think it was a large **wind-compass** *(rosa-dos-ventos)*. A flag flying from the center could immediately announce the wind's direction. Others speculate it's a large sundial. A pole in the center pointing toward the North Star (at a 37-degree angle, Sagres' latitude) would cast a shadow on the dial showing the time of day.

The row of buildings beyond the wind-compass is where the **school** once was. The **tower-cistern** (abutting the end of the modern exhibition center) is part of the original dorms. You can climb it for the view. The small, whitewashed **Church of Our Lady of Grace** (with St. Vincent and St. Francis flanking its humble altar)

They discovered the Madeira Islands (1420), which Henry planted with vineyards, and the Azores (1427), which Henry colonized with criminals. But the next expeditions returned empty-handed, having run into a barrier—both a psychological and physical one. Cape Bojador (at the southwest corner of modern Morocco), with its reefs and currents, was seen as the end of the world. Beyond that, sea serpents roamed, while the hot equatorial sun melted ships, made the sea boil, and turned white men black.

Henry ordered scared, superstitious sailors to press on. After 14 unsuccessful voyages, Gil Eanes' crew returned (1437), unharmed and still white, with new knowledge that was added to corporate Portugal's map library.

Henry himself gained a reputation as an intelligent, devout, nonmaterialistic, celibate monk who humbled himself by wearing horsehair underwear. In 1437, Henry faced a personal tragedy. His planned invasion of Tangier failed miserably, and his beloved little brother Fernão was captured. As ransom, the Muslims demanded that Portugal return Ceuta. Henry (and others) refused, Fernão died in captivity, and Henry was devastated.

In later years, he spent less time at court in Lisbon and more in desolate Sagres, where he died in 1460. (He's buried in Batalha; see page 214.) Henry died before finding a sea route to Asia and just before his voyages really started paying off commercially. A generation later, Vasco da Gama would sail to India, capping Henry's explorations and kicking off Portugal's Golden Age.

THE ALGARVE

replaced Henry's church. The former Governor's House is now the restaurant/gift shop complex (with some interesting photos of huge waves crashing onto the cape). Attached to the gift shop is a **windbreak wall** that dates from Henry's time, but is largely rebuilt.

The Sagres school taught mapmaking, shipbuilding, sailing, astronomy, and mathematics (for navigating), plus botany, zoology, anthropology, languages, and salesmanship for mingling with the locals. The school welcomed Italians, Scandinavians, and Germans, and included Christians, Muslims, and Jews. Captured Africans gave guest lectures. (The next 15 generations of Africans were not so lucky, being sold into slavery by the tens of thousands.)

Besides being a school, Sagres was Mission Control for the explorers. Returning sailors brought spices, gold, diamonds, silk, and ivory, plus new animals, plants, peoples, customs, communicable diseases, and knowledge of the routes that were added to the maps. Henry ordered every sailor to keep a travel journal that could be studied. Ship designs were analyzed and tweaked, resulting in the square-sailed, oceangoing caravels that replaced the earlier coast-hugging versions.

It's said that Ferdinand Magellan (circumnavigator), Vasco da Gama (found sea route to India), Pedro Cabral (discovered Brazil), and Bartolomeu Dias (Africa-rounder) all studied at Sagres (after Henry's time, though). In May of 1476, the young Italian Christopher Columbus washed ashore here after being shipwrecked by pirates. He went on to study and sail with the Portuguese (and marry a Portuguese woman) before beginning his American voyage. When Portugal denied Columbus' request to sail west, Spain accepted. The rest is history.

Beyond the buildings, the granite **point** itself is windswept, eroded, and largely barren, except for hardy, coarse vegetation admired by botanists. Walk on level paths around the edge of the bluff (a 40-minute round-trip walk), where locals cast lines and tourists squint into the wind. You'll get great seascape views of Cape St. Vincent, with its modern lighthouse on the site of an old convent. At the far end of the Sagres bluff are a naval radio station, a natural cave, and a promontory called "Prince Henry's Chair."

Sit on the point and gaze across the "Sea of Darkness," where monsters roam. Long before Henry's time, Romans dubbed it Promontorium Sacrum—Sacred ("Sagres") Promontory. Pilgrims who came to visit this awe-inducing place were prohibited from spending the night here—it was for the gods alone.

In Portugal's seafaring lore, capes, promontories, and land's ends are metaphors for the edge of the old, and the start of the unknown voyage. Sagres is the greatest of these.

Cape St. Vincent, a few minutes' drive from Cape Sagres, is actually the most southwestern tip of Europe. It has a desolate lighthouse that marks what was thought of even in prehistoric times as "the end of the world." Outside the lighthouse (at the parking lot), salt-of-the-earth merchants sell seaworthy sweaters (€25 average), cotton tea towels (a bargain at €1), and the *"Letter Bratwurst or Amerika"* (last hot dog before America).

The St. Vincent Lighthouse Museum is open to the public, though the lighthouse is not (€1.50, Tue-Sun 10:00-18:00, closed Mon). It's worth a few minutes for its exhibits on ship technology, ancient legends, celestial navigation, and on the lighthouse itself. In 1846 you could see the light of the oil lamp from six miles away. Now the beam is one of the strongest in Europe, said to reach 60 miles. In the courtyard there's a salty café, a WC, and wild views of the often stormy coastline.

Fortalezza de Beliche, the eroded remains of a 16th-century castle hanging precariously on a bluff over the sea, is just off the road, about a half-mile before the St. Vincent Lighthouse Museum if you're coming from Sagres. It was used as a kind of headquarters by the English pirate "sir" Francis Drake. Drake, who pillaged with the queen's blessing, waited here for his Mediterranean-bound victims.

Beaches

Many beaches are tucked away on the drive between Salema and Cape Sagres. Most of them require a short walk after you stop along N-125. In some cases, you leave your car on access roads or cross private property to reach the beaches—be considerate. Furnas beach is fully accessible by car. You can access Ingrina and Zavial beaches by turning south in the village of Raposeira. Many beaches have bars (the one at Ingrina beach is famous for its spicy garlic prawns—*camarão piri-piri*).

The best secluded beach in the region is **Praia do Castelejo,** just north of Cape Sagres (from the town of Vila do Bispo, drive inland and follow the signs for 15 minutes). If you have a car and didn't grow up in Fiji, this really is worth the drive. Overlooking the deserted beach is **Castelejo Restaurante,** which specializes in octopus dishes, *percebes* (goose barnacles), and *cataplana,* the hearty seafood stew (daily 12:00-22:00, 7.5 miles from Salema at Praia do Castelejo, tel. 282-639-777). While beaches between Salema and Sagres offer more of a seaside landscape, beaches north of São Vicente are more rugged and wild because they're exposed to ocean wind and weather. If there's no sand in Castelejo when you visit, blame it on nature and enjoy the rock formations instead.

Mareta Beach, just below the town of Sagres, has rental gear and showers in the summer and a fun little restaurant. For a resort beach, consider **Luz** (the first town west of Lagos), which feels like a Portuguese Riviera playground with a fine promenade and all the trappings of a beach-vacation destination.

Activities

Cape Cruiser down at Cape Sagres' port takes guided boat trips out to Cabo São Vincente (around €20/person, 90 minutes) and also does fishing trips (cash only, mobile 919-751-175, www.capecruiser.org, capecruiser@gmail.com).

Mar Ilimitado offers several daily boat trips, including dolphin watching (€32/person, 1.5 hours, July-Sept tours go hourly 9:30-15:30, March-June and Oct-Nov at 11:30 only). On their seabird-watching trips, they toss in ground-up fish and you observe the hungry spectacle (€40/person, 3 hours; daily tours at 9:00—book ahead, especially off-season). They'll also take you to Cabo

THE ALGARVE

São Vincente (€20/person, 1 hour, March-Nov at 16:00, no tours Dec-Feb, board at Sagres Harbor next to shipyard, mobile 916-832-625, www.marilimitado.com, tours@marilimitado.com, Ricardo and Sara).

Divers Cape Sagres, located at the port, is a diving school offering dive classes and various excursions (tel. 282-624-370, www.diverscape.com).

Sagres Natura Sport and Adventure Shop gives surf classes and offers canoeing and mountain bike expeditions (just behind Surf Planet on Rua São Vincente, tel. 282-624-072, www.sagresnatura.com, sagresnatura@hotmail.com). They also rent bikes (€15/day with ID).

Sleeping in Cape Sagres

$$$ Pousada do Infante, on a bluff overlooking the sea, provides a touch of lavish elegance in Sagres. This classy *pousada* (historic inn) is a reasonable splurge with a magnificent setting. At breakfast, you can sip coffee and enjoy the buffet while gazing out to sea (Sb/Db-€100-200, check website for discounts, tel. 282-620-240, www.pousadas.pt, recepcao.infante@pousadas.pt).

$$$ Memmo Baleeira Hotel, with views over the port of Sagres, is a 140-room resort-class hotel that caters to groups. It is chic and minimalist, with pure white bedrooms and sea views (July-Aug Sb-€145, Db-€180; off-season Sb-€95, Db-€105; see Web for two-night stay discounts, swimming pool, sauna, Turkish bath, tel. 282-624-212, www.memmobaleeira.com, hotel@memmobaleeira.com).

$$ Mareta View Boutique B&B, delightful and stylish, is perched on a bluff at the edge of town with 17 modern rooms, a fine garden, and hot tub with a sea view (Sb-€30-40, Db from €52, Db with view and balcony €67 to about €150 when surf's up, Wi-Fi, Beco D. Henrique, tel. 282-620-000, www.sagresholidays.com, info@sagresholidays.com). It's at the far west end of town past the park near the bus stop; look for the anchor in the roundabout. Its sister hotel Mareta Beach, a block away, is not so nice.

$ Quartos Atalaia, run by English-speaking Jorge, has seven clean, quiet, and comfortable rooms in the center of town (Sb/Db-€30-50, Qb-€60-80, extra bed-€10, no breakfast, Avenida Comandante Matoso, tel. 282-624-681, mobile 911-046-068, apart.atalaia@gmail.com).

Eating in Cape Sagres

Sagres feels designed to feed visitors with lots of inviting little eat-eries along its main drag, Avenida Comandante Matoso. **Mum's** (dinner only, closed Tue, tel. 968-210-411) and **Restaurante A Grelha** are reliably good.

Vila Velha Restaurante, the pricey gourmet option in town, offers wonderful meals, especially their rabbit stew (Tue-Sun 18:30-22:00, closed Mon, reservations smart, Rua Patrão Anto-nio Faustino, near *pousada* listed above, tel. 282-624-788, www. vilavelha-sagres.com).

Raposo Restaurante ("Fox") is right on the pristine, sandy, and picturesque Mareta Beach (Praia da Mareta). It's a fun spot for snacks (try *percebes*—barnacles—350-gram minimum plenty for two), drinks, or a serious meal, inside or outside on a terrace. Have a dip in the sea right after your meal (€3-5 milkshakes, €15-20 fish dishes, meals served daily 12:00-21:00, free Wi-Fi, tel. 282-624-168).

Bossa Nova Pizzeria, in a converted stable, caters to the surfing crowd, serving tasty pizzas, pastas, salads, and vegetarian dishes (daily 12:00-23:00 in summer; off-season Tue-Sat 17:00-23:00, closed Sun-Mon; eat in or take away, behind Dromadário Bar along Avenida Comandante Matoso, tel. 282-624-219).

Restaurante A Tasca, known for good seafood, has fine in-door seating and a sunny terrace overlooking the harbor a few blocks below the town (closed Wed, Porto da Baleeira, tel. 282-624-177).

Cape Sagres Connections

From Salema, Sagres is a 20-minute drive or a 30-minute bus trip (runs every 1-2 hours, stop is at the west end of Sagres near the park with the big anchor). You can check bus times online at www. algarvebus.info. Some buses continue to Cabo São Vincente; check schedules beforehand.

A taxi ride from Salema to Sagres costs about €25-30 (€60 for 1.25-hour round-trip, plus €10/hour for waiting time in Sagres; see Salema's "Helpful Hints," earlier in this chapter). Taxi driver José or Isabel can take you from Salema to Cabo São Vincente to Sagres and back with short photo stops (2 hours for €50, mobile 919-385-139).

Lagos

With a beach-party old town and a jet-ski marina, Lagos (LAH-goosh) is as enjoyable as a big-city resort can be. This major town on the west end of the Algarve was the region's capital in the 13th and 14th centuries. The first great Portuguese maritime expeditions embarked from here, and the first African slave market in Europe was held here. And today, with nothing of earth-shaking importance to see or do, it's just a purely enjoyable little bit of the Algarve.

Orientation to Lagos

The old town, defined by its medieval walls, stretches between the main square (Praça Gil Eanes) and the fort. It's a whitewashed

jumble of pedestrian streets, bars, funky craft shops, outdoor restaurants, mod fountains and sculptures, and sunburned tourists. Search out the sea-creature designs laid in the pavement—some of them will probably be on your plate at dinner. The beaches with the exotic rock formations—of postcard fame—begin just past the fort, with easy access via beachy boardwalks and higher trails. Except for a stroll among the rocks on the beach, there are no major sights. The town walk (described later) makes for a delightful morning or afternoon.

TOURIST INFORMATION

The TI, which covers Lagos and the entire Algarve, is in the former City Hall on the south side of Praça Gil Eanes. Stop in for a town map and transportation schedules (daily 9:30-19:00, tel. 282-763-031).

ARRIVAL IN LAGOS

By Train or Bus: The train and bus stations are a five-minute walk apart, separated by the marina and a ramped pedestrian bridge over a river. Neither station has baggage storage.

By Car: If you're coming from Spain on the A-22 freeway, exit at Lagos and follow signs to *centro*. The most convenient free parking lot is just outside the old city wall off Rua Infante de Sagres. There are other pay lots near the marina and a large, long-term, underground parking garage on Avenida dos Descobrimentos, near Praça do Infante. And you can use pay-and-display along the harborfront promenade.

HELPFUL HINTS

Internet Access: For the cost of a drink, you can get online at cafés and bars all over town.

Car Rental: English-speaking Nuno at **Lagorent Rent-a-Car** can set you up with four wheels for around €45 a day (Avenida dos Descobrimentos 43, tel. 282-762-467, www.lagorent.com, info@lagorent.com).

Local Guide: Carla Andrez de Sousa is a good licensed guide who lives and works in Lagos (€80 per family or group for a two-hour private town tour, longer tours available, mobile 964-670-661, carlasousa64@gmail.com).

Lagos Town Walk

While the actual sights of Lagos are humble, the town itself has an endearing charm that is best experienced by strolling. This simple self-guided walk, worth ▲▲, takes about an hour and covers the essence of the city. It starts on the main square, cuts straight up the main street to the town museum, and then down to the site of the slave market and harborfront, where you can walk the promenade and/or hike the exotic beaches.

Praça Gil Eanes

This city of 27,000 and its inviting cobbled pedestrian streets seem to converge in this square around the playful statue of King Sebastian (Sebastião). The big building housing the TI is the former City Hall. The local, free-spirited hippie community provides street music, and the cafés are tempting. While Lagos was a regional power from 1578 to 1756—in fact, the capital of the Algarve—today it feels like the capital of not much.

The statue commemorates the romantic King Sebastian who ventured from Portugal into Africa to Christianize "the Dark Continent" and was killed. With his death, Spanish royalty came to power here and Portugal entered into a kind of Spanish-dominated Dark Age (1580-1640). And the Portuguese have never given up hope of finding him. Sebastian is symbolic of ridiculous hopefulness. When he returns, so will the good times. This statue is poignant because it was inaugurated in 1973, the year before the

THE ALGARVE

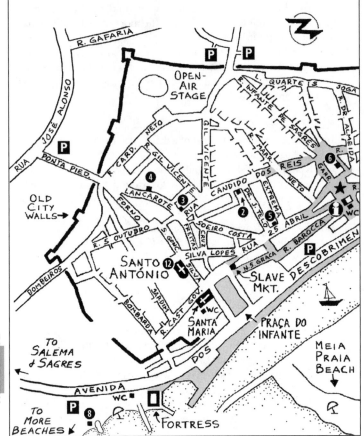

Carnation Revolution, when the people of Portugal were hungry to toss out their dictator and win their freedom.

• *From the square, head down Lagos' main drag.*

April 25 Street (Rua 25 Abril)

Forca Portugal, a patriotic soccer gear shop, marks the start of April 25 Street—named for the date of the 1974 military coup. Follow the street through Lagos' restaurant row. Enjoy the colorful tiles on building fronts. This was the town's finest street, and home to its noble families in the 19th century. The crest of the hill marks the start of the most popular night spots, with boisterous bars and popular discos, such as Bon Vivant.

• *Eventually you come to the...*

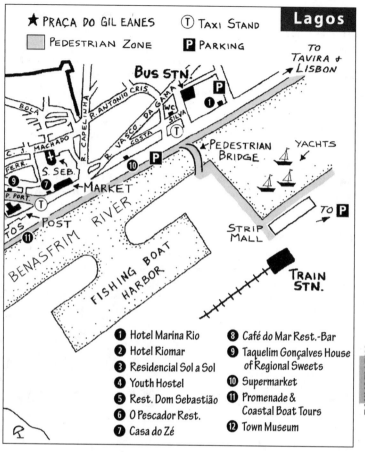

★ PRAÇA DO GIL EANES   Ⓣ TAXI STAND

▢ PEDESTRIAN ZONE   🅿 PARKING

Lagos

TO TAVIRA & LISBON

BUS STN.

PEDESTRIAN BRIDGE

YACHTS

MARKET

STRIP MALL

POST

BENASFRIM RIVER

FISHING BOAT HARBOR

TRAIN STN.

TO 🅿

❶ Hotel Marina Rio
❷ Hotel Riomar
❸ Residencial Sol a Sol
❹ Youth Hostel
❺ Rest. Dom Sebastião
❻ O Pescador Rest.
❼ Casa do Zé
❽ Café do Mar Rest.-Bar
❾ Taquelim Gonçalves House of Regional Sweets
❿ Supermarket
⓫ Promenade & Coastal Boat Tours
⓬ Town Museum

THE ALGARVE

▲Church of St. Anthony (Santo António) and the Town Museum

Tourists enter the Church of St. Anthony through the town museum. Lagos' humble little museum, while old-school, has some fascinating exhibits with good English descriptions (€3, Tue-Sun 10:00-17:30, closed Mon). You'll see ancient Roman mosaics, amphorae, and busts, models of traditional boats, octopus jugs, and other fishing gear. The chimneys, so character-istic of those you see all over the Algarve, are nicknamed "chimneys of the new Christians." According to tour guides, while Muslim Moors forced to convert

in the 13th century became nominal Christians, they worshipped privately under chimneys like these, which were inspired by and reminiscent of the minarets of their destroyed mosques.

The Church of St. Anthony was built in 1707, then rebuilt around 1800 after the 1755 earthquake. Considered one of the finest Baroque/Rococo churches in Portugal, it's dedicated to the patron saint of the military. The altar is shiny with Brazilian gold leaf. Paintings show the miracles of St. Anthony (each described in English), the ceiling is a festival of 3-D, and the exuberant cupids are all very expressive.

• *Exit the church, take two rights, and walk a block downhill to the next church, Santa Maria (daily 9:00-12:00 & 15:00-18:00). After being rebuilt many times, it's more modern and vibrant. Across the square, standing as if hoping you won't notice, is the...*

▲Slave Market Museum (Mercado de Escravos)

A humble one-room museum, located on the site of the original Lagos slave market, documents the tragic history of slavery in the region, which began at this very spot in 1444. Displays include some 15th-century coins, African ceramics and beads, and a skeleton—one of several found in a nearby rubbish dump (€1.50, Mon-Sat 10:00-17:30, closed Sun). In the small portico outside, chained slaves were paraded around to be bid on. From 1444 until the mid-1700s, over 100,000 individual slaves were sold under these arches. In the early days of Portuguese exploration, the king made a rule that ships needed to bring back dirt, plants, and people from "discovered" lands. Slaves were quarantined for 40 days. Survivors were cleaned up and sold. Now a memorial, the building is painted red (for the blood of the slaves) and gold (for the power of the crown). The spices hanging from the ceiling symbolize the various imports that made Portugal wealthy (yams, chile peppers, coconuts, and gold).

• *The square between the slave market and Santa Maria Church is...*

Praça Infante Dom Henrique

This square honors its namesake, Henry the Navigator, with a statue (erected along with the city's fine harborfront promenade in 1960 to celebrate the 500th anniversary of his death; he died just down the coast in Sagres in 1460).

Portugal's age of discovery started in 1415 in Lagos under Prince Henry (before he earned his nickname "the Navigator"). Up to 400 ships would depart on huge royal-sponsored expeditions from this port. The glory days of Lagos lasted through the 1400s, but by 1500 the action shifted to Lisbon. The slave trade enriched the city in the 15th and 16th centuries. Later, Lagos was a tuna-fishing center and the military capital of the Algarve. But the 1755 earthquake/tsunami devastated the city, spelling the end of its importance.

• *From the square, walk along the old city walls toward the striking fort on the harbor. The walls of Lagos, measuring nearly two miles, are the longest in the Algarve. Pause at the fortified Moorish gate with its stout twin crenelated towers. The first wall here dates from the ninth century.*

Fort Ponta da Bandeira

Fort Ponta da Bandeira was a state-of-the-art defense back in the 17th century, built to protect the city against pirates and Spaniards. Today it offers the visitor only stony ramparts and harbor views (€3, 10:00-18:00, closed Mon).

• *Continue walking beyond the fort, passing the Lagos Nautical Club (which rents canoes and kayaks), a public WC, and a boardwalk across*

the sand leading to Praia da Batata (Potato Beach), a popular student hangout. At low tide, you can enjoy a fascinating beach walk through exotic rocks and tunnels for nearly a mile. At high tide, a stepped and paved path takes you along the beach but higher up, with fine views of remote, photogenic little beaches with striking rock formations.

From Praia da Batata, a trail leads up to Café do Mar, which crowns a bluff with wonderful outdoor tables overlooking the harbor and sea (described in "Eating in Lagos," later).

Activities in Lagos

Lagos Market Hall

The small market hall faces the harbor as if waiting for the fishermen to unload their catch (as they do almost daily at 8:00 and 11:00). The Algarve's third-biggest fish market welcomes visitors to peruse an impressive array of fish, all netted within a few miles of town. Upstairs are fresh fruits and vegetables, dried figs, and nuts. You'll also see fun, gifty local products like spicy homemade *piri-piri* sauce and "flower of salt" from Tavira's salt beds, respected all over Europe (Mon-Sat until 13:00, closed Sun). Snails *(caracois)*, which come out after rain, are sold by merchants, but their prices are generally undercut by street-sellers.

▲Lagos' Promenade

This pedestrian avenue stretches about a mile from the fort to the marina. It's a joy to stroll along the black-and-white patterned cobbles (Portugal's unique *calçada* stonework), with views of palm trees and busy little boats, a soundtrack of gulls and hustlers of various sea activities, and the smell of "the perfume of the Atlantic."

Coastal Boat Tours

Along the harborfront promenade, you'll be hustled to take a sightseeing cruise. There's plenty of creativity and competition, giving you lots of options (which are usually cash only). Old fishermen ("who know the nickname of each rock along the coast") sit at anchor on board, while their salespeople on the promenade hawk 45-minute exotic rock-and-cave tours for around €10 (2-person minimum).

More serious maritime adventures are sold by a string of established companies with offices in the marina strip mall over the marina bridge (credit cards accepted). Some pleasant cafés are in the mall—sip a *sumo de laranja* (fresh orange juice) while observing the comings-and-goings of the yachts.

Bom Dia offers several different tours by sailboat: a two-hour grotto tour (with a chance to swim) for €25; a half-day BBQ cruise that's basically a grotto tour with a meal for €49; and a three-hour family-friendly fishing trip for €35 (buy tickets at kiosk on the promenade in marina at Lagos 10, WC on board, smart to reserve at least a day ahead in Aug, tel. 282-087-587, www.bomdia-boattrips.com).

Sleeping in Lagos

When a price range is given, the lowest is the winter rate and the highest is the August rate. Lagos is enjoyable for a resort its size, but remember that Salema, a village paradise, is a short taxi or bus ride away.

$$$ Hotel Marina Rio is big, slick, and comfortable, and faces the marina and the busy main street immediately in front of the bus station. Its 36 modern, air-conditioned rooms have all the amenities. Pricier marina views come with noise; quieter rooms are in the back. All rooms have twin beds (Sb-€74-130, Db-€77-133, extra bed- €28-42, includes breakfast, elevator, guest computer, Wi-Fi, small heated rooftop pool and sun terrace, Avenida dos Descobrimentos, tel. 282-780-830, www.marinario.com, marinario@net.vodafone.pt).

$$ Hotel Riomar, popular with tour groups, provides 42 dimly lit rooms for a decent price in a blocky, 1980s-feeling building (Sb/Db-€33-60, Tb-€47-71, Qb-€62-75, best prices available by booking online, Wi-Fi, air-con, elevator, back rooms lack street noise, Rua Candido dos Reis 83, tel. 282-770-130, www.hotelriomarlagos.com, hotelriomar@sapo.pt).

$$ Residencial Sol a Sol is basic but well-run, with 15 decent rooms in the heart of town (Sb/Db-€40-65, no breakfast, Wi-Fi, 24-hour reception, Rua Lançarote de Freitas 22, tel. 282-761-290, www.residencialsolasol.hostel.com, residencialsolasol@gmail.com).

$ The youth hostel is a busy, social, hammocks-in-the-courtyard experience (64 beds total, dorm bed in quad-€10-17 depending on the season, five Db-€28-45, includes breakfast, kitchen facilities, guest computer, Wi-Fi, priority given to hostel members, nonmembers of any age welcome, Rua Lançarote de Freitas 50, tel. 282-761-970, www.pousadasjuventude.pt, lagos@movijovem.pt).

Eating in Lagos

You'll find a variety of lively choices for dinner branching out in all directions from Praça Gil Eanes. Most of them offer a similar sampling of grilled fish with plenty of vegetables, but other options range from Italian to Indian. Home-style cooking is likely better closer to the market.

Restaurante Dom Sebastião, with elegant service, gourmet cuisine, and a huge wine cellar, is busy with in-the-know expats enjoying a splurge. Antonio runs one of the best restaurants in the West Algarve in a hands-on way with thoughtful touches, including a basket of sun-dried figs and almonds with port wine as a free meal-capping thank you. While the people-watching is great from the outside tables, I like the energy inside. Portions (€12-15 plates) are big and you're welcome to split. When split, the €17 *cataplana* becomes an amazing value (daily 12:00-22:00, reservations smart, air-con, Rua 25 de Abril 20, tel. 282-780-480, www.restaurantedonsebastiao.com).

O Pescador, popular with locals and tourists alike, serves good, inexpensive grilled fish and meat in a simple, bright atmosphere. Portions are large and easily splittable (daily 12:00-22:00, until 23:00 in summer, Rua Gil Eanes 6, tel. 282-767-028). Hardworking João speaks little English but is eager to please.

Casa do Zé is a very traditional, family-run diner facing the harbor next to the market. It's just right if you want to feel like a temporary local and write a poem (daily 12:00-22:00, €10 plate of day, Rua Portas de Portugal 65, tel. 282-762-038).

Café do Mar Restaurante Bar is perched on a bluff overlooking the sea and the city, just above the first of the exotic beaches. It's at the end of my town walk and is good for a drink, snack, light meal, pizza, or full-blown dinner (€9 pizzas and pastas, inside or outside seating, just above and beyond the fortress overlooking Praia da Batata, tel. 282-788-006).

Taquelim Gonçalves House of Regional Sweets is the local favorite for fresh-baked pastries, ice cream, and coffee. It offers a fine vantage point on the square for enjoying the scene. Their almond and custard tarts and marzipan are hits (Rua da Porta de Portugal 27, tel. 282-762-882).

Picnics: **Intermarché** supermarket has a wide selection of food (daily 8:00-21:00, on the waterfront opposite the marina, look for the black facade).

Lagos Connections

From Lagos by Train and Bus to: Lisbon (5 trains/day, 4 hours, transfer in Tunes or Faro, €24; 5 buses/day, 4 hours; €20), **Évora** (3 trains/day, 5-6 hours, transfer in Pinhal Novo and Tunes or Faro; 3 buses/day with transfer in Albufeira or Faro, 1 bus/day direct in summer only, 5 hours), **Tavira** (9 trains/day, 3 hours; 6 buses/day, 4 hours, both transfer in Faro). Confirm times locally. Train info: tel. 808-208-208, www.cp.pt. Bus info: tel. 289-899-760 or 282-762-944, www.eva-bus.com or www.algarvebus.info.

Connecting Lagos and Sevilla, Spain, by Bus: There are four buses per day in each direction during summer (€21, about 5.5 hours from Lagos bus station to Sevilla's Plaza de Armas bus station, buy ticket a day or two in advance May-Oct, 2/day in off-season). Ask the TI or a local travel agency for the latest bus schedule, or check www.algarvebus.info or www.eva-bus.com. This is the usual schedule, but confirm it locally: Buses for Sevilla depart Lagos at 6:15, 7:30, 12:30, and 14:45. Buses for Lagos depart Sevilla at 7:30, 8:00, 13:30, and 16:45. Note that Spanish time is one hour ahead of Portuguese time, so you'll arrive in Lagos about three hours after you depart Sevilla and arrive in Sevilla about five hours after departing Lagos. In summer, be sure to purchase your ticket at least one day in advance.

From Lagos to Salema: Take a bus (every 1-2 hours, fewer on weekends, 30 minutes, €2.60) or a taxi (€25-30, 20 minutes); see "Orientation to Salema" on page 139 for details. In Lagos, to get to the bus station from the train station, walk left out of the train station, go through the pink strip mall, cross the arched pedestrian bridge and then the main boulevard, and angle right over to the white-and-yellow EVA bus station (bus info: tel. 289-899-760 or 282-762-944, www.eva-bus.com). Before heading to Salema, pick up return bus schedules and train schedules for your next destination.

Tavira

Straddling a river, with a lively park, chatty locals, and boats that share its waterfront center, Tavira (tah-VEE-rah) is a low-rise,  easygoing alternative to the other more aggressive Algarve resorts. It's your best eastern Algarve stop.

Because Tavira has good connections by bus and train (it's on the trans-Algarve train line, with frequent departures both east and west), the town is more accessible than Salema. If you're driving from Sevilla to Salema, it's the perfect midway stop on the four-hour trip (just two miles off the freeway). You can also get to Tavira by bus from Sevilla.

You'll see many churches and fine bits of Renaissance architecture sprinkled throughout the town. These clues are evidence that 500 years ago, Tavira was the largest town on the Algarve (with 1,500 dwellings according to a 1530 census) and an important base for Portuguese adventurers in Africa.

The silting up of its harbor, a plague in 1645, the offshore 1755 earthquake, and the shifting away of its once-lucrative tuna industry left Tavira in a long decline. Today, the town has a wistful charm and lives off its tourists.

Orientation to Tavira

Tavira straddles the Rio Gilão two miles from the Atlantic. Everything of sightseeing and transportation importance is on the south bank. A clump of historic sights—the ruined castle and main church—fills its tiny fortified hill and tangled Moorish lanes. But today, the action is outside the old fortifications along the riverside Praça da República square and the adjacent shady fountain- and bench-filled park. The old market hall is beyond the park. And beyond that is the boat to the beach island. The old pedestrian-only Roman Bridge leads from Praça da República to the north bank (with most of the evening and restaurant action). With the exception of Clive's fun, fascinating Câmara Obscura show (described in "Sights in Tavira," later), the town's sights are pretty dull.

TOURIST INFORMATION

The TI is on the main square, Praça da República, right across from City Hall (June-Sept daily 9:00-18:00; Oct-May Tue-Thu 9:00-

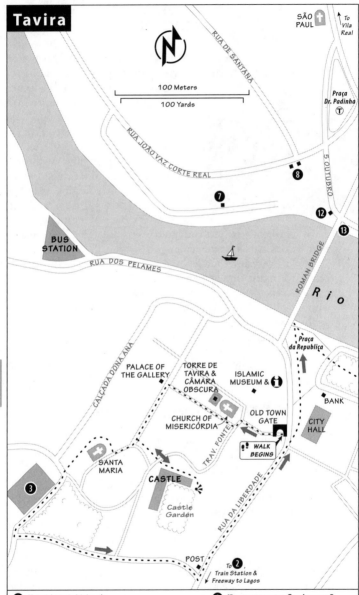

Tavira

THE ALGARVE

1. Residencial Marés
2. To Tavira House Hotel
3. Convento da Graça Pousada
4. Residencia Princesa do Gilão
5. Residencial Lagôas
6. Aquasul Restaurante
7. Restaurante Beira Rio
8. Restaurante Os Arcos & Casa Abilio Bike Rental
9. Supermarket
10. Pasteleria Ramos
11. Soares Wine Shop
12. Internet Shop
13. Tourist Train

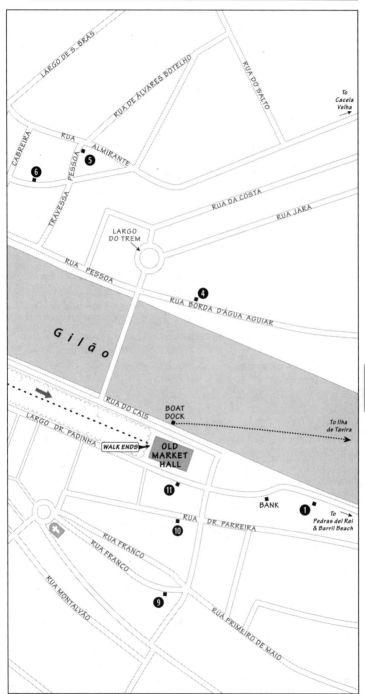

18:00, Fri-Mon 9:00-13:00 & 14:00-18:00; Praça da República 5, tel. 281-322-511). Their €0.50 town leaflet is helpful.

ARRIVAL IN TAVIRA

By Train: The train station is a 20-minute walk from the town center. To get there, leave the station via the roundabout and follow the signpost to *centro* (center). Follow this road downhill to the river and Praça da República (or take a cab from the station for around €4). The riverside bus station is three blocks from the town center; simply follow the river into town.

By Car: Drivers can park on the street in much of the old town. It's pay-and-display for up to two hours (€0.40/hour, Mon-Fri 9:00-19:00, Sat 9:00-14:00, Sun free, look for *zona pago* signs, pay at blue boxes marked *caixa,* change required). Free parking is available farther from the center.

HELPFUL HINTS

Internet Access: Free Wi-Fi is available throughout the city center, in the old market hall, at many cafés, and at the modern library in town. The **Internet Shop** is just over the bridge (30 minutes-€1.50, daily 9:00-21:00, Rua 5 de Outubro 7).

Bike Rental: You can rent bikes at **Casa Abilio** (€9/day, €20 deposit includes padlock, Mon-Sat 9:00-19:00, closed Sun, Rua João Vaz Corte Real 23-A, just across the Roman Bridge to the left, tel. 281-323-467).

Taxi: A taxi stand is across the Roman Bridge on Praça Dr. António Padinha.

Shopping Tip: You can buy your own copper cataplana pot for about €35 at the yellow hardware store at the far end of Rua Alexandro Herculano (behind City Hall). And for a wonderful selection of port wine, visit the helpful **Soares Wine Shop** (Mon-Sat 10:00-24:00 in summer, otherwise 10:00-19:00, closed Sun, facing market hall at Rua José Pires Padinha 66).

Sights in Tavira

The sights are listed here in a logical walking order starting near the TI on Praça da República (the town square).

Old Town Gate

This unimpressive gate (to the left of the TI) is one of the few sections left from Tavira's 16th-century wall. Check out the gate's crown and spheres—meant to remind visitors that they are in the kingdom of Portugal—and the holes for bars that once locked the door.

• *At the top of the lane, above the gate, stands a church.*

Church of Misericórdia

Dating from 1541, the Renaissance facade is considered the finest in the Algarve. Inside, you'll see a multitude of blue-and-white tile panels that illustrate how to lead a good Christian life and an over-the-top, gold-plated altar. A zealous attendant will make sure you don't take any photos. Throughout the year, the church transforms into a beautiful concert venue. Ask the attendant if any performances are scheduled during your visit.

Cost and Hours: Church entry free, Mon-Sat 9:00-12:30 & 14:00-19:00, off-season until 17:30, closed Sun.

• *Continue walking west to...*

Palace of the Gallery

This 17th-century Baroque palace, nearly the town's highest point, is nicknamed "Tavira's Acropolis." It's the biggest private mansion in town and houses an exhibition center, open to the public, with rotating themes: contemporary art or Tavira's maritime history. Even if you don't go into the museum itself, pop inside the door to see some Phoenician ritual pits, visible through glass covers on the foyer floor.

Cost and Hours: €2, Tue-Sat 10:00-12:30 & 15:00-18:30, off-season until 17:30, closed Sun-Mon.

• *Climb uphill to the big Church of Santa Maria. Across the way, on your left, is a hunk of castle with a door leading to the...*

Castle Garden

The base of the castle wall is supposedly Neolithic, while later inhabitants—the Phoenicians in the eighth century B.C., the Moors in the eighth century A.D., and the Portuguese in the thirteenth century—added their own layers. The castle grounds are now a fragrant garden, offering a fine city view. Overlooking the city, notice Tavira's unique "treasury" rooftops—a little roof for each room of a building. Tour guides have two explanations for this: The small roofs were inspired by visions brought home from Asia by local explorers. Or they are the result of this region having a shortage of big trees and therefore using small timbers for beams. (Portugal has long been short on timbers, naming its major colony "Brazil," the Portuguese word for a very valuable type of wood—apparently the colonists were particularly excited about that raw material.) Gaze to the right and see tower-wall remnants sprouting up between houses.

Cost and Hours: Free, Mon-Fri 8:00-17:00, Sat-Sun 10:00-17:00, daily until 19:00 in July-Sept.

Church of Santa Maria

Once a mosque, this church was transformed in the 13th century. It may be closed for repairs when you visit. If it's open, go inside

THE ALGARVE

and check out the second chapel on the left—the only part of the church that survived the 1755 earthquake. The third chapel has fine pink columns. The "marble" is actually painted wood, since there was no marble in the Algarve and no money to import it. I was told that while the town has 21 churches, there's only one active priest.

There's a small charge to enter the church's museum (crude but beautiful art in three rooms) and bell tower (peer past the bells to enjoy a commanding city view, with surviving bits of town wall and coastline nearby). Japanese-inspired paintings show Portuguese sailors braving the stormy seas off Tavira (WC at base of bell tower).

• *Facing the rear of the church, turn right. Just around the corner is the...*

Torre de Tavira and Câmara Obscura (Tavira Tower and Darkroom)

This 1931 water tower has been converted into a viewpoint, with a darkroom designed to accommodate an early optical device called

a camera obscura. Clive, the British owner, narrates an entertaining 15-minute, 360-degree view of Tavira in real time with the help of his 1899 lens as he describes the town's history. It's not "rain or shine"—without the sun, there's no image. This is the best show in this sleepy town (€3.50, daily May-Sept 10:00-18:00, Oct-April 10:00-17:00, shorter and variable hours and closed weekends in winter, elevator, tel. 281-321-754, www.cdepa.pt).

• *Head north along Rua da Liberdade to reach the...*

Roman Bridge

The "Roman Bridge" may not be Roman, but it was here when the Moors came. The current structure is from 1657, with parts rebuilt after a 1989 flood. The more functional bridge on your right was designed to be temporary, until the Roman Bridge was fixed, but it was better than the Roman Bridge for car traffic—so since 1989, the old bridge has been pedestrian-only.

• *Walk east along the river to reach the...*

Riverside Park and Old Market Hall

This is where old folks gossip and children play. Walk past the bandstand to the old market hall. In the 1990s, this was a noisy, colorful fish and produce market. Today, the hall has gift shops, free Wi-Fi, cafés, and one restaurant with riverside seating.

Beyond the market hall are a few fishing boats. Fishermen are weathering tough times as the "natural park" classification of the coastal areas makes aggressive netting illegal, and Spanish fishermen are selling their catch for far less.

Nearby: **Pasteleria Ramos,** near the market end of the park opposite a green kiosk, produces sweet and sticky *tartes de almendoas partidos* (almond cakes-€2), perfect with a *galão* (milky coffee) at their red outside tables (daily 8:00-24:00).

Sights near Tavira

▲Ilha de Tavira

Tavira's beach island is a hit with travelers. Ilha de Tavira is an almost treeless, six-mile-long sandbar with a campground, several restaurants, and a sprawling beach. A summer-only boat takes bathers painlessly from downtown Tavira to the island (€2 round-trip, June-mid-Sept about hourly 8:00-20:00, timetable at TI, departs from dock just past the old market hall). A year-round water taxi provides service in the off-season (5-minute walk beyond the old market hall, opposite Barclays Bank, mobile 966-615-071). It's an enjoyable ride even if you just go round-trip without getting off.

For an all-year shuttle ferry service, you can also bus, taxi, ride a rental bike, or hike a shadeless mile out of town, past the salt pans and fish farms, to Quatro Aguas, where a five-minute ferry shuttles sunbathers to Ilha de Tavira (€1.50 one-way, year-round ferry runs constantly with demand, last trip at 19:00 or near midnight in high season to accommodate diners).

A cheesy **tourist train** runs out to Quatro Aguas on its hour-long tour of Tavira's highlights (€3.50, first departure at 10:00, then usually every 30-60 minutes until around 20:00, leaves from across the Roman Bridge).

▲Barril Beach

This fine beach resort is two miles from Tavira. Walk, rent a bike, or take a city bus to Pedras del Rei, and then catch the little train (usually runs year-round), or walk 10 minutes through Ria Formosa Natural Park to the resort. Get details at the TI.

Cacela Velha

This tiny village lies through the orange groves about eight miles east of Tavira (half-mile off the main road and the bus route). It sits happily ignored on a hill with its fort, church, one restaurant, a few *quartos* and apartments (try Maria Antoinetta, mobile 965-858-630), and a beach with the open sea just over the sandbar a short row across its lagoon. The restaurant—Casa De Igreja—serves sausages *(chouricos)* and cheese *(queijo)* specialties fried at your table, along with local oysters (€10/dozen, great with *vinho verde;* daily July-Sept, March-June weekends only, closed Oct-Feb, tel. 281-952-126, Patricio speaks English). If you're driving, swing by, if only to enjoy the coastal view and to imagine how nice the Algarve would be if people like you and me had never discovered it.

Sleeping in Tavira

In Tavira, prices usually shoot up in August.

$$$ Residencial Marés, on the busy side of the river amid all the strolling and café ambience, has 24 good rooms, a friendly reception, an upscale restaurant, and an inviting rooftop terrace with lounge chairs. Some rooms have balconies overlooking the river, but also come with a little noise from cafés immediately below (Sb-€30-65; Db-€85-100 in summer, otherwise €55; extra bed-€10, includes breakfast, air-con, Wi-Fi, sauna-€5; Rua José Pires Padinha 134/140, just beyond old market hall; tel. 281-325-815, www.residencialmares.com, maresresidencial@mail.telepac.pt).

$$$ Tavira House Hotel is a charming nine-room boutique B&B filling a lovingly renovated and decorated army officer's house from 1860. The place is thoughtfully run with lots of flowers, a popular wine-tasting, and an inviting roof terrace. It's buried in the old town under the castle, a two-minute walk from the main square (Db around €120, Wi-Fi, Rua Miguel Bombardo 47, tel. 281-370-307, www.tavirahousehotel.com).

$$$ Convento da Graça is a *pousada* (government-sponsored historic inn) with 36 sumptuously appointed rooms inside a former Augustine convent. The cloister is perfect for relaxing, and there's even a pool if you can't tear yourself away to go to the beach. It's at the top of the old town, a five-minute walk from the main square (Db around €120, discounts often available online, Rua D. Paio Peres Correia, tel. 281-442-001, www.pousadas.pt, guest@pousadas.pt).

$$ Residencia Princesa do Gilão is a low-energy place offering 22 small, old-fashioned, basic rooms. Choose between riverfront or quiet rooms on the back with a terrace (Sb-€42-52, Db-€48-58, Tb-€58-68, Qb-€78-88, includes breakfast, grumpy management, Wi-Fi, Rua Borda de Agua de Aguiar 10, cross Roman Bridge and turn right along river, tel. 281-325-171, www.residencial-gilao.com, maresa@residencial-gilao.com).

$ Residencial Lagôas is spotless, homey, and a block off the river. Friendly Claudia and Miquel offer 17 rooms, a communal refrigerator, laundry washboard privileges, and a rooftop patio with a view made for wine and candles (S-€20, D-€25-30, Db-€30-40, Tb-€50, no gouging in July and Aug, cheaper off-season, no breakfast, cash only, some rooms with air-con, Wi-Fi, Rua Almirante Candido dos Reis 24, tel. 281-328-243, al.lagoas@hotmail.com). Cross the Roman Bridge from Praça da República, follow the middle fork on the other side, and turn right where it ends.

Eating in Tavira

Tavira is filled with reasonable restaurants. Your best bets lie across the river (where lively, top-end places face the riverbank just beyond the old market hall) and inland a couple of blocks (where hole-in-the-wall options offer more fish per dollar). It's fun to walk around and scout out your options.

Aquasul—mod, bright, cheery, on a back lane, and open only for dinner—is my favorite. Wenda runs it with passion, serving a modern fusion of Italian and Mediterranean dishes, including nightly vegetarian specials, good pizzas out of the wood oven (€10), and tasty homemade desserts (€7 starters, €15 plates, three-course meals-€22, Tue-Sat 18:30-22:30, closed Sun-Mon; go over the bridge, continue one block and turn right on to Rua Dr. A. S. Carvalho 13; tel. 281-325-166). If it's full or doesn't do it for you, check out several other appealing places spilling out onto the same street.

On the River: I recommend two riverside restaurants. For both, cross the Roman Bridge, turn left, go through the tunnel, and look for tables on the waterfront.

Restaurante Beira Rio is Irish-owned, as reflected in the menu and the fun Irish bar next door. It has good seating inside and riverside, with an extensive menu and lots of fish (€15 meals, nightly 18:30-22:30, Rua Borda d'Agua da Asseca 46, tel. 281-323-165, mobile 916-822-117).

Restaurante Os Arcos is simpler, with cheap and tasty grilled fish served at rustic little riverside tables or inside a characteristic dining hall. They offer €5-7 seafood specials and a slew of fun €2 dishes (Mon-Sat for lunch and dinner, closed Sun, Rua João Vaz Corte Real 15, tel. 963-583-527).

Supermarket: **Minipreço** has all the groceries you'll need for a good picnic. It's centrally located, a couple of blocks inland from the market hall (daily 9:00-21:00, Rua D. Marcelino Franco 40).

Tavira Connections

From Tavira by Train and Bus to: Lisbon (5 trains/day, 4-5 hours, transfer in Faro, arrive at Oriente; 5 direct buses/day, 4.25 hours), **Lagos** (9 trains/day, change in Faro, 3 hours; 6 buses/day, 4 hours,

THE ALGARVE

change in Faro), **Sevilla** (4 buses/day in summer, 2/day in winter, 3-4 hours; summer bus leaves at 8:10, 9:05, 14:25, and 16:20, check TI or bus station to verify schedules; buy ticket a day or two in advance May-Oct, note that Spain is an hour ahead when calculating arrival times). Luggage storage is not available. Train info: tel. 808-208-208, www.cp.pt. Bus info: tel. 281-322-546, www. eva-bus.com or www.algarvebus.info, bus ticket office open 7:30-19:00, closed 12:00-15:00 on weekends.

ROUTE TIPS FOR DRIVERS IN THE ALGARVE

Lisbon to Salema (185 miles, 3.5 hours): Following the blue *Sul Ponte* signs, drive south over Lisbon's 25th of April Bridge. A short detour just over the bridge takes you to the giant concrete statue of Cristo Rei (Christ in Majesty). Continue south by freeway until you hit the coast, and follow signs west to Lagos. Take the Lagos/Vila do Bispo exit and follow signs to *Vila do Bispo* and *Sagres*. If you pay attention, you'll see the turnoff for Salema before Vila do Bispo. A modern freeway, less traffic, and the glory of waking up on the Algarve make doing this drive in the evening after a full day in Lisbon a good option.

Algarve to Sevilla (175 miles, 3 hours): Drive east along the Algarve. It's a 1.5-hour drive from Salema to Tavira, with some hills crowned by rotting windmills and others by mobile-phone towers. In Lagos, parking is most convenient in the free lot near the old city wall off Rua Infante de Sagres (pay parking at marina and underground parking garage near Praça do Infante). From Lagos, hit the freeway (A-22, direction: Lisboa/Faro, then Espanha) to Tavira. Leaving Tavira, follow the signs to *Espanha*. You'll cross the bridge into Spain (where it's one hour later) and glide effortlessly (1.5 hours by freeway) into Sevilla. Be aware that there is an electronic tolling system on the A-22 highway from the Spanish border to Lagos (for details, see "Tolls" on page 387).

THE ALGARVE

ÉVORA

Deep in the heart of Portugal, in the sizzling, arid plains of the southern province of Alentejo, historic Évora (EH-voh-rah) has been a cultural oasis for 2,000 years. With an untouched provincial atmosphere, a fascinating whitewashed old town, museums, a cathedral, a chapel of bones, and even a Roman temple, Évora (pop. 56,600) stands proudly amid groves of cork and olive trees.

Évora—a traditional, conservative city with a small-town feel—reopened its historic university about 40 years ago. You'll see plenty of college-age students here, along with lots of retirees, but comparatively few 30- to 40-year olds. There's not much to keep graduates around, and this generation gap gives the town an intriguing mix of old and new—strong traditions underlie its younger side.

PLANNING YOUR TIME

With easy bus and train connections to Lisbon (buses almost hourly, four trains a day; both take 1.5 hours), Évora makes a decent day trip from Portugal's capital city. You can stop by for an overnight stay en route to or from the Algarve, which is five hours away (3-4 buses a day). Drivers can sandwich Évora between Lisbon and the Algarve, exploring dusty droves of olive groves and scruffy seas of peeled cork trees along the way. Take the freeway from the Algarve to Beja, and the nearly-as-fast highway from Beja to Évora. A super freeway zips you from Évora to Lisbon in 90 minutes.

With a day in Évora, follow my self-guided walk outlined on page 184, have a quick lunch, see the remaining sights, and enjoy a leisurely, top-notch dinner. After dinner, stroll the back streets and ponder life, like the retired men of Évora seem to do so expertly.

Orientation to Évora

Évora's old town, contained within a medieval wall, is surrounded by the sprawling newer part of town. The major sights—the Roman Temple and early Gothic cathedral—crowd together at the old town's highest point. A subtle yet still-powerful charm is contained within the medieval walls. Find it by losing yourself in the quiet lanes of Évora's far corners.

TOURIST INFORMATION

Pick up a free map at the TI on the main square at Praça do Giraldo 73 (April-Oct daily 9:00-19:00, Nov-March Mon-Fri 9:00-18:00, Sat-Sun 10:00-14:00 & 15:00-18:00, tel. 266-777-071, www.cm-evora.pt/en).

ARRIVAL IN ÉVORA

By Bus: The bus station is west of the center, on Avenida São Sebastião. To reach the town center, take a short taxi ride (€5) or a 10-minute walk (exit station right, continue straight all the way into town, past the cemetery wall and through the city gates at the halfway point).

By Train: The train station is south of the center, on Avenida Dr. Barahona. To get to the center, take a taxi (€7), or walk a long 25 minutes up Avenida Dr. Barahona, continuing straight on Rua da República after you enter the city walls.

By Car: Drivers will find Évora's old town frustrating because of its tiny one-way streets. Park in one of the big, free parking lots that circle the town just outside the walls (see map on page 182 for locations). The green-and-white Trevo shuttle bus (see below) serves the parking lots and most hotels.

HELPFUL HINTS

Internet Access: The town hall, on Praça de Sertório, has free Wi-Fi and free computers that are often busy (Mon-Fri 9:00-17:00, closed Sat-Sun; this is a stop on my self-guided town walk, page 184). You can also find free Wi-Fi at many cafés and on both Praça do Giraldo and Praça de Sertório.

Taxis: Cabs wait on the main square (€3.90 minimum for 2.5 miles—4 kilometers—likely the farthest you'd go in compact Évora).

Shuttle Bus: The blue line on the streets marks the route of the green-and-white Trevo shuttle bus that circles through the town, offering tourists easy transport to and from the parking lots outside the walls. Hop on for a city joyride (€1); they stop for anyone who waves.

Fado Entertainment: Although fado is not as popular here as it is in Lisbon or Coimbra, the recommended **Adega Típica Bota Alta** has live fado music on Friday and Saturday evenings (see page 201). The TI can suggest other places to hear fado.

Fun Ice-Cream Stop: Zoka, a local favorite for ice cream, has tables on a quiet, inviting square just 100 yards off the main square, Praça do Giraldo (daily 9:00-22:00, off Largo de S. Vicente, Rua Miguel Bombarda 14, tel. 266-703-133).

Tours in Évora

Walking Tour

A group of local guides offers excellent two-hour city walks every morning, departing from the TI at 10:00 (€12, 2-person minimum, call ahead to confirm tour will run, mobile 963-702-392, info@alentejoguides.com). The tour hits the sights described in this chapter, but it's a great opportunity to connect with a local and enliven your visit. They are also happy to schedule tours at other times (€24, 2-person minimum).

Bus Tours

A bus tour is a good option if you want to see the prehistoric sights near Évora, since getting there by public transport is nearly impossible. **Ebora Megalithica Guided Tours** runs an interesting daily minivan tour led by archaeologists to four megalithic sites: Cromeleque dos Almendres, the Zambujeiro burial mound, the standing stone of Menhir dos Almendres, and Alto de São Bento (€25/half-day, morning and afternoon departures, 6-person maximum; reserve a day ahead through the TI, at most hotels, by phone, or via email; tel. 964-808-337, www.eboramegalithica.com, eboramegalithica@gmail.com).

RSI offers several half-day bus and minivan tours into the surrounding countryside. Their "Megalithic Circuit Tour" visits the main prehistoric sights, including Cromeleque dos Almendres (€30/half-day, 2-person minimum, discounts for larger groups, pick up flyer at TI, smart to reserve a day ahead, tel. 268-333-228, www.rsi-viagens.com, info.evora@rsi-viagens.com).

Local Guides

Professor **Libânio Murteira Reis**—who has a passion for his native Alentejo region and loves to share it with others—organizes town and regional tours; he'll even take you around in his car (€100/half-day, €190/day for a family up to 4, transport—when required—and admission fees not included, confirm price on reserving, tel. 917-236-025, but best to contact via email at m.murteira@mail.telepac.pt).

ÉVORA

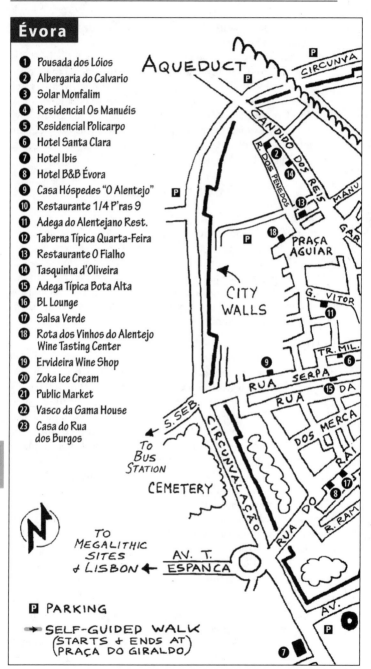

Évora

1. Pousada dos Lóios
2. Albergaria do Calvario
3. Solar Monfalim
4. Residencial Os Manuéis
5. Residencial Policarpo
6. Hotel Santa Clara
7. Hotel Ibis
8. Hotel B&B Évora
9. Casa Hóspedes "O Alentejo"
10. Restaurante 1/4 P'ras 9
11. Adega do Alentejano Rest.
12. Taberna Típica Quarta-Feira
13. Restaurante O Fialho
14. Tasquinha d'Oliveira
15. Adega Típica Bota Alta
16. BL Lounge
17. Salsa Verde
18. Rota dos Vinhos do Alentejo Wine Tasting Center
19. Ervideira Wine Shop
20. Zoka Ice Cream
21. Public Market
22. Vasco da Gama House
23. Casa do Rua dos Burgos

ÉVORA

AQUEDUCT

CIRCUNVA

CANDIDO DOS REIS

R. DOS PENEDOS

MANU

GAR

CITY WALLS

PRAÇA AGUIAR

G. VITOR

TR. MIL.

RUA SERPA

RUA DA

DOS MERCA

RAI

RUA DO

R. RAM

S. SEB.

To BUS STATION

CEMETERY

CIRCUNVALAÇÃO

N

To MEGALITHIC SITES & LISBON ←

AV. T. ESPANCA

AV.

P PARKING

→ SELF-GUIDED WALK
(STARTS & ENDS AT)
(PRAÇA DO GIRALDO)

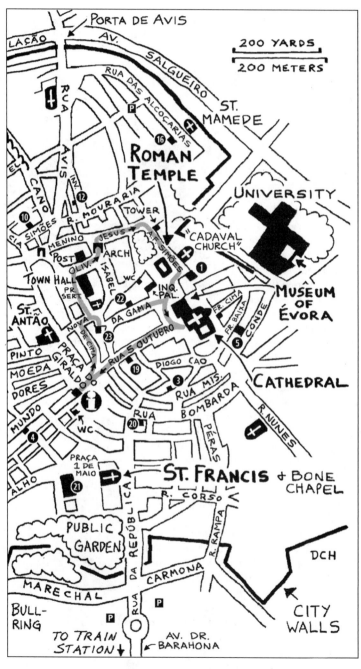

Maria Pires does walking tours of Évora as well as car tours of the surrounding area (€90/half-day, €180/day, price of car tours varies with distance, tel. 917-232-147, m-jose-pires@hotmail.com).

Évora Walk

Évora's walled city is compact, and its key sights are all within a five-minute walk of the main square, Praça do Giraldo (PRA-suh doo zhee-RAHL-doo). This self-guided walk takes about an hour (longer if you visit sights). If it's going to be a hot day, go early in the morning (the cathedral opens at 9:00).

Background: Named a World Heritage Site in 1986, the city has strictly preserved the old center. It works hard to be people-friendly and inviting. The charming colors you see are traditional in Alentejo: Yellow trim is believed to repel evil spirits, and blue actually does keep away flies. Monster garbage cans hide under elegant smaller ones; at night, trucks lift entire hunks of sidewalk to empty them. Jacaranda trees—imported from Brazil 200 years ago—provide shade through the summer and purple flowers in the spring.

From Romans to Moors to Portuguese kings, this little town has a big history. Évora was once a Roman town (second century B.C. to fourth century A.D.), important because of its wealth of wheat and silver, as well as its location on a trade route to Rome. We'll see Roman sights, though most of Évora's Roman past is buried under the houses and hotels of today (often uncovered by accident when plumbing work needs to be done in basements).

The Moors ruled Évora from the 8th to the 12th century. Around the year 1000, Muslim nobles divided the caliphate into small city-states (like Lisbon), with Évora as this region's capital. And during its glory years (15th-16th century), Évora was favored by Portuguese kings, often serving as the home of King John (João) III (1502-1557, Manuel I's son who presided over Portugal's peak of power...and its first decline).

• *Start at Évora's main square.*

Praça do Giraldo: This square was the market during the

Moorish period, and it remains a center of commerce and conviviality for country folk who come to Évora for their weekly shopping. The square is named for Giraldo the Fearless, the Christian knight who led a surprise attack and retook Évora from the Moors in 1165. As thanks, Giraldo was made governor of the town, and he's become the symbol of the city. (Évora's coat of arms is a knight on a horse, usually walking over two beheaded Moors; see it crowning the lampposts.) On this square, all that's left of several centuries of Moorish rule is their artistry, evidenced by the wrought-iron balconies of the buildings that ring the square (and the occasional, distinctive Mudejar "keyhole" window found throughout the town).

Until the 16th century, the area behind the TI was the Jewish quarter. At the time, Christians believed that the Bible prohibited them from charging interest for loans. Jews did the moneylending instead, and the streets in the Jewish quarter still bear names related to finance, such as Rua da Moeda (Money Street) and Rua dos Mercadores (Merchants' Street).

The Roman triumphal arch that once stood on Praça do Giraldo was demolished in the 16th century to make way for the looming Church of Santo Antão. In front of the church is a 16th-century marble fountain—once an important water source for the town (fed by the end of the aqueduct we'll see in a minute) and now a popular hangout for young and old.

King John III lived in Évora off and on for 30 years. The TI is inside the palace where the king's guests used to stay, but others weren't treated as royally. A fervent proponent of the Inquisition, John was king when its first victims were burned as heretics on this square in 1543.

Until recently, the square was a traditional cattle-and-produce market. While ranchers and farmers no longer gather here to make deals, old-timers still gravitate here out of habit. Notice the C.M.E. board (opposite the TI, near the start of Rua 5 de Outubro), where people gather to see a list of who has died recently. You'll see the initials "C.M.E." all over town, from lampposts to manhole covers. It's an abbreviation for Câmara Municipal de Évora—meaning the municipality of Évora. The characteristic arcades you see on buildings around the square fit the weather—providing shelter in the winter and shade in the summer.

• *Leave the square on Rua 5 de Outubro (opposite the TI office). On the first corner, Alforge (daily 10:00-19:00) is a good little shop for gifty gourmet goodies from the region. Outside, note how the back of the shop incorporates the old Roman-Arab wall. From here head left (past Mr. Pickwick's Restaurante) on Alcárcova de Cima. A few steps farther on, you'll see another portion of a Roman wall built into the buildings on your right.*

Roman Remnants: A series of modern windows shows more

Alentejo Region

Southeastern Portugal is very sunny and very dry. The rolling plains of the Alentejo (ah-len-TAY-zhoo) are dotted with large orchards and estates, Stone Age monoliths, Roman aqueducts, Moorish-looking whitewashed villages, and thick-walled, medieval Christian castles.

During the Christian reconquest of the country, Alentejo was the war zone. When Christian conquerors were victorious over the Muslims, they turned over huge tracts of recaptured land to the care of soldier-monks. These recipients came from various religious-military orders, including the Knights Templar and the Order of Christ (which Prince Henry the Navigator once headed—see the Prince Henry sidebar on page 154). Évora was governed by the House of Avis, which produced the kings of Portugal's Age of Discovery.

Despite its royal past, the Alentejo (the land "beyond the River Tejo") is an unpretentious land of farmers. Having been irrigated since Roman and Moorish times, the region is a major producer of wheat, cattle, wine...and trees. You'll see cork oak trees (green leaves, knotted trunks, red underbark of recently harvested trunks), other types of oak (native to the country, once used to build explorers' caravels), olive (dusty green-silver leaves, major export crop), and eucalyptus (tall, cough drop-smelling trees imported from Australia, grown for pulp).

Today, the Alentejo region is known for being extraordinarily traditional, and it is even considered backward by snooty Lisboans. The people of Alentejo don't mind being the butt of jokes. Libanio, my guide in Évora, said it was the mark of a people's character to be able to laugh at themselves. He asked me, "How can you tell a worker is done for the day in Alentejo?" I didn't know. He said, "When he takes his hands out of his pockets." My guide continued more philosophically: "In your land, time is money. Here in Alentejo, time is time. We take things slow and enjoy ourselves." I'm impressed when a region that others are inclined to insult has a strong local pride.

of the Roman wall, which used to surround what is now the inner core of the town. Through the last window, you can see the red paint of a Roman villa built over by the wall. If you look at your town map, you'll notice how the Roman wall, which surrounded the ancient city, left its footprint in the circle of streets defining the city core. The bulk of the wall that currently encircles Évora is from the 14th century, with a more modern stretch from Portugal's 17th-century fight for independence from Spain.

• *Walk straight, sniffing the wonderful scent of pastries coming from the kitchen of Café Arcada (we'll visit the café at the end of this walk), and cross the intersection to find the...*

Aqueduct: This blunt granite-columned end of the town's aqueduct is a relic from the 16th century. The Portuguese have such a fondness for their aqueduct reservoirs that they give them a special name—*Mãe d'Agua* (Mother of Water). Notice the abnormally high sidewalk to your left—it's the aqueduct channel. (On the outskirts of town, the channel sets higher, supported by stone pillars that kept the water flowing downhill.)

• *Return to the intersection at Mãe d'Agua and walk uphill until you reach the large, irregular plaza called Largo de Alexandre Herculano. Take a right to enter the large green doors at #5, the...*

Casa do Rua dos Burgos: This 17th-century house with a Roman foundation contains a small museum, with temporary exhibits on the main floor and a section of Roman wall below (free, Mon-Fri 9:00-18:00, closed Sat-Sun). The house is also home to a regional cultural organization, and staff at the entrance will point the way inside. Walk through the courtyard to view a small collection of Roman artifacts and a large section of the original town wall (including the other side of the section you saw earlier in this walk).

• *Exit the building left and continue one block down Rua de S. Tiago. You'll reach a square that was once congested with parked cars and is now a good example of how the town has become very pedestrian-friendly.*

Praça de Sertório and the Town Hall: The tallest white building on the square is the town hall. Any up-and-coming project for Évora is displayed inside here, including aerial views and scale models that visualize what the future city will look like (Mon-Fri 8:00-17:30, closed Sat-Sun, free Wi-Fi and terminals inside; free Wi-Fi on the square).

Inside the town hall, in the corner on the right, is a view of a Roman bath that was uncovered during a building repair. Step through the glass door to the right of this overlook for a peek at the ongoing excavation.

• *Exit the town hall to the right. Look up to see a church and convent built into a Roman tower (once part of the Roman wall you saw earlier). The grilled windows on the top of the tower enabled the cloistered sisters to enjoy looking at the busy town without being seen. Take a right turn and walk under the arcades past the post office (correios) and take the first left, on Rua de Dona Isabel. You'll immediately see a...*

Roman Arch: This arch, the Porta de Dona Isabel, was once a main gate in the Roman wall. Below are some of the original Roman pavement stones, large and irregular in size and placement.

When you pass under the Roman wall, you're entering a neighborhood called Mouraria (for the Moors). After Giraldo the Fearless retook Évora, the Moors were still allowed to live in the area, but on the other side of this gate, beyond the city walls. They were safe here for centuries...until the Inquisition expelled them in about 1500.

• *Passing under the old arch, turn right, and walk along the road past sod-capped water reservoirs to a patch of grass showing Évora's coat of arms: Giraldo on horseback again. Turn right at the tower, called the Cinco Esquinas (Five Corners) for its five sides, and walk a block up Rua A. F. Simões to...*

Évora's Sight-Packed Square: Here, at the town's high point (1,000 feet above sea level), you'll see the Roman Temple, a public garden, and the dressy Jardim do Paço restaurant, known for its beautiful garden setting (and €10 buffet lunches and dinners). Also on the square is the recommended Pousada dos Lóios, once a 15th-century monastery but now a luxurious hotel with small rooms (blame the monks).

• *To the left of the pousada, stairs lead down into the...*

Church of the Lóios: Stop in to see the church's impressive gold altarpiece. This is the lavish mausoleum chapel of the noble Cadavals, who are still a big-time family, which is why they charge €3 to enter (skip €5 combo-ticket that includes Cadaval palace, Tue-Sun 10:00-12:30 & 14:00-17:00, closed Mon). You'll walk upon Cadaval tombstones throughout your visit; taped chants and liturgical music add to the ambience. Look for the two small trapdoors in the floor that flank the aisle, midway up the church. The one on the right opens up to a deep, dark well (the palace and its church sit upon the remains of a Moorish castle—this was its cistern); the one on the left reveals an ossuary stacked with bones, supposedly belonging to former monks. The noble box (mid-church, high above the pews) is a reminder that the aristocratic family didn't worship with commoners below. The tilework around the altar is from the 17th century—mere decoration with traditional yellow patterns. Along the nave, the tiles are 18th-century, with scenes illuminating Bible stories. The popularity of these tiles (inspired by the blue-and-white Delft tiles of the Netherlands) coincided with the flourishing of tapestries in France and Belgium that had the same teaching purpose.

The grilled windows allowed the Cadaval family to worship without being seen. The room to the right of the altar contains religious art, including a cleverly painted Crucifixion and rare Muslim tilework.

• *Located across from the church is the...*

Roman Temple: With 14 Corinthian columns, this temple was part of the Roman forum and the main square in the first century A.D. Today, the town's open-air concerts and events are staged here against an evocative temple backdrop. It's beautifully floodlit at night. While previously known as the Temple of Diana, it was more likely dedicated to the emperor.

Museum of Évora: This museum stands where the Roman forum once sprawled. An excavated section of the forum is in the museum's courtyard, surrounded by a delightful mix of Roman finds, medieval statuary, and 16th-century Portuguese, Flemish, Italian, and Spanish paintings (€3, free Sun before 14:00, open Tue-Sun 10:00-18:00, last entry 30 minutes before closing, closed Mon, English info sheets, Largo Conde de Vila Flor, tel. 266-702-604, www.museudevora. imc-ip.pt). The museum also contains megalithic artifacts, including some found near Évora at the tomb known as the Anta Grande do Zambujeiro (described on page 196).

• *Across the square from the museum is a white building with the top windows trimmed in yellow. This is the...*

Tribunal of the Inquisition: This building may be closed for renovation when you visit. When finished, it will house a new modern art museum. The building itself stands as a reminder of Évora's notorious past as a tribunal site during Portugal's Inquisition. Here, thousands of innocent people, many of them Jews, were tried and found guilty of crimes against faith. Punishment could be anything from whipping, imprisonment, banishment, slave labor, or, for the most unlucky, death by burning on the main square.

• *Go to the left of the Inquisition headquarters to find a little street called...*

Rua de Vasco da Gama: Globetrotting da Gama is said to have lived on this street after he discovered the water route to India in 1498. His house is 30 yards down the street—find the smudged #15 on your right. Note the fine circa-1500 horseshoe-arch window above. This complex of adjoining buildings—the former Inquisition tribunal and Vasco da Gama's home—are now a cultural exhibition space called the Fórum Fundação Eugenio de Almeida. If it's open, you may be able to get a peek at the 16th-century murals supposedly painted for the global explorer.

• *Backtrack and turn right for the...*

Cathedral: Located behind the museum, this cathedral was built after Giraldo's conquest—on the site of the mosque. (For a description of the cathedral, its cloister, and its museum, see "Sights in Évora," later.)

• *Head downhill on the little street opposite the cathedral's entrance. You're walking on...*

Rua 5 de Outubro: This shopping street, which has served this same purpose since Roman times, connects Évora's main sights with its main square. Its name celebrates October 5, 1910, when Portugal shook off royal rule and became a republic. The street is lined with products of the Alentejo region: cork (even used as postcards), tile, leather, ironwork, and Arraiolos rugs (handmade, with a distinctive weave, in the nearby town of the same name).

For a great opportunity to taste Alentejo wines, stop in at the **Ervideira Wine Shop** at #56. It sits in the old family home of the Count of Ervideira—look for the shrine remnants holding some of the oldest bottles from the winery (located 20 miles outside Évora). They make crisp whites (even from the red tempranillo grape), earthy reds from a secret family recipe, rosés, and the occasional sparkling wine (€2.50 tasting fee for 4 wines, daily 11:00-19:00, Rua 5 de Outubro 56, tel. 266-700-402, www.ervideira.pt).

As you stumble down the shopping street, after passing the intersection with Rua de Burgos, look left to see a blue **shrine** protruding from the wall of a building. The town built it as thanks to God for sparing it from the 1755 earthquake that devastated much of Lisbon. Ahead of you is the main square. The Chapel of Bones and town market are just a few blocks away on your left. But first, stop by the venerable **Café Arcada,** under the arcade near the church. Considered the best pastry shop in town (with the surliest staff), it serves good coffee and the local specialty: fresh, sweet cheese tarts (*queijada,* kay-ZHAH-duh, pay at the bar).

Sights in Évora

▲▲Cathedral of Évora (Sé de Évora)

Portugal has three archbishops, and one resides here in Évora. This important cathedral of Santa Maria de Évora, built in the late 12th century, is a transitional mix of Romanesque and Gothic styles. As happened throughout Iberia, this church was built upon a mosque after the Reconquista succeeded here. That mosque was built upon a Christian Visigothic chapel, proving that religious and military tit for tat is nothing new.

Cost and Hours: Church and cloister-€2.50; view terrace-€1; museum-€3.50; combo-ticket covers everything-€4.50; daily July-Sept 9:00-17:00, Oct-June 9:00-12:30

& 14:00-16:00 (audioguide not very useful, photos OK except in museum, WC under cloister entry).

Visiting the Cathedral: Inside the **cathedral,** in a sumptuous Baroque chapel midway down the nave on the left, is a 15th-century painted marble statue of a pregnant Mary. It's thought that the first priests, hoping to make converts out of Celtic pagans who worshipped mother goddesses, felt they'd have more success if they kept the focus on fertility. Throughout Alentejo, there's a deeply felt affinity for this ready-to-produce-a-savior Mary. Loved ones of mothers giving birth pray here for blessings during difficult deliveries.

Across the aisle, a more realistic Renaissance Gabriel, added a century later, comes to tell Mary her baby won't be just any child. The 16th-century pipe organ still works, and the 18th-century high altar is Neoclassical. Step up close to the high altar to view the ornately decorated chapel filling the apse. The royal box (high on the right, covered in gold leaf) looks down on the space, which is decorated almost entirely by colored marble. Only the muscular Jesus is not marble—he's carved in wood, yet matches the marble all around.

The **Museum of Sacred Art** (Museu de Arte Sacra) is to the right of the main altar. Descend the ramp and steps, then scan the barcode on your ticket to open the door (*empurre* means push). Signage is sparse, but make your way through the chapel reproduction at the entrance, go past the elevator, then turn right. You'll enter a long series of rooms displaying ornaments and artifacts used in the cathedral over the centuries. The highlight (at the end) is a sparkling reliquary heavily laden with more than a thousand gems—diamonds, rubies, emeralds, and sapphires—and supposedly containing pieces of the True Cross (in a cross shape). Backtrack and go up a flight of steps to floor 2 to find an intricate 14th-century, French-made, puzzle-like ivory statue of Mary *(Virgem do Paraiso)*. Her "insides" open up to reveal scenes of her life. A photo below shows Mary folded up and ready to travel. Not much else of interest is on this floor except perhaps Our Lady of Good Death—*Nossa Senhora da Boa Morte*—displayed toward the chapel.

Return to the church (scan your ticket again to leave the museum). The entrance to the Gothic **cloister** is past the ticket booth to the left. The cloister's openness and orange trees make it a cool haven, even on the hottest of Alentejo afternoons. Carvings of the four evangelists decorate the corners. Near where you enter, a tight spiral stairway leads to the "roof," with close-up views of the cathedral's fortress-like crenellations and grand views of the Alentejo plains. This "fortress of God" design was typical of the Portuguese Romanesque style. Notice the small relief (carved in the wall toward the tower) showing the local Christian hero Giraldo the Fearless with two severed Muslim heads. Back on ground level, a simple chapel niche (opposite the cloister entry) has a child-sized statue of another pregnant Virgin Mary (midway up wall on left).

For the best views of the plains, return to the ticket booth and climb even more stairs to reach the church's rooftop terrace (*terra-ço*). Get up close to the church bells and the cathedral's fine lantern tower. Baroque flaming vases provide an interesting foreground to the rolling hills.

▲▲Church of St. Francis and the Chapel of Bones (Igreja de São Francisco/Capela dos Ossos)

This church, dedicated to St. Francis, and its Chapel of Bones are worth the stroll to the southern edge of the old town. The main attraction is the macabre chapel, with the skulls and bones of 5,000 monks tightly cemented to the walls, with barely a gap in sight.

Cost and Hours: Church-free; Chapel of Bones-€2 (additional €1 to take photos); June-Aug Mon-Sat 9:00-12:50 & 14:30-17:45, Sept-May Mon-Sat until 17:15, opens at 10:00 Sun and holidays. From the main square (Praça do Giraldo), take the road to the left of the Bank of Portugal. Turn right when you reach Rua da República. You'll see the church ahead on the right; swing right to find the entrance on Praça 1 de Maio.

Visiting the Church and Chapel: Imagine the **church** in its original, pure style—simple, as St. Francis would have wanted it. It's wide, with just a single nave lined by chapels. In the 18th century, it became popular for wealthy families to buy fancy chapels, resulting in today's gold-leaf hodgepodge. The huge Baroque chapel to the left of the altar is dedicated to St. Francis and Claire, his partner in Christ-like simplicity. But they're surrounded by anything but poverty—the chapel is slathered in gold leaf from Brazil. The fine 18th-century tiles tell stories of St. Francis' life.

The entrance to the **bone chapel** (Capela dos Ossos) is outside, to the right of the church entrance. The message above the chapel translates: "We bones in here wait for yours to join us." Inside the macabre chapel, bones line the walls, and a chorus of skulls stares blankly from walls and arches. They were unearthed from various

Évora churchyards. This was the work of three monks who were concerned about society's values at the time. They thought this would provide Évora, a town noted for its wealth in the early 1600s, with a helpful place to meditate on the transience of material things in the undeniable presence of death. The bones of the three Franciscan monks who founded the church in the 13th century are in the small white coffin by the altar.

▲Public Market (Mercado Público)

Pop into the modernized yet still charming farmers market, across the square in front of the Church of St. Francis. It's busiest in the morning and on Saturday (Tue-Sun 7:00-18:00, generally closed Mon though a few rogue stands might be open). Wander around. It's a great slice-of-life look at this community. People are proud of their produce. *"Posso provar?"* (POH-soo proo-VAHR) means "Can I try a little?" *Provar* some cheese and stock up for a picnic (perhaps in the adjacent gardens).

▲Public Gardens (Jardim Publico)

Take a refreshing break in the town's public gardens (main entrance across from market, at the bottom of Praça 1 de Maio). Just inside the gate, Vasco da Gama looks on with excitement as he discovers a little kiosk café nearby selling sandwiches, freshly baked goodies, and drinks. For a quick little lunch, try an *empada de galinha* (tiny chicken pastry) and perhaps a *queijada* (sweet cheese tart—a local favorite). The gardens, bigger than they look, contain an overly restored hunk of the 16th-century Royal Palace (right of the entry gate). Behind the palace, look over the stone balustrade to see a kids' playground and playfields. Life goes on—make no bones about it.

▲▲University of Évora (Universidade de Évora)

First known as the College of the Holy Spirit, this institution was established as a Jesuit university in 1559 by Henrique, brother of King John III and the cathedral's first archbishop (1512-1580). Henrique later became king himself after his great-nephew Sebastian (Sebastião, who had succeeded John III) died in a disastrous attempt to chase the Moors out of North Africa. Because Henrique was a cardinal—and therefore chaste—he left

no direct descendants when he died only two years later. Portugal's throne passed to Sebastian's uncle, King Philip II of Spain, beginning 60 years of Spanish rule—and the start of Évora's decline.

Two hundred years after the founding of the Jesuit university, Marquês de Pombal (see sidebar, page 45), the powerful minister of King José I, decided that the Jesuits had become too rich, too political, and—as the sole teachers of society—too closed to modern thinking. He abolished the Jesuit society in 1759, confiscated their wealth, and closed the university. Another 200 years later, in 1973, it reopened, but this time as a secular university. Injecting 8,000 students into this town of almost 57,000 people (with 11,000 inside the walls) brought Évora a new vitality—and discos. Unlike an American-style centralized campus, the colleges are scattered throughout the town. While it's fun to visit when classes are in session, you'll have better access on Sunday, when all the rooms are wide open for visitors.

Cost and Hours: Free to enter, usually open long hours daily, Largo dos Colegiais 2, info tel. 266-740-800, www.uevora.pt.

Visiting the University: The university's main entrance is the old courtyard on the ground level (downhill from the original Jesuit chapel). Enter the inner courtyard. Attractive blue-and-white tiles (one of the biggest and best-preserved collections south of Lisbon) ring the walls of the courtyard as well as the classrooms lining the courtyard arcades. The tiles within classrooms portray the subject originally taught in each room. Notice the now-ignored pulpits. (Originally, Jesuit priests were the teachers, and information coming from a pulpit was not to be questioned.)

On Sundays, you can enter the room directly across the courtyard from the entrance. Major university events are held here under the watchful eyes of Cardinal Henrique (the painting to the left) and young King Sebastian (to the right).

Sala 114 to the right of this room gives you a great look at more tiles. In the 16th century, this was a classroom for students of astronomy—note the spheres and navigational instruments mingled with cupids and pastoral scenes. Imagine the class back then. Having few books, if any, the students (males only) took notes as the professor taught in Latin from the lectern in the back.

To find the university's **cafeteria,** head to the second smaller courtyard behind the main one (notice the big marble washbasin just outside). The cafeteria thrives with students and offers anyone super-cheap meals (Mon-Fri 8:30-18:00, closed Sat-Sun, WC).

From the cafeteria, wander along the row of offices to the left. Take the staircase (behind glass doors) up to the next level, and stroll down the long hall until it intersects with another hallway—you're at the "center of the universe." Tile panels representing the four elements (earth, air, wind, and fire) surround paintings of the

Jesuit founding fathers. From this level, you can exit through the original chapel.

Rota dos Vinhos do Alentejo Wine Tasting Center

This inviting place offers free tastings of four to six local wines, bottles of which are available for purchase. Familiarize yourself with little-known Portuguese grape varietals *(castas)*. Wines change weekly and are posted on the front door. Large info-panels in English hold perfume sprays that capture the essence of each varietal. Try to identify the various scents—it's more difficult than you think. The staff can give you details about the Alentejo wine route and schedule visits to nearby cellars.

Cost and Hours: Free, Mon 14:00-19:00, Tue-Fri 11:00-19:00, Sat 10:00-13:00, closed Sun, Praça Joaquim António de Aguiar 20-21, tel. 266-746-498, www.vinhosdoalentejo.pt.

Bullfighting

Evora's bullring (Arena d' Évora, just outside the southern city wall) was recently turned into a multipurpose pavilion, and routinely draws crowds as a concert venue. While bullfights are still held here, they're rare (about 4/year), in contrast to nearby towns that advertise fights on Saturday and Sunday throughout the summer (details from TI). Notice that women are on the program now, perhaps to give a tired sport a little kick.

MEGALITHIC SITES NEAR ÉVORA

Near Évora, you'll find stony sights, including menhirs (solitary standing stones, near Nossa Senhora de Guadalupe and elsewhere), cromlechs (monolith circles, at Cromeleque dos Almendres), and dolmens (stone slabs such as the rock tombs of Anta Grande do Zambujeiro, near Valverde, and Anta Capela de São Brissos). The most interesting to visit are Cromeleque dos

Almendres and the Anta Grande do Zambujeiro, described later.

Depending on how much you want to see, you can do a 15- to 45-mile loop from Évora by **bus tour** or hire a **guide** with a car (see "Tours in Évora," earlier), or **rent a car** to do the loop on your own (Évora's TI has a list of rental-car agencies and a map of the sites).

▲Cromeleque dos Almendres

This Portuguese Stonehenge, dating from about 5500 B.C., stands in the midst of cork trees down a dirt road. If you're in a rush, skip the first signposted site (a lone 10-foot menhir) and continue to the second—95 rounded granite stones erected in the shape of an oval.

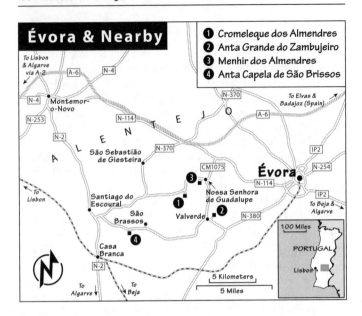

Évora & Nearby

❶ Cromeleque dos Almendres
❷ Anta Grande do Zambujeiro
❸ Menhir dos Almendres
❹ Anta Capela de São Brissos

It's the largest megalithic monument in Iberia and one of the oldest in Europe, some 2,000 years older than Stonehenge. Look closely at the stones; some have raised carvings, barely visible, of circles and shapes resembling a shepherd's hook.

Some believe that Stone Age sun-worshippers gathered at this pagan sanctuary in search of harmony between the "micro" environment on earth and the "macro" environment of the entire cosmos. The stones functioned as a celestial calendar, with the far ends of the ellipse lining up with the rising and setting sun on each solstice. A posted description (in English) at the site tells more. Stop and comfort a peeled cork tree, or pet the sheep that are often grazing nearby.

Getting There: The cromlech is five miles (20 minutes) west of Évora. Take N-114 toward Montemore/Lisbon; from Nossa Senhora de Guadalupe, follow clear signposts to the stones (and to the solitary Menhir dos Almendres, which is along the same road).

▲Anta Grande do Zambujeiro

This large megalithic dolmen, a burial tomb, is one of the tallest of its kind and dates to 4,000-3,000 B.C. When it was discovered in 1964, the tomb was completely covered by a large mound of dirt. Excavation left the structure exposed to the elements, and although now protected by a roofed enclosure, it's believed the tomb will eventually collapse. Walk up behind the dolmen and look into the bare interior, which once contained one of the largest artifact caches ever found in Iberia. Weapons, ceramics, gold and ivory jewelry,

---

Sleep Code

Abbreviations (€1 = about $1.40, country code: 351)
S = Single, **D** = Double/Twin, **T** = Triple, **Q** = Quad, **b** = bathroom, **s** = shower only
Price Rankings
  $$$ **Higher Priced**—Most rooms €100 or more.
   $$ **Moderately Priced**—Most rooms between €50-100.
    $ **Lower Priced**—Most rooms €50 or less.
Unless otherwise noted, credit cards are accepted, English is spoken, breakfast is included, and Wi-Fi is free. Prices change; verify current rates online or by email. For the best prices, always book directly with the hotel.

---

as well as 30 male skeletons had all been buried here over several generations (some of these items are now on display at the Museum of Évora). Off to the side you can see the original capstone, which was blasted off with dynamite during excavation.

Getting There: The dolmen is located a 20-minute drive southwest of Évora, near the town of Valverde (take N-380 toward Valverde and follow posted signs).

Sleeping in Évora

$$$ Pousada dos Lóios, formerly a 15th-century monastery, is now a luxury hotel renting 30 well-appointed cells. While the rooms are tiny, this hotel sprawls with fine public spaces, courtyards, and a swimming pool in a peaceful garden (Db-€216, less Nov-March, book ahead online for best price, discounts for longer stays, air-con, Wi-Fi in public areas, free parking, Convento dos Lóios, across from Roman Temple, tel. 266-730-070, www.pousadas.pt, recepcao.loios@pousadas.pt).

$$ Albergaria do Calvario is a stylish 22-room hotel on the site of a 16th-century olive mill. Friendly Peter and Nina will take very good care of you. When you reserve a three-night stay directly by email or phone and mention this book, they'll throw in one load of free laundry service—and may offer an upgrade (confirmed on arrival) to their best available room (Sb-€80-98, Db-€90-108, "premium" room-€110-120, prices depend on season and room size, extra bed-€25, air-con, Wi-Fi, free private parking, excellent organic breakfast, just inside the old town walls at the Porta Nova entrance, Travessa dos Lagares 3, tel. 266-745-930, www.adcevora.com, hotel@adcevora.com).

$$ Solar Monfalim, the labyrinthine house of a 16th-century noble, seems unchanged from when it received its first hotel guests in 1892. This elegant hacienda-type accommodation, with homey

ÉVORA

lounges and a Valium ambience, rents 25 rooms in a quiet central location (Sb-€50-60, Db-€70-85, extra bed-€25, air-con, pleasant breakfast room with balcony, Largo da Misericordia 1, tel. 266-750-000, www.monfalimtur.pt, reservas@monfalimtur.pt).

$$ Residencial Os Manuéis rents 14 cozy rooms surrounding an airy central patio. Breakfast can be served on the terrace with views of the sweeping Alentejo plains, while the Church of St. Francis looms in the distance. Vasco makes you feel at home and loves to share his knowledge of Portugal (Sb-€30-45, Db-€45-60, suite-€55-80, extra bed-€15, 10 percent discount when you book directly with the hotel and pay cash, air-con, no elevator, Wi-Fi, free parking, Rua do Raimundo 35, tel. 266-769-160, no website but can reserve through Booking.com, res.osmanueis@sapo.pt).

$$ Residencial Policarpo, filling another 16th-century nobleman's mansion, also has a homey feel, with 20 simple rooms—each one unique—tucked around a courtyard. There are fine public spaces and an inviting sun terrace. Joaquim, Michele, and David Policarpo carry on the family tradition of good hospitality (S-€30, Sb-€60, D-€36, Db-€55, Tb-€68, about €10 less in low season, cash only, double-paned windows, air-con in rooms with bathroom, Wi-Fi, no elevator, terrace, fireplace, free and easy parking, two entrances: Rua da Freiria de Baixo 16 and Rua Conde da Serra, near university, tel. 266-702-424, www.pensaopolicarpo.com, mail@pensaopolicarpo.com). For those on a very tight budget, their doubles without private bathrooms are perhaps the best cheap beds in town.

$$ Hotel Santa Clara, renting 41 comfortable rooms on a quiet side street, is solid, professional, and tour-friendly. Part of the Best Western chain, it lacks character, but comes with a good location and price (Sb-€60-65, Db-€65-75, air-con, Wi-Fi, free parking, Travessa do Milheira 19; from Praça do Giraldo, take Rua Pinto Serpa downhill, then right on Milheira; coming from the bus station, continue up Rua Pinto Serpa, turn left at the closed Santa Clara Church, look for the arch and signpost, then right at the end of the road; tel. 266-704-141, www.bestwesternhotelsantaclara.com, reservas@hotelsantaclara.pt).

$$ Hotel Ibis, a cheap chain hotel, has 87 identical Motel 6-type rooms that are a 15-minute walk from the center, just outside the city walls. Simple to find and offering easy parking, it's a cinch for drivers—but staying here is like eating at McDonald's in Paris (Sb/Db-€35-59, check website for deals, one child under 12 sleeps free, breakfast-€6, air-con, Wi-Fi, elevator, parking, Rua de Viana 18, tel. 266-760-700, www.ibishotel.com, h1708@accor.com).

$ Hotel B&B Évora is a minimalist oasis offering 80 professional, crisp rooms in a residential part of the walled city. The building incorporates part of the facade of Évora's first bullring, and the decor is equestrian-inspired. An interior patio with a reflecting pool is relaxing even on the hottest of afternoons (Sb-€37, Db-€45, Tb-€66, breakfast-€4.50, Wi-Fi, secure garage-€5/day, Rua do Raimundo 99, tel. 220-407-000, www.hotelbb.pt, evora@hotelbb.com).

$ Casa Hóspedes "O Alentejo," an old noble house renting 22 well-worn but thoroughly cared-for rooms, comes with a homey TV salon and endearing attention to quaint detail (Sb-€25-30, Db-€38-48, Tb-€45-59, Qb-€50-75, no breakfast, air-con, Rua Serpa Pinto 74, tel. 266-702-903, residencial.oalentejo@gmail.com, charming Rosa speaks very little English).

Eating in Évora

The region has its own proud cuisine—rustic and hearty, with lots of game and robust red wines. Don't ask for *vinho verde* here. And don't ask for *porto* either. A good local *vinho licoroso* (sweet dessert wine) is Mouchão.

Restaurante 1/4 P'ras 9 ("Quarter to Nine") has a big, rustic dining room with an open kitchen that steams up with local families and tourists chowing down on favorites such as *arroz de tamboril*, a rice and seafood stew, and *açorda de marisco*, a soup with clams, shrimp, and bread spiced with Alentejo herbs like cilantro (Thu-Tue 12:00-15:00 & 19:30-22:00, closed Wed, some outdoor seating, Rua Pedro Simões 9, near exposed kink in aqueduct off Rua do Menino Jesus, tel. 266-706-774).

Adega do Alentejano is like an aboveground wine cellar. Locals choose from affordable traditional dishes, including tasty pork options. The menu is scrawled on paper tablecloths and chalkboards. Ask to watch them pour your *jarro* of house wine from the large earthenware vats at the back. If you didn't try *ginjinha* in Lisbon or Óbidos, finish your meal with a glass of this housemade cherry liqueur. Come at lunch to avoid crowds, or elbow in at dinnertime for a festive night out (€8-12 plates, Mon-Sat 12:00-15:00 & 19:00-22:00, closed Sun, cash only, Rua Gabriel Victor do Monte Pereira 21-A; from main square go alongside church on Rua João de Deus, then take third left and keep walking; tel. 266-744-447).

Taberna Típica Quarta-Feira is a rustic 14-table tavern, festooned with patriotic Portuguese decor, where Zé Dias and his family proudly and expertly serve country cooking, including rabbit and partridge in season. Don't expect to order from a menu—they usually serve just the food they felt like cooking that day. Sit down and enjoy the "Trust Zé Special" (€25)—he'll bring out the works, offering fun samples of whatever's in season, including his

ÉVORA

Versatile Cork

The cork extracted from the bottle of wine you're having with dinner is very local. The Alentejo region is known for its cork. (The wine you're drinking is likely local, too— the Alentejo produces lots of wine as well.) Besides bottle-stoppers, cork is used for many things, from bulletin boards to floor tiles, and from car-engine gaskets to the center of a baseball. Cork is a remarkable substance, spongy and pliable but resistant to water.

Cork comes from the bark of the cork oak *(Quercus suber)*, a 30-foot tree with a sprawling canopy and knotty trunk that grows well in dry heat and sandy soil. After 25 years, a tree is mature enough for harvest.

The outer bark is stripped from the trunk, leaving a "wound" of red-colored "blushing" inner bark. It takes nine years for the bark to grow back, and then it's harvested again. A cork tree keeps producing for more than 100 years. After harvesting, the bark is boiled to soften it up, then flattened. Machines cut the cork into desired shapes or punch out bottle stoppers.

Portugal produces more than half the world's supply of cork (with Spain making much of the rest). These days, many wine stoppers are made from plastic, which could become a threat to cork production. So far the business remains strong, thanks to cork's insulating and acoustical applications, but some fear that if cork eventually loses its economic value, the survival of the forests—and the special ecosystem they support—will be at risk.

house wine (there's no wine list...just one decent house wine), fine desserts, dessert wine, and coffee (Mon 12:30-15:00, Tue-Sat 12:30-15:00 & 19:30-22:00, closed Sun, hidden on a narrow street just north off Rua da Mouraria at Rua do Inverno 16, tel. 266-707-530). This is no place for vegetarians.

Restaurante O Fialho is expensive and enjoyably pretentious, with white-coated waiters serving Alentejo cuisine to Bogart-like locals. Enjoy the photos of VIP diners on the wall, or ask for a look at the photo album showing O Fialho's great moments since it opened in 1948. For decades, this was virtually the only fine restaurant in town, and it arguably still offers Évora's best food. Go all-local with your waiter's recommendations. For a delightful mix of nun-inspired sweets, ask for the *misto de convento* (€30 plates, Tue-Sun 12:30-24:00, closed Mon, arrive before 20:00 or make a reservation, Travessa das Mascarenhas 16; from the main square go right alongside the church—Rua João de Deus—for 5 minutes, take first left after public square with theater; tel. 266-703-079, www.restaurantefialho.com).

At **Tasquinha d'Oliveira,** Manuel (who was a cook for years at O Fialho) and his wife, Carolina, offer an intimate dining experience with all the quality of his mentor's restaurant, but less pretense. In a tiny, 14-seat abode of cooking love, they work with a respect for Alentejo cuisine and heritage. Note that you will be brought several plates of appetizers—if you nibble, you will pay. Most are €6-8, but the crab appetizer is €18. Just leave them on the table or refuse the dish (€15-25 main dishes are easily splittable, closed Sun, reservations smart, Rua Cândido dos Reis 45, tel. 266-744-841).

Adega Típica Bota Alta is a charming eight-table eatery, worth checking out on weekends for their live fado music. Esperança runs "her house" with a loving passion for the art of fado (see page 98 for more on fado). You'll find yourself singing along with the locals. Arrive no later than 20:30 to finish your meal before the music starts at 22:00. You're welcome to come just for fado; you'll pay €10 for a seat (€25-30 plates, fado music Fri-Sat 22:00-late, closed Aug, Rua Serpa Pinto 93, tel. 968-655-166).

At **BL Lounge,** friendly Antonio offers a break from the traditional by serving Alentejo cuisine with a modern and international twist. Try the *risotto com espargos e gambas* (asparagus risotto with prawns), and be sure to save room for the chocolate cake, which is *muito bom* (€10-20 meat and seafood plates, extensive wine list, Mon-Sat 12:30-15:00 & 19:30-22:00, closed Sun, Rua das Alcoçarias 1, near São Mamede Church, tel. 266-771-323).

Salsa Verde, a good choice for a light, inexpensive lunch or dinner, caters to the vegetarian crowd in a crisp, clean cafeteria (Mon-Fri 11:00-15:30 & 19:00-21:30, Sat 11:00-15:30, closed Sun, Rua do Raimundo 93, tel. 266-743-210).

Évora Connections

From Évora by Bus to: Lisbon (hourly, 1.5 hours), **Lagos** (3/day, 4.5-5 hours, direct in summer only, otherwise transfer in Albufeira), **Coimbra** (2/day direct, 4 hours, almost hourly with transfer in Lisbon), **Madrid** (2/day, 7 hours, tickets at Eurolines/Intersul office on second floor of bus station). Portugal bus info (no English spoken): tel. 266-769-410.

From Évora by Train to: Lisbon (4/day, 1.5 hours, arrives at Lisbon's Oriente Station), **Coimbra** (3/day direct, 4-5 hours, more options with change in Lisbon), **Lagos** (3/day, 5 hours, change in Pinhal Novo and Tunes or Faro). Check with TI or online at www. cp.pt for schedules.

NAZARÉ AND NEARBY

Nazaré • Batalha • Fátima • Alcobaça • Óbidos

Nazaré, an Atlantic-coast fishing town turned resort, is both black-shawl traditional and beach-friendly. Several worthy sights are within easy day-trip distance of Nazaré (nah-zah-RAY). You can drop by Batalha to see its monastery, the patriotic pride and architectural joy of Portugal. If the spirit moves you, the pilgrimage site at Fátima is nearby. Alcobaça has Portugal's largest church (and saddest romance). And Portugal's incredibly cute walled town of Óbidos is just down the road.

PLANNING YOUR TIME

While the far north of Portugal has considerable charm, those with limited time can enjoy maximum travel thrills here—in its "Midwest." This area is an ideal stop if you're interested in a small, resort-town side-trip north from Lisbon, or if you're coming in from Salamanca or Madrid, Spain. Expect crowds in July and August, particularly on weekends.

On a two-week trip through Portugal, Nazaré merits a day. Another day's worth of sightseeing is in Alcobaça, Batalha, and Fátima (I'd prioritize in that order). See Óbidos on the way between Nazaré and Lisbon.

Nazaré

I got hooked on Nazaré back when colorful fishing boats littered its long, sandy beach. Now, rather than crashing through the surf to reach the beach in the town center, the boats motor comfortably into a new harbor 30 minutes' walk south of town. Today Nazaré's beach is littered with frolicking families, and it seems that most of the town's 10,000 inhabitants are in the tourist trade. But I still like the place.

You'll be greeted by the energetic applause of the surf, widows with rooms to rent, and big plates of *percebes* (barnacles). Relax in the Portuguese sun in a land of cork groves, eucalyptus trees, ladies in petticoats, and men who stow cigarettes and fishhooks in their stocking caps.

Even with its summer crowds, Nazaré is a fun stop that offers a glimpse of old Portugal amid the tourists. Somehow the traditions survive, and the townspeople are able to go about their old-school ways. Wander the back streets for a fine look at Portuguese family-in-the-street life. Laundry flaps in the wind, kids play soccer, and fish sizzle over tiny curbside hibachis. Squadrons of sun-dried and salted fish are crucified on nets pulled

tightly around wooden frames and left under the midday sun. (Locals claim they are delightful...but I don't know.) Off-season Nazaré is almost empty of tourists—inexpensive, colorful, and relaxed, with enough salty fishing-village atmosphere to make you pucker.

Nazaré doesn't have any blockbuster sights. The beach, tasty seafood, and the funicular ride up to Sítio for a great coastal view are the bright lights of my lazy Nazaré memories.

Plan some beach time here. Sharing a bottle of chilled *vinho verde* (young white wine, a specialty of Portugal) on the beach at sundown is a good way to wrap up the day.

Orientation to Nazaré

Nazaré faces its long beach, stretching north from the new harbor to Sítio (SEE-tee-oo), the hill-capping old part of town. Survey the town from Avenida da República, which lines the waterfront. Scan the cliffs. The funicular climbs to Sítio. Also to your right, look at the road kinking toward the sea. The building (on the kink) with the yellow balconies is the recommended Ribamar Hotel.

Nazaré Fashions: Seven Petticoats and Black Widows

Nazaré is famous for its women who wear skirts with seven petticoats (one for each day, or for the seven colors of the rainbow, or...make up your own legend). While this is partially just a creation for the tourists, there is some element of truth to the tradition. In the old days, women would sit on the beach waiting for their fishermen to sail home. To keep warm in the face of a cold sea wind while staying modestly covered, they'd wear several petticoats in order to fold layers over their heads, backs, and legs. Even today, older and more traditional women wear short skirts made bulky by several—but not seven—petticoats. The ensemble is completed with house slippers, an apron (embroidered by the wearer), a small woolen cape, head scarf, and flamboyant jewelry, including chunky gold earrings (often passed down from generation to generation).

You'll see some women wearing black, a sign of mourning. Traditionally, if your spouse died, you wore black for the rest of your life. While this tradition is still observed, mourning just ain't what it used to be—in the last generation, widows began remarrying.

Just beyond the Ribamar, you'll find the main square (Praça Sousa Oliveira, with banks and ATMs) and most of my hotel listings.

Sitting quietly atop its cliff, the Sítio neighborhood feels like a totally separate village. Its people don't fish; they farm. Take the funicular up to the top for a spectacular view.

Tourist Information: The TI faces the beach on Avenida Manuel Remigio, a 10-minute walk south of the main square, inside the Cultural Center building (look for *Centro Cultural* signs, daily Aug 9:00-21:00, April-July and Sept 9:30-12:30 & 14:30-18:30, Oct-March 9:30-13:00 & 14:30-18:00, tel. 262-561-194, www.cm-nazare.pt). Ask about summer activities and bullfights in Sítio.

HELPFUL HINTS

Markets: The colorful **town market** bustles with fresh fish, produce, and caged rabbits in the morning (daily 8:00-13:00 except closed Mon Oct-May, a few blocks up from the beach on Avenida Vieira Guimarães, in the green building just behind the taxi stand), and a **flea market** pops up near Nazaré's town hall every Friday, except in August (9:00-13:00, also on Avenida Vieira Guimarães).

❶	Hotel/Rest. Mar Bravo & Rest. O Casalinho	❽	To Restaurante O Luis
❷	Hotel Maré	❾	Taberna da Adélia
❸	Hotel Praia	❿	Restaurante A Tasquinha
❹	Hotel A Cubata	⓫	Mr. Pizza
❺	Ribamar Hotel-Restaurant	⓬	To Taverna "do 8 ó 80" & Internet Access (2)
❻	Hotel Âncora Mar	⓭	Laundry
❼	Julia Pereira Rooms		

Internet Access: Café.com offers the fastest connection in town (daily 10:00-23:00, four terminals, Wi-Fi, in Edifício Atlântico on Avenida da República toward the new port), but the **Municipal Library** offers 30 minutes for free (Mon-Fri 9:30-13:00 & 14:00-19:00, Internet center closed Sat-Sun, in blocky gray building a few blocks behind the Cultural Center at Rua Grupo Desportivo "Os Nazarenos").

Laundry: At **Lavanderia Nazaré,** Fátima will wash, dry, and fold your laundry for pickup the next day (€3.50/kg—about 2 lbs, Mon-Sat 9:00-13:00 & 15:00-19:00, open all day July-Aug, closed Sun, Rua Branco Martins 17, tel. 262-552-761).

Regional Guide: Manuela Rainho, who works out of Alcobaça, is a helpful guide for anyone interested in seeing this part of Portugal (€150/day, mobile 968-076-302, manuelarainho@gmail.com).

Sights in Nazaré

THE BEACH

It's the domain of the summertime beach tents, a tradition in Portugal. In Nazaré, the tents are run as a cooperative by the old women you'll see sitting in the shade ready to collect €6 or more a day. The beach is groomed and guarded, and in the evening, piped music is played. Flags indicate danger level: red (no one allowed in the water), yellow (wading is safe), and green (no problem).

If you see a mass of children parading through town down to the beach, they're likely from a huge dorm in town, where poorer kids from inland areas of this part of the country are put up for a summer break.

Boats used to line the beach in summer and fill the squares in winter, but when the harbor was built in 1986, that's where the boats ended up. Today, only re-creations occur (on most Sundays in May), when boats line the main square to show the hands-on fishing process of the past (confirm exact days with the TI).

If you stroll south along the promenade toward the new harbor, you'll come to a few traditional boats in the sand, with prows

high to cut through the surf. Try to imagine the beach before 1986, littered with boats like these, with old men mending their nets. Oxen (and later, tractors) hauled the boats out each day. (Across the street is the town's Cultural Center—with interesting exhibits and the TI.) Near the boats is a mackerel crucifixion zone—where ladies still sun-dry their mackerel and sardines. (They may try to sell them to you, but the fish need to be cooked again before eating.) Preparing and selling fish is the lot of Nazaré women married to fishermen. Stroll to people-watch. Traditions survive even among younger women.

The buildings beyond this point are new. While it may seem

that in Nazaré most of the people are older than most of the buildings, the town is a Portuguese Coney Island—thriving with young people who flock here for fun-in-the-sun on the beach.

Head back into town. Just under the bluff (near the funicular to Sítio) is the oldest square in Nazaré, Praça Sousa Oliveira. This square is lined with the oldest buildings in the lower town.

IN SÍTIO

To get to Sítio, take the **funicular.** It was originally built in 1889—the same year as the Eiffel Tower—by the same disciple of Eiffel who built the much-loved Elevador de Santa Justa in Lisbon. The equipment and stations, however, have been modernized. To get to the lift, follow signs to *ascensor;* it goes every 15 minutes (€1.20 each way, June-Sept 7:30-24:00, Oct-May 7:30-20:30, WCs at each station).

Off-season, red line *(linha vermelha)* buses replace funicular service after 20:30, but run only hourly. If dining in Sítio off-season, check bus times at the funicular station before you eat (funicular round-trip ticket valid for bus ride down).

Upon arrival at the top, walk downhill and turn left to reach the main square and the promontory.

Sítio's Main Square

Historic Sítio seems to gather around its dominant square. Survey the square to see...

The Church of Our Lady of Nazaré: The town's main church, built in the late 16th century and proudly restored by small local

Nª SENHORA DA NAZARÉ

donations, is on the pilgrimage trail. The faithful circulate around and then go up to the high altar to venerate the Black Madonna, brought here by two fishermen in the seventh century from Jesus' hometown of Nazareth (hence the name of this town: Nazaré). The Madonna, hidden in nearby rocks throughout the Muslim Moorish rule, was rediscovered during the Christian Reconquista in the 12th century, when interest in the relic led to the establishment of the town. Today the church, with its gilded Baroque-Neoclassical interior and 17th-century Delft tiles (from the Netherlands), is popular for weddings and other family religious occasions (which is why it has lots of flowers).

On the left side of the nave at the entrance, a large painting shows the story you'll find all over town: Dom Fuas, a noble from the area, was hunting deer and became so absorbed in the chase that he didn't realize he was about to go over the cliff. The Virgin Mary appeared suddenly and stopped him, saving his life. (The un-

NAZARÉ & NEARBY

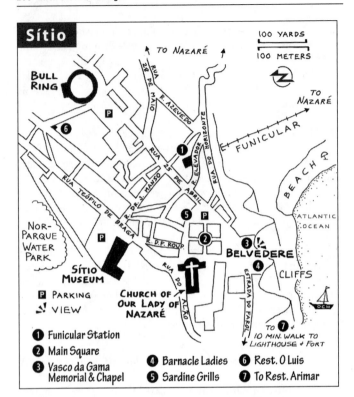

Sítio

100 YARDS
100 METERS

TO NAZARÉ

BULL RING

TO NAZARÉ

FUNICULAR

TO NAZARÉ

BEACH

ATLANTIC OCEAN

NOR-PARQUE WATER PARK

SÍTIO MUSEUM

BELVEDERE

CLIFFS

CHURCH OF OUR LADY OF NAZARÉ

TO 10 MIN. WALK TO LIGHTHOUSE & FORT

P PARKING
VIEW

1 Funicular Station
2 Main Square
3 Vasco da Gama Memorial & Chapel
4 Barnacle Ladies
5 Sardine Grills
6 Rest. O Luis
7 To Rest. Arimar

fortunate deer didn't see Mary in time.) Exit the church through the gift shop. In front of the church, admire the view from...

The Belvedere: From the edge of the bluff you can survey Nazaré and its golden beach stretching all the way to the new harbor. In the distance are the mostly uninhabited Berlenga Islands. The pillar on the belvedere ("beautiful view") is a stone **memorial** for Vasco da Gama, erected in 1497 after he stopped here before leaving Europe for India. The tiny chapel next to the monument sits on the spot where the Black Madonna hid in the rocks for 400 years, as if waiting for the Moors to leave and for the Christians to return.

Several women (mostly from the same family, but competitive nevertheless) camp out here in their over-the-top traditional fashions, selling munchies and Nazaré knickknacks. This is a fine opportunity to buy *percebes*—boiled, addictively tasty, and ready-to-

NAZARÉ & NEARBY

eat **barnacles.** Two euros will get you 100 grams (that's the size of their tiny wooden box). From here the road dead-ends a 10-minute walk away at the Farol lighthouse, where you can enjoy panoramic views of the north beach *(praia norte)*.

The bandstand marking the center of the square is a reminder that this is the main venue for the town's busy festival schedule. In the summer, smoke rises from the many outdoor grills, and the savory fragrance entices you to sit down for a plate of sardines.

Sítio Museum (Museu Etnográfico e Arqueológico

Dedicated to Dr. Joaquim Manso, this museum is the only place in Nazaré where you can see artifacts of the colorful traditional fishing culture—boats, gear, costumes, historic photos, and so on.

Cost and Hours: €1, April-Oct Tue-Sun 10:00-19:00, Nov-March Tue-Sun 10:00-18:00, closed Mon year-round, one block inland from Sítio's main square, Rua Dom Fuas Roupinho, tel. 262-562-801, mdjm-nazare.blogspot.com.

Activities at Sítio

Sítio stages Portuguese-style **bullfights** on Saturday nights in summer (July-mid-Aug, tickets from €10 at kiosk in Praça Sousa Oliveira). Sítio's NorParque is a family-friendly **water park** with a pool, slides, and Jacuzzi (€12 for adults, €9.50 for kids ages 6-11, cheaper after 17:00, June-mid-Sept 10:00-19:00, closed mid-Sept-May, opening may be delayed until July depending on weather, confirm hours at TI, watch for free shuttle bus parked on the main drag, tel. 262-562-282).

Restaurante Arimar, on the left along the way to the lighthouse, is a good place to **take in the sunset** with drinks or dinner (avoid windy days). Restaurante O Luis, also in Sítio, is worth finding (see "Eating in Nazaré," later).

Sleeping in Nazaré

You should have no problem finding a room, except in August, when the crowds, temperatures, and prices are all at their highest (particularly during the Nazaré Beach Party in mid-Aug). I've never arrived in Nazaré without a welcoming committee of eager hustlers inviting me to sleep in their *quartos* (rooms in private homes). They line the street coming into town, hit up tourists on the beachfront promenade, and meet each bus as it pulls into the station (you may enjoy dropping by for the commotion as the grannies fight over the tourists).

Prices vary wildly with the season. I've listed rough prices for the medium-high season (approximately April-mid-July and Sept-Dec). Expect to pay about 50 percent more from mid-July through mid-August. Outside of this highest season, you'll save

Sleep Code

Abbreviations   **(€1 = about $1.40, country code: 351)**
S = Single, **D** = Double/Twin, **T** = Triple, **Q** = Quad, **b** = bathroom, **s** = shower only.
Price Rankings
$$$ **Higher Priced**—Most rooms €50 or more.
  $$ **Moderately Priced**—Most rooms between €30-50.
    $ **Lower Priced**—Most rooms €30 or less.
Unless otherwise noted, credit cards are accepted, English is spoken, breakfast is included, and Wi-Fi is generally free. Prices can change; verify current rates online or by email. For the best prices, always book directly with the hotel.

serious money if you arrive with no reservations and try your hand at bargaining, even at hotels. Most hotels don't have single and triple rooms as such—instead, they generally offer single travelers a double room at about €10 off, and they make a triple by cramming in an extra bed for €10 to €20 more.

HOTELS

$$$ Hotel Mar Bravo is on the main square and the waterfront. Its 16 comfy rooms are great—modern, bright, fresh—and they come with balconies, nearly all of them with views (Db-€60-90, higher in Aug, owner Fátima promises a 10 percent discount with cash and two-night stay, double-paned windows, view breakfast room, air-con, elevator, Wi-Fi, attached restaurant serves good seafood with a sea view, Praça Sousa Oliveira 71-A, tel. 262-569-160, www.marbravo.com, info@marbravo.com). Parking for the Mar Bravo is several blocks away at Hotel Praia on Avenida Vieira Guimarães.

$$$ Hotel Maré, just off Praça Sousa Oliveira, is a big, modern, American-style hotel with 46 rooms, some tour groups, and a rooftop terrace (Db-€50, €100 in July, €120 in Aug; extra bed-€15, one kid under 10 stays free, air-con, balconies, double-paned windows, elevator, Wi-Fi, parking-€5/day, Rua Mouzinho de Albuquerque 10, tel. 262-550-180, www.hotelmare.pt, geral@hotelmare.pt).

$$$ Hotel Praia, run by the folks who run Hotel Mar Bravo, shares the Bravo's modern look and design, but not its beach location (instead, it's on the main road into town). It does, however, have a rooftop terrace with a pool, 80 bright rooms with double-paned windows, and parking in an adjacent underground garage for €5 per day (Db-€70 in low season, €140 in Aug; singles-€10 less, extra bed-€20, air-con, Wi-Fi, Avenida Vieira Guimarães 39, tel. 262-569-200, www.hotelpraia.com, geral@hotelpraia.com).

NAZARÉ & NEARBY

$$$ Hotel A Cubata, a nice place on the waterfront on the north end, has 22 small rooms with remodeled bathrooms (Sb-€30-65, Db-€35-75, depends on view, Wi-Fi, noisy bar below, Avenida da República 6, tel. 262-569-150, www.hotelcubata.com, geral@hotelcubata.com). For a peaceful night, forgo rooms with private balconies and take a back room on the top floor (saving some money).

$$ Ribamar Hotel-Restaurant has a prime location on the waterfront, a rare Old World atmosphere, and 25 small rooms with dark wood and four-poster beds. To spot the hotel from the waterfront, look for its yellow awnings and balconies (Db-€30-65, a couple of suites cost same as doubles in off-season, four rooms with balconies, good attached restaurant downstairs, Wi-Fi, parking-€10/day, €15 in Aug; Rua Gomes Freire 9, tel. 262-551-158, www.ribamarnazare.net, geral@ribmarnazare.com).

$$ Hotel Âncora Mar is a big, modern, almost institutional place, with 26 spacious, bright, and functional rooms and a generous roof terrace with a pool. It's on a quiet street a block from the bus station (Db-€35-45, €60-80 in July, €95 in Aug; free parking, Wi-Fi in lounge, Rua Sub-Vila 49, tel. 262-569-010, www.ancoramar.com, info@ancoramar.com).

QUARTOS

I list no dumpy hotels or cheap pensions, because the best budget options are *quartos*. Like nowhere else in Iberia, locals renting spare rooms clamor for your business here. Except perhaps during weekends in August, you can stumble into town any day and find countless women hanging out on the streets (especially along the waterfront and near the bus station) with fine modern rooms to rent. I promise. If you need an inexpensive room, they've got it. Their rooms are generally better than cheap hotel rooms—for half the cost. Your room is likely to be large and homey, with old-time-elegant furnishings (with no plumbing, but plenty of facilities down the hall). Many *quartos* are located in a quiet neighborhood, six short blocks off the beachfront action. I'd come into town and have fun looking at several places. Hem and haw, and the price goes down.

$ Julia Pereira rents five nice rooms with private baths in a small building over her daughter's café. Rooms overlook a charming square that faces the beach and comes with night noise (Db-€30, €50 July-Aug, no breakfast, reception desk at ground-floor café run by same family, on Praça Dr. Manuel Arriaga, mobile 967-468-011, or call Julia's daughter Eduarda at mobile 262-189-458, eduardacorreia@gmail.com).

Eating in Nazaré

Nazaré is a fishing town, so don't order *hamburguesas*. Fresh seafood is tasty all over town, more expensive (but plenty affordable) along the waterfront, and cheaper farther inland. Waiters will usually bring you food (such as olives or bread) that you didn't order. Nibble and you pay—or ask for it to be removed. Double-check your bill to make sure you're not being charged for something you didn't eat.

In this fishing village, even the snacks come from the sea. *Percebes* are boiled barnacles, sold as munchies in bars and on the street. Merchants are happy to demonstrate how to eat them and let you sample one for free (say *"Posso provar?"*). They're great with beer in the bars. Connoisseurs know that they are fresh only April through September (otherwise they're frozen). Sardines are fresh only in July, August, and the first half of September, but yummy any time of year.

Try Portugal's light, young wine, *vinho verde;* with its champagne-like taste, it's perfect with shellfish. *Amêndoa amarga* is the local amaretto. For a tasty pastry, try a *pastel de feijão* (fay-ZHOW) from any café. This small tart with a puff-pastry shell has a filling similar to pecan pie, but it's actually made of white beans.

Restaurante O Luis in Sítio serves excellent seafood and regional cuisine to an enthusiastic crowd in a cheery atmosphere. While few tourists go here, the friendly white-coated waiters make you feel welcome (€10-20 dinners, Fri-Wed 12:00-24:00, closed Thu, reserve on weekends, air-con, Rua Dos Tanques 7, tel. 262-551-826, David speaks English). This place is worth the trouble if you want to eat well: Ride the funicular up to Sítio and exit right; turn right on the main drag and walk to the bullring; it's one block downhill to the left of the bullring (Praça de Touros). Off-season, the funicular stops running at 20:30; remember to check the hourly bus schedule down to Nazaré before eating.

Taberna da Adélia is a family-run *restaurante típico* popular with Portuguese visitors for its honest service, fresh fish, and unpretentious jovial ambience. You can enjoy the menu and the appetizers without being ripped off. Marco and his family pride themselves on respecting the customer (daily 12:00-15:30 & 18:30-22:30, reservations smart in summer, one block off the beach at Rua das Traineiras 12, tel. 262-552-134).

Restaurante A Tasquinha dishes up authentic Portuguese cuisine with a cozy blue-and-white picnic-bench ambience. Friendly, hardworking Carlos and his family serve their fish with the best bread in town and a special sauce that's good on just about everything (Tue-Sun 12:00-15:00 & 19:00-22:30, closed Mon, Rua Adrião Batalha 54, tel. 262-551-945).

Taverna "do 8 ó 80" defies Nazaré's fishing heritage. Nuno and his staff specialize in beef and pork dishes—a great break from seafood—in a stylish, modern setting. With 350 different bottles of wine on-site and over 200 available by the glass, the wine list is a mini-course in Portuguese enology. Sidewalk tables let you watch the tide roll in (Fri-Wed 12:00-23:00, closed Thu, Edifício Atlântico, Loja 8, tel. 262-560-490).

Mr. Pizza has decent pizzas that you can order to go and eat down on the beach (€6-12 pizzas, daily 12:00-23:00, across the street from Hotel Maré at Rua Mouzinho de Albuquerque 15, tel. 262-560-999).

Eating on the Beachfront: Competitive restaurants line the beach. These two places offer good value: **Mar Bravo's** friendly staff serves fresh seafood at charming on-square tables overlooking the beach (April-Oct 12:00-23:00, Nov-March 12:00-15:30 & 18:30-22:30, 10 percent discount for readers of this guidebook, inside hotel of same name, Praça Sousa Oliveira 71-A). **Restaurante O Casalinho,** on the main square by the sea, has good outdoor seating, plain decor, and a solid reputation (daily 12:00-23:00, Praça Sousa Oliveira 7, tel. 262-551-328).

Public Market for a Picnic: To experience the colorful market, buy a picnic there and enjoy it on the beach. The covered market is just up the street from the bus station (daily 8:00-13:00, closed Mon Oct-May, produce and bread sold below, fish above). Other to-go and picnic options can be found in any number of mini-markets along Rua Sub-Vila.

Nazaré Connections

BY BUS

Nazaré's bus station was demolished in 2012 to make way for an apartment building. A temporary ticket office is in a small portable building behind the library on Avenida do Municipio, a few blocks inland from the Cultural Center and beach. Buses merely stop along the avenue. A new, permanent station will likely be built within the next few years, but it's anyone's guess where. Service diminishes on Sundays, so verify schedules beforehand at the station. Two bus companies serve Nazaré: Rede Expressos, which covers most of Portugal (tel. 707-223-344, www.rede-expressos.pt) and RodoTejo, which focuses on central Portugal (tel. 967-449-868, www.rodotejo.pt).

If you're heading to Lisbon, buses are faster and more direct than trains. You will arrive at Lisbon's Sete Rios bus station, a Metro (or taxi) ride away from the center.

Nazaré by Bus to: Alcobaça (stopping at Valado, about every half-hour, 20 minutes), **Batalha** (6/day, 1 hour), **Óbidos** (4/day,

40-60 minutes, some direct, most transfer in Caldas da Rainha), **Fátima** (4/day, 1.5 hours), **Coimbra** (5/day, 2 hours), **Lisbon** (6/day, 2 hours). Buses are scarce on Sunday.

BY TRAIN

The nearest train station is at Valado (three miles toward Alcobaça, connected by semi-regular €1.25 buses and reasonable, easy-to-share €8-10 taxis). The train to Lisbon requires a bus or taxi ride from Nazaré to the station in Valado, then several transfers—not worth the hassle. To avoid this train-station headache, consider using intercity buses instead of trains.

From Nazaré/Valado by Train to: **Coimbra** (3/day, 2.5 hours, transfer in Bifurcação de Lares; bus is faster), **Lisbon** (3-5/day, 3.5-4 hours, involves 2-3 transfers in Caldas da Rainha, Cacém, and possibly Melecas; bus is better). Train info: Tel. 808-208-208.

DAY-TRIPPING FROM NAZARÉ TO ALCOBAÇA, BATALHA, FÁTIMA, OR ÓBIDOS

If you're traveling by bus, you can see both Alcobaça and Batalha in one day (but not on Sunday, when bus service is sparse). Alcobaça is easy to visit on the way to or from Batalha (and both are connected by bus with Óbidos). Ask at the bus station or TI for schedule information, and be flexible. Fátima has the fewest connections and is farthest away. Without a car, Fátima is not worth the trouble for most, but if you're heading by bus to Coimbra, you can go via Fátima. A taxi from Nazaré to Alcobaça costs a little more than €15; agree on the price before leaving town.

Batalha

On August 14, 1385, two armies faced off on the rolling plains of Batalha (bah-TAHL-yah) to decide Portugal's future—independence or rule by Spanish kings? King John (João) I of Portugal ordered his 7,000 men to block the road to Lisbon. The Spanish Castilian king, with 32,000 soldiers and 16 modern cannons, ordered his men to hold their fire. But when the Portuguese knights dismounted from their horses to form a defensive line, some hotheaded Spaniards—enraged by such a display of unsportsmanlike conduct by supposedly chivalrous knights—attacked.

Shoop! From the side came 400 arrows from English archers fighting for Portugal. The confused Castilians sounded the retreat, and the Portuguese chased them, literally, all the way back to Castile. A mere half-hour (and several hundred deaths) after it began, the Battle ("Batalha") of Aljubarrota was won. King John I claimed

Nazaré & Nearby

Atlantic Ocean

São Pedro de Moel

Marinha Grande

Leiria

To Coimbra & Porto

IC-1

IC-2

Batalha

N-242

IC-1

A-1

IP-1

Ourém

To Tomar

N-356

Fátima

Sítio

Nazaré

Valado

N-8

Alcobaça

Aljubarrota

A-1

São Martinho

N-1

IC-2

Caldas da Rainha

Óbidos

100 Miles

PORTUGAL

SPAIN

Lisbon

IC-1

A-15

Rio Tejo

10 Kilometers

10 Miles

N-1

A-1

IP-1

A-13

Santarém

To Lisbon

To Lisbon

To Algarve

the Portuguese crown, and thanked the Virgin Mary with a new church and monastery.

The only reason to stop in the town of Batalha is to see its great monastery, considered Portugal's finest architectural achievement. Batalha's market day is Monday morning (market is 200 yards behind monastery).

Tourist Information: The TI, behind the monastery, has free maps, information on buses, and free Internet access for up to 15 minutes (daily 9:00-13:00 & 14:00-18:00, Praça Mouzinho de Albuquerque, tel. 244-765-180).

Arrival in Batalha: If you take the bus to Batalha, you'll be dropped off a block behind the monastery and TI, near an Intermarché supermarket. To get to the monastery, walk toward the Gothic spires. If you have difficulty finding it, ask anyone to point you toward the *mosteiro*. There's no official luggage storage, but you can leave luggage at the TI if you ask nicely. If you're driving, follow the signs to *Batalha* and park free alongside the church.

Sights in Batalha

▲▲▲MONASTERY OF SANTA MARÍA

This monastery, the symbol of Portugal's national pride, was built by King John I after winning the Battle of Aljubarrota. Unfortunately, the highway runs directly in front of the monastery, but at least you can't miss it from the road.

Cost and Hours: Church—free, cloisters—€6 except free first Sun of every month; open daily April-Sept 9:00-18:00, Oct-March 9:00-17:00, last entry 30 minutes before closing; tel. 244-765-497.

Getting In: On your way in to the church, buy a ticket for the cloisters (at the ticket counter on your immediate left); the staff at the Founders' Chapel will ask to see it.

❍ Self-Guided Tour: Here's a walk through Batalha's most important sight. Start by surveying the...

Exterior (1388-1533): The Church of Our Lady of Victory (c. 1388-1550) is a fancy late Gothic (pointed-arch) structure decorated with lacy Gothic tracery—stained-glass windows, gargoyles,

railings, and Flamboyant pinnacles representing the flickering flames of the Holy Spirit. (Inside, we'll see even more elaborate Manueline-style ornamentation, added toward the end of its construction.) The church's limestone has mellowed over time into a warm, rosy, golden color.

The equestrian statue outside the church is of Nuno Alvares Pereira, who commanded the Portuguese in the battle and masterminded the victory over Spain. Before entering the church, study the carvings on the main entrance (much-restored after serious damage in the 1755 earthquake). Notice the six lanes of heavenly traffic in the archway over the entrance: inside track—angels with their modesty wings; second track—the angel band with different instruments, including a hillbilly washboard; third—evangelists (those holding scrolls are from the Old Testament, those holding books are from the New Testament); fourth—Biblical kings and secular kings (those with globes in their hands); fifth—doctors of the Church with symbols of their martyrdom; and the express lane—female saints. Overseeing all this traffic is Jesus with the four evangelists in the tympanum. And the 12 apostles provide a foundation for it all. The statues are 19th-century copies of 14th-century originals. At the top of the pointed arch are two small coats of arms: Portugal's on the right and the House of Lancaster's on the left (a reminder of the

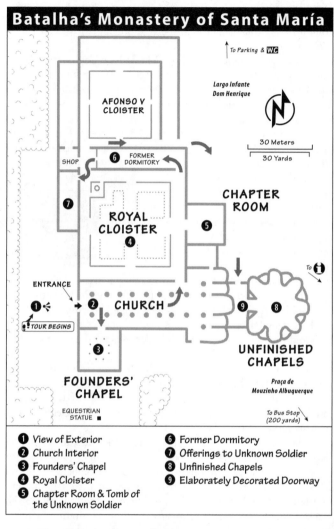

Batalha's Monastery of Santa María

To Parking & WC

Largo Infante
Dom Henrique

N

30 Meters
30 Yards

AFONSO V
CLOISTER

SHOP

❻ FORMER
DORMITORY

❼

CHAPTER
ROOM

ROYAL
CLOISTER

❹

❺

ENTRANCE

❶ ❷ CHURCH

TOUR BEGINS

❸

❾ ❽

To ℹ

FOUNDERS'
CHAPEL

UNFINISHED
CHAPELS

EQUESTRIAN
STATUE ■

Praça de
Mouzinho Albuquerque

To Bus Stop
(200 yards)

❶ View of Exterior
❷ Church Interior
❸ Founders' Chapel
❹ Royal Cloister
❺ Chapter Room & Tomb of
the Unknown Soldier

❻ Former Dormitory
❼ Offerings to Unknown Soldier
❽ Unfinished Chapels
❾ Elaborately Decorated Doorway

marriage of John I and Philippa that cemented centuries of friendship between Portugal and England).

• *Enter the church.*

Church Interior: The tall pillars leading your eye up to the "praying hands" of pointed arches, the warm light from stained-glass windows, the air of sober simplicity—this is classic Gothic, from Europe's Age of Faith. The church's lack of ornamentation reflects the vision of the project's first architect, Afonso Domingues (worked 1388-1402). Compared with Alcobaça's monastery (described later), this interior is dimmer and feels more somber,

NAZARÉ & NEARBY

though the stained glass more dramatically colors the floors and columns (only the glass around the altar is original).

• *The first chapel on the right is the...*

Founders' Chapel (Capela do Fundador): Center-stage is the double sarcophagus (that's English style) of King John I and his English queen, Philippa. The tomb statues lie together on their backs, holding hands for eternity. This husband-and-wife team ushered in Portugal's two centuries of greatness.

John I (born 1357, ruled 1385-1433), the bastard son of Dom Pedro I (King Peter I, see sidebar on page 230), repelled the Span-ish invaders, claimed the throne, consolidated his power by confiscating enemies' land to reward his friends, gave Lisbon's craftsmen a voice in government, and launched Portugal's expansion overseas. His five-decade reign greatly benefited Portugal. John's motto, *"Por bem"* ("For good"), is carved on his tomb. He established the House of Avis (see the coat of arms carved in the tomb) that would rule Portugal through the Golden Age (and eventually challenge the House of Hertz in the car-rental business). John's descendants (through both the Avis and Bragança lines) would rule Portugal until the last king, in 1910.

John, indebted to English soldiers for their help in the battle, signed the friendship Treaty of Windsor with England (1386). To seal the deal, he was requested to marry Philippa of Lancaster, the granddaughter of England's king. You can see their respective coats of arms carved at the head of the tomb.

Philippa (c. 1360-1415)—intelligent, educated, and moral—had already been rejected in marriage by two kings. John was also reluctant, reminding the English of his vow of celibacy as Grand Master of the Order of the Cross. He retreated to a monastery (with his mistress) before finally agreeing to marry Philippa (1387). Exceeding expectations, Philippa won John's admiration by overseeing domestic policy, boosting trade with England, reconciling Christians and Jews, and spearheading the invasion of Ceuta (1415) that launched the Age of Discovery.

At home, she used her wide knowledge (she was trained personally by Geoffrey Chaucer and John Wycliffe) to inspire her children to greatness. She banished John's mistress to a distant convent, but raised his bastard children almost as her own, thus sparking the rise of the Bragança line that would compete for the throne.

John and Philippa produced a slew of talented sons, some of whom rest in tombs nearby. These are the golden youth of the Age of Discovery that the Portuguese poet Luís de Camões dubbed "The Marvelous Generation" *(Ínclita Geração).*

Henrique (wearing a church for a hat and marked by a metal wreath on the floor in front) is Prince Henry the Navigator (1394-1460, see sidebar on page 154). When Philippa was on her deathbed with the plague, she summoned her son Henry to her side and made him swear he would dedicate his life to finding the legendary kingdom of Prester John—sending Henry on his own journey to explore the unknown.

Fernando (tomb on far left), Henry's kid brother, attacked the Muslims at Tangier (1437) and was captured. When his family refused to pay the ransom (which would have meant returning the city of Ceuta), he died in captivity. Son Pedro (tomb on far right), a voracious traveler and student of history, ruled Portugal as regent while his six-year-old nephew Afonso grew to manhood (heir Afonso's father, Duarte—John and Philippa's eldest—died of the plague after ruling for only five years).

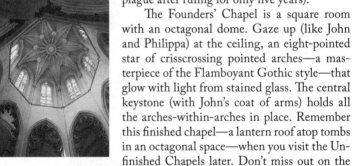

The Founders' Chapel is a square room with an octagonal dome. Gaze up (like John and Philippa) at the ceiling, an eight-pointed star of crisscrossing pointed arches—a masterpiece of the Flamboyant Gothic style—that glow with light from stained glass. The central keystone (with John's coat of arms) holds all the arches-within-arches in place. Remember this finished chapel—a lantern roof atop tombs in an octagonal space—when you visit the Unfinished Chapels later. Don't miss out on the original paint job of red-and-green arches.

• *From the church, you enter the adjoining...*

Royal Cloister (Claustro Real): Architecturally, this open courtyard (show your ticket again to enter) exemplifies Batalha's essence: Gothic construction from circa 1400 (the pointed arches surrounding the courtyard) filled in with Manueline decoration from circa 1500. The tracery in the arches features the cross of the Order of Christ (headed at one time by Prince Henry the Navigator) and armillary spheres—skel-

etal "globes" that showed what was then considered the center of the universe: planet Earth. The tracery is supported by delicate columns with shells, pearls, and coils of rope, plus artichokes and lotus flowers from the recently explored Orient.

Portugal's House of Avis and Its Coat of Arms

Seen on monuments at Belém, Batalha, Sagres, and even on the modern Portuguese flag, the Avis coat of arms is a symbol of the glorious Age of Discovery, when Portugal was ruled by kings of the Avis family.

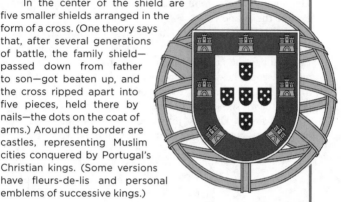

In the center of the shield are five smaller shields arranged in the form of a cross. (One theory says that, after several generations of battle, the family shield—passed down from father to son—got beaten up, and the cross ripped apart into five pieces, held there by nails—the dots on the coat of arms.) Around the border are castles, representing Muslim cities conquered by Portugal's Christian kings. (Some versions have fleurs-de-lis and personal emblems of successive kings.)

Some Important House of Avis Kings

Pedro I (Peter I, r. 1357-1367)—Buried with his beloved Inês de Castro at Alcobaça (see sidebar on page 230).

John I (r. 1385-1433)—Pedro's bastard son, who protected Portugal from a Spanish takeover and launched overseas expansion.

Manuel I (r. 1495-1521)—Ruler when all the overseas expansion began to pay off financially. He built the Monastery of Jerónimos at Belém, decorated in the ornamental style that bears his name (see architecture sidebar on page 87).

John III (r. 1521-1557)—Ruler during Portugal's peak of power... and at the beginning of its decline.

Sebastian (r. 1557-1578)—Because he was lost in battle, the nation lost its way, leading to takeover by Spain.

Stop here and picture Dominican monks in white robes, blue capes, and tonsured haircuts (shaved crown) meditating as they slowly circled this garden courtyard. They'd stop to wash their hands at the washbasin (*lavabo*, in the northwest corner, with a great view back at the church) before stepping into the adjoining refectory (dining hall) for a meal.

• *Continue to the...*

Chapter Room: The self-supporting star-vaulted ceiling spans 60 feet, an engineering tour-de-force by Master Huguet, a foreigner who became chief architect in 1402. Huguet brought Flamboyant Gothic decoration to the church's sober style. The ceiling was considered so dangerous to build (it collapsed twice) that only prisoners condemned to death were allowed to work on it. (Today, unknowing tourists are allowed to wander under it.) The architect who helped Huguet come up with the strong-enough, interlocking, spider-web design for this vast vault supposedly silenced skeptics by personally spending the night in this room. (It even survived the 1755 earthquake.) He's remembered with a little portrait figurine supporting the column in the far-right corner of the room. Besides this ceiling, Huguet designed the Founders' Chapel and the Unfinished Chapels.

Portugal's **Tomb of the Unknown Soldier** sits under a mutilated crucifix called *Christ of the Trenches,* which accompanied Portuguese soldiers into battle on the western front of World War I. The three small soldiers under the flame—which burns Portuguese olive oil—are dressed to represent the three most valiant chapters in Portuguese military history: fighting Moors in the 12th century, Spaniards in the 14th century, and Germans in the 20th century.

• *Leaving the Chapter Room, turn right and enter the former dormitory through the archway (notice the tiny ornamental knots). Pass through the dormitory while immersing yourself in the walk-through audiovisual history of the church and monastery. Exit left to the refectory, through the door near the fountain in the corner.*

The **refectory** contains a collection of all the offerings from various countries to the Portuguese unknown soldier. Of particular interest is a photograph taken in the trenches of the WWI crucifix (the crucifix itself is the one displayed in the Chapter Room you just visited).

• *Go back past the former dormitory and continue through the Afonso V Cloister—not nearly as interesting as the Royal Cloister (although you may see art students learning about sculpture on the far side). Follow the exit signs to a square outside the church. Head right, to the...*

Unfinished Chapels (Capelas Imperfeitas): The Unfinished Chapels are called by that name because, well, that's not a Gothic sunroof overhead. This chapel behind the main altar was intended as an octagonal room with seven niches for tombs, topped with a rotunda ceiling (similar to the Founders' Chapel). But only the walls, support pillars for the ceiling, and a double tomb were completed.

King Duarte and his wife, Leonor, lie hand in hand on their backs, watching the clouds pass by, blissfully unaware of the work left undone. Duarte (1391-1438), the oldest of John and Philippa's sons, was the golden boy of the charmed family. He wrote a how-to book on courtly manners. When, at age 42, he became king (1433), he called a *cortes* (parliament) to enact much-needed legal reforms.

NAZARÉ & NEARBY

He financed and encouraged his brother Prince Henry's initial overseas explorations. And he began work on these chapels, hoping to make a glorious family burial place. But Duarte died young of the plague, leaving behind an unfinished chapel, a stunned nation, and his six-year-old son, Afonso, as the new king.

Leonor became the regent while Afonso grew up, but she proved unpopular as a ruler, being both Spanish and female. Duarte's brother Pedro then ruled as regent before being banished by rivals.

In 1509, Duarte's grandson, King Manuel I, added the elaborately decorated **doorway** (by Mateus Fernandes), a masterpiece of the Manueline style. The series of ever larger arches that frame the door are carved in stone so detailed that they look like stucco. See carved coils of rope with knots, some snails along the bottom, artichokes (used to fend off scurvy), corn (from American discoveries), and Indian-inspired motifs (from the land of pepper). Contrast the doorway's Manueline ornamentation with the Renaissance simplicity of the upper-floor balcony that crowns the grand doorway, done in 1533.

Manuel abandoned the chapel after Vasco da Gama's triumphant return from India, channeling Portugal's money and energy instead to building a monument to the Age of Discovery launched by the Avis family—the Jerónimos Monastery in Belém (where both Manuel and, some believe, da Gama are buried).

Sleeping in Batalha

If you spend the night, don't count on nightlife—this town shuts down early.

$$$ Hotel Villa Batalha offers 93 modern rooms with high-class comfort, complete with an in-house spa and swimming pool (Sb-€65-75, Db-€75-90, Rua D. Duarte I 248, tel. 244-240-400, www.hotelvillabatalha.pt, geral@hotelvillabatalha.pt). With the monastery behind you, walk left on Rua Dona Filippa de Lencastre, continue straight through the roundabout, and you'll see the hotel.

Batalha Connections

From Batalha by Bus to: Nazaré (6/day, 1 hour), **Alcobaça** (8/day, 30 minutes), **Fátima** (4/day, 1 hour), **Coimbra** (5/day, 1 hour), **Porto** (6/day, 3 hours), and **Lisbon** (5/day, 2 hours). Expect fewer buses on weekends. The café across the street from the Batalha bus stop sells bus tickets (not sold by drivers).

By Car: Batalha is an easy 10-mile drive from Fátima. You'll see signs from each site to the other.

Fátima

On May 13, 1917, three children were tending sheep when the sky lit up and a woman—Mary, the mother of Christ, "a lady brighter than the sun"—appeared standing in an oak tree. (It's the tree to the left of the large basilica.) In the midst of bloody World War I, she brought a message that peace was coming. The war raged on, so on the 13th day of each of the next five months, Mary dropped in again to call for peace and to repeat three messages. Word spread, bringing many curious pilgrims. The three kids—Lucia, Francisco, and Jacinta—were grilled mercilessly by authorities trying to debunk their preposterous visions, but the children remained convinced of what they'd seen.

Finally, on October 13, 70,000 people assembled near the oak tree. They were drenched in a rainstorm when suddenly, the sun came out, grew blindingly bright, danced around the sky (writing "God's fiery signature"), then plunged to the earth. When the crowd came to its senses, the sun was shining and the rain had dried.

In 1930, the Vatican recognized the Virgin of Fátima as legit. And today, tens of thousands of believers come to rejoice in this modern miracle. Many walk from as far away as Lisbon. Depending on the time of year you visit, you may see scores of pilgrims with reflective vests walking along the smaller highways. Fátima, Lourdes (in France), and Međugorje (in Bosnia-Herzegovina) are the three big Mary sights in Europe.

Orientation to Fátima

The pilgrim-friendly, modern Fátima (FAH-tee-mah) is a huge complex, with two big churches bookending a vast esplanade, adjacent to a practical commercial center. Wandering through the religious and commercial zones, you see the 21st-century equivalent of a medieval pilgrimage center: lots of beds, cheap eateries, fields of picnic tables and parking lots, and countless religious souvenir stands—all ready for the mobs of people who inundate the place each 12th and 13th day of the month from May through October. Any other day, it's just big and empty.

At the start of the commercial zone, browse through the horseshoe-shaped mall of stalls selling religious trinkets—wax body parts, rosaries (which pilgrims get blessed after attending Mass here), and so on.

Those arriving by car can simply follow the *Sanctuario parques* signs to vast lots behind the church.

Tourist Information: The TI is near the church (daily April-

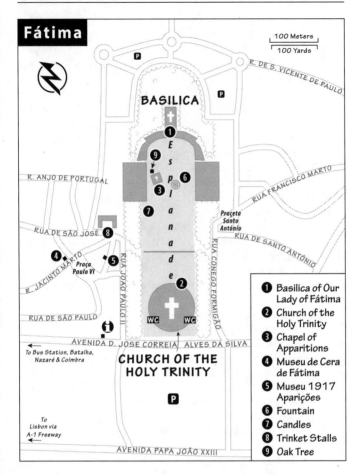

Fátima

100 Meters
100 Yards

BASILICA

Esplanade

Praçeta
Santo
António

R. DE S. VICENTE DE PAULO
R. ANJO DE PORTUGAL
RUA FRANCISCO MARTO
RUA DE SANTO ANTÓNIO
RUA DE SÃO JOSÉ
RUA JACINTO MARTO
Praça Paulo VI
R. JACINTO MARTO
RUA JOÃO PAULO II
RUA CONEGO FORMIGÃO
RUA DE SÃO PAULO
AVENIDA D. JOSÉ CORREIA ALVES DA SILVA
AVENIDA PAPA JOÃO XXIII

To Bus Station, Bataiha,
Nazaré & Coimbra

To
Lisbon via
A-1 Freeway

WC   WC

CHURCH OF THE
HOLY TRINITY

1 Basilica of Our
Lady of Fátima
2 Church of the
Holy Trinity
3 Chapel of
Apparitions
4 Museu de Cera
de Fátima
5 Museu 1917
Aparições
6 Fountain
7 Candles
8 Trinket Stalls
9 Oak Tree

Sept 10:00-13:00 & 14:00-19:00, Oct-March 10:00-13:00 & 14:00-18:00, Avenida José Alves Correia da Silva 126, tel. 249-531-139, www.rt-leiriafatima.pt).

Sights in Fátima

Esplanade

The huge assembly ground facing the basilica is impressive even without the fanfare of a festival day. The fountain in the middle provides holy water for pilgrims to take home. You'll see the information center; the oak tree and Chapel of the Apparitions marking the spot where Mary appeared; a place for lighting and leaving candles (with an inferno below where the wax melts into a trench and flows into a vat to be resurrected as new candles); and a long

Mary's Three Messages

1. Peace is coming. (World War I is ending. Later, during World War II, Salazar justified keeping Portugal neutral by saying it was in accordance with Mary's wishes for peace.)

2. Russia will reject God and communism will rise, bringing a second great war.

3. Someone will try to kill the pope. (This third message was kept a secret for decades, supposedly lying in a sealed envelope in the Vatican. On May 13, 1981—the first pilgrimage day of Fátima each year—Pope John Paul II was shot. He visited Fátima in 2000, meeting the surviving visionary, beatifying the two who had died, and publicly revealing this long-hidden third secret.)

smooth route on the pavement for pilgrims to approach the chapel on their knees.

Basilica of Our Lady of Fátima

The towering Neoclassical basilica (1928-1953) has a 200-foot spire with a golden crown and crystal cross-shaped beacon on top. Its

facade features Mary of the Rosary, flanked by mosaics in the porticoes of the 14 Stations of the Cross (under the statues of the four Portuguese saints). At the top of the steps, an open-air altar, cathedra (bishop's chair), and pulpit await the next 13th of the month, when the masses will enjoy an outdoor Mass.

Dress modestly to enter the church. Inside, huge letters arc across the ceiling above the altar, offering up a request for Mary in Latin, "Queen of the Holy Rosary of Fátima, pray for us." A huge painting depicting the vision is flanked by chapels dedicated to the Stations of the Cross and the tombs of the children who saw the vision. Two died in the flu epidemic that swept the world shortly after the visions. Francisco's tomb (died 1919) is to the right of the altar. Jacinta (died 1920) and Lucia rest in a chapel to the left of the altar. Lucia (the only one with whom Mary actually conversed) passed away at the age of 97 in 2005. She lived as a Carmelite nun near Coimbra for most of her life. The basilica is busy with many Masses throughout each day.

Cost and Hours: Free, daily 6:00-21:00.

Church of the Holy Trinity (Igreja da Santíssima Trindade)

In 2005, Pope John Paul II began the construction of this grand church with a stone from St. Peter's actual tomb in the Vatican.

Completed in late 2007, it can hold 9,000 devotees, 10 times the capacity of the older basilica. The striking architecture and decoration is intentionally multinational—the architect was Greek; the large orange iron crucifix in front is German; the dazzling, golden mosaic mural inside (the left side depicts Mary with the three children she visited and all the people who witnessed her in the last apparition in October 1917) is Slovenian; and the crucifix at the altar (with the strikingly different Jesus) is Irish. The church is circular, symbolizing the world. Each of its 12 doors is named for an apostle. Outside, statues of two popes kneel facing the esplanade (Paul VI, who was here on the 50th anniversary in 1967, and John Paul II, who had a special place for Fátima in his heart and visited three times). The long, smooth approach for pilgrims making their way to the Chapel of Apparitions on their knees starts here, with a pilgrims' prayer posted.

Cost and Hours: Free, daily 9:00-19:00, services Sat at 11:00 and Sun at 15:00 and 16:30, www.santuario-fatima.pt.

Chapel of Apparitions

This marks the spot where Mary appeared to the three children (located outside the church, next to the big old oak tree, beneath a canopy). Services take place daily 6:30-21:30 in a variety of languages; check the posted schedule for English.

Pilgrimage

On the 13th of each month from May through October, and on August 19, up to 100,000 pilgrims come to Fátima. Some shuffle on their knees, traversing the mega-huge, park-lined esplanade (which is more than 160,000 square feet) leading to the church. Torch-lit processions occur on two nights (usually the 12th and 13th). In 1967, on the 50th anniversary of the miracle, 1.5 million pilgrims—including the pope—gathered here.

Museums

Unfortunately the Catholic Church hasn't yet put together an exhibition befitting this beautiful sight. Instead, two tacky and overpriced for-profit "museums" compete for your euros—each within a couple of blocks of the esplanade in the modern town. The **Museu de Cera de Fátima** is a series of rooms filled with wax figures that tell the story of Fátima's visitation one scene at a time. Its €7.50 tickets—the proceeds from which don't go to a good cause—make it the worst sightseeing value in Portugal (daily April-Oct 9:30-18:30, Nov-March 10:00-17:00, English leaflet describes each vignette). The **Museu 1917 Aparições,**

telling the same story with a 15-minute-long low-tech sound-and-light show, is a better value and experience (€3.50, daily April-Oct 9:00-19:00, Nov-March 9:00-18:00, deep inside a shopping complex behind enormous Hotel de Fátima, worthless without English soundtrack—ask at the ticket window). Both exhibits are pretty cheesy for those not inclined to take Fátima too seriously.

Fátima Connections

From Fátima by Bus to: Batalha (4/day, 1 hour), **Alcobaça** (3/day, 1 hour, more frequent with transfer in Batalha), **Coimbra** (hourly, 1 hour), **Nazaré** (3/day, 1.5 hours), and **Lisbon** (hourly, 1.5-2.5 hours, depending on route); service drops on Sunday. Note that the stop closest to the basilica is listed on bus schedules as Cova de Iria, *not* Fátima. Baggage storage is available at the bus station (€2.40/day).

Alcobaça

This pleasant little town is famous for its church, one of the most interesting in Portugal. I find Alcobaça (ahl-koh-BAH-sah) a better stop than Batalha.

Tourist Information: The English-speaking TI is in the shopping district, between the monastery and the market (daily 9:00-13:00 & 14:00-18:00, Rua 16 de Outubro 9, tel. 262-582-377).

Arrival in Alcobaça: If you arrive by bus, it's a five-minute walk to the town center and monastery. Exit right from the station (on Avenida Manuel da Silva Carolino), walk a half-block uphill (car parking lot visible in distance), take the first right, and continue straight (on Rua Dom Pedro V). Hang a left just after passing a small plaza, and you are in the main square.

If you're arriving by car, follow the *Mosteiro* or *estação rodoviário* (bus station) signs at the roundabout. A parking lot just uphill from the bus station is currently free, and streets in front of the monastery have plenty of pay-and-display parking.

Sweets: Pastelaria Alcôa, across from the entrance to the monastery, wins awards yearly for their traditional convent pastries, including the best *pastel de nata* in all of Portugal in 2014. Do your own taste test (daily 8:00-19:30, Praça 25 de Abril 44, tel. 262-597-474).

Sights in Alcobaça

▲▲Cistercian Monastery of Santa Maria

This abbey church, despite its mainly Baroque facade, represents the best Gothic building in Portugal. It's also the country's largest church, and a clean and bright break from the heavier Iberian norm. Afonso Henriques began construction in 1178 after taking the nearby town of Santarém from the Moors.

The first Cistercian monks arrived in 1228 and proceeded to make this one of the most powerful abbeys of the Cistercian Order and a cultural center of 13th-century Portugal. This simple abbey was designed to be filled with hard work, prayer, and total silence.

Cost and Hours: €6, free first Sun of every month, daily April-Sept 9:00-19:00, Oct-March 9:00-17:00, last entry 30 minutes before closing, tel. 262-505-128.

◐ Self-Guided Tour: As you view the church from the expansive square facing it, you can sense its former importance. The wings stretching to the right and left from the facade housed monks and pilgrims. As was generally the case with monasteries, the monastery was an industrial engine (making ceramics and other products), and by the 16th century a town had grown around the abbey. When the abbey was dissolved in 1834, the town declined, too.

Stepping inside, you find a suitably grand yet austere house of prayer—just straight Gothic lines. The only decor is organic (such as leafy capitals).

Nave and Tombs of Dom Pedro and Inês: A long and narrow central nave leads to a pair of finely carved Gothic tombs (from

1360). These are of Portugal's most tragic romantic couple, Dom Pedro (King Peter I, 1320-1367, on the right) and Dona Inês de Castro (c. 1323-1355, on the left). They rest feet-to-feet in each transept, so that on Judgment Day they'll rise and immediately see each other again. Pedro, heir to the Portuguese throne, was hopelessly in love with the Spanish aristocrat Inês (see sidebar).

Notice the carvings on the tombs. Like religious alarm clocks, the attending angels are poised to wake the couple on Judgment

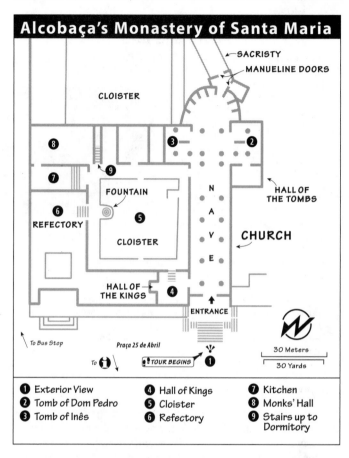

Alcobaça's Monastery of Santa Maria

SACRISTY
MANUELINE DOORS

CLOISTER

❸ ❷

N
A
V
E

HALL OF
THE TOMBS

CHURCH

❽

❾

❼

FOUNTAIN

❻

❺

REFECTORY

CLOISTER

HALL OF
THE KINGS

❹

ENTRANCE

To Bus Stop

Praça 25 de Abril

To ℹ

🔊 TOUR BEGINS ❶

30 Meters
30 Yards

❶ Exterior View
❷ Tomb of Dom Pedro
❸ Tomb of Inês
❹ Hall of Kings
❺ Cloister
❻ Refectory
❼ Kitchen
❽ Monks' Hall
❾ Stairs up to
   Dormitory

Day. Pedro will lie here (as inscribed on the tomb) *"Até ao fim do mundo"*—until the end of the world, when he and Inês are reunited. The "Wheel of Life" below Pedro's finely combed head features the king on the throne at the top and the king in his tomb at the bottom, with the good things in life on the left and the bad things (including Inês' beheading) on the right.

Scenes from the life of St. Bartholomew—famous for being skinned alive (Pedro's patron saint, reflecting his life of sacrifice)—circle the tomb. The martyrdom of St. Bartholomew is depicted on a relief directly below the king's head on his left side—along with the creepy aftermath. Pedro's tomb is supported by lions, a symbol of royalty. Opposite, Inês' tomb is supported by

Pedro and Inês

Twenty-year-old Prince Pedro met 17-year-old Inês, a Galician noblewoman, at his wedding to Inês' cousin Constance. The

politically motivated marriage was arranged by Pedro's father, the king. Pedro dutifully fathered his son, the future king Fernando, with Constance in Lisbon, while seeing Inês on the side in Coimbra. When Constance died, Pedro settled in with Inês. Concerned about Spanish influence, Pedro's father, Afonso IV, forbade their marriage. You guessed it—they were married secretly, and the couple had four children. When King Afonso, fearing rivals to his ("legitimate") grandson's kingship, had Inês murdered, Prince Pedro went ballistic. He staged an armed uprising (1355) against his father, only settled after much bloodshed.

Once he was crowned King Pedro I the Just (1357), the much-embellished legend begins. Pedro summoned his enemies, exhumed Inês' body, dressed it in a bridal gown, and put it on the throne, making the murderers kneel and kiss its putrid rotting hand. (The legend continues...) Pedro then executed Inês' two murderers—personally—by ripping out their hearts, eating them, and washing them down, it is said, with a fine *vinho verde*. Now that's *amor*.

the lowly scum who murdered her...one holding a monkey, a symbol of evil. Inês' tomb features vivid scenes from the life of Christ, and the relief at her feet features Heaven, the dragon mouth of Hell (pictured at bottom of previous page), and jack-in-the-box coffins on Judgment Day. Although Napoleon's troops vandalized the tombs (that's why so many heads are missing), the story of Pedro and Inês endures *até ao fim do mundo*. Stroll through the ambulatory to the sacristy entrance. The two Manueline doors, courtesy of King Manuel I, add a touch of grandeur (think of Lisbon's Monastery of Jerónimos) to the rather plain but elegant church. Return toward the entrance and find the doorway on the right to the...

Hall of Kings: This hall features terra-cotta ceramic statues of most of Portugal's kings. The last king portrayed is Joseph, who ruled when the earthquake hit in 1755. Since then there has been no money for fancy statues. The next empty pedestal (to the left of Joseph) is wider than the rest—in anticipation of the reign of Portugal's first queen, Mary I, and her big fancy dress. The walls feature 18th-century tiles telling the story of the 12th-century conquest of the Moors and the building of the monastery (each with Latin supertitles and Portuguese subtitles). In the last scene, the first king lays the monastery's first stone.

The sculpture facing the entrance features a fantastical image of Afonso Henriques, first king of Portugal and founder of this monastery, being crowned by Pope Innocent III and St. Bernard. From here, steps lead to the...

Cloister: Cistercian monks built the abbey in 40 years, starting in 1178. They inhabited it until 1834 (when the Portuguese king disbanded all monasteries). The monks spent most of their lives in silence, and were allowed to speak only when given permission by the abbot. To enjoy this cloister like the monks did: Meditate, pray, exercise, and connect with nature. As you multitask, circle counterclockwise until you reach the fountain—where the monks washed up before eating. Traditionally, in any cloister, the fountain marks the entry to the...

Refectory (Dining Hall): Imagine the hall filled with monks eating in silence as one reads from the Bible atop the "Readers' Pulpit." Food was prepared next door.

Kitchen: The 18th-century kitchen's giant three-part oven could roast seven oxen simultaneously. The industrious monks rerouted part of the River Alcoa to bring in running water. This kitchen fed huge numbers: The population of monks here maxed out at 999 (triple the Trinity), and peasants who worked the church-owned land were rewarded with meals here.

Monk's Hall (Sala dos Monges): This large common space contains the short audiovisual presentation "Portugal—Between Heaven and Earth," with nice aerial views of different cities...good inspiration for future travel.

Dormitory: Take the stairs up to the bare dormitory, from which you can peer down on the transept of the church where Inês and Pedro lie buried. On this floor, there is also a terrace onto the

adjacent cloister, with a rose garden and a stairway to the upper cloister with two views: overlooking the kitchen's giant oven, and the main cloister and up-close gargoyles.

▲Mercado Municipal

An Old World version of Safeway is housed happily here under huge steel-and-fiberglass arches. Inside the covered market, black-clad dried-apple-faced women choose fish, uncaged and feisty chickens, ducks, and rabbits from their respective death rows. Wander among figs, melons, bushels of grain, and nuts (Mon-Sat 9:00-13:00, closed Sun, best on Mon). Imagine having a lifelong relationship with the person who grows your produce. Women from Nazaré—with their distinctive dress—sell fish in a separate room. The market is a five-minute walk from the TI (just down the block from the bus station); ask a local, *"Mercado municipal?"* Also, a flea market happens Mondays by the Alcoa River.

Alcobaça Connections

From Alcobaça by Bus to: Lisbon (6/day, 2 hours, some transfer in Caldas da Rainha), **Nazaré** (2/hour, 20 minutes, stops at Valado), **Batalha** (8/day, 30 minutes), **Fátima** (3/day, 1 hour, more frequent with transfer in Batalha), **Óbidos** (6/day, 1.5 hours). Bus frequency drops on weekends, especially Sunday. A taxi to the Nazaré/Valado train station costs about €10; to Nazaré, a little over €15. Bus info: Tel. 808-200-370.

Óbidos

Postcard-perfect Óbidos (OH-bee-doosh) sits atop a hill, its 14th-century wall (45 feet tall) corralling a bouquet of narrow lanes and flower-bedecked whitewashed houses. Its name, dating from ancient Roman times, means "walled town." The 16th-century aqueduct connecting it like an umbilical cord to a nearby spring is a reminder of the town's importance during Portugal's boom century. Óbidos—now protected by the government from modern development—is ideal for photographers who want to make Portugal look as pretty as it can be.

Founded by Celts (c. 300 B.C.), then ruled by Romans, Visigoths, and Moors, Óbidos was known as Portugal's "wedding city." In 1282, when King Dinis brought his bride Isabel here, she liked the town so much he gave it to her. (Whatta guy.) Later kings carried on the tradition—the perfect gift for a king to give to a queen who has everything. (Beats a toaster.) Today, this medieval walled town is popular for lowly commoners' weddings. Preserved in its entirety as a national monument since 1951, it survives on tourism. Every summer morning at 9:30, the tour groups flush into town. Óbidos is especially crowded in August, but it's worth a quick visit anyway. Ideally, arrive late one day and leave early the next, enjoying the town as you would a beautiful painted tile. Or arrive midday and encounter the crush of tour groups.

Tourist Information: The TI is at Óbidos' main pay parking lot (€0.60/hour, TI open daily May-Sept 9:30-19:30, shorter hours off-season, tel. 262-959-231). The TI rents bikes for €10 a day (€6/half-day).

Internet Access: Net, across from the pillar on the main street at Rua Direita 107, has 14 terminals and offers free Internet access (daily in summer 10:00-19:00, shorter hours off-season).

Arrival in Óbidos: There's no official place to store luggage in town, so it's smart to travel light.

If you arrive at the train station, you're faced with a 20-minute uphill hike into town. The bus drops you off much closer, right outside the main gate (upon arrival, go up the steps and through the archway on the right). If leaving by train, you can catch a taxi to the station in the lot outside the main gate (about €10).

If you arrive by car, don't drive into tiny, cobbled Óbidos. Ample tourist parking is provided just outside the main gate. The closest lot (by the TI and a public WC) is pay-and-display (€0.60/hour). The huge lot across the street (lined by the 16th-century aqueduct) is a bit cheaper (€0.50/hour), but first check for a space in the perfectly good free lot just south of here, or in the small free lot near the *pousada*. If you're staying inside the town walls and want to park near your hotel, be sure to get details beforehand. Some hotels inside the walls have one or two spots, but it's generally easier to park outside the walls.

Óbidos Walk

WELCOME TO ÓBIDOS

Main Gate: Enter through the main gate in Óbidos' 14th-century wall. Stop to gaze up at the scenes related to the town's history—depicting centuries of battles and religion in blue-and-white tiles. Tiles like these covered the entire face of the walls here until the 1755 quake shook them down.

Step into the town, and like Dorothy entering a medieval Oz, you're confronted by two wonderful cobbled lanes.

The top lane is the town's main drag, littered with tourists shopping and leading straight through Óbidos to its castle (ahead, you can see its square tower, where this walk finishes).

Town Wall: After entering the old town through the main gate, notice the steep stairs (to your left) accessing the scenic if treacherous sentry path along the wall (other access points are near the castle/*pousada*, and uphill from the main church). Climb the steps for views of the city and surrounding countryside from the 45-foot-high walls. The west (uphill) wall is best, letting you look over the town's white buildings with red roofs and blue or yellow trim. You can almost gaze at the Atlantic, six miles away. Until the 1100s, when the bay silted up, the ocean was half as far away, making this a hilltop citadel guarding a natural port. The aqueduct is from the 16th century.

• *Bypass the wall walk for now, descend the staircase, and head into town. Follow...*

Rua Josefa d'Óbidos: Continue straight along this mini-restaurant row and notice the whitewash that keeps things cool; the bright blue-and-yellow trims, traditionally designed to define property lines; and the potted geraniums, which bloom most of the year, survive the summer sun well, and keep mosquitoes away. The **Church of St. Peter** has a fine, restored Baroque altar covered with Brazilian gold leaf. The Maltese-type crosses carved into the rock throughout the church are a constant reminder that this fine building was "brought to you by your friends in the Order of Christ" (daily 9:30-12:30 & 14:30-19:00, until 17:00 Oct-March). After peeking in, exit the church and climb uphill to the main tourist drag.

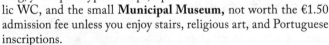

• *Then turn right on...*

Rua Direita: Walking toward the castle on this main shopping drag, you'll pass typical shops, a public WC, and the small **Municipal Museum,** not worth the €1.50 admission fee unless you enjoy stairs, religious art, and Portuguese inscriptions.

• *Continue on and enter the...*

Town Square: The lone column at the side of the road (opposite the church) is the 16th-century **pillory.** Bad boys were tied to this to endure whatever punishment was deemed appropriate. Studying it closely, you'll notice it's capped by Queen Leonor's crown. On the side facing the castle, the carved hanging shrimp net represents how fishermen found the body of 16-year-old Afonso, son of Manuel I and Leonor, in the Rio Tejo after a tragic and mysterious death. The net eventually became part of the queen's

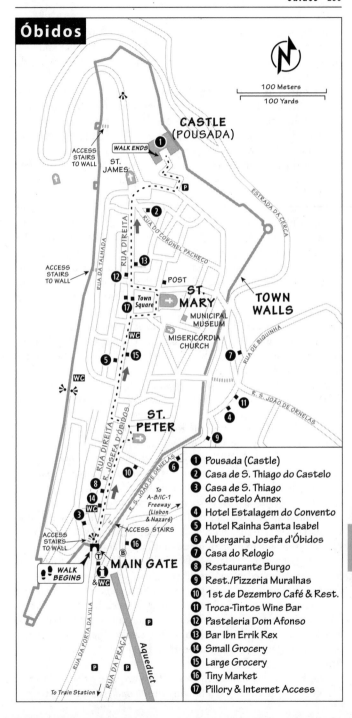

Óbidos

100 Meters
100 Yards

CASTLE
(POUSADA)

WALK ENDS ➊

ACCESS
STAIRS
TO WALL

ST.
JAMES

ESTRADA DA CERCA

P

➋

RUA DIREITA

RUA DO CORONEL PACHECO

ACCESS
STAIRS
TO WALL

RUA DA TALHADA

RUA DIREITA

➌

➊➋

POST

Town
Square

ST.
MARY

TOWN
WALLS

➊➐

MUNICIPAL
MUSEUM

MISERICÓRDIA
CHURCH

RUA DE BIQUINHA

WC

➎ ➊➎

WC

ST.
PETER

RUA DIREITA

R. JOSEFA D'ÓBIDOS

R. S. JOAO DE ORNELAS

➊➊

➍

➒

➏

➊➐

➑

➊➍

WC

➌

ACCESS
STAIRS
TO WALL

➊➏

B

T

**WALK
BEGINS**

MAIN GATE

i & WC

R. S. JOAO DE ORNELAS

To
A-8/IC-1
Freeway
(Lisbon
& Nazaré)

ACCESS STAIRS

RUA DA PORTA DA VILA

Aqueduct

RUA DA PRAÇA

P

P

P

To Train Station ↓

➊ Pousada (Castle)
➋ Casa de S. Thiago do Castelo
➌ Casa de S. Thiago
   do Castelo Annex
➍ Hotel Estalagem do Convento
➎ Hotel Rainha Santa Isabel
➏ Albergaria Josefa d'Óbidos
➐ Casa do Relogio
➑ Restaurante Burgo
➒ Rest./Pizzeria Muralhas
➊ 1st de Dezembro Café & Rest.
➊➊ Troca-Tintos Wine Bar
➊➋ Pasteleria Dom Afonso
➊➌ Bar Ibn Errik Rex
➊➍ Small Grocery
➊➎ Large Grocery
➊➏ Tiny Market
➊➐ Pillory & Internet Access

NAZARÉ & NEARBY

coat of arms. The huge pots you see beneath the awning overlooking the square on the left were once in the central market and held olive oil instead of flowers. But at the bottom of the square, do enter the...

Church of St. Mary of Óbidos: Grab a seat on a front pew, surrounded by classic 17th-century tiles (church open daily). Notice the fine painted-wood ceiling over each of the three naves. To the left of the altar is a niche with a delicate Portuguese Renaissance tomb, featuring a pietà carved out of local limestone. To the right of the altar are three paintings, including *The Mystical Marriage of St. Catherine,* all by Óbidos' most famous artist, the nun Josefa d'Óbidos (1634-1684).

To peek into another church, exit left and head a few steps down (behind the terrace bar). Look for Our Lady of Mercy sculpted in blue and white ceramic above the entrance. The **Misericórdia church** was built as part of the queen's charity institution, hence the royal coat-of-arms painted on the ceiling. It's lined with 16th-century "carpet tiles." To the right of the altar you can see one of the "religious floats" and a cross that's carried through town during Holy Week festivities.

• *Return to the main shopping drag and turn right for the...*

Final Stretch to the Castle: On the left, pop into the **Pasteleria Dom Afonso** (#113). This welcoming little coffee bar, dominated by a big old grape press, serves good pastries and sandwiches. Try the local version of *pastel de nata* with chocolate (open daily 8:00-20:00, on the main drag). Farther down the street, **Bar Ibn Errik Rex** (#100) is the most characteristic—and touristy—of several Óbidos *ginjinha* bars—the town is famous for its much-loved Portuguese cherry liqueur. Bruno will take good care of you, with a backdrop of his dad's 30-year-old collection of mini liquor bottles (but you'll pay €2.50 a glass here, as opposed to only €1 a shot in several other small shops along the main street).

• *The main drag dead-ends at the top of town and the...*

Pousada: This former castle is now a fancy hotel with nine rooms (Db-€170-265, tel. 262-955-080, www.pousadas.pt). Visitors are welcome to drop in for a fancy cup of coffee.

On January 11, 1148, Afonso Henriques (Portugal's first king) led a two-pronged attack to liberate the town from the Moors. Afonso attacked the main gate at the other end of town (where tourists enter), while the Moorish ruler huddled here in his castle. Meanwhile, a band of Afonso's men, disguised as cherry trees, snuck up the steep hillside behind the castle. The doomed Moor ignored his daughter when she turned from the window and asked him, "Daddy, do trees walk?"

A lane to the left leads to the stairs accessing the town wall. But go uphill to the right, following the *pousada* signs to the terrace with the telescope for a look at the city. After savoring the view, go back to the top of Rua Direita and enter the archway to your right. Walk uphill for a minute until you see the town wall. Turn around for a spectacular view of the castle—it's yours for the taking.

• *You can return to your starting point three ways: hiking along the upper town wall, exploring photogenic side lanes, or shopping and drinking your way back down the main drag.*

Sights in Óbidos

The main sight in Óbidos is the town itself. Wander the postcard-perfect streets, climb the town walls, and sample some *ginjinha* (cherry liqueur) in a chocolate cup. You will find several shops selling chocolates and *ginjinha* along the main street, Rua Direita. Then explore the side streets, away from the throngs of tourists.

NEAR ÓBIDOS
Caldas da Rainha
A 10-minute drive or taxi ride from Óbidos, Caldas da Rainha is famous for its therapeutic springs, which have attracted royalty looking for rheumatism cures and aristocrats wanting to make the scene. A venerable hospital now sits on the source of those curative waters. The charming old center is more workaday than Óbidos, as mono-block development has swamped the outskirts. But the town is still filled with unexpected surprises. Stroll the lovely public gardens near the hospital, uncover the hidden meanings of the various stenciled graffiti, and gaze at a multitude of Art Deco buildings. Caldas da Rainha provides a good glimpse of everyday Portugal, with the charm punched up just a notch. Ideally, drop by any morning (except Mon), when its farmers' market fills Praça da República with fruits, veggies, nuts, flowers, and lots of busy locals.

Sleeping in Óbidos

To enjoy Óbidos without tourists, spend the night. Here are reasonable values in this overpriced toy of a town. In the first three weeks in August, prices spike up beyond those listed here.

$$$ Casa de S. Thiago do Castelo, a fancy and characteristic little guesthouse at the base of the *pousada*/castle, rents eight elegantly appointed rooms around a chirpy *Better Homes and Tiles* patio. Lower levels offer three different, welcoming salons to relax in, including one with a classy billiards table (Sb-€65, Db-€80, free parking, Largo de S. Thiago, tel. 262-959-587, www.casas-sthiago.com, reservas@casas-sthiago.com, Alice speaks English). They also have an annex near the main gate, where they book overflow guests in six rooms (without breakfast) at busy times.

$$$ Hotel Estalagem do Convento was built to house nuns—but they never showed up. Now it welcomes guests to its 28 rooms with solemn charm (Sb-€80, Db-€95, suites-€116-150, extra bed-€40, located outside wall with easy parking, Rua Dom João d'Ornelas, tel. 262-959-216, www.hotelestalagemdoconvento. com, estconventhotel@mail.telepac.pt).

$$$ Hotel Rainha Santa Isabel is an old-school, hotelesque place marked by flags on the main drag in the center of the old town. If you're driving, call first to let them know you're approaching, stop long enough to drop your bags and get a parking permit, and drive on to the town square to park. If no one's at the front desk, the staff at the Doce Rainha café next door can help (Sb-€40-65, Db-€65-90, Tb-75-95, price depends on room, prices soar in Aug, air-con, elevator, Wi-Fi in public areas, on the main one-lane drag, Rua Direita 63, tel. 262-959-323, www.obidoshotel. com, arsio@mail.telepac.pt).

$$$ Albergaria Josefa d'Óbidos, located just outside the town walls, is a fine value. Its 34 rooms are clean and well-appointed. Half the rooms have been updated with modern bathrooms and new furnishings; the older rooms are somewhat dated, but have nice *azulejo*-tiled bathrooms (Sb-€45-65, Db-€60-80, Tb-€70-90, suites-€110-115, air-con, Wi-Fi in reception and bar, free parking, Rua Dom João d'Ornelas, tel. 262-959-296, www.josefadobidos. com, josefadobidos@iol.pt). The attached restaurant serves nice fish and meat dishes starting at €13, and also offers vegetarian options.

$$ Casa do Relogio is a rustic eight-room place at the downhill end of town, just outside the wall. It's friendly and easygoing, providing no-stress parking and great comfort for the price. English-speaking Sara offers a big sun terrace and happily does her guests' laundry for no extra charge (Sb-€35-45, Db-€45-60, Tb-€60-70, same prices in peak of summer, ask for Rick Steves discount, cash only, Rua da Graça 12, tel. 262-959-282, www. casadorelogio.com, reservas@casadorelogio.com).

Eating in Óbidos

Óbidos is tough on the average tourist's budget. Consider a picnic or one of the many cafés that offer cheap, basic meals.

Restaurante Burgo, just inside the main gate on the lower road, is a lively place with good seating inside and out on the cobbled street (€12-15 meat and fish dishes, open long hours daily, good ice cream, Rua Josefa d'Óbidos 11).

Restaurante/Pizzaria Muralhas serves traditional Portuguese and Italian cuisine outside the city wall. Dine indoors or on the back patio (€7-10 pizzas, €13-16 meat and fish dishes, Thu-Tue

12:00-15:00 & 19:00-22:00, closed Wed, Rua Dom João d'Ornelas 6, tel. 262-958-550).

1st de Dezembro Café & Restaurante serves inexpensive pizza, salads, and omelets. Daily specials start at €11 (€7 meat and fish plates, Mon-Sat 8:00-24:00, closed Sun, next door to Church of St. Peter on Largo de San Pedro, tel. 262-959-298).

Troca-Tintos is a good spot for a glass of wine and light meal of *petiscos* (Portuguese tapas) in an intimate atmosphere. The only downside is that smoking is allowed. Sit at one of the outdoor tables if possible (€4-14, Mon-Sat 18:00 until late, closed Sun, Rua Dom João de Ornelas, next to recommended Hotel Estalagem do Convento, tel. 966-928-689). They have fado weekly (Mon 20:30-23:30, €4 cover, €3 if you buy food).

Picnics: Pick up your picnic at the small grocery store just inside the main gate (on the lower brick road), the larger grocery in the center on Rua Direita, or the tiny market just outside the town wall.

Óbidos Connections

From Óbidos to: Nazaré (4 buses/day, 40-60 minutes, some direct, most transfer in Caldas da Rainha), **Alcobaça** (6 buses/day, 1.5 hours). Far fewer buses run on weekends; be sure to check schedules at the TI.

By Bus to/from Lisbon: The bus (hourly, 1.25 hours, www.rodotejo.pt) is a much better option than the train (3/day, 2.25-3 hours, transfer in Cacém or Mira Sintra-Melecas). If coming from Lisbon: Buses leave Campo Grande (on yellow Metro line) from numerous open-air stops. To find your stop, exit the Metro station with the giant, tiled stadium in view (don't exit on the highway side). Walk around the right side of the station to the dark green high-rise building. Across the street from the building, look for the RodoTejo stop to Óbidos.

By Car to Lisbon: From Óbidos, the tollway zips you directly into Lisbon in about an hour (€8).

NAZARÉ & NEARBY

COIMBRA

The college town of Coimbra—just two to three hours north of Lisbon by train, bus, or car—is Portugal's Oxford, and the country's easiest-to-enjoy city.

Don't be fooled by the drab suburbs. Culturally and historically, Coimbra (koo-EEM-brah) is second only to Lisbon. It was Portugal's leading city while the Moors controlled Lisbon (8th to 12th century) and the country's capital for more than 100 years (12th to mid-13th century). Only when Portugal's maritime fortunes rose did the ports of Lisbon and Porto manage to surpass landlocked Coimbra.

The earthquake that devastated Lisbon in 1755 spared Coimbra. Coimbra's "earthquake" came much later, in the form of the 20th-century dictator Salazar—who demolished much of the old center for his bombastic building projects.

Today, Coimbra (pop. 143,000) is home to the country's oldest and most prestigious university (founded 1290). When school is in session, Coimbra bustles—although many students go home on Friday, so weekend nights aren't as crazy as you might expect from a college town. During summer holidays, it's sleepy.

Any time of year, Coimbra's inviting Arab-flavored old town—a maze of people, narrow streets, and tiny *tascas* (restaurants with just a few tables)—awaits exploration.

PLANNING YOUR TIME
On a two-week swing through Portugal, give Coimbra two nights and a full day. Browse through its historic university, fortress-like cathedral, and lively old town.

Orientation to Coimbra

Coimbra is a mini-Lisbon, with everything good about urban Portugal without the intensity of a big metropolis. I couldn't design

a more delightful city for a visit. Skip Coimbra's modern center and stick to the charming old town.

From Largo da Portagem, the main square by the river, everything is within a short (if occasionally steep) walk. The TI and plenty of good budget rooms are within several blocks of the train station. The best views are from its low and high points: looking up from the far end of Santa Clara Bridge (Ponte Santa Clara) and looking down from the observation deck of the old university.

Coimbra's old town—a maze of timeworn shops, houses, and stairways—has two parts: the lower (Baixa) and the upper (Alta). The dividing line between these two sections is the main pedestrian street, which is named Visconde da Luz at one end and Rua de Ferreira Borges at the other. It runs from the Praça 8 de Maio to the Mondego River.

To get to the university from this main pedestrian thoroughfare, follow the streets that wind their way up the side of the hill. These little lanes meander like the alleyways of a Moroccan medina up to the city's highest point, the old university. To save yourself some uphill climbing, use Coimbra's elevator, take a taxi, or ride the little electric minibus (see "Getting Around Coimbra," later).

TOURIST INFORMATION

Pick up an info-packed map and the monthly cultural calendar at the helpful English-speaking TI at Largo da Portagem (June-Sept Mon-Fri 9:00-20:00, Sat-Sun 9:00-18:00; Oct-May Mon-Fri 9:00-18:00, Sat-Sun 9:30-13:30 & 14:00-17:30; entrance on Avenida Emídio Navarro, tel. 239-488-120, www.turismodocentro. pt). You can get bus schedules printed out for you here and find information on sights in central Portugal.

ARRIVAL IN COIMBRA
By Train
There are two Coimbra train stations, Station B (Estaçã Velha) and Station A (Estaçã Nova). Think B for "big": Nearly all major trains—such as those to and from Lisbon or Porto—stop only at Station B (some local trains do stop at both). But any ticket to or

from Coimbra includes a shuttle train that connects Station B with the more centrally located Station A (5 minutes, 4/hour). To find which train will get you from B to A, check the electronic schedule boards or ask any station employee, *"Para Coimbra A* (ah)*?"* Taxis wait across the tracks from Station B (figure about €4 to Station A or your hotel).

Both stations provide train information and schedules, and have windows selling train tickets and reservations (daily 6:15-23:00, tel. 808-208-208), including an international window for trips to Spain (Station A—daily 10:00-12:00 & 14:00-18:00, Station B—daily 15:00-20:30). Car-rental offices are only at Station B. Neither has baggage storage.

By Bus

The bus station, on Avenida Fernão de Magalhães (tel. 239-855-270), has two ATMs (one inside, one outside) and baggage storage (Mon-Fri 8:00-18:30, closed Sat-Sun). The station is an easy 15-minute walk from the center; exit the bus station to the right, and follow the busy street into town.

There's no need to make a special trip to the station just to get bus schedules (the TIs print timetables upon request) or to buy tickets (travel agencies sell them; see "Helpful Hints," later). If you're walking to the station to catch a bus to leave Coimbra, take Avenida Fernão de Magalhães almost to its intersection with Cabral, and look to the left—the Neptuno café is by the station's subtle entrance.

By Car

From Lisbon, it's an easy two-hour straight shot on the slick *auto-estrada* A-1 (toll). You'll pass convenient exits for Fátima and the Roman ruins of Conímbriga along the way. Leave the freeway on the easy-to-miss first Coimbra exit (Coimbra Sul), then follow the *Centro* signs. Two and a half miles after leaving the freeway, you'll cross the Mondego River. Take Avenida Fernão de Magalhães directly into town. Most recommended hotels are near Station A and the Santa Clara Bridge. If you arrive from northern Portugal or central Spain, follow signs for *Centro/Largo da Portagem.*

The large lot on the south bank of the river offers free parking (but it's not a safe choice for leaving a car overnight). You can also look for free parking along the streets along the river. In town, you'll find big, convenient, clearly marked pay garages. The largest in-town parking lot is centrally located under the government office, called Loja da Cidadão (on Avenida Fernão de Magalhães, 800 spots, €1/hour 7:00-20:00, €0.70/hour overnight). Most hotels can provide advice on the best parking options, and many offer parking in city lots (as little as €5/day).

HELPFUL HINTS

Internet Access: Internet Coimbra Câmara Municipal has free Wi-Fi plus six computers offering free Internet access (bring passport to use computers, Mon-Fri 10:00-20:00, Sat-Sun 10:00-22:00; coming from the pedestrian street, it's past Praça 8 de Maio on your left at #38).

Car Rental: Avis is in the modern part of town (Rua General Humberto Delgado 297, tel. 239-834-786), **InterRent Car** is in Station B (tel. 239-496-559), and **Hertz** is near the bus station at Rua Padre Estevão Cabral, tel. 219-426-300). These agencies have similar hours (roughly Mon-Fri 9:00-13:00 & 15:00-18:00, Sat 9:00-13:00, closed Sun).

Long-Distance Bus Tickets: The **InterVisa travel agency** sells Intercentro company international tickets to Salamanca, Spain, and beyond. They charge a small commission, but it's worth it (Mon-Fri 9:00-12:30 & 14:30-18:30, closed Sat-Sun; Avenida Fernão da Magalhães 11—leaving Station A, walk 100 yards to your left, then take the first left; tel. 239-823-873).

Local Guides: I've enjoyed working with three good private guides in Coimbra. Each can give you and your travel partners a private half-day tour in town (€100) or around the region on an outing tailored to your interests: **Cristina Bessa** (mobile 917-200-180, ccfb64@hotmail.com), **Maria Jose Fernandes** (mobile 934-093-542, mariajf@portugalmail.pt), and **Rosa Lopez** (mobile 966-103-277, mrosatoscano@gmail.com). **Sara Cruz** and her colleagues at **Go! Leisure & Heritage** lead a variety of cultural town walks (tel. 910-163-118, www.gowalksportugal.com).

GETTING AROUND COIMBRA

While most visitors do the entire city on foot, **taxis** are cheap (€4-5 for a short ride) and a good option if you've been up and down too many hills.

Most **buses** skip the old town, but a few run through the university (€1; better-value 3-ride, 10-ride, and one-day passes available and shareable; all are sold at kiosks or the SMTUC hut at Santa Clara Bridge—directly across from TI, www.smtuc.pt). Bus passes are also valid for Coimbra's Elevador do Mercado that runs between Mercado Municipal and the top of town (described on page 250), and for the electric minibus that shuttles between the lower and upper town.

This cute little electric **minibus** (nicknamed *pantufinhas,* or "grandma's slipper") is silent and easy, designed to get grandmas— and anyone else—up and down the steep hills of the old town. It makes a continuous 20-minute loop through the lower old town (Baixa) and around the upper old town (Alta), passing through

COIMBRA

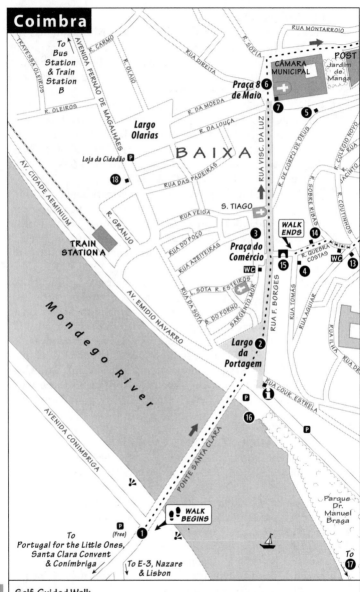

Coimbra

To Bus Station & Train Station B

RUA MONTARROIO

R. CARMO

K. OLAIO

RUA DIREITA

RUA SOFIA

CÂMARA MUNICIPAL

POST

Jardim de Manga

Praça 8 de Maio ❻

❼

❺

AVENIDA FERNÃO DE MAGALHÃES

K. OLEIROS

R. DA MOEDA

R. DA LOUÇA

Largo Olarias

B A I X A

RUA VISC. DA LUZ

R. DE CORPO DE DEUS

RUA COLÉGIO NOVO

RUA

Loja da Cidadão Ⓟ

❶⑧

RUA DAS PADEIRAS

S. TIAGO

R. SOBRE RIBAS

RUA JACINTO

AV. CIDADE AEMINIUM

R. GRANJO

RUA VEIGA

RUA DO POÇO

RUA AZETEIRAS

❸

Praça do Comércio

WALK ENDS ⑭

RUA COUTINHOS

TRAIN STATION A

WC

❶⑤

R. QUEBRA COSTAS

WC ⑬

AV. EMÍDIO NAVARRO

L. SOTA R. ESTEIROS

❹

RUA DA SOTA

B. DO FORNO

SARGENTO-MOR

RUA F. BORGES

RUA TOMÁS

RUA AGUIAR

RUA ILHA

RUA DR

M o n d e g o   R i v e r

Largo da Portagem ❷

RUA COUR. ESTRELA

AVENIDA CONÍMBRIGA

Ⓟ

ⓘ

❶⑥

Ⓟ

PONTE SANTA CLARA

Parque Dr. Manuel Braga

WALK BEGINS 👣

To Portugal for the Little Ones, Santa Clara Convent & Conímbriga

Ⓟ (Free)

❶

To E-3, Nazaré & Lisbon

To ⑰

Self-Guided Walk

❶ Santa Clara Bridge
❷ Largo da Portagem
❸ Praça do Comércio
❹ Chiado Building/ Municipal Museum
❺ À Capella Fado

❻ Church of Santa Cruz
❼ Café Santa Cruz
❽ Mercado Municipal
❾ Elevador do Mercado
❿ Machado de Castro Museum/ Cryptoporticus

COIMBRA

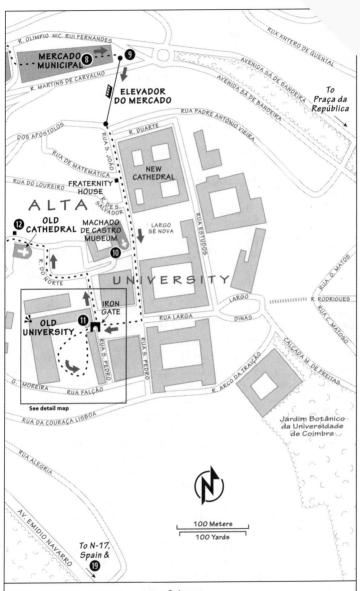

11 Iron Gate to Old University
12 Restaurante O Trovador
13 Café Sé Velha
14 Fado ao Centro
15 Arco de Almedina

Other
16 Boat Tours
17 To Kayak Tours
18 InterVisa Travel Agency (Bus Tickets)
19 To Pedro & Inês Bridge

down the pedestrian shopping lane to Praça
market and elevator, then circling up to the
high point) before returning down to Largo
are just three regular stops—but you can wave
here you like, and the driver will let you off
wherever you ask (€1.60, pay driver or use multiple-ride pass).

Coimbra Old Town Walk

Coimbra is fun on foot, especially along its straight (formerly
Roman) pedestrian-only main drag. This self-guided tour takes
two to three hours, including a visit to the university.

• *Start your walk at the...*

❶ **Santa Clara Bridge:** This bridge, Ponte Santa Clara, has
been an important link across the Mondego River since Roman
times. For centuries, it had a tollgate *(por-*
tagem). The far end of the bridge offers a
fine Coimbra view.

Coimbra is redeveloping its long-
neglected riverside. A park stretches past
several recommended restaurants to the
romantic pedestrian bridge, linking the
town with the far riverbank, where an
improved, people-friendly zone is en-
visioned. The bridge is named for Dom
Pedro and Dona Inês (Portugal's Romeo and Juliet—see page 230).

• *At the end of the bridge on the Coimbra side is...*

❷ **Largo da Portagem:** Much of the old center is ornamented
with fin-de-siècle architecture (circa 1900) from a boom period;
notice the fancy bank building and the exterior of Hotel Astória
behind it. This square is a great place for coffee or a pastry. The
best goodies are at Pastelaria Briosa; enjoy their creative window
displays. The shop's name, meaning "pure, proud, respectable," is
the nickname for the people of Coimbra (and their football team):
Go Briosa! Another popular place is Café Montanha, with a big
brass palm tree inside and delightful seating on the square. The
town's two special treats are *pastel de Santa Clara* (pastry made with
almonds and marmalade) and *pastel de Tentúgal* (rolls of puff pastry
stuffed with eggs and cream, and dusted with powdered sugar). In
the center of the square is a statue of the prime minister who, in
1834, shut down the city's convents and monasteries, and earned
the nickname "friar killer."

• *Stroll down the delightfully pedestrianized Rua de Ferreira Borges.*
After a 200-yard-long gauntlet of clothing stores, take the stairs (to your
left) leading to a terrace overlooking the square below (pay public WC,
sanitários, in the stairwell).

Coimbra in History

1064 Coimbra is taken from the Moors.

1139 Portugal's first king, Afonso Henriques, makes Coimbra his capital.

1211 Portugal's first parliament of nobles *(cortes)* convenes at Coimbra.

1256 Lisbon replaces Coimbra as Portugal's capital.

1308 The university (founded in Lisbon in 1290 under King Dinis, r. 1279-1325) moves to Coimbra.

1537 The university, after another short stint in Lisbon, resettles permanently in Coimbra under Jesuit administration.

1810 Napoleon's French troops sack Coimbra, then England's Duke of Wellington drives them out.

1928 António Salazar, professor of political economy at Coimbra, becomes Minister of Finance and eventually dictator of Portugal.

❸ **Praça do Comércio:** This pleasant square is, literally, the place of commerce. It was originally just outside the city walls—a kind of medieval duty-free zone where merchants could trade tax-free. The streets branching off the square were named for the type of product traditionally made or traded there (such as Rua das Azeiteiras, named for olive-oil producers). Two churches bookending the square are a reminder that religious orders also set up just outside the city walls. Beyond Praça do Comércio stretches the rough end of town.

Look at your map. The circular street pattern outlines the wall used by Romans, Visigoths, Moors, and Christians to protect Coimbra. Historically, only the rich could afford to live within the protective city walls of the Alta, or high town. Even today, the Baixa, or low town, remains a poorer section, with haggard women rolling wheeled shopping carts, children running barefoot, and men lounging on the square as if wasting time is their life's calling. But it's a fine area for wandering around during the day to explore small shops and eateries, and to get thoroughly disoriented.

• *Return to the pedestrian street.*

Across the way, notice the balconied building trimmed with lacy ironwork. This innovative iron structure, opened as the ❹ **Chiado** department store in 1909, was big news in town when it was built. (Today it's an insignificant museum with textiles and artwork; see page 261.)

Next door is **Casa da Sorte,** a lottery shop—these are much

COIMBRA

loved in Portugal. Step inside and feel the energy of gamblers un-wittingly letting the state take their money to fund social programs. What's the total for the Euromilhões (European-wide "euro mil-lions" lottery)? You may see circles of friends huddling here who've invested collectively in a gambling partnership. (If you like to send postcards, this shop is a convenient place to buy stamps.)

At the corner (on your right), steps lead up through an ancient arched gateway—Arco de Almedina—into the old city and to the old cathedral and university. Later, after visiting the university, we'll finish this walk by going downhill through this arch.

A block farther along the pedestrian drag, stop at the pictur-esque corner (where the building comes to a triangular corner). The steep road climbs into Coimbra's historic former Jewish quarter and the wonderful and recommended ❺ À Capella fado nightclub (see "Entertainment in Coimbra," later).

Check out the newsstands, where the daily papers have mostly sport news fixated on football (meaning soccer). The **Bragas men's store** (at #35), with hats and ties, is one of a shrinking number of old-time shops left on this street. Malls are sucking this kind of business out to the suburbs as a rising tide of tourism changes the character of this venerable street.

As you stroll along, you'll know it's graduation time if stu-dents' photos are displayed in photographers' windows. Check out the graduates decked out in their traditional university capes (dis-playing the time-honored rips on the hem—left side for family, right side for friends, backside for girl- or boyfriends) and color-coded sashes indicating their field of study.

• *The pedestrian street ends at Praça 8 de Maio with the...*

❻ **Church of Santa Cruz:** Enjoy this church's grand facade. While almost invisible, wires on the statuary are electrified to keep

pigeons from dumping their corrosive loads on the tender limestone. Go in-side; it's the most active religious spot in town. (If a Mass is under way, you can generally slip quietly around on the right to enter the sacristy and cloister.)

The musty church is lavishly decorated with 18th-century tiles that tell the sto-ries of the discovery of the Holy Cross (by Roman Emperor Constantine's mother, Saint Helen, on the left) and the life of St. Augustine (on the right; the

church is of the Augustinian order). The pulpit is considered one of the finest pieces of Renaissance work in Portugal. St. Anthony of Padua is known as St. Anthony of Lisbon around here. He studied in Coimbra as a young monk in the 13th century. A statue of him dressed as an Augustinian monk is the centerpiece of a side altar on the left.

Step behind the altar for a close-up look at two fine 16th-century tombs. On the left lies the first Portuguese king, Afonso Henriques (1095-1185). Afonso "The Conqueror" reclaimed most of Portugal from the Moors, declared himself king, got the pope to approve the title, and settled down in his chosen capital—Coimbra. There, his wife gave birth to young Sancho, who later became king. Sancho I (1154-1211, tomb on right) was known as "The Populator." He saw the destruction that war had brought to the country, and set about rebuilding and repopulating, inviting northern European Crusaders (such as the Knights Templar) to occupy southern Portugal and giving trade privileges to border towns to strengthen his country's economy.

Notice that these tombs are carved in the richly ornamented Manueline style. In the 16th century, while headed on a pilgrimage to Santiago de Compostela, the great King Manuel I dropped by this church and was underwhelmed by the two kings' original tombs. He commissioned these beautifully carved replacements—much more fitting for royalty. Study the intimate faces. Notice how the kings seem only to be resting. (To make themselves more comfortable, they've "hung" their helmets and arm guards just behind them.)

Church of Santa Cruz Sacristy and Cloister: For a small fee, you can explore the sacristy (entrance to right of main altar), see the treasures of the church, and pass through the impressive chapter room into the Manueline Cloister of Silence (€2.50, Mon-Sat 9:00-17:00, Sun 16:00-17:30). The first room is the actual sacristy (with "carpet tiles" blanketing the walls and huge banks of drawers for priests' vestments). The room to the right has relics, including the skull of St. Teotonio, the first Portuguese saint. Opposite is the chapter room with St. Teotonio's tomb and a few paintings.

In the chapter room, note the painting of the Augustinian monks. Imagining you are a fellow monk, step outside into the Cloister of Silence, with its fine Manueline arches and late-18th-century tiled scenes of Christ teaching the beatitudes. Walk pensively clockwise, hands folded, pondering worshipfully each parable from Matthew and Luke as a meditative monk would have in this space 200 years ago. Feel the tranquility. Notice that you are walking upon the tombs of the very monks who took this same stroll so long ago—and who chose to be buried so humbly, to be trod upon by those who came after them. You're in the city center, but here, in the Cloister of Silence, about the only sound is the splash of the fountain.

• *Exit the church into the main square. Once called the Square of Samson, it was renamed for the date when French Revolutionary ideas ar-*

rived in Portugal (a little behind the European trends, as usual) and the state asserted its secular power over the Church—on May 8, 1833. People (and pigeons) survey the Praça 8 de Maio scene from the terrace of the recommended...

❼ Café Santa Cruz: Located to the right of the church, this recommended coffeehouse was itself built as a church. It was abandoned with the dissolution of the monasteries in the 1830s, when the government took possession of many grand religious buildings and their surrounding land. As a café, this was the 19th-century haunt of the town's intellectuals. The altar is now used for lectures, poetry readings, small concerts, and art exhibits (the women's restroom is in a confessional). They offer free fado performances many nights at 22:00.

• *Continue past the church and the city hall (Câmara Municipal). At the noisy street, turn right, and go a block to find a park with a fountain (once a monastery cloister and Renaissance garden) and the cheap, handy, and recommended self-service restaurant* **Jardim da Manga.** *Keep going uphill along the busy Rua Olímpio Nicolau di Fernandes past the big post office to the...*

❽ Mercado Municipal: This modern covered market is fun to explore and great for gathering picnic supplies (Mon-Sat 8:00-14:00, closed Sun, busiest on Tue and Fri). It's clean and hygienic, but maintains the colorful appeal of an old farmers' market. See the "salt of the earth" in the faces of the women selling produce (their men are off in the fields...or in the bars—a.k.a. their beloved "little chapels"). These ladies aren't shy about trying to sell their goods, even to tourists. For about the cheapest meal in town, pop into the Bar do Mercado Requinte at the end of the ground floor (menu posted on wall, €5.50 meals for two, public WC around the corner). Check out the photos of the old market on the wall. Then go upstairs for bread, more meat, and veggies. Follow your nose through the glass doors at the far end, with all the fresh fish and dried cod. The Portuguese are the world's biggest cod eaters, but because cod is no longer found in nearby waters, the local favorite is imported from Norway. To the Portuguese, cod *(bacalhau)* tastes much better dried and salted than fresh. This section housed the original market—you can recognize the wrought-iron work from the photos you've just seen on the ground floor at the bar.

• *Swim through the fish hall and head outside, where you'll find the sleek city elevator.*

❾ Elevador do Mercado: A combination elevator/funicular ride whisks you up the long, steep hill (stop midway to transfer to funicular), offering commanding views of Coimbra en route (€1.60/trip,

Mon-Sat 7:30-21:00, Sun 10:00-21:00). At the top, jog right, then left, heading uphill toward the university buildings at the top of the hill. Fifty yards up this lane (Rua da Couraça Apóstolos), at the first intersection, you'll find a fraternity house called Real República Corsários das Ilhas ("Royal Commune of the Island Pirates"). Notice the prominent skull-and-crossbones graffiti on the wall, linking McDonald's and the G8 (group of the eight most powerful countries). Look around for other examples of graffiti. These small university frat houses, called *repúblicas,* are communes that traditionally house about a dozen students from the same region or provincial town. While some are highly cultured, the rowdier ones are often decorated with plunder from their pranks—stolen traffic signs and so on—giving rise to the local saying, "At night, many things happen in Coimbra."

• *Walk three blocks on past the* ❿ *Machado de Castro Museum (on right, consider visiting before climbing back down to town, described on page 258, recommended lunch buffet) and the big, fascist-style university square (Praça da Porta Férrea). The* ⓫ *Iron Gate entry to the old university is on your right.*

University: Explore the university (described later, under "Sights in Coimbra"), then continue this town walk.

• *Leave the university—pass back out through the Iron Gate, turn left immediately and take the steps down toward the back of the Machado de Castro Museum, then follow the steep lanes left toward the old cathedral and into the old town. You're walking along the stone wall built by ancient Romans to give their forum, or main market square, a level surface. Farther down, look through the metal grate on your right to see the old Roman street and remains of ancient houses.*

As you wander, notice the white-paper squares and diamonds in the windows—they indicate that there's a student room available for rent. Continuing on, you'll come to the **old cathedral** (Sé Velha, described later, under "Sights in Coimbra"). Facing the cathedral is the ⓬ **Restaurante O Trovador,** offering fado performances nearly every night in summer (reservations essential; see "Entertainment in Coimbra"). The colorful little ⓭ **Café Sé Velha,** on the corner immediately below the cathedral and tiled with traditional Coimbran scenes, is a good place to sit and watch people climb up and down. From here, a blue line on the cobbles marks the route of the electric minibus (described earlier). Take the steep stairway leading down (past the public WCs) to Rua Quebra Costas, the "Street of Broken Ribs." At one time, this lane had no steps, and literally *was* the street of broken ribs. During a strong rain, this becomes a river. The lane's many tourist and gift shops show off the fine local blue-and-white ceramic work called *faiança.*

Descending farther, you come to the recommended ⓮ **Fado ao Centro**—consider making a reservation for a performance (see

COIMBRA

page 264 for details). Notice the charming statue of Tricana (the term given for a local woman in traditional folk dress) resting after a trip to the well. She represents the usual target of fado love songs—and student Romeos. Local men from the lower town had a tough time competing for the Tricana of Coimbra with all the rich and witty students in town.

• *Rua Quebra Costas ends at...*

🅖 **Arco de Almedina:** This is the double set of arches (named "Gate to the Medina" in Arabic by the Moors) we saw earlier from the pedestrian street Rua de Ferreira Borges. Part of the old town wall, the arches act as a double gate with a 90-degree kink in the middle for easier defense. Pause at the gift shop between the gates to enjoy the lilting, nostalgic sound of fado and the 12-string Portuguese guitar. That's sweet. But don't linger too long because—look up: In times of attack, soldiers used those two square holes in the ceiling to pour down boiling oil, turning attacking Moors into fritters. The holes are rudely nicknamed *mata-cães* (dog killers).

A few steps farther down, before the second gate, admire from all sides the monument to fado. Featuring the Coimbra-style Portuguese guitar, draped both with the cape of the male student and the shawl of the woman, this bronze statue celebrates how fado connected the all-male-at-the-time university world with the women of the town. Locals say a good musician plays his guitar with art and passion, as if loving a woman.

• *Passing under the second arch, you're back on the pedestrian street near where this walk began.*

Sights in Coimbra

▲▲▲COIMBRA'S OLD UNIVERSITY (VELHA UNIVERSIDADE)

This venerable centuries-old university, founded in 1290, was modeled after Bologna's university (Europe's first, founded in 1139). It's a stately three-winged former royal palace (from when Coimbra was the capital), beautifully situated overlooking the city. At first, law, medicine, grammar, and logic were taught. Then, with the rise of seafaring in Portugal, astronomy and geometry were added. While Lisbon's university is much larger, Coimbra's university (with 25,000 students) is still the country's most respected. For visitors, the university marks the top of the old town. While most of it is mid-20th-century sprawl, the old core of the university (the palace section, with its iron gate, courtyard, fancy ceremonial halls, chapel, and library) makes for an interesting visit.

Cost and Hours: A €9 combo-ticket covers the Grand Hall, St. Michael's Chapel, King John's Library, and a handful of other rooms. Open April-Oct daily 9:00-19:30, Nov-March Mon-Fri

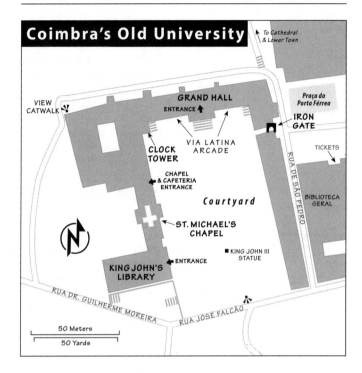

Coimbra's Old University

To Cathedral
& Lower Town

VIEW
CATWALK

GRAND HALL
ENTRANCE

Praça da
Porta Férrea

IRON
GATE

TICKETS

VIA LATINA
ARCADE

CLOCK
TOWER

CHAPEL
& CAFETERIA
ENTRANCE

Courtyard

BIBLIOTECA
GERAL

ST. MICHAEL'S
CHAPEL

RUA DE SÃO PEDRO

KING JOHN III
STATUE

ENTRANCE

KING JOHN'S
LIBRARY

RUA DR. GUILHERME MOREIRA

RUA JOSÉ FALCÃO

50 Meters

50 Yards

9:30-17:30, Sat-Sun 10:00-16:00, €3 audioguide gives 90 minutes of info. Buy your ticket at the counter located inside the Biblioteca Geral (the large building to the left as you approach the Iron Gate; ticket office closes 30 minutes before sights; TI at same desk). Your library

entry time will be printed on the receipt that comes with your ticket—be mindful of that time as you tour; you'll need to show the receipt later to enter the library, tel. 239-242-745, www.uc.pt/en.

Getting There: To get to the university, you could take the "Coimbra Old Town" walk (earlier), using the elevator from the Mercado Municipal to get to the top of the hill. Or take a taxi to the Iron Gate (on Praça da Porta Férrea), see the university, and then sightsee Coimbra downhill.

Iron Gate (Porta Férrea)

Before entering the old campus, stand with your back to the iron gate and look across the stark, modern square at the fascist archi-

COIMBRA

tecture of the new university. In the 1940s, in what's considered one of the worst cultural crimes in Portuguese history, the dictator António Salazar tore down half of Coimbra's old town to build these university halls. The grandiose ceremonial approach to the university, bombastic and utilitarian to fit fascist taste, is flanked by the faculties of letters, medicine, science, and the library (with the ticket office). The law school is behind you, inside the old campus.

Salazar, proud that Portugal was the last European power to hang onto its colonial empire, wanted a fittingly monumental university here. After all, Salazar—along with virtually everyone of political influence in Portugal—had been educated at Coimbra, where he studied law and then became an economics professor. If these bold buildings are reminiscent of Mussolini's E.U.R. in Rome, perhaps it's because they were built in part by Italian architects hired by Portugal's little Mussolini.

OK, now turn and walk through the Iron Gate. Traditionally, freshmen—proudly wearing their black capes for the first time—pass through the Iron Gate to enroll. Also traditionally, they had to pass through an Iron Gate gauntlet of butt kicks from upperclassmen to get out.

Old University Courtyard

The university's most important sights all face this square: the Grand Hall (up the grand stairway on the right), St. Michael's Chapel (straight ahead, through the door, then to the left), and King John's Library (across the square, farthest door on left, flanked by columns).

The statue in the square is of King John III. While the university was established in 1290, it went back and forth between Lisbon and Coimbra (back then, university students were adults, privileged, and a pain to have in your town). In 1537, John III finally established the school permanently in Coimbra. Standing like a good humanist (posing hand on hip, much like we're used to seeing his contemporary, England's King Henry VIII), John modernized Portugal's education system in the Renaissance style. But, unlike Henry, who broke the local power of the Church, John (grandson of the ultra-Catholic Queen Isabel of Spain) empowered the Church. He let the Jesuits—the guardians of orthodoxy—run this university, which became the center of Portugal's Inquisition.

The black capes famously worn by local students originated with the capes worn by Jesuits and clergy during this period. Wearing the same clothing—like the uniforms of students at American Catholic schools—removes the focus on power-dressing and equalizes people of all classes. To this day, standards of modesty prevail, keeping class divisions at a minimum among the students, and between students and professors. (Students, when wearing their gowns, are not allowed to show off by wearing gold.)

Survey the square with your back to the gate. The dreaded sound of the clock tower's bell—named the "baby goat" for its nagging—calls students to class. On several occasions, the clapper has been stolen. (No bell...no class. No class...big party.) A larger bell (the "big goat") rings only on important, formal occasions.

The arcaded passageway (on the right, up the stairs) between the Iron Gate and the clock tower is called Via Latina, from the days when only Latin was spoken in this part of the university.

Grand Hall (Sala dos Capelos)

From the middle of the Via Latina, climb the tiled stairway and enter the Grand Hall, site of the university's major academic ceremonies, such as oral exams and graduations. Tourists look down

from balconies above the room. This regally red room was originally the throne room of the royal palace. Today, the rector's green chair sits like a throne in front. During ceremonies, students in their formal attire fill the benches, and teachers sit along the perimeter as gloomy portraits of Portuguese kings watch from above.

The fine, old, painted ceiling features "Indo-Portuguese" themes, reminding Portugal's next generation of leaders of the

global reach of their nation. There is no clapping during these formal rituals, but a brass band (on the wooden platform in the back) punctuates the ceremonies with solemn music.

View Catwalk *(Varanda):* Continue around the Grand Hall, past an ornately decorated former royal stateroom (until recently a place where students take their oral exams as portraits of past university rectors look on). Just past this room a door leads to a narrow observation deck offering the best views of Coimbra (closed in bad weather). If the door is closed, open it.

From the viewpoint, scan the old town from right to left. Remember, before Salazar's extension of the university, this old town surrounded the university. The Baroque facade breaking the horizon

COIMBRA

The Burning of Ribbons

Europe's third-oldest university has long-standing traditions to match. If you're lucky enough to be in Coimbra at the end of the academic year (early to mid-May), you'll witness a big party.

The "Burning of Ribbons" (Queima das Fitas) began in the 1850s, when a group of students who passed their final fourth-year exams gathered outside the Iron Gate and marched together to the lower town. They burned their ribbons (which were used to bind and carry their books) in a small fire, representing their passage from student life to professional life. Eventually, that simple event evolved into the biggest academic festival of the year, complete with floats and parades.

Students entering their last year of studies as well as recent graduates (finalistas) participate in the party these days, but of course the graduates get the most attention. Women wear simple white shirts with black skirts and black stockings. Men dress more formally in a long black suit, university cape, wide sash with various badges, top hat, and cane. Different accent colors, proudly displayed on the top hats and canes, represent the different academic departments, indicating which degree the student earned (yellow for medicine, red for law, blue for science, and so on). For good luck after graduation, men take their canes and tap other students' top hats three times. (The taps can get out of control, and lots of students end up losing the tops of their hats.)

Much drinking accompanies this rite of passage. Ribbon-burning parties are also celebrated in Porto, and to a lesser extent in Lisbon. Join the fun, and offer an appropriately colored flower to a new graduate. You may be invited to the party.

is the "new" cathedral—from the 16th century. Below that, with the fine arcade, is the Machado de Castro Museum, housed in the former bishop's palace and located atop a Roman site (with an appealing terrace restaurant, all described later). And below that, like an armadillo, sits the old cathedral with its tiled cupola.

Gaily painted yellow-and-blue windows mark *república* frat houses. If you visit during late October, November, or May, you might see a student festival: Parades of rowdy students in funny costumes, draped in signs, dragging tin cans—these are all part of the traditional initiation rites marking the beginning and end of the school year. May provides the biggest spectacle, when new students receive—and graduating students burn—the small colored ribbons of their chosen major (see sidebar). Look beyond the houses to the Mondego River, the longest river that flows entirely in Portugal. Over the bridge, beyond the university's sports facilities, stretches the 17th-century Santa Clara Convent—at 590 feet, the longest building in Coimbra.

St. Michael's Chapel (Capela de São Miguel)

This chapel is behind a 16th-century facade (enter through door to the right of facade—once inside, push the door on the left marked *capela*). The architecture of the church interior is Manueline—notice the golden "rope" trimming the arch before the altar. The chapel was begun in 1517, but much of the decor is from a later time. The altar is 17th-century Mannerist, with steps unique to Portugal (and her South American colonies); based on Jacob's Ladder, they symbolize the steps the faithful take on their journey to heaven. The "carpet tiles" covering the aisle date from the 17th century and kept the chapel cool in the summer. The 2,100-pipe, 18th-century German-built organ is notable for its horizontal "trumpet" pipes. Found only in Iberia, these help the organist perform the allegorical fight between good and evil—with the horizontal pipes trumpeting the arrival of the good guys. The box seats for the royal family are high above the musicians' loft in the rear. Students and alums enjoy the privilege of having their weddings here.

Student Cafeteria: In the corridor just outside the chapel, you'll find WCs and a cheap student-filled café with a lovely view of the river from the terrace. Visitors are perfectly welcome to eat here. During busy lunch times, every seat gets taken, people share tables, and you may find yourself sitting with law students and their professors.

▲King John's Library (Biblioteca Joanina)

In this elegant building, one of Europe's best surviving Baroque libraries displays 55,000 books in 18th-century splendor. The zealous doorkeeper locks the door at every opportunity to keep out humidity. Buzz (on left) to get into this 300-year-old temple of thought. Inside, at the "high altar," stands the library's founder, the absolute monarch King John (João) V (1698-1750), who considered France's King Louis XIV an

inspiration (and they have similar hairstyles).

The reading tables, inlaid with exotic South American woods (and ornamented with silver ink wells), and the precious wood shelves (with clever hideaway staircases) are reminders that Portugal's wealth was great—and imported (mostly from Brazil). Built Baroque, the interior is all wood. Even the "marble" on the arches of triumph that divide the library into rooms is just painted wood. (Real marble would add to the humidity.) The small doors with glass windows lead to professors' tiny studies with big windows to read by. The resident bats—who live in the building, but not the library itself—are well cared for and appreciated. They eat insects, providing a chemical-free way of protecting the books, and alert the guard to changing weather with their "eee-eee" cry. Look for the trompe l'oeil Baroque tricks on the painted ceiling. Gold leaf (from Brazil) is everywhere, and the Chinese themes are pleasantly

reminiscent of Portugal's once vast empire. The books, each dating from before 1755, are in Latin, Greek, and Hebrew. Imagine being a student in Coimbra centuries ago, when this temple of learning stored the world's knowledge like a vast filing cabinet (and consider how readily accessible the world of information is to our age). As you leave, watch how the doorman uses the giant key as a hefty doorknob.

MORE SIGHTS IN COIMBRA

▲▲Machado de Castro Museum and Cryptoporticus of Aeminium

Housed in an elegant old bishop's palace, the huge Machado de Castro Museum (Museu Nacional Machado de Castro) has two parts: many floors of mostly religious 14th- to 16th-century paintings and statues (taken mostly from dissolved monasteries) plus ceramics and jewels, and the vast, barren understructure (Criptoportico de Aeminium) of the ancient Roman forum upon which the palace was built. At the entry level, you'll find a great restaurant (Loggia, with a classy €7 buffet lunch—one of the best deals in town) on a terrace with a fine old-town view (free entry). To save needless climbing, visit this sight before or after the old university (since both are at roughly the same altitude).

Cost and Hours: €6 for museum and Roman site, €3 for just the Roman site, free first Sun of every month, Tue-Sun 10:00-18:00, closed Mon, audioguide-€1.50, Largo Dr. José Rodrigues, tel. 239-853-079, www.museumachadocastro.pt.

Visiting the Museum: At the entry level, the collection (which is well-described in English) starts with a fine example of the layers

COIMBRA

of history you find when you dig—a 2,000-year-old rubble layer-cake of Coimbra's past.

The main floor includes statues from the 14th, 15th, and 16th centuries. The highlight: a powerfully realistic 14th-century *Cristo Negro* carved in wood. Until a decade ago, when this statue was cleaned (and the candle soot was removed), it was considered to be a portrait of a black Christ. If this dramatic statue has an impact on you today, imagine its power in the 14th century. Gothic lasted here long after the Renaissance hit Italy and France. Viewing the stately Renaissance Treasurers' Chapel (moved here from a now-gone 16th-century monastery), consider how Coimbra with its university was Portugal's center of humanism and the Renaissance. The collection continues upstairs with two more floors of exhibits: northern European statues and paintings (a reminder of this country's wealth in its Golden Age heyday), royal and ecclesiastical treasures and jewels, and tiles and ceramics. Note how aspects of Moorish culture and design were absorbed into the Christian culture that threw them out.

Visiting the Cryptoporticus: You'll find stairs down to the Roman ruins on the entry level. Aeminium was the Roman city that became Coimbra. Two thousand years ago, its two main streets crossed here, marking the forum. Because the city was built on a slope, a vast understructure was required to provide a level place for the town square, and that "cryptoporticus" is what survives today. Walking through the two-level maze of the vaulted galleries, evocative and beautifully lit, will leave you marveling at what you can do with slave labor.

Leaving the Museum: As you exit the museum and hike downhill (swing around to the right and the backside of the museum), you'll understand the need for a sturdy foundation to support a sprawling and level town square. Notice the actual Roman wall with two internal structural arches overlooking the steep cobbled lane. A block farther downhill, look through a black metal grill (on your right) to see the remains of a Roman street and homes.

▲Old Cathedral (Sé Velha)

Same old story: Christians build a church on a pre-Christian holy spot (Visigoths in sixth century), Moors destroy the church and build a mosque (eighth century), then Christians push out the Moors (1064), tear down their mosque, and build another church (consecrated in 1184).

If this structure reminds you of Lisbon's cathedral, it should. As in Lisbon, this was essentially a church-fortress, built in the middle of the Reconquista and designed by the same French architect. Notice the crenellations along the roof of this Romanesque church; the Moors, though booted out, were still considered a risk.

COIMBRA

Cost and Hours: Church and cloisters—€2, open Mon-Sat 10:00-18:00 and generally Sun after Mass.

Visiting the Cathedral: Before entering, stand back and study the west portal. Notice how Moorish-style columns are decorated by neo-Byzantine capitals, but there are no Christian motifs. It is an unbreakable facade—fortified and practical, complete with arrow slits.

Study the stone blocks, set up in the 12th century. You can see mason's marks and even some Arabic writing (on a block six rows up by the north portal), indicating that the conquered Moors worked within Christian society.

The north portal was added later, in Renaissance times. Made of soft limestone, it was cheap and easy to carve but hasn't weathered very well.

Now enter the cathedral. The giant holy-water font shells are a 19th-century gift from Sri Lanka, and the walls are lined with some of the oldest tiles in the country—imported in the 16th century from Sevilla, Spain. The three front altars are each worth a look. The main altar, a fine example of the late Flamboyant Gothic style, was made by Flemish artists (circa 1500). The 16th-century chapel to the right contains one of the best Renaissance altars in the country. The apostles all look to Jesus as he talks, while musical angels flank the holy host. Notice how the Renaissance passion for balance and proportion trumped fact—the composition had room for only 10 apostles. To the left of the main altar, the Chapel of St. Peter shows Peter being crucified upside down.

On the right of the nave, just before the transept, is a murky painting of Queen Isabel (St. Elizabeth) with a skirt full of roses. This 13th-century Hungarian princess—with family ties to Portugal—is a local favorite with a sweet legend. Against the wishes of the king, she always gave bread to the poor. One day, when he came home early from a trip, she was busy doling out bread from her skirt. She pulled the material up to hide the bread. When the king asked her what was inside (suspecting bread for the poor), the queen—unable to lie—lowered the material and, miraculously, the bread had turned to roses. For this astonishing act, she was canonized as a saint in 1625.

The peaceful cloister (entrance near back of church) is the oldest Gothic cloister in Portugal. Well-maintained with an inviting lawn, the courtyard offers a fine, framed view of the cathedral's dome. A tomb from 1064 in the cloister belongs to Coimbra's first Christian post-Reconquista governor.

Chiado Building/Municipal Museum
(Edifício Chiado/Museu Municipal)

Originally the site of Coimbra's first Chiado department store (a chain common throughout Portugal in the early 20th century), this refurbished building is notable for its construction—it was one of the first structures in Portugal to be built around an iron framework, like the then-revolutionary American skyscrapers. It now houses an eclectic assortment of artworks and textiles donated by local collector José Telo de Morais.

Cost and Hours: €1.80, Tue-Sun 10:00-18:00, closed Mon, Rue Ferreira Borges 85, tel. 239-840-754, www.cm-coimbra.pt ("Cultura" tab).

Visiting the Museum: Take the elevator up to the top floor and walk your way down, noticing the exposed iron beams. The third floor has ceramics, drawings, and a collection of silverware. The second floor has 17th- and 18th-century furniture as well as religious paintings and objects. The first floor holds oil and pastel paintings from the 19th and early 20th centuries. The ground floor houses a free temporary exhibit.

Parque Dr. Manuel Braga

Coimbra's pleasant riverside park sprawls upstream from the Santa Clara Bridge to the Pedro and Inês Bridge. You'll find boat tours, some recommended restaurants, a strip of trendy evening spots, and the Portuguese Pavilion from the Hannover Expo (2000 World's Fair in Hannover, Germany).

River Cruise

To take advantage of Coimbra's Mondego River, try a cruise: Basófias boats float up and down the river on a 50-minute joyride (€6.50; Tue-Sun at 15:00, 16:00, and 17:00, also 18:00 and 19:00 in summer; schedule posted at dock across from TI, no narration, tel. 969-830-664).

Portugal for the Little Ones (Portugal dos Pequenitos)

Across the Santa Clara Bridge is a children's (or tourists') look at the great buildings and monuments of Portugal and its former empire in miniature, scattered through a park a couple of blocks south of town. Wanting to boost national pride, Salazar commissioned architect Cassiano Branco to build these mini-replicas in 1940. If you've been through some of Portugal already, it's fun to try and identify the buildings you've already seen. Doll fans may enjoy the recent addition of an enormous Barbie collection, including one of the very first ever produced.

Cost and Hours: €9, kids ages 3-13-€5.50, kids under 2 free, daily March-May 10:00-19:00, June-mid-Sept 9:00-20:00, mid-

Sept-Feb 10:00-17:00, last entry 30 minutes before closing, Rossio de Santa Clara, tel. 239-801-170, www.portugaldospequenitos.pt.

NEAR COIMBRA
▲Conímbriga Roman Ruins (Conimbriga Ruínas)

Portugal's best Roman sight is impressive...unless you've been to Rome. What remains of the Roman city of Conímbriga is divided in two, in part because its inhabitants tore down buildings to erect a quick defensive wall against an expected barbarian attack. You'll see what's left of homes, shops, and baths from the second and third centuries A.D. (some remnants are even older), amazingly detailed mosaic floors, and peaceful gardens. Informative exhibits tell the city's history with excavated artifacts at the on-site museum (closed Mon, though site open daily).

Cost and Hours: €4.50 admission covers ruins and museum, ruins—daily June-Sept 10:00-19:00, Oct-May 10:00-18:00, last

entry 45 minutes before closing, museum—same hours as ruins but closed Mon, www.conimbriga.pt.

Getting There: The ruins are nine miles southwest of Coimbra, just outside the town of Condeixa-a-Nova on the road to Lisbon. On weekdays, four **buses** leave for the ruins each morning across from Coimbra's Station A (€2.45; Mon-Fri at 9:00, 9:30, 12:30, and 15:30; Sat-Sun at 9:30, 12:30, and 15:30; bus stop is on the river side, opposite the station, look for the *Joalto* sign, 30-minute trip). Return buses leave from Conímbriga's parking lot (Mon-Fri at 12:55, 16:25, and 17:55; Sat at 13:25 and 18:25; Sun at 13:55 and 18:25). Confirm the destination by asking, *"Vai para Conímbriga?"* Otherwise, you could end up on one of the frequent buses to Condeixa (run twice hourly) that stop a mile short of the ruins.

Drivers should consider going to Conímbriga on the way to or from Coimbra; the Conímbriga freeway exit is clearly marked from the A-1. To get there from the town center, cross the Santa Clara Bridge and go uphill, following signs to *Condeixa*. Continue straight through town, and you will see brown signs guiding you to the ruins.

Eating: The museum's café is an excellent spot to have lunch before catching the return bus to Coimbra (€7 meals, same hours as museum). Or bring a picnic lunch and eat in the gardens.

Visitng the Ruins: Purchase tickets inside the main building, then enter the ruins before visiting the museum. Helpful arrows guide you through the sight. Explore the remnants of the old town first, and save the mansion—under the protective modern roofing—for the grand finale. You'll first see remains of different houses and shopping arcades, most with wonderful mosaics intact. Note how the columns are made of preformed wedges. After you see the public baths, walk around the wall.

The Wall: Locals hastily built this immense structure for their own protection, and it shows. Once the Roman Empire retreated from this area, invaders from the north went on the offensive (beginning around A.D. 465). A Christian Germanic tribe conquered the city and built a basilica at the end of this wall.

Continuing along the wall, you'll see parts of a house belonging to a local landowner. Walk through the fields to the rest of the ruins. Other houses and public baths are out there, even though they're poorly signposted. As you explore, you'll see the sparse ruins of the old forum. Backtrack to pass under the aqueduct and go around it. Look for the fallen stones, which once supported the structure, until you reach the most important find (under a protective roof). The **House of the Fountains** is an entire dwelling, with most of its rooms and mosaics intact. Don't spend €0.50 on the lazy fountain show (wait for one of the school groups to do it for you), but enjoy the stories told in the mosaics. Simple portraits, horses, and numerous hunting scenes illustrate the daily routine in this town during Roman times.

The Museum: Return to the delightful museum that shows the discoveries from decades of excavation. The room to the right of the ticket counter describes daily life in Conímbriga. You'll see coins, dinnerware, and even grooming utensils (find the spoon-shaped ear cleaners)—all with good English descriptions. The opposite room contains a miniature replica of the forum, along with fine mosaics and a few tombstones. The best mosaic is of the mythological, bull-headed Minotaur—follow the maze from the center until you are safely out.

Kayaks and Adventure Sports

Kayaking: The company called **O Pioneiro do Mondego** buses you from Coimbra to Penacova (15 miles away), where you can kayak down the Mondego River for about four hours back into Coimbra (€22.50, 10 percent discount with this book, daily June-Sept, one- and two-person kayaks available, book by phone or email, meet at park near TI, tel. 239-478-385, www.opioneirodomondego.com, info@opioneirodomondego.com, Kristien and Jonas speak English). Most people stop to swim or picnic on the way back, so it often turns into an all-day journey. For the first 12.5 miles, you'll go easily with the flow, but you'll get your exercise paddling the remaining stretch. To avoid the workout (and the more boring part

COIMBRA

of the Mondego River), ask to be picked up 2.5 miles before Coimbra, at Portela do Mondego, where the river's current slows down.

Adventure Sports: Located in the nearby town of Foz da Figueira, **Capitão Dureza** specializes in at-your-own-risk activities: rappelling, rafting, mountain biking, hiking, and canyoning (pickup and drop-off in Coimbra, tel. 239-476-701, mobile 918-315-337, www.capitaodureza.com).

Entertainment in Coimbra

▲▲Fado Music

Portugal's unique, mournful traditional music, fado, is generally performed by women. But in Coimbra, men sing the fado. Roving bands of male students—similar to the *tuna* bands in Spain's Salamanca—serenade around town for tips and the hearts of women. The best performers are probably at À Capella or Fado ao Centro.

Fado ao Centro is an all-male ensemble of current and former Coimbra university students who sing fado in the unique local style. The 50-minute shows, held in a cute little hall, end with a glass of port and a little Q&A time with the musicians (daily at 18:00 and occasionally, with demand, at 19:00). This is a nice alternative to late-night shows, but can be popular with tour groups; reservations are smart in summer (just past the Arco de Almedina on Rua Quebra Costas #7, tel. 913-236-725, www.fadoaocentro. com/en). Money raised here supports musicians and promotes local culture.

À Capella, on the hill above the Church of Santa Cruz, offers an intimate fado nightclub experience. The tiny chapel has been turned into a temple for Coimbra-style traditional music, and it's fado almost every night all year long (three musicians perform from 22:00 to about 24:00). Come for the music, the cool scene, the slick background videos adding context to each song, and the snacks and drinks (€10 cover, reservations wise in summer, at the triangular corner midway down the main drag, climb the steep Rua do Corpo de Deus 100 yards until you see the old chapel on your left, tel. 239-833-985, www. acapella.com.pt). If you're coming to eat, note that the chapel opens nightly at 18:00 and serves snacks and wine by the glass.

Diligência is a fado bar famous for its informal music schedule—locals love to come here and just jam (guitar and voice).

Recently renovated, the interior is less homey than in the past, but the food has improved. Mushrooms stuffed with *alheira* sausage are popular, but a deconstructed *francesinha* (the famous meat sandwich from Porto) is the biggest hit. Along with the occasional sing-along, up-and-coming groups often play here. If the music moves you, jump right in (kitchen opens at 18:00, shows daily 22:30-2:00 in the morning; from Praça 8 de Maio, take Rua Sofia to your second left, Diligência is 2 blocks up on your right at Rua Nova 30; tel. 239-827-667).

Restaurante O Trovador is your best place for dinner with fado (music nearly nightly in summer from 21:00, Fri-Sat only off-season, no cover; €15-20 meals Mon-Sat 19:30-22:30, closed Sun, facing the old cathedral on Largo de Sé Velha 15, reservations essential to eat with the music—ask for a seat with a music view, tel. 239-825-475). When busy, the musicians alternate between two dining rooms. You can always drop in late for a drink and enjoy the live music for the cost of a drink.

More Fado: During the tourist season, you'll find sit-down fado most nights at Café Santa Cruz. The mayor organizes Thursday street concerts that feature fado music through the summer.

Sleeping in Coimbra

These listings are an easy walk from the central Station A and Santa Clara Bridge. For the cheapest rooms, simply walk a block from Station A into the old town, and choose one of countless *dormidas* (cheap pensions). River views come with traffic noise.

TRADITIONAL HOTELS AND PENSIONS

$$$ Hotel Astória gives you the thrill of staying in the city's finest old hotel with Coimbra's first Art Deco lounges. Though it's a bit worn around the edges, this venerable place retains its charm (Sb-€92, Db-€117, superior Db-€130, extra bed-€35, 10 percent discount if you mention this book when you reserve directly by email or phone—show it at check-in, includes breakfast, air-con, Wi-Fi, elevator, public parking opposite hotel-€0.50/hour but  free overnight, central as can be at Avenida Emídio Navarro 21, tel. 239-853-020, www.astoria-coimbra.com, astoria@themahotels.pt). Rooms with river views don't cost extra, but come with some street noise. I prefer the quieter city-view rooms at the back.

Sleep Code

Abbreviations   (€1 = about $1.40, country code: 351)
S = Single, **D** = Double/Twin, **T** = Triple, **Q** = Quad, **b** = bath-room, **s** = shower only
Price Rankings
  $$$ **Higher Priced**—Most rooms €80 or more.
   $$ **Moderately Priced**—Most rooms between €50-80.
    $ **Lower Priced**—Most rooms €50 or less.
Unless otherwise noted, credit cards are accepted, English is spoken, and Wi-Fi is generally free. Prices change; verify current rates online or by email. For the best prices, always book directly with the hotel.

$$ Hotel Bragança's brown-on-brown lobby leads to 83 clean and comfortable rooms with modern bathrooms. The wood panel-ing and furniture transport you back to Portugal in the 1950s (Sb with shower-€28, Sb with tub-€46, smaller Db with shower-€46, larger Db with tub-€56, Tb with tub-€56, Qb-€70, 10 percent discount with this book, air-con, elevator, Wi-Fi, free parking in small lot at entrance if space available, Largo das Ameias 10 next to Station A, tel. 239-822-171, www.hotel-braganca.com, geral@hotel-braganca.com).

$ Hotel Vitória is a spotless, well-located hotel renting 21 renovated and modern rooms over a good restaurant, which is its main business. Some rooms have uphill views to the university (Db-€50-55, Tb-€65, air-con, elevator, Wi-Fi, a block from Sta-tion A at Rua da Sota 9, tel. 239-824-049, www.hotelvitoria.pt, reservas@hotelvitoria.pt).

$ Residência Lusa Atenas, which rents 20 old-time rooms and has a fine TV room, is on a big noisy street but is reasonably quiet (Sb-€20-25, Db-€30-40, third person-€10, cheaper rooms in annex, breakfast extra, air-con, two blocks from Station A at Ave-nida Fernão de Magalhães 68, tel. 239-826-412, fax 239-820-133, www.residencialusatenas.com, mail@residencialusatenas.com, no English spoken).

$ Hotel Domus, tucked away in a corner of a side street, has 15 fine rooms with renovated bathrooms and a cozy atmosphere (Sb-€28, Db with air-con-€40-45, Tb-€45, 10 percent discount with this book, Wi-Fi, parking-€5/day, Rua Adelino Veiga 62, tel. 239-828-584, www.hoteldomus.com.pt, hoteldomus@sapo.pt, Sra. and Sr. Santos). They rent five small, basic, cheaper rooms in the simpler **Annex Manuela** across the street (Ds-€28-35, WC on floor).

$ Hotel Larbelo, with Old World character, mixes frumpiness and former elegance in its 17 rooms. The old-fashioned staircase, classic reception rooms, and gentle non-English-speaking management take you to another age (Sb-€25-30, Db-€30-45, Tb-€50, no breakfast, air-con, Wi-Fi, in front of the Santa Clara Bridge at Largo da Portagem 33, tel. 239-829-092, fax 239-829-094, www.larbelo.net, residencial.larbelo@sapo.pt).

MODERN AND HIGH-RISE HOTELS

$$$ Hotel Tivoli Coimbra, a classy, Houston-esque skyscraper, is the handiest place offering contemporary luxury, such as flat-screen TVs and a swimming pool. It rents 80 big rooms with all the modern amenities, but it's a 10-minute walk from Station A and any Coimbra charm (Db-€85-160 depending on demand, book on their website for best deal, Rua João Machado 4, tel. 239-858-300, www.tivolicoimbra.com, htcoimbra@tivolihotels.com).

$ Ibis Hotel, a modern high-rise, has 110 orderly little rooms that come with all the comforts. Well-located near the riverside Parque Dr. Manuel Braga, this impersonal but reliable chain hotel is three blocks past the Santa Clara Bridge and the old town (Sb/Db-€45-55, breakfast-€6, elevator, easy €6/day parking in basement, Avenida Emídio Navarro 70, tel. 239-852-130, www.ibishotel.com, h1672@accor.com).

$ RiverSuites, once an abandoned apartment building, is now a modern, 25-room hotel, just across the Santa Clara Bridge. A walk from the hotel across the bridge is the perfect way to view Coimbra (Db-€45, bigger Db-€47-49, Tb-€69, Qb-€79, air-con, Wi-Fi, at the foot of the Santa Clara Bridge at Avenida João das Regras 82, tel. 239-440-582, www.riversuites.pt, geral@riversuites.pt).

HOSTEL

$ Pousada de Juventude, the youth hostel, offers 71 rooms on the edge of town in the student area past Praça da República. It's friendly, clean, and well-run, but is no cheaper than a simple *pensão* (€12/bed in 4- to 6-bed rooms, S-€28, Db-€30, Rua Dr. Henriques Seco 14, tel. 239-822-955, www.pousadasjuventude.pt, coimbra@movijovem.pt).

Eating in Coimbra

Specialties of this hilly Beira region include *leitão* (suckling pig), *cabrito* (baby male goat), *chanfana* (goat cooked in wine), *Serra* cheese, and rich, red *Bairrada* and *Dão* wines. For a sweet and herby *digestivo*, try Licor Beirão. The local pastries are *pastel de Santa Clara* (made with almonds and marmalade) and *pastel de Tentúgal* (flaky puff pastry with a sweet egg filling and a dusting

COIMBRA

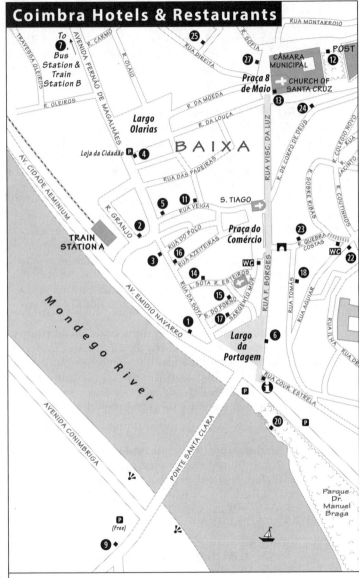

Coimbra Hotels & Restaurants

RUA MONTARROIO

To 7, Bus Station & Train Station B

AVENIDA FERNÃO DE MAGALHÃES

TRAVESSA OLEIROS

R. CARMO

R. OLAIO

R. OLEIROS

AV. CIDADE AEMINIUM

R. GRANJO

TRAIN STATION A

Largo Olarias

Loja da Cidadão 🅿️ ❹

B A I X A

RUA DAS PADEIRAS

RUA DA MOEDA

RUA DA LOUÇA

❺

RUA VEIGA

RUA DO POÇO

❷

❸

RUA AZEITEIRAS

❶❻

L. SOTA R. ESTEIROS

WC

RUA DA SOTA

B. DO FORNO

SARGENTO-MOR

AV. EMIDIO NAVARRO

M o n d e g o   R i v e r

AVENIDA CONIMBRIGA

PONTE SANTA CLARA

🅿️ (Free)

❾

RUA DIREITA

R. SOFIA

❷⁵

❷⁷

Praça 8 de Maio

CÂMARA MUNICIPAL

POST

⓬

CHURCH OF SANTA CRUZ

⓭

②④

RUA VISC. DA LUZ

R. DE CORPO DE DEUS

R. COLÉGIO NOVO

RUA JACINTO

R. SOBRE RIBAS

R. COUTINHOS

S. TIAGO

Praça do Comércio

②③

R. QUEBRA COSTAS

WC

②②

RUA F. BORGES

⓰

⓮

⓯

⓱

⓫

⓲

RUA TOMÁS

RUA AGUIAR

RUA ILHA

❻

Largo da Portagem

RUA COUR. ESTRELA

🅿️ ℹ️

②⓪

🅿️

Parque Dr. Manuel Braga

COIMBRA

❶ Hotel Astória
❷ Hotel Bragança
❸ Hotel Vitória
❹ Residência Lusa Atenas
❺ Hotel Domus
❻ Hotel Larbelo
❼ To Hotel Tivoli Coimbra

❽ Ibis Hotel
❾ RiverSuites
❿ To Pousada de Juventude
⓫ Adega Paço do Conde
⓬ Restaurante Jardim da Manga
⓭ Café Santa Cruz
⓮ Restaurante O Serenata

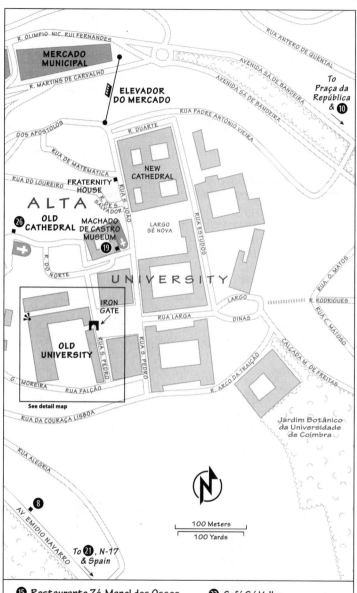

15 Restaurante Zé Manel dos Ossos	**22** Café Sé Velha
16 Restaurante Solar do Bacalhau	**23** Fado ao Centro
17 O Bizarro	**24** À Capella Fado
18 Fangas Mercearia Bar	**25** Diligência Fado
19 Loggia Restaurante	**26** Restaurante O Trovador
20 Restaurante Itália	**27** Internet Café
21 To Avenida da Lousã Eateries	

of powdered sugar). Be aware that many of these restaurants shut down—along with most of Coimbra—on Sunday.

EATING NEAR THE MAIN DRAG

Adega Paço do Conde knows how to grill, and Coimbra's students know it. Choose your seafood or meat selection from the display case as you enter. They'll pop it right on the grill and then bring it to your table. Students, travelers, families, and pigeons like this homey place that just seems right, even without English menus (big, splittable €5-12 plates, Mon-Sat 11:30-15:00 & 18:30-22:00, closed Sun, Rua Paço do Conde 1; from Praça do Comércio, take the last left—Rua Adelino Veiga, opposite the church, and walk 2 blocks to small square—Largo Paço do Conde; tel. 239-825-605, Alfredo).

Restaurante Jardim da Manga is handy for a quick, cheap, self-service meal with locals. Sit indoors or outdoors next to a cool and peaceful fountain. It's family-friendly and cheap enough to be a popular choice for children's birthday parties. Just slide a tray down the counter and pick what you like (€7-10 meals, daily 12:00-15:00 & 19:00-22:00, in the Jardim da Manga garden behind Church of Santa Cruz, tel. 239-829-156).

Café Santa Cruz, next to the Church of Santa Cruz, is Old World elegant, with great coffee, simple toasted sandwiches, Wi-Fi, and outdoor tables offering great people-watching over Praça 8 de Maio. Their signature pastry *cruzios* (named for the church's friars) is a new confection inspired by nun-baked sweets. Coffee costs €0.60 at the bar and just €0.80 outside at a table (Mon-Sat 7:00-24:00, plus Sun 8:00-20:00 in summer, closed Sun off-season). The café hosts free live fado most nights in season at 22:00.

CHARACTERISTIC RESTAURANTS IN THE OLD TOWN

These restaurants serving typical Portuguese fare are just behind Hotel Astória.

Restaurante O Serenata is country-kitchen cozy, with about 20 tables and a fresh, bright atmosphere. Hardworking and helpful Pedro serves hearty and splittable meals for €10-15. Goat, cod, and mixed grill are his fortes (Mon-Sat 12:00-15:00 & 19:00-23:00, closed Sun, Largo da Sota 6, tel. 239-826-729).

Restaurante Zé Manel dos Ossos is tiny, rustic, and authentic. Judging from the walls—caked with notes from happy eaters—and the line of people waiting hungrily in the alley, this place is a favorite. They serve a dozen good, typical Coimbran dishes. To order, I'd trust Mario, who speaks a lee-tle English. The *ossos*—meaty bones cooked with veggies—are the popular dish here (€8 for one person, €14 for two, Mon-Sat 12:00-15:00

& 19:30-22:00, closed Sun and off-season, no reservations taken, arrive early or wait; Beco do Forno 12, tel. 239-823-790).

Restaurante Solar do Bacalhau serves good Portuguese and Italian meals in a large dining area (€6 salads, €5-10 pizzas, €10 pastas, €12 meat and fish plates, daily 12:00-14:30 & 19:00-24:00, Rua da Sota 12, tel. 239-098-990).

O Bizarro is a small, family-run, white-tablecloth hole-in-the-wall that serves up tasty Portuguese food at a good price. *Chanfana* (goat simmered in wine) is the house specialty (great €7.50 lunch special, one regular €7 plate—or "*dose*"—is designed to serve—and fill—two, daily 12:00-15:00 & 18:00-22:00, Rua Sargento Mor 44, Rafael speaks English).

FINER DINING IN THE OLD TOWN

Fangas Mercearia Bar, my Coimbra favorite, is a small, intimate five-table wine bar where English-speaking Luisa serves delightful *petiscos* (Portuguese tapas) matched by a nice selection of quality Portuguese wines by the glass (small plates around €5 each, 3 or 4 will fill 2 people, €13 for a sampler plate, Tue-Sun 12:00-16:00 & 19:00-24:00, closed Mon, Rua Fernandes Tomás 45, reserve ahead, tel. 934-093-636).

Loggia Restaurante is a dressy place at the Machado de Castro Museum with seating inside or outside on the view terrace overlooking the old town. It's a convenient stop while sightseeing, as it's next to the university, and there's an amazing €7 lunch buffet (including drink and coffee). And, if you don't mind the long hike above the old town, it's a romantic and classy option for dinner when it's open (€12 plates, €20 fixed-price menu, Tue and Sun open 10:00-18:00 for lunch only, Wed-Sat 10:00-22:30 with dinner from 19:30, closed Mon, tel. 239-853-076).

DINING ON THE RIVER

Restaurante Itália—at Parque Dr. Manuel Braga, opposite the TI—literally hangs over the river. It serves Italian food indoors and out. Dinner reservations are smart (€8-12 pizza and pastas, €12-23 fish and meat plates, pizza available to go, daily 12:00-24:00, riverside tables limited to parties of four when busy, tel. 239-838-863).

Avenida da Lousã **Eateries:** A modern building on this street houses a strip of trendy restaurants, each with modern, air-conditioned seating indoors and breezy riverside tables on a common patio. They are below ground level and not visible from Avenida da Lousã; to reach them, walk past Restaurante Itália and hug the river for about 150 yards heading south. The restaurants (open daily from 12:00 until late) include:

A Portuguesa Restaurante, the most expensive and contemporary choice, is romantic, serving traditional dishes with a modern twist (€15-20 fish and meat plates, tel. 239-842-140).

The Mondego Irish Pub is fun, noisy, and youthful, with live music many nights (generally Irish). It serves burgers, steaks, dinner salads, Guinness on tap, and all you'd expect from an Irish bar, plus a traditional favorite—*francesinha*. Locals love these egg, cheese, and sausage sandwiches made with a spicy sauce (tel. 239-837-092).

Picnics: Shop at the colorful covered market (Mercado Municipal), behind the Church of Santa Cruz (Mon-Sat 8:00-14:00, closed Sun) or at tiny *mini-mercados* in the side streets. The well-maintained gardens along the river across from the TI are picnic-pleasant.

Coimbra Connections

If you're traveling by train, remember that Coimbra has two stations—A and B—but any ticket covers you for the five-minute shuttle train that runs between the stations (see page 241 for details).

From Coimbra by Bus to: Alcobaça (2/day, 1.5 hours), **Batalha** (3/day, 1 hour, transfer in Leiria), **Fátima** (hourly, 1 hour), **Nazaré** (5/day, 2 hours), **Lisbon** (hourly, 2.5 hours), **Évora** (2/day direct, 4 hours, almost hourly with transfer in Lisbon), **Porto** (almost hourly, 1.5 hours). Bus info: tel. 239-855-270. Frequency drops on weekends, especially Sunday.

By Train to: Nazaré/Valado (3/day, 2.5 hours, transfer in Bifurcação de Lares; the bus is a better option—see above—because Nazaré/Valado train station is 3 miles outside Nazaré), **Porto** (nearly hourly, 1 hour on Alfa Pendular line or Intercidades service, 2 hours on regional line; most long-distance trains end at Porto's non-central Campanhã station but include a transfer to the more central São Bento Station), **Lisbon** (almost hourly on Alfa Pendular or Intercidades service, 2 hours; regional service equally frequent but takes 4 hours; for Lisbon center, get off at Santa Apolónia Station; for Lisbon airport, hop off at Oriente Station and take the Metro to airport; all Coimbra/Porto trains stop at both Lisbon stations, 7 minutes apart). Train info: tel. 808-208-208, www.cp.pt.

To Salamanca, Spain: The best option is the direct InterNorte **bus** (€45, departs daily at 10:15, arrives at 17:30 in Salamanca on Spain time—add one hour from Portugal). To guarantee a place, book a couple of days in advance. You can confirm schedules and buy your bus ticket by phone or in person at the friendly InterVisa

travel agency in Coimbra (see "Helpful Hints," page 243) more easily than at Coimbra's bus station (InterCentro office, tel. 239-827-
588, no English spoken).

I'd avoid taking the **train** to Salamanca because of its inconve-
nient early-morning arrival time: One train per day on the Sud-Ex-
presso line departs Coimbra at 23:37 and drops you in Salamanca
at 4:56 (4.5 hours).

PORTO

To get a complete picture of Portugal, visit Porto—the capital of the north and the country's second city (with 238,000 residents and a sprawling metropolitan area that includes 1.7 million people). Porto, proud of the things that make it different, fiercely clings to its long-standing rivalry with Lisbon...especially where soccer is concerned.

Porto (POR-too) is less polished than Lisbon, but it's also full of Old World charm. Houses with red-tiled roofs tumble down the hills to the riverbank, prickly church towers dot the skyline, mosaic-patterned stones line streets, and flat-bottomed boats called *rabelos* ply the lazy river. The old town was spared the devastation of the great 1755 earthquake, and today is preserved as a World Heritage Site.

The city's name comes from the Romans, who dubbed the port town Portus Cale. When Porto's Christians conquered the Moors in the southern half of the country, the city's name became the name of the whole country. The British, who have a long-standing trading association with the city, refer to the town as "Oporto" (a combination of two Portuguese words meaning "the port"). While various guidebooks and postcards call it this, locals never do.

Porto has a gritty character, warts and all. It's a solid city—it seems made entirely of granite—with solid people. In fact, the residents of what's nicknamed "the granite city" like to say they have granite in their DNA. Locals claim they're working too hard to worry about being pretty. As an oft-repeated saying goes, "Coimbra studies, Braga prays, Lisbon parties...and Porto works."

Straight-laced, nose-to-the-grindstone Porto has enjoyed something of a cultural renaissance in the last decade. In 2001,

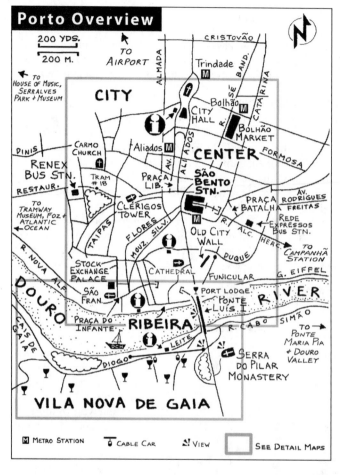

Porto Overview

200 YDS.
200 M.

N

TO
AIRPORT

TO
HOUSE OF MUSIC,
SERRALVES
PARK + MUSEUM

CITY

CRISTOVÃO

Trindade M

ALMADA

SÉ BAND.

CATARINA

Bolhão

CITY HALL &

Bolhão M

BOLHÃO MARKET

DINIS

CARMO CHURCH

Aliados M

AV. ALIADOS

CENTER

FORMOSA

RENEX BUS STN.

TRAM #18

PRAÇA LIB.

SÃO BENTO STN.

RESTAUR.

TO
TRAMWAY MUSEUM, FOZ +
ATLANTIC
OCEAN

CLÉRIGOS TOWER

TAIPAS

FLORES

MOUZ. SILV.

OLD CITY WALL

PRAÇA BATALHA

AV. RODRIGUES FREITAS

R. ALC.

HERC.

REDE EXPRESSOS BUS STN.

TO
CAMPANHÃ STATION

R. NOVA ALF

STOCK EXCHANGE PALACE

SÃO FRAN.

CATHEDRAL

DUQUE

FUNICULAR

G. EIFFEL

DOURO

RIVER

CAIS DE GAIA

PRAÇA DO INFANTE

RIBEIRA

PORT LODGE

PONTE LUIS I

R. CABO

SIMÃO

TO
PONTE MARIA PIA
+ DOURO VALLEY

DCH

DIOGO

LEITE

SERRA DO PILAR MONASTERY

VILA NOVA DE GAIA

M METRO STATION   CABLE CAR   VIEW   SEE DETAIL MAPS

it was designated as a European Capital of Culture. Two exciting showpieces of contemporary architecture have been built: the Serralves Museum and the House of Music. European Union money has poured in, funding a revamping of the public transportation system and more. With this ongoing construction, Porto is ever-changing, often chaotic, and worth a visit now more than ever. (And discount airlines like Ryanair fly here, putting the city within easy reach of budget travelers.) As a bonus, Porto serves as a handy gateway to the stunning Douro Valley.

Porto offers two high-impact sightseeing thrills: the postcard-perfect ambience of the riverfront Ribeira district and the opportunity to learn more about (and taste) the port wine that ages here. Porto also features other unexpected treats, including sumptuous

PORTO

Baroque churches and civic buildings, a bustling real-world market hall, and quirky but worthwhile museums.

The weather is always changing, blown in and out by the steady sea breeze. You're likely to get sun and rain at the same time—causing the locals to exclaim, "A widow's going to remarry."

PLANNING YOUR TIME

Porto offers one very busy day's worth of sightseeing (or better yet, two relaxed days). Begin your day by exploring the city center above the town (poke around the market hall and climb Clérigos Tower for a visual orientation). Wander past the cathedral and clamber down one of the steep lanes to the Ribeira district for lunch. Enjoy touring the breathtaking interiors of the Stock Exchange Palace and São Francisco Church. Then head across the river to tour a couple of port-wine lodges before returning to the Ribeira for dinner. With a second day, slow down, taste more port, cruise the river, and add a visit to the Serralves Museum, its Art Deco mansion, and its plush park.

Ideally, combine your visit to Porto with a trip up the Douro Valley (about two hours away—see next chapter).

Orientation to Porto

Porto sprawls on the hilly north bank of the Douro River, near where the river meets the Atlantic Ocean. The tourist's Porto is

compact, but confusing and steep. Get a good map and wear comfortable walking shoes (or just grab a taxi whenever you need a quick connection). It helps to think of the tourist's Porto in three parts.

Ribeira (ree-BAY-rah): Right on the river, the Ribeira neighborhood has a twisty street plan and oodles of atmosphere. Praça Infante Dom Henrique (Henry the Navigator Square), two blocks above the Ribeira, hosts two intriguing sights: the Stock Exchange Palace and São Francisco Church.

City Center: Ramshackle old homes scramble steeply uphill toward the second part of town, the modern city center, which hovers above the Ribeira and surrounds the broad boulevard called Avenida dos Aliados (Avenue of the Allies). This area is the urban business center of Porto, packed with office buildings and shoppers, and peppered with hotels. You'll also find a smattering of squares, monuments, and sights (including the market hall and cathedral). Clérigos Tower stands as the city's most recognizable landmark.

Vila Nova de Gaia: Across the river shine the neon signs of Porto's main tourist attraction, the port-wine cellars *(caves do vinho do porto)* in Vila Nova de Gaia, the third part of Porto, although it's technically another town.

The Douro is spanned by six bridges (two steel, four concrete). The only one you're likely to cross is the monstrous steel **Ponte Dom Luís I** (cars use lower level, Metro trains run along upper level; pedestrians can use either level).

Visitors venturing farther out find Porto to be a city of contrasts. Its outskirts boast bright, spacious, prim residential neighborhoods, such as the areas surrounding the Boavista Rotunda and the Serralves Museum and park.

TOURIST INFORMATION

Porto has two main TIs: in the **city center** across from City Hall (at the top of Avenida dos Aliados, Rua Clube dos Fenianos 25) and on **cathedral square** (both open daily 9:00-20:00, until 19:00 off-season, tel. 223-393-472). On the **Ribeira** waterfront, a small green info kiosk is staffed in high season (April-Oct daily 10:00-19:00). You'll also find TIs at the **Campanhã train station** (June-Oct daily 10:00-18:00, shorter hours off-season), the **airport** (daily 8:00-23:30, on the arrivals level near Vodafone store and Café Aeroporto), and in **Vila Nova de Gaia,** officially outside the city limits. The TIs share a website: www.visitporto.travel.

At any TI, pick up the free one-page city map (with sights and hotels) and the *Useful Information* pamphlet (€0.50). The city-walk guide (€1) lays out four themed walks. The free quarterly *Agenda Cultural* guide lists cultural events in the city in Portuguese. The monthly *Casa da Música* guide lists events at the House of Music (www.casadamusica.com). The TI also sells the Porto Card (for sightseeing—described next) and the Andante card (for transit—described later).

Porto Card: This card offers free entry to some sights and discounts for others, plus discounts on bus tours and some restaurants. It generally pays for itself if you visit four or more sights. The card comes in several versions, but the best choice for most visitors is either the one-day Walker card (€5, covers sights) or the one-day Standard card (€10.50, covers sights and includes a 24-hour transit pass, which covers all public transit—except trams). If you plan to get around mostly on foot or by taxi, the Walker card is your best bet. If using public transit, the Standard card is a pretty good deal. Either card is good for 24 hours—you choose the start date and time, which are written on the card. Don't get the card for Monday, when many sights are closed; skip it if you're under 26 or a senior (you can get into most sights free or half-price). The card is sold at Porto's TIs, travel agencies, and some hotels, but not at participating sights. A handy guidebook is included. See www.visitporto. travel for details.

ARRIVAL IN PORTO

By Train: Porto has two train stations. Regional trains, including those serving the Douro Valley, use the very central **São Bento Station** (a sight in itself for its magnificent tiles; see page 289). Facing the exit in the left corner is the helpful Loja da Mobilidade **transport office** (daily 7:30-20:30, international ticket window daily 8:00-12:30 & 13:30-16:30). Here you can purchase train tickets as well as the hassle-free Andante card (described later, under "Getting Around Porto"), and get answers to your questions about transportation within or out of Porto. The helpful staff can help you understand the bus-station mess and get a handle on the ever-changing local transit picture (tel. 808-208-208, www.stcp.pt).

Trains coming from farther away, including Lisbon and Coimbra, arrive at **Campanhã Station,** on the east edge of town. If your train stops at both stations, get off at São Bento (closer to central hotels). If you have to get off at Campanhã, you have three options for getting into the center: Take a taxi directly to your hotel (€7 with luggage to most city-center accommodations); catch another train to São Bento Station (6/hour, free with any ticket to Porto); or use the Metro across the street (take it to the Trindade stop, then transfer to the yellow line for either Aliados or São Bento stations).

Note that the Metro does not have a stop directly at the Ribeira, but the neighborhood is an easy, downhill walk from the São Bento Metro stop and train station.

By Bus: As each of Porto's many bus companies operates its own garage, there's no central bus station. All of the bus garages are more or less in the city center. The main ones are: **Rede Expressos** (to Lisbon and Coimbra; Rua Alexandre Herculano 366, tel. 222-006-954, www.rede-expressos.pt); **RENEX** (to Lisbon; Campo Mártires da Pátria 37, tel. 222-003-395, www.renex.pt); **Rodonorte** (to points north; Rua Ateneu Comercial do Porto 19, tel. 222-004-398, www.rodonorte.pt); and **Internorte** (to Spain, including Madrid; Praça da Galiza 96, tel. 226-052-420, www. internorte.pt). You can also buy bus tickets to Spain from the Abreu Travel Agency on Avenida dos Aliados (at #207, tel. 222-043-500).

By Car: Central Porto is a headache by car—and parking is very expensive (over €30/day). Stow it at your hotel. Approaching from Lisbon and Coimbra on the A-1 expressway, pay a toll and then follow signs for *Ponte da Arrábida*. After crossing the bridge, take the first right and follow *centro* signs (or the little bull's-eyes) into downtown.

By Plane: Porto's Francisco Sá Carneiro Airport (airport code: OPO) is 11 miles north of the city center. Since it's an international airport (with connections beyond Iberia), it's used by people throughout northern Portugal and Spain. The Metro connects the airport to the center (3/hour, 30 minutes to the Trindade stop), or catch a taxi (figure €25). Airport info: tel. 229-432-400.

HELPFUL HINTS

Closed Day: Most Porto museums are closed on Monday.

Festivals: Porto's big holiday is São João Day (for St. John the Baptist, the city's patron saint) on June 24. Festivities start the night of June 23 with partying and fireworks at Ponte Dom Luís I bridge, and continue on the 24th with a *rabelo* regatta.

Internet Access: OnWeb Cyber Bar is a handy Internet café with fast access and a youthful, musical ambience (€2/2 hours, Mon-Sat 10:00-2:00 in the morning, Sun 15:00-2:00 in the morning, a block below TI at the top of Avenida dos Aliados across from City Hall at #289).

Laundry: A small self-service laundry hides almost underground at the west end of the Ribeira district (between São Francisco Church and the river at the top of Rua da Reboleira). Look for the silver *Câmara Municipal* sign (€6/load, daily 8:00-19:00, closed afternoons in Aug, tel. 222-084-621).

Best Views: There are fine views all along the Ribeira riverfront embankment, but they're even better from across the river in Vila Nova de Gaia (looking back toward Porto, especially from the cable car). You can also enjoy the views from the top of Clérigos Tower, from the terrace next to the cathedral, from the old town wall, or from Mosteiro da Serra do Pilar (the monastery across the river, just above the big steel Ponte Dom Luís I bridge). But the best vantage point of all is from a boat on the river itself (see "Cruising the Douro," page 297).

Updates to This Book: For updates to this book, check www.ricksteves.com/update.

GETTING AROUND PORTO

The city is investing heavily in its public transportation infrastructure. As a result of all the construction, Porto's transit system is often changing and a bit confusing. The network includes buses, trams, the Metro, a funicular, and some trains.

Andante Card: This non-shareable card is required to ride the Metro, and covers other forms of public transit (including buses and the train linking Campanhã and São Bento stations), but not trams or the funicular. Your fare depends on which "zone" you

Porto at a Glance

▲▲Strolling the Cais da Ribeira Porto's picturesque riverfront, with arcades and colorful traditional homes. **Hours:** Always open. See page 296.

▲▲Stock Exchange Palace Astonishing monument to civic pride, with room after sumptuous room. **Hours:** By tour only, daily April-Oct 9:00-18:30, Nov-March 9:00-12:30 & 14:00-17:30. See page 294.

▲▲Port-Wine Lodges in Vila Nova de Gaia Porto's most popular tourist activity: touring the cellars where its most famous product ages...and tasting some, too. **Hours:** Vary, but generally daily, last tours at 18:00. See page 298.

▲Cruising the Douro Lazy one-hour cruises up and down the river, offering the city's top views. **Hours:** Generally daily 10:00-18:30 in summer (until 17:00 off-season). See page 297.

▲São Francisco Church Gothic church dripping with Baroque gold. **Hours:** Daily March-June 9:00-19:00, July-Sept 9:00-20:00, Oct-Feb 9:00-17:30. See page 294.

▲Avenida dos Aliados Porto's top urban street, where the city goes to work in elaborate buildings. **Hours:** Always open; quiet at night. See page 285.

▲Clérigos Church and Tower Porto's towering landmark, with a 225-step climb to sweeping views over the urban sprawl. **Hours:** Daily 9:00-19:00. See page 288.

▲São Bento Train Station Entry hall decorated with impressive *azulejo* (tile) murals. **Hours:** Always open. See page 289.

▲Cathedral (Sé) Huge church overlooking the town, with fine *azulejo*-decorated cloister and otherwise dull interior. **Hours:**

travel in. Zone 2 covers all the recommended sights in this book (€1.20/trip); the airport is in Zone 4 (€1.85/trip). The regular **Andante** card is reloadable—you can buy as many trips, or *títulos*, as you want (one-time €0.50 card fee, one free trip credited with the purchase of 10).

Unless you're taking just a few rides, it's a better value to buy a 24-hour pass—called **Andante 24** (€4.15 for Zone 2, €6.40 for Zone 4, plus €0.50 card fee). But be aware that once a card has been used as a 24-hour pass, you can't load it with individual trips—you can only reload it with another 24-hour pass. While the city pro-

Church—daily in summer 9:00-12:30 & 14:30-19:00, until 18:00 in winter; cloister and sacristy—daily in summer 9:00-12:30 & 14:30-19:00, until 17:30 in winter, closed Sun morning. See page 290.

▲**Rua de Santa Catarina** The main shopping drag, with Art Nouveau and Art Deco landmarks. **Hours:** Traffic-free during the day; quiet at night. See page 293.

▲**Market** Lively old-fashioned produce and meat market...with old-fashioned sanitary conditions. **Hours:** Mon-Fri 8:30-17:00, Sat 8:30-13:00, closed Sun. See page 293.

▲**Serralves Foundation Contemporary Art Museum and Park** Sprawling park with impressive museum, Art Deco mansion, and relaxing grounds. **Hours:** April-Sept Tue-Fri 10:00-17:00, park open until 19:00, Sat-Sun 10:00-20:00; Oct-March Tue-Fri 10:00-17:00; Sat-Sun 10:00-19:00; closed Mon year-round. See page 304.

Port and Douro Wines Institute Classy one-stop spot for port tasting. **Hours:** Mon-Fri 11:00-19:00, closed Sat-Sun. See page 295.

Tramway Museum Collection tracing the history of electrical transport. **Hours:** Mon 14:00-18:00, Tue-Fri 10:00-19:00, Sat-Sun 14:00-19:00. See page 303.

House of Henry the Navigator Birthplace of the explorer, with history exhibits. **Hours:** Tue-Sun 9:30-13:00 & 14:00-17:30, closed Mon. See page 296.

House of Music New Modernist concert hall with performances of jazz, fado, and more. **Hours:** English tour daily at 16:00, concerts nearly nightly. See page 305.

motes its €7 **AndanteTour** card, the Andante 24 pass is a better deal.

To use any Andante card, pass it over the scanner on the Metro, bus, or train. The cards are sold at ticket machines and at TIs, the Loja da Mobilidade transport office in the São Bento Station, Andante stores (at the airport and at Trindade Station), and some bus, Metro, and train ticket offices (www.linhandante.com).

By Bus

Several local **buses** are useful for tourists, such as the routes that go to the port-wine lodges in Vila Nova de Gaia across the river

(#900, #901, and #906). Buses also run from the Ribeira to Foz (#500), and from the beach in Foz to the Serralves Museum (#203). Service is generally speedy, but avoid buses during rush hour, when traffic slows to a crawl.

Individual bus tickets cost €1.85 if purchased from driver; if riding public transportation more than once, it's cheaper to buy an Andante card (described earlier, www.stcp.pt).

By Tram

Three interconnecting tram lines for tourists are #1, #18, and #22 (each marked *Porto Tram City Tour*). Tram #1 (Infante/Passeio Alegre) uses a historic car that shudders along the river from the Ribeira, past several museums to the Jardim do Passeio Alegre, a 10-minute walk to the Foz district and the Atlantic Ocean. Tram #18 (Restauração/Cordoaria) begins at Carmo Church and wobbles to the Tramway Museum. Tram #22 (Guindais/Carmo) makes a loop through the city center, from the shopping street Rua de Santa Catarina, down Rua de Passos Manuel, cutting through Avenida dos Aliados, and turning near Carmo Church to return along Rua 31 de Janeiro, with a jog across Praça da Batalha to the funicular (see map on page 286).

Trams are not covered by the Andante card. Individual tickets cost €2.50 per ride (purchase from driver). You can also buy an €8 pass that covers unlimited rides on all three lines for a 24-hour period (purchase from driver, travel agencies, and some hotels).

By Metro

Metro lines include blue, red, green, purple, and orange; these five connect Campanhã Station to the center (www.metrodoporto.pt). All Metro lines converge at the Trindade stop, two blocks behind City Hall and Avenida dos Aliados. The purple line connects the airport to the center and Campanhã Station; the yellow line includes São Bento Station and Vila Nova de Gaia, across the river. To ride the Metro you must have an Andante card, described earlier. You have a little over an hour to complete your ride. If you transfer, you must validate your card before getting on the next line. Don't worry—you aren't paying another fare. The system is just checking if your trip falls within your travel-time window.

By Funicular

A handy funicular (Elevador dos Guindais) connects the Ribeira district (at the base of the Ponte Dom Luís I bridge) to the top of the steep hill above (at the remains of the city wall, down the Rua de Augusto Rosa from Praça da Batalha). Note that the funicular stops running earlier in the off-season (€2, every 10 minutes; May-

July and Sept-Oct Sun-Wed 8:00-22:00, Thu-Sat 8:00-24:00; Aug daily 8:00-24:00, Nov-April 8:00-20:00).

By Cable Car

The overpriced Teleférico de Gaia cable car soars above Vila Nova da Gaia, connecting the riverfront with the Jardim do Morro, just under the Mosteiro da Serra do Pilar monastery and the upper part of the Ponte Dom Luís I bridge. The five-minute ride gives a unique view over the port wine lodges and across the river to the city, and can be handy for connecting the upper and lower parts of Vila Nova da Gaia (€5 one-way, €8 round-trip, daily 10:00-20:00 in summer, 10:00-18:00 off-season, www.gaiacablecar.com).

By Taxi

Taxis are a good option in this hilly city. Most rides are fairly short and cost only around €5. For rides within the city limits, the meter should be on "T1" during the day (€2 drop charge) and "T2" at night (21:00-6:00 in the morning, €2.50 drop charge). Each kilometer costs about €0.40. A luggage surcharge of €1.60 is legit. It's easy to find taxi stands, and you'll pay €0.80 more to call one (try Invicta, tel. 225-076-400).

Tours in Porto

The city of Porto operates an ingenious, extremely useful tour co-op—ATC/Porto Tours—allowing all the small tour companies to share one office in an old medieval watchtower next to the cathedral (daily April-Sept 10:00-19:00, shorter hours off-season, Calçada Dom Pedro Pitões 15, tel. 222-000-073, www.portotours. com, reservas@portotours.mail.pt). This organization, which takes no commission and is not biased toward any particular company, will help you sort through all of the walking, bus, boat, bike, Segway, taxi, and even helicopter tour options in Porto and up the Douro. They'll confirm times, answer questions, and sell tickets for the tours. Walking tours on different topics can be reserved online through their website (tours average €25/person, but prices vary depending on the number of people in your group).

ON WHEELS

In this steep, tiring city, a **bus tour** is worth considering.

Two companies offer hop-on, hop-off bus tours, with tickets good for 48 hours. Choose between City Sightseeing's red buses (€12, 2-hour circuit with 9 stops, 10 buses/day, daily 9:30-18:30, tel. 222-080-677, www.city-sightseeing.com) and Yellow Bus tours (€15, 2 different 2-hour circuits, 1-2 buses/hour, daily 9:00-18:00, mobile 967-659-257, www.yellowbustours.com). Yellow Bus also

---

Lisbon versus Porto: Teams and Terms

Lisbon and Porto are proud rivals. Lisboners, known as "cabbage eaters," drink an *imperial* (as a small glass is called) of Sagres beer while rooting for Benfica (the working-class soccer team) or Sporting (the upper-class rival). Meanwhile, the people of Porto, known as "tripe eaters," drink a *fino* (small glass) of Super Bock beer while rooting for FC Porto. Differences extend to coffee breaks, too. When it's time for a shot of espresso, Lisboners ask for a *bica* while in Porto they request a *cimbalino*.

---

sells a €22 combo-ticket that includes a "Six Bridges" river cruise (see page 297).

If you prefer a typical stay-mainly-on-the-bus tour, figure on paying €32 (half-day, live guide in 4 languages, details at ATC/Porto Tours).

A silly **tourist train** includes a stop at a port-wine lodge across the river (€7, 1.25 hours, 2/hour, leaves from in front of cathedral daily on the hour, 10:00-17:00 in high season, less frequently off-season, tel. 800-203-983).

Taxi tours of the town and side-trips to the Douro Valley and even Santiago are also available (details at ATC/Porto Tours).

ON FOOT

A good local guide or tour can be well worth the expense.

Maria Jose Aleixo is a private guide whom I've found very helpful (€110/half-day per group, mobile 969-468-347, aleixo19@sapo.pt).

The City Tailors Tours are led by your friend in Porto, Ricardo Brochado, who truly loves his work. He tailors half-day Porto experiences for groups of one to four for €65 per person (cheaper for larger groups). This rate includes snacks, drinks, and perhaps a light meal along the way (mobile 917-574-983, www.thecitytailors.com, ricardo@thecitytailors.com).

Taste of Porto Food and Wine Tours is run with gusto by tour guide André, who has a contagious enthusiasm for good food and embracing life Portuguese-style. André takes small groups (up to 10) on a two-mile walk with six tasty stops. It's fun socially, really educational, relaxed, and delicious. André enjoys his work so much he'll happily do the tour if just one person signs up (€55, Tue-Sat at 10:30 and 16:00, lasts 3.5 hours, tel. 920-270-136, www.tasteporto.com, info@tasteportofoodtours.com).

BY BOAT

The city's well-promoted **"Six Bridges" river cruises** leave from the waterfront in the Ribeira district (see page 297).

If you want a longer cruise, **day trips along the Douro** can be reserved through ATC/Porto Tours (daily to Peso da Régua-€54-99, 5/day; to Pinhão-€70-100, 4/day; includes lunch on board).

Sights in Porto

IN THE CITY CENTER

The modern urban sector of Porto has few museums, but there are a handful of interesting squares, churches, and monuments here. These sights are all within a few minutes of each other by foot.

▲Avenida dos Aliados (Avenue of the Allies)

This is the main urban drag of Porto—named for the alliance created when Portugal joined the winning side before the outbreak

of World War I. The wide boulevard, lined with elaborate examples of various architectural eras (mostly Art Nouveau and Art Deco), reminds me of Prague's Wenceslas Square. The twin bank towers flanking the street midway up were designed by Portuguese architect Marques da Silva (circa 1920). This strip is where the city goes to work, watched over by the huge **City Hall** (Câmara Municipal). Behind that is the Trindade Church, and nearby you'll find the station (also called Trindade) where all of Porto's Metro lines converge.

The bottom of the avenue is known as **Praça da Liberdade** (Liberty Square) with an equestrian statue of King Pedro IV, a hero in the 1832 Civil War, who advocated for a limited constitutional monarchy in Portugal (while maintaining his title as Emperor of Brazil). King Pedro prevailed...and he's holding the constitution to prove it. A true "peoples' king," he left his heart to the people of Porto—buried in a local church. The square itself is a strong statement for a secular and modern Portugal. The City Hall (rather than a church) stands at the top (actually hiding a church).

Throughout Porto, after the king confiscated church property in the 1830s, large tracts of land that had been the domain of the church became the domain of the people. Then, in the 1920s and 1930s (especially with the coming of the dictator António Salazar), Portugal demonstrated its national pride by razing many character-

PORTO

Porto

- ⌐ VIEW
- Ⓣ TAXI STAND
- 🚈 TRAM (NOT ALL STOPS SHOWN)

N

RUA JORGE

ALMADA

CARMO CHURCH
PRAÇA LÉNCASTRE
R. CARMO
RUA S. TERESA
PRAÇA TEIXEIRA
RUA FABRICA
CAMPO

(TO TRAMWAY MUSEUM)
#18
Ⓣ #22
CARM.
CITY
CLÉRIGOS TOWER
RUA CLÉRIGOS

1/4 MILE
400 METERS

MARTIRES
JARDIM DE CORDOARIA
R. DE TRAS
R. DOS CALD.
RUA DAS TAIPAS
DA PATRIA
VITORIA
RUA DAS FLORES

MISERICORDIA CHURCH
RUA
RUA MOUZ. DA SILVEIRA
BAINHARIA
VENTOSA

RUA BELOMONTE
PORTO
STOCK EXCHANGE PALACE
MKT.
RUA S. JOÃO
MERC.

TO FOZ
SÃO FRAN.
PRAÇA INFANTE
RUA DO
INFANTE

Ⓣ Ⓣ
TRAM #1 (OR BUS)
CAIS DA

DOURO
HOUSE OF HENRY THE NAVIGATOR
PRAÇA RIBEIRA
RIB

RIVER

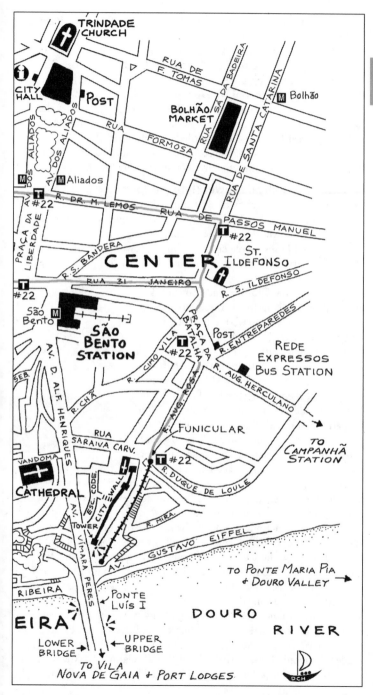

istic medieval quarters to build bigger squares (like this) and bigger buildings (like those dominating the scene here).

Orient yourself using an imaginary clock for a compass. Start by standing at the bottom of the square facing the horse. The City Hall is at the top of the square. At about 2 o'clock (behind the trees) is the **"Imperial McDonald's,"** perhaps the fanciest in Europe (formerly the Imperial Café). Check it out, and ponder the battle of cultural elegance against global economic efficiency. At 3 o'clock, a street leads to the blue-tiled church of St. Ildefonso. At 4 o'clock (50 yards away) is the corner of São Bento Station. And at 9 o'clock is Clérigos Church, with its famous view tower.

▲Clérigos Church and Tower (Igreja e Torre dos Clérigos)

This oval-shaped church with a disproportionately tall tower is the masterwork of Nicolau Nasoni, a prolific Baroque architect who left his mark all over the city (see sidebar).

Cost and Hours: Free entry to church, tower-€2, daily 9:00-19:00, free city maps at ticket window, Rua São Filipe de Nery, tel. 222-001-729.

Visiting the Church and Tower: This church, which consumed three decades of Nicolau Nasoni's life (1731-1763), shows his flair for theatrics. He fit the structure into its hilltop location, putting the tower at the back on the highest ground, dramatically reinforcing its height. Nasoni worked in stages: first the church, then the hospital and the Chapter House (residence for priests and monks). He topped it all off with the outsized tower.

The church facade displays Nasoni's characteristic frills, garlands, and exuberant cornices. Inside is an oval-shaped Baroque nave built out of granite and marble, but covered with ornate carvings. See the high altar—a wedding-cake structure with Mary on top—and the tomb of Nasoni, who asked to be buried here.

The real attraction is going up the tower—one of Porto's icons. After climbing 225 steps and 250 feet up to the top, you get a close-up look at the carillon and commanding views of the city with its jumble of tightly packed red roofs. Nasoni built the tower in six sections, each one more elaborate than the last, topped with a round dome and spiked with pinnacles.

Nearby: A fancy bookstore a few blocks away is worth a peek. Built in 1906, the **Lello & Irmão bookstore** boasts a lacy exterior and a fancy Art Nouveau interior. It looks like wood, but it's mostly made of painted plaster with gold leaf. Locals claim J. K. Rowling, who worked in Porto for a year, was inspired by this Harry Potter-

---

Nicolau Nasoni
(1691-1773)

In the 1720s—a boom time in Porto—the Italian Nasoni found work as a painter here. His swirling, colorful paintings wowed Porto, and Nasoni got plenty of work. He married a Portuguese woman, had five kids, and made Porto his home. Soon, he was employed as an architect, hiring skilled local artisans to turn granite, wood, and poured plaster into his trademark cherubs, garlands, and cumulus clouds. Even stark medieval churches had their facades topped with Baroque towers and their interiors paneled and spackled in billowy gilded designs. Prolific to the max, Nasoni redid Porto in the Baroque style (much as Bernini did in Rome), creating palaces and churches throughout the area. His tour de force was the hill-topping Clérigos Church, where he was later buried.

---

esque interior. Follow the quaint tracks to the book trolley. Climb the sagging staircase to a cute tearoom. The store has a good selection of books in English by leading Portuguese authors (Mon-Sat 10:00-19:30, closed Sun, Rua das Carmelitas 144).

• *Backtrack, crossing Avenida dos Aliados, and continue on to the...*

▲São Bento Train Station (Estação São Bento)

The main entry hall of this otherwise forgettable station features some of Portugal's finest *azulejos*. These vivid, decorative hand-painted tiles show histori-cal and folk scenes from the Douro region. Upper tiles on the left (when facing the tracks) show medieval battles back when Spain and Portugal were at war. Tiles on the opposite wall (far right when looking at the tracks) show a pivotal event from Porto's past—the 1387 wedding of Portugal's King John (João) I and the English princess Philippa, which established the Portuguese-English alliance. (Notice the fine portrait of Philippa and the depiction of the cathedral as it looked in the 14th century.) Below is the result of the marriage—their son, Prince Henry the Navigator, shown conquering Ceuta for Portugal in 1415. While humble Ceuta was just a small chip of Morocco (across from Gibraltar), it marked an important first step in the creation of a soon-to-be vast Portuguese empire. The trackside tiles celebrate the tradition-

PORTO

al economy, such as the transport of port wine. The multicolored tiles near the top show different modes of transportation, as they evolved from Roman chariots (just to the right of the big clock), progressing counterclockwise 360 degrees to the arrival of the first train (left corner above Philippa). Notice the words *Douro* and *Minho* overhead. These are the major rivers in this part of Portugal, and the key regions linked by these trains (basically the north of the country). All this art seems old, but it's really Portuguese revival art from the period just after World War I, celebrating the country's heritage.

To orient yourself from the station, stand outside with your back to the main entrance. Over your right shoulder (two blocks up the hill) is Praça da Batalha (Battle Square), the gateway to Porto's shopping district and old-fashioned market hall (described later). At 2 o'clock is the bottom of Avenida dos Aliados, the main square of the modern town. On the hill to your left is the cathedral. Ahead at 10 o'clock is the pedestrian street, Rua das Flores—with a series of delightful shops selling jewelry, antiques, chocolates, and more. This and the streets to your left lead down to the Ribeira.

▲Cathedral (Sé)

This hulking, fortress-like, 12th-century Romanesque cathedral, while graced with fine granite stonework typical of northern Portugal and lavish 18th-century Baroque altars, feels gloomy and stark inside. But the history is palpable. Henry the Navigator was baptized here, and it was the scene of many royal marriages (including John I and Philippa).

Cost and Hours: Cathedral—free, open daily in summer 9:00-12:30 & 14:30-19:00, until 18:00 in winter; cloister and sacristy—€3, daily in summer 9:00-12:30 & 14:30-19:00, until 17:30 in winter, closed Sun morning; Terreiro da Sé, tel. 222-059-028.

Visiting the Cathedral: The **main altarpiece** sums up the exuberance of Porto in the 1720s, when the city was booming, the local bishop was temporarily away in Lisbon, and Italian Baroque was sweeping through town. On the side walls flanking the altar are faded faux-architecture paintings by Nicolau Nasoni (see sidebar on page 289), the Italian who came to Porto to paint the cathedral's sacristy and soon became the city's most influential architect.

Look at the chapel just left of the high altar. Inside is a dreamy, carved-and-painted limestone statue of the Lady of Vendôme, brought to Porto in the 14th century by monks from France. It originally stood at one of the fortified gates of the city and remains close to the hearts of the townsfolk. Just left of the Lady of Vendôme is the Silver Altar of the Holy Sacrament (circa 1700)—1,500 pounds of silver. When French troops under Napoleon pillaged Porto, the church guards plastered over the altar to hide it.

The **cloister** and its adjacent rooms are worth the time and entrance fee. The cloister's walls are decorated with elaborate *azulejo* tiles illustrating the amorous poetry of the Bible's "Song of Songs." (The €0.50 pamphlet is skimpy, but the €5 English guidebook explains it all, including the text that inspired the *azulejos*.) The adjacent **Chapel of St. Vincent,** with 17th-century painted carvings of Bible scenes, has a trapdoor into a crypt, where centuries of bishops' bones were ultimately tossed. Upstairs, the richly ornamented chapter room is where the bishop and his gang met in the 17th century to wield their religious and secular power. Note the holy figures depicted on the ceiling and the fine city views from the windows.

Cathedral Square

From the cathedral's small square—until the 1920s a congested medieval quarter—you'll get a great **view** of the old town. The Baroque spiral pillory (20th-century copy) is a reminder of the harsh justice once doled out here. Look for the massive **Bishop's Palace,** still the home of the bishop and his offices: The immensity of this 18th-century building, dominating the skyline of Porto, reflects the bishop's past power. The stone tower in front of the cathedral houses the **ATC/Porto Tours** office (see page 283); a TI is also on the square (between the tower and cathedral).

Facing the cathedral, walk around to the left to the **statue** of Vímara Peres, a Christian warrior who reconquered this region from the Moors in 868. (It was lost again within two generations, and remained under Muslim control until the final reconquest in about 1100.) Step into the portico on the side of the cathedral to admire the original 18th-century blue tiles. From the banister to the left of Vímara Peres, survey the city and find the church with the blue facade in the distance. São Bento Station is just to its right, and the green copper dome of the City Hall breaks the skyline above it. Below you spreads the seedy district called **Sé** (meaning "cathedral," it refers to the *Se*at of the Catholic Church). This neighborhood, the oldest in town, was famously run-down and depopulating. Things may be changing, as the government is encouraging people to move in by offering economic incentives. The streets beyond the medieval gate—once a ratatouille of drug users and prostitutes—twist their way down into the Ribeira district.

City Wall View

A segment of the city wall is open and leads to a tower high above the river; from here you can enjoy a grand city and river view. To get there, walk 300 yards up the street behind the cathedral on Rua de Saraiva de Carvalho to a leafy square (Largo Primeiro de Dezembro) and through the arched doorway to the **Santa Clara Church** (with an impressive Baroque interior, decorated with carved wood and lots of gold leaf). Exiting the church, go right, through another gate (Instituto Nacional de Saúde), and ahead on your left you'll see the impressive crenellated remains of the 14th-century **town wall** (free, Mon-Fri 8:00-17:00, closed Sat-Sun). From the tower you can survey the Ribeira district, see three bridges upstream crossing the Douro River (including one designed by Gustave Eiffel), and look down at the funicular tracks (watch the cute car accordion in and out as it crests).

To ride that gadget down to the river, go back through the square to the bottom of Rua da Augusto Rosa. Here's where the **funicular** (Elevador dos Guindais) departs for the Ribeira riverfront. Or you can hike two blocks up Rua da Augusto Rosa to Praça da Batalha (described next) and the start of the shopping district.

PORTO'S SHOPPING NEIGHBORHOOD

Porto's bustling, local-feeling shopping district is a wonderful place to people-watch. Most of the action occurs along Rua de Santa Catarina, which runs roughly parallel to Avenida dos Aliados a few blocks east. Begin at Praça da Batalha (just up Rua 31 de Janeiro from São Bento Station), and follow this route to the Old World market hall.

Praça da Batalha (Battle Square)

This square has a fine tiled church (Santo Ildefonso), the 19th-century National Theater (originally the Opera House), and the impressive Art Deco Cinema Batalha (now closed). The church's *azulejo* tiles, reminiscent of Ming dynasty blue-and-white ceramics, were all the rage in Baroque Portugal. But these tiles, depicting scenes from the life of the church's patron saint, aren't Baroque. They were fitted into the walls of the church during the early 1930s, an era that celebrated Portuguese heritage.

This square, with its inviting benches, is where the old guys hang out. If you'd like a classic little hot dog with the local gang, drop by **Cervejaria Gazela** (just to the right of the National Theater, described in "Eating in Porto").

• *At the north end of the square, branching off to the left of the blue-tiled church, is...*

▲Rua de Santa Catarina

Porto's main shopping street is busy and (mostly) traffic-free by day, quiet by night. A stroll along here gives you a sense of today's Porto—as well as yesterday's, including the venerable Art Nou-

veau Café Majestic, the circa-1900 hangout for the local intelligentsia, a block down on your right. Step in. Porto's pet name for a little coffee is *cimbalino*—named for the traditional Italian espresso-making machines. Outside Café Majestic (on the nearby corner) is the FNAC department store—handy for whatever you might need.

The Rua de Santa Catarina sidewalk is a good example of *calçada portuguesa*, Portugal's unique limestone and basalt mosaic work. It's handmade and high-maintenance...but apparently worth the effort and expense to locals. Notice all of the shoe stores. Along with wine, textile and shoe factories power northern Portugal's industry.

• *If you head up the street two blocks and turn left on Rua Formosa (note the 1917 Art Deco facade of the Pearl of the Market shop at #279, filled with traditional and edible souvenirs), you'll run into the...*

▲Market (Bolhão)

Porto's traditional market still manages to stay in business, despite competition from newer shopping malls. This is a great place to wander—especially in the morning—and take in the sights, sounds, and smells of real-world Porto (Mon-Fri 8:30-17:00, Sat 8:30-13:00, closed Sun).

As you enter, the butchers and fishermen are on the left and right; produce and flowers (along with cheap eateries serving €3 sardine lunches) are dead ahead. Check out the butcher section, with half-pigs hanging from the ceiling, and display cases full of unusual specialties...such as *sangue cozido* (coagulated pig blood). Then wander through the seafood section. If it's springtime, you may see a favorite local delicacy pulled from the river: *lampreia* (eel). They say eels are so tasty because they dine on the flavorful garbage in the Douro. Climb the stairs for farmers' stalls. The market's old-fashioned sanitary conditions aren't quite up to European Union snuff, but the EU seems to be looking the other way...for now.

Inside and around the market are lively shops. At one corner is Casa Horticula, with a wide variety of seeds. In bakery windows, the big, round, dark *broa* breads, made with corn and rye, are moist inside and hard outside. The breads with bits of sausage baked in are called *folar*. The cheeses on display are either *ovelha* (sheep) or *cabra* (goat). *Bom-apetite!*

NEAR PRAÇA INFANTE DOM HENRIQUE

These sights are on or near Praça Infante Dom Henrique (Henry the Navigator Square), a long block uphill from the Ribeira district.

▲São Francisco Church

This is Porto's only church in the Gothic style—complete with a rose window, stair-step buttresses, and a statue of St. Francis of Assisi on the front. Today, a visit comes in two parts: the extravagantly decorated church and its jam-packed catacombs.

Cost and Hours: €3.50, daily March-June 9:00-19:00, July-Sept 9:00-20:00, Oct-Feb 9:00-17:30, no photos in church, Rua Infante Dom Henrique.

Visiting the Church: Although the church was ravaged by Napoleon and by the Portuguese during their 19th-century civil war, the interior remains stunning, with lavish chestnut carvings slathered in gold leaf. Wander down the main aisle like a bewildered 18th-century peasant. On the right, find the ornate altar showing how Franciscans weren't always warmly received—at the top they are being cruelly tortured and crucified by Japanese (portrayed with Muslim features), and at the bottom they are being beheaded by Moors. Still, in the center, St. Francis encourages his followers on. Across the nave, find the extremely fertile Tree of Jesse (1718), which is a very literal interpretation of the family tree of Jesus, resting upon a sleeping Jesse. Below that, Mary lies in a boat as Our Lady of Good Voyage, a patron saint of navigators. Note the wooden boards on the floor—once graves of parishioners. These graves are now empty but you can see the bones in the crypt.

Visiting the Crypt: Opposite the church entry, at the ticket desk, steps lead down to the church's crypt, its walls and floors neatly lined with tombs. The remains of former parishioners eventually end up in an inglorious bone heap or ossuary. Peer down through the trapdoor near #32 (look for signs to the *ossário*) to see their final refuge.

▲▲Stock Exchange Palace (Palácio da Bolsa)

Today this unassuming building is neither a stock exchange nor a palace, but a breathtaking monument to civic and commercial pride, with some of the most lavishly decorated rooms in Portugal.

The people of Porto have always taken pride in being hard workers. Commerce came to define Porto, as royalty or religion would define other cities (like Lisbon and Braga, respectively). The Commercial Association of Porto (Associação Comercial do Porto) even

had its own system of courts and a representative to the king. In 1832, the monastery of the São Francisco Church burned down, and the queen offered the property to the Commercial Association. They seized the opportunity to show off, crafting a building that would demonstrate the considerable skill of Porto's tradesmen.

Cost and Tours: The "Palace" can only be visited on a 30-minute guided tour (€7). Tours leave every 30 minutes in whatever language is necessary (often English plus another language). To avoid the wait, you can call to ask when the next English tour departs.

Hours: Daily April-Oct 9:00-18:30, Nov-March 9:00-12:30 & 14:00-17:30, last visit 30 minutes before closing, no flash photos inside, in big building marked *Associação Comercial do Porto* on Rua Ferreira Borges, tel. 223-399-013 or 223-399-007, www.palaciodabolsa.com. Note that the building still houses the offices of the Chamber of Commerce, and often closes when rented out for events.

Visiting the Stock Exchange: You'll tour eight rooms. The place is rife with symbolism and intricate, time-consuming craftsmanship intended only to impress: the complex patterned floors, carefully pieced together with Brazilian and African wood (from Portugal's colonies); an incredibly detailed inlaid table, created over three years using wood scraps from those same floors; and a room that looks like it's made of finely carved woodwork and bronze—until you realize it's all painted plaster and gold leaf.

The knock-your-socks-off finale is the sumptuous Arabian Room. This grand hall—inspired by Granada's Alhambra and 18 years in the making—was painstakingly decorated in the Moorish style with wood, plaster, and gold leaf.

Before exiting, consider a break in the **Wines of Portugal Tasting Room.** A sister organization of the tasting venue located in Lisbon's Praça do Comércio, they offer unique wines difficult to find in other locations. Buy a rechargeable chip card for €2 and you'll be given a glass to enjoy as many wines as you like (pours range from €0.50-1.50). A guide to regional differences goes for €1, but a general orientation is free (Tue-Sat 11:00-19:00, closed Sun-Mon, tel. 223-323-072, www.winesofportugal.com).

Port and Douro Wines Institute

This is a very good spot for sampling an array of ports. The price per taste starts at €1 a glass (or 4 glasses for €6). If they call it "port," you'll find it here. While it's more fun to tour the cellars across the river, this is a handy one-stop opportunity to try several ports. They also give short tours for €5 that finish with a tasting.

Cost and Hours: Mon-Fri 11:00-19:00, closed Sat-Sun, Rua Ferreira Borges 27, near Stock Exchange Palace, tel. 222-071-669, www.ivdp.pt.

House of Henry the Navigator (Casa do Infante)

Six hundred years ago, Porto's favorite son was supposedly born in this mansion (once the largest house in town and later the main customs house). This scant museum has few artifacts, but fans of ancient history enjoy the Roman mosaics found on-site and the re-construction of the building when it was the customs house. A free revolving exhibit of town history drawn from the city archives is located in the same building.

Cost and Hours: €2.20, free on weekends, Tue-Sun 9:30-13:00 & 14:00-17:30, closed Mon, last entry 30 minutes before closing, Rua da Alfândega 10, tel. 222-060-400. For more on Hank, see page 154.

THE RIBEIRA, PORTO'S ROMANTIC RIVERFRONT

The riverfront Ribeira (ree-BAY-rah, meaning "riverbank") district is the city's most scenic and touristy quarter, with the highest concentration of restaurants (and postcard racks). Before tourism, this was a working port. The city wall fortified the city from the river, and until the 20th-century embankment was built, the water came right up to the arches, many of which were loading zones for merchants, or "watergates."

Praça da Ribeira, the main square facing the river, was long the city's front door. City fathers attempted to clear it out and make a vast wasteland like Lisbon's Praça do Comércio, but the proud people of Porto (who, remember, have granite in their DNA) asserted themselves—as they like to do—and that construction project was stopped. Today, this square is a place of the people. Stand on the riverfront and look inland: Left is the unfinished facade of that urban renewal vision; on the right is a classic line of Porto houses that survive. (Do a "Where's Waldo?" for old ladies looking out at the crowd from their windows.) Check out the artwork in the square—the cube fountain and the statue of St. John the Baptist with his rough cloak, who overlooks the happy scene from above.

▲▲Strolling the Cais da Ribeira (Embankment)

Walking along the waterfront is a fine lazy-afternoon activity in Porto. As you stroll, imagine the busy port scene before the promenade was reclaimed from the river—cargo-laden riverboats lashed to the embankment, off-loading their wine and produce into 14th-century cellars (still visible). The old arcades lining the Ribeira promenade are jammed with hole-in-the-wall restaurants (made to look more "local" than they actually are) and souvenir shops. Behind the arcades are skinny, colorful houses draped with drying laundry fluttering like flags, while the locals who fly them stand on their little balconies, gossiping. The contrast of bright tourism and vivid untouched neighborhoods within 30 yards of each other is amazing.

The Ribeira neighborhood looks up at the Ponte Dom Luís I bridge, rising 150 feet above the river. In the 1880s, Teofilo Seyrig, a protégé of Gustave Eiffel, stretched this Eiffel Tower-sized wrought-iron contraption across the 500-foot-wide Douro. Eiffel himself designed a bridge in Porto, the Ponte Dona Maria Pia, a bit upstream (barely visible from here).

Shoppers might seek out **O Cântaro,** run by the English-speaking Oliveira family (Mon-Sat 9:00-19:00, closed Sun, a block back from embankment near the east end—toward the bridge—at Rua da Lada 50-56, tel. 223-320-670). Among the trinkets for sale are ceramics, hand-painted tiles, embroidery, and filigree. Ask them for a filigree-making demonstration to see tiny gold and silver wires twisted and soldered into intricate patterns.

▲Cruising the Douro

"Six Bridges" cruises, operated by several different companies, leave continually from the Ribeira riverfront. These relaxing 50-minute excursions float up and down the river, offering a fine orientation and glimpses of all of Porto's bridges (including the majestic steel Ponte Dona Maria Pia, right next to

the concrete Ponte de São João). The boat trips, which generally run daily from 10:00 to 18:30 in summer (until 17:00 off-season), are all essentially the same—offering scenic joyrides with no real commentary (€10). You might shop around, as you'll find lots of competition for essentially the same tour.

Moored in Porto and all along the Douro River are the old-fashioned boats called *rabelos.* These were once the only way to transport wine downriver to Porto. These boats, which look Asian, have flat bottoms, a big square sail, and a very large rudder to help them navigate the rough, twisty course of the river (for more info, see page 328). The region's famous port wine is produced about 60 miles up the river and aged in lodges here.

Vinologia

This wine boutique, just uphill from Praça da Ribeira, offers an intimate wine-tasting experience focused on smaller producers—a big difference from the corporate sellers on the opposite side of the river. You can sample flights of three port wines for €10-19 and six wines for €20. Tastings can showcase different types of port wine (see page 300) or can be the same type but made by different producers. Over 200 bottles are available for sampling (daily 16:00-24:00, Rua de São João 46, mobile 936-057-340, www.lamaisondesporto.com).

PORT-WINE LODGES IN VILA NOVA DE GAIA

Just across the river from Porto, the town of Vila Nova de Gaia, or just Gaia (GUY-yuh), is where much of the world's port wine comes

to mature. Port-wine grapes are grown, and a young port is produced, about 60 miles upstream in the Douro Valley. Then, after sitting for a winter in silos, the wine is shipped downstream to Vila Nova de Gaia, to age for years in lodges on this cool, north-facing bank of the Douro. Eighteen companies run these lodges, holding down the port fort and offering tours and tastings. For wine connoisseurs, touring a port-wine lodge *(cave do vinho do porto)* and sampling the product is a ▲▲ attraction. Like so many miniature Hollywood signs climbing the riverbank, you'll see the 18 different company names proudly marking their lodges here.

Gaia is technically a separate town from Porto, even though it's just across the river and feels like part of the city. Venturing here is well worth the trip. To taste port from all the different lodges under one roof, visit the Port and Douro Wines Institute (see page 295).

Getting There: From the Ribeira district, walk (or catch a cab) across the Ponte Dom Luís I bridge. From the city center, take bus #900, #901, or #906 (every 30 minutes, stop across from São Bento Station). After crossing the bridge, the bus stops first at the Cálem lodge, then near Sandeman and the TI, then climbs the hill.

Services: Vila Nova de Gaia operates its own handy **TI** with information about the lodges (daily 10:00-18:00, closed Sun off-season, on the riverbank near Sandeman lodge at Avenida Diogo Leite 242, tel. 223-703-735, www.cm-gaia.pt). A string of **eateries**

Vila Nova de Gaia

100 Meters
100 Yards

RIBEIRA DISTRICT

To Porto Center

PONTE LUÍS I
UPPER LEVEL
LOWER LEVEL →

SERRA DO PILAR MONASTERY

D o u r o   R i v e r

Largo Miguel Bombarda

BOAT TRIPS

AV. D. LEITE

Jardim do Morro

Largo Cruz

Cable Car

Jardim do Morro

AVENIDA RAMOS PINTO
RUA 7 PASS.

R. FERN.

R. COSTA SANTOS

R. DO CHOUPELO

R. SERRA PINTO

R. BARÃO

R. RAMADA ALTA

R. AZENHAS

R. LEO. DE FREITAS

RUA DR. A. GRANJO

R. SEI RAMIRO

RUA PILAR

RUA GENERAL TORRES

R. CÂNDIDO DOS REIS

R. LUÍS JAU

RUA JAU

CAMÕES

General Torres

❶ Sandeman
❷ Cálem
❸ Taylor & Restaurante Barão de Fladgate
❹ Croft
❺ Ferreira
❻ Kopke Shop
❼ Adega E Presuntaria Transmontana Restaurante
❽ Ar de Rio Restaurante
❾ Cais de Gaia Eateries

face the river, just past the Ramos Pinto lodge. Drinks-with-a-view options are available all along the waterfront. A pricey **cable car** links the riverfront with the Jardim do Morro (see page 283).

▲▲Tours and Tastings

Port tasting is a subjective business, and no single lodge is neces-sarily the best. If you're a port enthusiast, you probably already have a favorite (or can quickly decide on one, with a little enjoyable research). Though more seri-ous European visitors choose one lodge to visit, American tourists are known to hop between three or four in a single day...before stumbling back to their ho-tels.

At any lodge, the procedure is about the same. Individual travelers simply show up and ask for a tour. Pass any wait time by learning about the port (via posted information or a video), or simply get started on the

Port-Wine Crash Course

Port is a medium-sweet wine (20 percent alcohol), usually taken as a *digestif* after dinner, sometimes with strong cheese to balance its powerful flavor. The wine is fortified with *aguardente* (grape brandy, more like grappa, sometimes called "grape essence") at a ratio of about 4:1. This brandy is also distilled from wine, so it blends nicely with the port. The introduction of brandy halts fermentation early, killing the yeast and leaving more sugar in the port (standard wines ferment for 10-12 days; port for only 2-3 days). Vintners constantly monitor sugar levels to attain the precise sweetness they want. After the brandy is added, the wine ages in wood or in bottles, anywhere from two years to (for big spenders) longer than a century.

For most people, "port" means a tawny port aged 10-20 years—the most common type. But there are multiple varieties of port; the two general categories are wood ports (aged in wooden vats or barrels) and vintage ports (aged in bottles). More than 40 varieties of grapes, both red and white, can be used for port production.

The basics: Inexpensive **ruby** is young (aged three years), red, and has a strong, fiery taste of grape and pepper. Note that some ports are **white**—young and robust, but with white grapes. (Some white "ports" sold today are an attempt to approximate Spain's dry *fino* sherries, but sweet versions exist—look for *lágrima* on the label for these.)

Tawny, the wood port with a leathery color, is the most typical version—the one most Americans imagine when they think of port. It's older, lighter, mellower, and more complex than L.B.V. (described later). It's aged in smaller barrels, maximizing exposure to wood (and, therefore, oxygen)—which gives it a nuttier flavor than the more fruity, younger ports. Tawny port is aged 10, 20, 30, or 40 years, but it's not all the same vintage; to enhance

tasting. Sometimes the tours and tastings are free; at other lodges, there's a modest entry fee (which may be refunded if you buy a more-expensive bottle). Before you go (or while you're waiting for your tour), read the "Port-Wine Crash Course" sidebar, "Brits on the Douro" (page 325), and "Growing—and Stomping—Grapes in the Douro Valley" (page 324).

Allow 30 minutes per visit. Tours in English depart three or four times per hour. Occasionally, if the lodge is busy, you'll be the complexity of the flavor, any tawny is a combination of several different ages. So a "30-year-old tawny" is predominantly 30 years old, but also has minor components that are 10 or 20 years old. Once blended, it takes about eight months for the various ports to "marry," though no producer would release an immature tawny. It's ready to consume when you buy it.

Vintage port (if you can afford it) is a ruby. Rather than being a blend from many different years, it comes from a single harvest. Only wine from the very best years is selected by lodges to become vintage. After port ages for two years in wooden casks, it's tested by the Port and Douro Wines Institute to determine whether it's worthy of the vintage label. (If not, it may be kept in wooden casks longer to become L.B.V.) There are usually only two or three vintage years per decade, and the year 2000 was deemed as one of the best ever. If the port is good enough to be classified as vintage, it's bottled and aged another 10-30 years or more. Using glass, rather than wood, makes the difference in the aging process. Sediment is common, so bottles must be decanted. And if a bottle is really old, the cork may deteriorate—so the top of the bottle is heated up with a pair of red-hot tongs, then cold water is poured over it to break it off cleanly. Bottles of port can be stored upright, rather than on their side like regular wines.

Late Bottle Vintage (L.B.V.) was invented after World War II, when British wine lovers couldn't afford true vintage port. L.B.V. is a blend of wines from a single year, which age together in huge wooden vats for four to six years. The size of the vats means less exposure to wood, which makes it age more quickly, but without losing its fruitiness and color. After five years, it's bottled (later than a vintage port, which ages for only two years—hence the name) and sold. This more-affordable alternative saved the port-wine industry.

Port's stodgy image makes it unpopular among young Portuguese. Lodges have not escaped the multinational conglomerate game, but new owners often retain the brand name to keep loyal customers and invent marketing techniques to attract new ones. Many Americans consider port an acquired taste; for this reason, many port producers along the Douro also make a more straightforward red wine. But as I always say, "Any port in a storm..."

given a tour time and can come back. Tours generally come with a walk through the warehouse, perhaps a tiny museum tour, a 5- to 10-minute video produced by that label giving you a quick peek at their process and the scenic Douro River Valley, and, finally, two to four tastings. Serious students may opt for more involved tours (generally €12-15, with smaller groups, 5 tastings, book in advance if possible).

Sandeman, the most high-profile company, is sort of the Budweiser of port—a good first stop for novices. They were the first port producer to create a logo for their product, which you'll see everywhere: a mysterious man wearing a black cloak (representing a Portuguese student's cape) and a rakish *Shadow* hat (worn by Spanish horse-riders, symbolizing the sherry that Sandeman makes in Jerez). Sandeman provides the most corporate, mainstream, accessible experience for first-timers—with a short walk led by a caped guide, a 10-minute video, and two tastings. It's also the most crowded, often giving times for you to return or sending you to their sister manufacturers (€5, also more extensive €15 tour, daily March-Oct 10:00-12:30 & 14:00-18:00, Nov-Feb 9:30-12:30 & 14:00-17:30, right on the riverfront at Largo Miguel Bombarda 3, tel. 223-740-533, www.sandeman.com). It's exciting to think that the entire Portuguese production of Sandeman Port ages right in this building.

Cálem, the first place you see after crossing the bridge, offers a fine tour wandering among its huge oak casks (€5 includes 2 samples, 20-minute tours depart 4/hour, daily 10:00-17:30, offseason fewer tours offered, tel. 223-746-672, www.calem.pt). They also offer 45-minute fado shows that include a port tasting (€17.50, Tue-Sun at 18:30, none on Mon).

Taylor, for more discriminating tastes, is a growing label that bought one competitor, Croft (described next) in 2001. I toured the classy Taylor lodge—near the top of the hill, with stunning views back on Porto—and enjoyed it. After watching an informative video, I learned a little about the history of the company (which, like many port producers, began in the sheep business) and about the unique microclimates of the Douro Valley. Then I saw the various sizes of wooden vats in which different kinds of ports are aged (€5 including 3 tastings, Mon-Fri 10:00-18:00, Sat-Sun 10:00-17:00, high up but worth the hike at Rua do Choupelo 250, tel. 223-742-800, www.taylor.pt). Their restaurant, **Barão de Fladgate,** offers stunning lunchtime views along with an opportunity to recharge for more tastings. Many consider it among the best dining spots in Porto (daily 12:30-15:00 & 19:30-22:00, no dinner served Sun).

Croft offers a similar tour, but you also get to see vintage port being aged in bottles, as well as a fun "library" of dusty old ports (the oldest is from 1834). While the views are not as good as the lodges described earlier, you'll learn how to properly open and present an old bottle of port (€3.50, daily 10:00-18:00, Rua Barão de Forrester 412, tel. 223-756-433, www.croftport.com).

Ferreira's lodge comes with classical music "to help age the wine." It's an interesting tour and shows off some fine museum artifacts (€5 includes 2 tastings, daily 10:00-12:30 & 14:00-18:00, look for big sign at the end of the riverfront promenade at Avenida Ramos Pinto 70, tel. 223-746-107).

Kopke is recognized as one of the best in the business because they were the first. Unfortunately, their lodge doesn't receive visitors, but they've opened a shop along the waterfront to allow people to experience—one delightful sip at a time—what they've been doing well since 1638. The staff offers concise explanations and some fine ports by the glass in an elegant, upstairs tasting room far from the crowds outside (€2-5, daily May-Oct 10:00-19:00, Nov-April 10:00-18:00, Avenida Diogo Leite 312, mobile 915-848-484).

SIGHTS AWAY FROM THE CENTER
Tramway Museum (Museu do Carro Eléctrico)

This clever museum-in-a-warehouse displays beautifully restored examples of trams from different eras, including 1950s buses and a brand-new hydrogen-powered city bus. You can climb aboard many for a fun, Rice-A-Roni-style experience...just ding the bell.

Trams have long been a part of Porto's history, and the city is committed to bringing them back as an integral part of the public-transit system. In 1872 (40 years after being invented in the US), the first trams in Iberia began operating in Porto, pulled by horses and oxen. Dubbed *americanos* based on their origin, the tram network was electrified in 1904. Essential for connecting suburbs with the city center, there were more than 100 tram lines still in use by the 1970s. However, buses and cars—by-products of modern prosperity—almost eliminated this important part of the city's heritage.

Cost and Hours: €4, Mon 14:00-18:00, Tue-Fri 10:00-19:00, Sat-Sun 14:00-19:00, Alameda Basílio Teles 51, tel. 226-158-185, www.museudocarroelectrico.pt.

Getting There: The most atmospheric way to arrive at the museum is via tram #1 or #18. Sit on restored wicker seats and see a little of workaday Porto, plus some river views from up above.

Foz

Foz do Douro (or simply "Foz") is one of Porto's trendiest, greenest, wealthiest, and most relaxing quarters, situated where the river meets the Atlantic. There's no real destination in Foz; simply wander through the park (Jardim do Passeio Alegre, with miniature golf, a fancy old WC pavilion, and a nondescript café), hike up to the lighthouse, ponder the sea, watch fishermen mend-

ing their nets, and smell the seaweed. If you have the time and good weather, take a boardwalk stroll to the beach, Praia dos Ingleses. It's a relaxing break from the busy downtown area.

Getting There: An antique tram car (line #1) scenically rattles its way from the Ribeira district, along the Douro River, to the Jardim do Passeio Alegre, a 10-minute walk to the center of the Foz district. From the tram stop, you can walk or catch bus #500 for an Atlantic coast ride. Or bypass the tram by taking bus #500 from the Ribeira all the way to Foz (catch tram or bus in front of São Francisco Church, departures roughly every 20 minutes 9:00-19:00, 20-minute trip).

Nearby: You can combine a trip to Foz with a visit to the Serralves Museum. From Foz, either catch bus #203—it runs near the beach on Rua de Dui—or take a taxi; it's easy to hail a cab or find a taxi stop *(praça de taxis).*

▲Serralves Foundation Contemporary Art Museum and Park (Fundação de Serralves)

Porto's contemporary art museum, surrounding park, and unique Art Deco mansion are a half-day excursion worth ▲▲▲ for art lovers...and worthwhile for anyone looking to relax in a lush green space.

The complex is managed by the Serralves Foundation. The Foundation was formed in 1989 with two goals: the advancement of contemporary art and the appreciation of landscape and environment as an artistic concept. These goals, symbolized by the giant red hand shovel near the front gate, drive the layout of the complex: a gigantic contemporary art facility on the edge of a carefully planned park. The whole thing is based around the Art Deco mansion of a count who lived here in the 1930s. When the Foundation was formed, the government bought them the house and surrounding land to encourage them to pursue their goals. A decade later, in 1999, the museum opened.

Cost and Hours: €4 for park/mansion only, €8.50 for museum, park, and mansion; April-Sept Tue-Fri 10:00-17:00, park open until 19:00, Sat-Sun 10:00-20:00; Oct-March Tue-Fri 10:00-17:00, Sat-Sun 10:00-19:00; closed Mon year-round; tel. 808-200-543, www.serralves.pt.

Eating: The museum's restaurant serves a lunch buffet from 12:00-15:00 (€13 Tue-Fri, €16 Sat-Sun, closed Mon). Coffee and snacks are available until 19:00 (17:00 in winter).

Getting There: The complex is about 1.5 miles west of the city center in a wealthy residential neighborhood at Rua Dom João de Castro 210, just south of the busy Avenida da Boavista. From the center, you can reach it most easily via taxi or on a hop-on, hop-off bus tour. Public bus service isn't great, but you can take bus #203 to the Serralves stop (less convenient from downtown—the most central place to catch it is at the big Boavista Rotunda near Casa da Música).

Visiting the Museum and Park: The **museum** presents temporary exhibits by Portuguese and global artists. The enormous, blocky U-shaped building was designed by prominent Portuguese architect Álvaro Siza, who was greatly inspired by the existing mansion. As in most important contemporary-art museums, its vast white exhibition spaces are modified to suit the art displayed (windows and walls continually disappear and reappear).

The **park** around the museum has been designed very carefully to compartmentalize each section; when you're in one part of the grounds, you can't see the rest. This is a very peaceful, romantic place to wander. Hiding in here somewhere are a pleasant rose garden, a tea house overlooking a former tennis court, a lake, a small farm with animals, a gardening school, and Casa de Serralves itself.

The **house (Casa de Serralves)** is, for many, the most interesting part of the whole experience: a huge pink Art Deco mansion that looks like the home of an Old Hollywood star. On two sides, long manicured hedges and fountains stretch to the horizon. Look for the private chapel in back—also pink Art Deco. You can usually go inside the house to check out the cavernous interior. As you step through the fancy gate inside the living room, remember that in the last century, someone actually lived here. Ponder how the design of this place is reflected in the museum. The best part is upstairs: the mirrored, pink-marbled bathroom, dramatically overlooking the grounds.

House of Music (Casa da Música)

This landmark 1,200-seat concert hall opened in 2005. The angular, white concrete building with rippling glass windows was designed by the firm of Dutch architect Rem Koolhaas, called OMA, which also built Seattle's Central Library. Contemporary-architecture fans will find it at the big Boavista Rotunda northwest of the city center (Metro: Casa da Música). Guided tours take you through the interior, or you can attend a concert of anything from world music to classical to jazz to fado. The building is operated by a nonprofit foundation established to promote musical culture—tickets are subsidized.

Cost and Hours: €5 tours, 1/day in English at 16:00, 1 hour, focus is on concert hall's unique architecture; concert tickets run €5-25—generally about €15, info/reservation tel. 220-120-220, www.casadamusica.com. For a schedule of upcoming, nearly daily events, pick up the free monthly *Casa da Música* brochure at any TI.

Nightlife in Porto

While fado is not a big deal in Porto, you can enjoy a live performance of this blues-like Portuguese music with dinner or a drink two blocks off the riverfront at **Restaurante Mal Cozinhado** (€32 for touristy dinner and show). Or drop by later to enjoy the music over just a drink (€10 cover for the music). Music starts nightly except Sunday at 21:00 (Rua do Outeirinho 11, tel. 222-081-319).

Other music venues include **Restaurante Guarany,** which has fado on Thursdays and Saturdays, Cuban tunes on Fridays, and piano on other nights, starting at 21:30 (Avenida dos Aliados 85, tel. 223-321-272; see page 315). The **House of Music (Casa da Música)** offers classical, jazz, fado, and more (described earlier).

Sleeping in Porto

There are lots of cheap sleeps in Porto—but none in the desirable Ribeira district (where prices are higher). I've listed two options right in the Ribeira, three just above (near the Stock Exchange Palace), and several better value places in the city center. The cheaper the place, the greater the chance that English isn't spoken (and the grottier the bathroom). You'll almost always have to climb a few stairs to get to the elevator, if they have one.

IN THE RIBEIRA
Neither of these two places is a particularly good value. But...location, location, location.

$$$ Pestana Porto Hotel is a stylish splurge, with Porto's best location, right on the Douro in the heart of the Ribeira action. Its 48 rooms occupy two old Ribeira buildings, now converted to plush accommodations and connected by glass walkways (standard Db-€188-229, river view Db-€224-275, extra bed-€72, discounts often available on its website, air-con, elevator, Wi-Fi, Praça de Ribeira 1, tel. 223-402-300, www.pestana.com, pestana.porto@pestana.com).

$$$ Guest House Douro is a nice splurge on the river in the center of the Ribeira. It has eight small but tastefully decorated rooms with all the modern comforts. Owners Carmen and João make you feel right at home (Sb/Db-€130-190, higher prices are for river views, air-con, elevator, Wi-Fi, curfew-1:00 in the morning, closed Jan, near House of Henry the Navigator at Rua Fonte Taurina 99-101, tel. 222-015-135, www.guesthousedouro.com, guesthousedouro@sapo.pt).

Sleep Code

Abbreviations (€1 = about $1.40, country code: 351)
S = Single, **D** = Double/Twin, **T** = Triple, **Q** = Quad, **b** = bathroom, **s** = shower only.
Price Rankings
 $$$ **Higher Priced**—Most rooms €85 or more.
  $$ **Moderately Priced**—Most rooms between €40-85.
   $ **Lower Priced**—Most rooms €40 or less.
Unless otherwise noted, breakfast is included, credit cards are accepted, Wi-Fi is generally free, and English is spoken. Prices can change without notice; verify the hotel's current rates online or by email. For the best prices, always book directly with the hotel.

NEAR THE STOCK EXCHANGE PALACE

$$ Hotel da Bolsa, a few blocks above the Ribeira scene, is swank and modern, with more comfort than character. It has a great location and 36 decent rooms (Sb-€60-80, Db-€74-95, Sb/Db with view-€112, extra bed-€18-21, higher rates are for April-Oct, air-con, elevator, Wi-Fi, Rua Ferreira Borges 101, tel. 222-026-768, www.hoteldabolsa.com, reservas@hoteldabolsa.com).

$$ InPátio Guest House provides a quiet, secluded oasis of comfort away from the Ribeira crowds. Five rooms with modern interiors and unique bathrooms hide inside a renovated 19th-century building. Fernando and Ogla make you feel very welcome in their city (Sb-€68-82, Db-€79-95, superior Db-€98-115, extra bed-€30, air-con, luggage elevator, Wi-Fi, Pátio de São Salvador 22, mobile 934-323-448, www.inpatio.pt, info@inpatio.pt).

$ Dixo's Hostel, just a few blocks down the hill from the São Bento Station and up from the Ribeira, is as central as can be. It's run by the friendly brother-and-sister team of Pedro and Joanna, who take pride in their hostel and treat their guests well (bed in 4-, 6- or 8-bed mixed dorms-€16-21, D-€44-50, higher rates are for April-Oct, one all-female dorm, free linens, includes breakfast, Wi-Fi, lounge, small rooftop deck, free walking tours and organized evening excursions, Rua Mouzinho da Silveira 72, tel. 222-444-278, www.dixosoportohostel.com, info@dixosoportohostel.com).

IN THE CITY CENTER

$$$ Quality Inn Praça da Batalha offers 113 predictable, big, business-class rooms near São Bento Station. It shares a square with a beautiful *azulejo* church and the beginning of Porto's pedestrian shopping drag (Sb-€65-90, Db-€70-120, third bed-€20, air-

PORTO

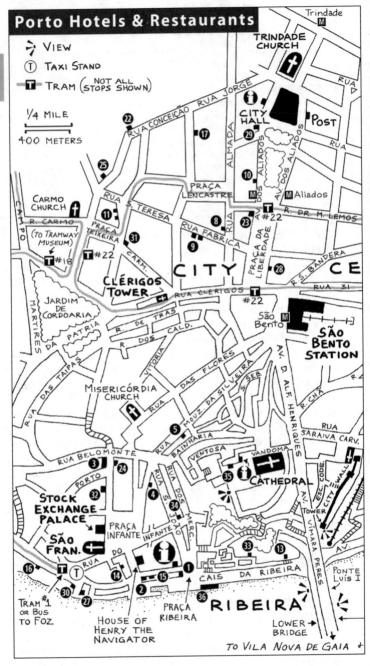

Porto Hotels & Restaurants

➤ VIEW
ⓣ TAXI STAND
🚊 TRAM (NOT ALL STOPS SHOWN)

¼ MILE
400 METERS

Trindade Ⓜ

TRINDADE CHURCH ✝

RUA

RUA JORGE

RUA CONCEIÇÃO

ⓘ CITY HALL Post

ALMADA

AV. DOS ALIADOS

RUA

22

17

29

25

CARMO CHURCH ✝

RUA

TERESA

PRAÇA LENCASTRE

Ⓜ Ⓜ Aliados

R. DR. M. LEMOS

R. CARMO
(TO TRAMWAY MUSEUM)

CAMPO

11

PRAÇA TEIXEIRA

31

CARM.

RUA FABRICA

8

9

23

ⓣ #22

Ⓣ #18 Ⓣ #22

PRAÇA DA LIBERDADE

28

R. S. BANDERA

CLÉRIGOS TOWER ✝

RUA CLÉRIGOS

ⓣ #22

C I T Y   C E

RUA 31

JARDIM DE CORDOARIA

R. DE TRAS

R. DOS CALD.

São Bento Ⓜ

SÃO BENTO STATION

MARTIRES DA PATRIA

VITORIA

RUA DAS FLORES

S. SEB.

AV. D. ALF. HENRIQUES

R. CHÃ

RUA DAS TAIPAS

MISERICÓRDIA CHURCH ✝

RUA

MOUZ DA SILVEIRA

RUA SARAIVA CARV.

5

BAINHARIA

RUA BELOMONTE

3

24

VENTOSA

VANDOMA

35 ⓘ

CATHEDRAL ✝

ESC. CODE.

CITY WALL

PORTO

32

STOCK EXCHANGE PALACE

4

34

RUA S. JOÃO

MERC.

Tower

AV. VIMARA PERES

SÃO FRAN.

PRAÇA INFANTE

RUA INFANTE

16

ⓣ ⓣ

RUA DO

14

ⓘ

2 15

33

13

PONTE LUÍS I

30

27

1

CAIS DA RIBEIRA

36

RIBEIRA

TRAM #1 or BUS TO FOZ

HOUSE OF HENRY THE NAVIGATOR

PRAÇA RIBEIRA

LOWER → BRIDGE

TO VILA NOVA DE GAIA ✛

PORTO

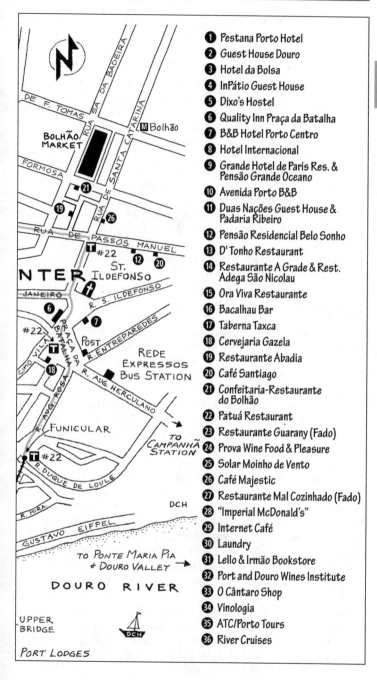

1 Pestana Porto Hotel
2 Guest House Douro
3 Hotel da Bolsa
4 InPátio Guest House
5 Dixo's Hostel
6 Quality Inn Praça da Batalha
7 B&B Hotel Porto Centro
8 Hotel Internacional
9 Grande Hotel de Paris Res. & Pensão Grande Oceano
10 Avenida Porto B&B
11 Duas Nações Guest House & Padaria Ribeiro
12 Pensão Residencial Belo Sonho
13 D' Tonho Restaurant
14 Restaurante A Grade & Rest. Adega São Nicolau
15 Ora Viva Restaurante
16 Bacalhau Bar
17 Taberna Taxca
18 Cervejaria Gazela
19 Restaurante Abadia
20 Café Santiago
21 Confeitaria-Restaurante do Bolhão
22 Patuá Restaurant
23 Restaurante Guarany (Fado)
24 Prova Wine Food & Pleasure
25 Solar Moinho de Vento
26 Café Majestic
27 Restaurante Mal Cozinhado (Fado)
28 "Imperial McDonald's"
29 Internet Café
30 Laundry
31 Lello & Irmão Bookstore
32 Port and Douro Wines Institute
33 O Cântaro Shop
34 Vinologia
35 ATC/Porto Tours
36 River Cruises

con, elevator, Wi-Fi, Praça da Batalha 127, tel. 223-392-300, www. choicehotelseurope.com, quality.batalha@grupo-continental.com).

\$\$ B&B Hotel Porto Centro has 125 slumbermill, economic-chic rooms occupying a remodeled movie theater. Black-and-white photos of movie stars decorate the walls in tribute to its former life. It's on Praça da Batalha, near the Santo Ildefonso *azulejo*-covered church (Sb/Db-€47-53, Tb-€70-79, Qb-€81-92, breakfast buffet-€6, air-con, elevator, Wi-Fi, parking, quiet back patio, Praça da Batalha 32-34, tel. 220-407-000, www.hotelbb.pt, booking.porto@hotelbb.com).

\$\$ Hotel Internacional fits 35 super-modern rooms into the heavy granite-and-tile shell of an old monastery just two blocks off the Avenida dos Aliados. It offers hotel formality, typical amenities, and a good location at a reasonable price (Sb-€50-65, Db-€60-75, third bed-€20, air-con, elevator, Wi-Fi, Rua do Almada 131, tel. 222-005-032, www.hi-porto.com, info@hi-porto.com).

\$\$ Grande Hotel de Paris Residencial brags it was the first hotel in Porto with running water in its rooms. Its 45 faded but fine rooms—all with antique furniture—are spread out over three interconnected buildings, each with a grand atrium and sloping floors. This proudly run place has big, classy public spaces strewn across its treehouse-style floor plan (Sb-€65, Db-€70, higher prices July-Sept, extra bed-€20, free glass of port with this book, elevator, guest computer, relaxing garden, one block up from Avenida dos Aliados at Rua da Fábrica 27-29, tel. 222-073-140, www. hotelparis.pt, info@hotelparis.pt, David).

\$\$ Avenida Porto Bed & Breakfast is stark but functional, renting 14 simple rooms on the fourth and fifth floors above a grand boulevard (Sb-€25-30, Db-€40-45, Tb-€55-65, higher rates are for May-Sept, Avenida dos Aliados 141, tel. 222-009-551, avenidaporto.com.pt, porto@avenidaporto.com.pt).

\$ Duas Nações Guest House is a well-run backpacker place with 16 dumpy rooms—as comfy as such a cheap place can be. It overlooks a square straight up Rua da Fábrica, a few blocks from Avenida dos Aliados. The "two nations" are Portugal and Brazil, still friends after all these years (bed in dorm-€9-15, S-€15, Sb-€20-25, D-€20, Db-€20-39, T-€30-48, Tb-€42-45, Q-€50, Qb-€52, cash only, Wi-Fi, no breakfast but adjacent to handy café, Praça Guilherme Gomes Fernandes 59, tel. 222-081-616, www. duasnacoes.com.pt, duasnacoes@sapo.pt). They also rent several apartments—all recently remodeled with small kitchens, washing machines, air-con, double-pane windows, and Wi-Fi (2-person studio-€45-65/night, apartment for up to 8-€110-115).

\$ Pensão Residencial Belo Sonho is well-maintained and family-run (no English spoken), and just up the street from Café Majestic and the main shopping drag, Rua de Santa Catarina. Its

15 rooms are a good value (Sb-€20-30, Db-€30-40, Tb-€40-45, higher prices June-Sept, noisy on Fri and Sat nights, no breakfast, Wi-Fi, Rua Passos Manuel 186, tel. 222-003-389, fax 222-012-850).

$ Pensão Grande Oceano, a good value in a central location, has 15 clean, basic rooms on four floors. All but two of the rooms have private baths and air-con (S/D-€20-30, Sb-€25-30, Db-€35-40, Tb-€45-50, Qb-€65-75, no breakfast, no elevator, Wi-Fi, Rua da Fábrica 45, just a few doors up the hill from Hotel Paris, tel. 222-038-770, www.pensaograndeoceano.com, geral@pensaograndeoceano.com).

Eating in Porto

Porto is famous for its tripe. Legend has it that when Porto's favorite son, Prince Henry the Navigator, set out for his explorations, the city slaughtered all of its mature livestock to send along with his crew—keeping only the guts for themselves. Porto's cooks then devised many ingenious ways of preparing innards. The tradition stuck, and to this day, people from Porto are known as *tripeiros.* These days, tripe plays a subtler role. You'll most typically see it prepared Porto-style *(tripas a moda do Porto):* barely present in a thick stew, with beans, sausage, chicken, and scant vegetables. The tripe itself doesn't have much taste—though I couldn't keep myself from thinking about digestive processes while I chewed.

For something easier to stomach, try *caldo verde*—a tasty soup made with potatoes and thinly chopped cabbage. For a quick meal, locals like a sandwich called a *francesinha* ("little French girl"), which usually comes with various meats dripping with a spicy tomato- or seafood-based sauce, though some restaurants and different regions have variations (egg, cheese, even vegetarian).

Remember, if the menu has two price columns, in general the cheaper list is for smaller portions *(meia dose,* or "1/2," plenty for one person), and the higher-priced list is for splittable dishes that will easily feed two (listed as *dose,* or "1").

Food Tours in Porto: To maximize your eating experience, consider **Taste of Porto Food and Wine Tours,** which amount to a mobile feast (lunch or dinner) and a tour at the same time. André meets a small group near the market and takes you on a two-mile walk with six yummy stops for €55 (see page 284).

IN THE RIBEIRA

There's a wide range of dining options in the Ribeira—and they're all touristy, with predictable tourist-trap quality and prices accompanying the fine views and fun scene. Strolling along the waterfront and following your nose is a good option. You can also try

PORTO

wandering the back lanes to find a spot that feels right—you'll be trading river views for lower prices and local color. The seafood's fresh, except on Mondays (since fishermen don't go out on Sundays).

D' Tonho, atop the arcade near the bridge, is everyone's top recommendation for a Ribeira splurge. The place is white-tablecloth classy, at once Old World and mod, with friendly and unpretentious service. A few outside tables are perched scenically above the Ribeira action. The dishes—traditional Portuguese cuisine, with an emphasis on fresh fish—are only slightly more expensive than nearby tour-group alternatives. Veal and cod dishes, the house specialties with huge and tasty portions, are a great value at €15-20. Reservations are a must (daily 12:30-15:00 & 19:30-23:00, Cais da Ribeira 13, tel. 222-004-307, www.dtonho.com). They also have a portable harborfront location set up directly across the river in Vila Nova de Gaia with wonderful outdoor seating (in front of Cálem Lodge, daily 12:30-15:30 & 19:30-23:00).

Restaurante A Grade is a small mom-and-pop restaurant on a delightful alley just off the Ribeira. Ferreria serves while wife Elena cooks good, home-style Portuguese food. The baked octopus is a favorite among regulars (€15 seafood and meat plates; big, splittable portions; Mon-Sat 12:00-16:00 & 18:30-22:30, closed Sun, Rua de São Nicolau 9, tel. 223-321-130, reservations smart for dinner).

Restaurante Adega São Nicolau, next to Restaurante A Grade, is homey, small, and sparkling, with a few outside tables and a tight interior under a shiplap vault. They serve traditional cuisine with lots of fish (€12-15 plates, closed Sun, Rua São Nicolau 1, tel. 222-008-232).

Ora Viva Restaurante is a humble but exuberantly decorated, long-and-skinny dining hall a block off the waterfront. The hardworking Pinto family specializes in traditional grilled meat and fish dishes—especially *cataplana*, a seafood stew. It's a little less touristy than the Ribeira norm, with locals, decent food, and good prices (€10-12 meals, daily 12:00-15:00 & 18:30-22:30, Rua Fonte Taurina 83, tel. 222-052-033). Antonio promises a free glass of port wine (before or after your dinner) if you show him this book.

Bacalhau Bar is a trendy little hole-in-the-wall at the quiet western end of the riverside rampart. Four tiny (unreservable) tables outside overlook the river, and a few tables are tucked in the mod interior (€10-13 plates, open daily for dinner only, Muro dos Bacalhoeiros 153, tel. 222-010-521).

IN VILA NOVA DE GAIA

Eating across the river in Vila Nova de Gaia, just a 10-minute scenic stroll over the bridge from the Ribeira, is a fine option. All of these recommended places are on the riverfront with views over to Porto. The last port lodges finish their tasting tours at 19:00, so working a dinner here into your sightseeing schedule is easy. While there is a good variety of places all along the riverfront, here are a few favorites:

Adega E Presuntaria Transmontana serves up quality Portuguese fish and meat plates (€13-17) as well as *petiscos*—Portuguese tapas—for €4-11. Their tapa sampler (listed on the menu as "Mixed of Titbits") stuffs two to four people for €33. And for an education in the sweet treats of Portugal, enjoy their all-you-can-eat dessert buffet for just €7 (daily 12:00-24:00, Avenida Diogo Leite 80, tel. 223-758-380).

Ar de Rio Restaurante, where modern design meets traditional Portuguese cuisine, is located in a park right on the river. Their €10 *francesinha* (a local super-grilled meaty sandwich that makes a triple cheeseburger seem like health food) is considered one of the best in town. You can eat inside or out on the deck (€11-20 meat and fish plates, daily 12:00-24:00, modern steel-and-glass "box" at Avenida Diogo Leite 5, tel. 223-701-797, www.arderio.pt). Consider a drink from their bar while enjoying a lounge chair on the riverbank here.

Cais de Gaia features a strip of six riverside, modern buildings housing a variety of restaurants—all with rooftop terraces overlooking the river. Choose from Indian, Japanese, BBQ, Italian, and more (a three-minute walk along the Vila Nova de Gaia riverfront).

Picnic on the Riverfront: The Vila Nova de Gaia mayor is determined to make his city (which is actually bigger than Porto) visitor-friendly. A sign of that is the inviting waterfront, welcoming picnickers with picnic tables, grass, rockery, piers, and the best views in town.

IN THE CITY CENTER
Basic Eateries

Good, cheap restaurants are scattered all around the city center. Menus are often handwritten (posted on paper tablecloths outside) with €1 soups and €5 plates. Remember that most coffee and pastry shops do double-duty as lunch spots, so wander around and see what people are having. Good locations abound on the pedestrian Rua do Sampaio Bruno and on the side streets of Rua do Almada (one block west of Avenida dos Aliados). The dining's more atmospheric in Ribeira, but these are convenient if you're staying in the center.

The charming little square, Praça Guilherme Gomes Fernandes, has several cheap and cheery, no-pretense eateries with pleasant outside seating. **Padaria Ribeiro**—a bright, happy bakery handy for a breakfast, light lunch, or snack—serves savory and sweet pastries, sandwiches, and popular cookies (at #21, no indoor seating but tables on square, tel. 222-005-067).

Taberna Taxca is like a man cave offering up beer, soup, and sandwiches (€2-3). The menu is extremely basic: two soups (great *caldo verde* or the much heavier *papas*—made with shredded pork, gravy, and cumin) and sandwiches that celebrate simplicity: smoked ham with fried egg, meat from black crockpots of cooked pork *(rojão)*, or typical-for-Porto spicy shredded pork *(bifanas)*. Order water and they'll hit the cowbell of shame. Hams hang with the TV from the ceiling. I like to sit at the bar to enjoy the scene (Mon-Sat 12:00-24:00, closed Sun, Rua da Picaria 26, tel. 222-011-807).

Cervejaria Gazela, a dark little hole-in-the-wall in the shopping district just off Praça da Batalha, is beloved among locals for its "little hot dogs" or *Cachorro Especial* (€3). Sit down at the bar, order one and a beer (the Super Bock is the local favorite on tap) and watch the staff lovingly lay the sausage and cheese on the fresh buns and then grill these little snacks just right (Mon-Fri 12:00-22:30, closed Sat-Sun, facing National Theater just to the right at #3, tel. 222-054-869).

Restaurante Abadia is a big, bright, friendly, family diner, with two floors of happy customers dining on large portions of straightforward Portuguese cuisine. Split a huge half-portion of their Porto-style tripe with your travel partner, balanced with something a little more predictable, such as a sizzling mini-hibachi of roasted chicken and potatoes (€15 *meia dose*s and tasty omelets, €20-25 splittable *dose*s, specialty is grilled cod, Mon-Sat 12:00-15:00 & 18:30-23:00, closed Sun, head one block east of Sá da Bandeira near Bolhão market to side street Rua do Ateneu Comercial do Porto 22, tel. 222-008-757, www.abadiadoporto.com).

Café Santiago is just a basic diner, but often wins awards in the very serious competition for Porto's best signature sandwich, the hearty *francesinha* beloved by carnivores. You won't walk away hungry (€10 sandwiches, Mon-Sat 12:00-23:00, busiest on Sat when lines can form, closed Sun, Rua Passos Manuel 226, tel. 222-055-797).

Confeitaria-Restaurante do Bolhão, which faces the market-hall entrance, has been pleasing local shoppers since 1896. This bustling bakery/brasserie offers enticing takeout items in front and an inviting old-time dining hall in the rear (the more elegant basement is less lively and soulful). You'll find fresh baked goods, omelets, and fish, along with daily specials for €5-8 (Mon-Sat 7:00-20:00, closed Sun, Rua Formosa 339, tel. 223-395-220).

Fancier Dining

Patuá Restaurant, a few blocks away from the tourist zone and totally local and modern, is the closest thing to a gourmet experience I'm recommending. This is where locals go for a fine and classy meal. Trying creative dishes from a fun and accessible menu, you'll enjoy twisted traditions with a global influence. The ground floor with the open kitchen has the best energy (€15-20 plates, Mon-Sat 19:00-24:00, closed Sun, reservations smart, Rua da Conceição 94, tel. 222-080-622, mobile 964-298-569).

Restaurante Guarany, established in 1933, has been the musicians' coffee shop for generations and is popular with tourists today. You'll enjoy Art Deco elegance with a Brazilian flair (read the brochure for the charming story of the murals) and crisp yet friendly service. They offer good €14-18 meat and fish plates and daily specials (daily 9:00-24:00, Avenida dos Aliados 85, tel. 223-321-272, www.cafeguarany.com). There's no extra charge for the live music starting at 21:30 (see "Nightlife in Porto," earlier).

Prova Wine Food & Pleasure is a great little wine bar. It's the passion of sommelier Diogo who speaks English and enjoys coaching visitors through his list of Portuguese wines (including ports) and then matching it with his selection of fine meats and cheeses. Dining and drinking here, you'll enjoy a jazzy interior where quality and relaxation go hand to mouth (Fri-Wed 13:00-24:00, closed Thu, across and just uphill from the Port and Douro Wines Institute on Rua Ferreira Borges 86, mobile 916-499-121, www.prova. com.pt).

Solar Moinho de Vento, on a small plaza just above Praça Guilherme Gomes Fernandes, offers proper-but-friendly service and Portuguese cuisine in a tile-covered, white-tablecloth dining room upstairs (€15 main dishes, daily 12:00-15:30 & 19:00-22:00, Rua de Sá Noronha 81, tel. 222-051-158, www. solarmoinhodevento.com).

Porto Connections

BY TRAIN

Regional trains use the more central São Bento Station; long-distance trains use Campanhã Station on the east edge of town. The two stations are connected by frequent trains (see "Arrival in Porto," page 278). All trains leaving São Bento also stop at Campanhã (the next station). Some trains only depart from Campanhã Station, so check the schedule carefully.

From Porto's São Bento Train Station to: Peso da Régua (3/day direct, 2 hours; many more with change in Caide, 2-2.5 hours), **Pinhão** (5/day, 2.5-3 hours, transfer in Peso da Régua).

From Campanhã Train Station: Fast Alfa Pendular and Intercidades trains (both require reservation, buy at station) go to **Coimbra** (almost hourly, 1 hour on Alfa Pendular line or Intercidades service but 2 hours on slower regional line—confirm before buying) and **Lisbon** (almost hourly, 3 hours). Note that Alfa Pendular and Intercidades trains are similarly speedy, but Alfa trains cost more.

To reach **Santiago de Compostela, Spain,** take a train bound for the Spanish port city of Vigo (2/day, departures at 8:15 and 19:15, 5 hours, ticket only purchased as far as Vigo, must buy another ticket in Spain to continue to Santiago; en route to Vigo, you may change at the border town of Valença). Once in Spain, you can change to the Santiago-bound train in Vigo, but most conductors will encourage you instead to change trains before that, in the town of Redondela. This works fine, since Vigo is on a dead-end track and any train going to Vigo also goes through Redondela on the way. (In other words, if you change in Vigo instead of Redondela, you'll simply spend more time on the train and less time at the station.) Frustratingly, rail-information people in Porto generally can't tell you much about parts of the journey beyond the Spanish border. Consider a bus instead (see below).

BY BUS

Remember, each bus company has its own mini-station; there's no central bus terminus (for addresses and telephone numbers, see "Arrival in Porto," page 278). Various companies compete on the same route (for example, four companies go to Lisbon). Ask the transport office at the TI about the handiest bus for your itinerary (see "Tourist Information," page 277; toll-free tel. 800-220-905). Don't bother trying to get to the Douro Valley (Peso da Régua or Pinhão) by bus; it takes twice as long as the train.

From Porto by Bus to: Coimbra (operated by Rede Expressos, Rodonorte, and others; best is Rede Expressos—almost hourly, 1.5 hours), **Lisbon** (best via RENEX or Rede Expressos, at least hourly, 3 hours), **Santiago de Compostela, Spain** (ALSA buses leave from bus terminal on Rua do Capitão Henrique Galvão near Casa da Música Metro station, daily at 12:45, 4 hours, may be additional runs in summer, Spanish tel. 34-902-422-242, www.alsa.es).

Santiago Bus Tour: To get a taste of Santiago de Compostela, Spain, consider taking an expensive but convenient all-day guided bus tour from Porto. It leaves daily at 8:00 and takes two to three hours via the expressway. But this is a pricey alternative—the fares are €98-120. For information on these tours, ask at the ATC/Porto Tours office (see page 283; www.portotours.com).

DOURO VALLEY

Vale do Douro

The best single activity in northern Portugal is exploring the scenic Douro (DOH-roo) Valley—the birthplace of port wine—with its otherworldly, ever-changing terrain sculpted by centuries of hardy farmers. The Douro River's steep, craggy, twisting canyons have been laboriously terraced to make a horizontal home for grape vines and olive and almond trees. Unlike the Rhine, the Loire, and other great European rivers, the Douro was never a strategic military location. So, rather than fortresses and palaces, you'll see farms, villages...and endless tidy rows of rock terraces, which took no less work—and are no less impressive— than those castles and châteaux. Locals brag, "God made the earth, but man made the Douro."

The Douro River begins as a trickle in Spain (where it's called the Duero), runs west for 550 miles (350 miles of which are in Portugal), and spills into the Atlantic at Porto. The name likely means "river of gold" (though some trace it to a Celtic word for water), perhaps because of the way the sun shines on the water, or the golden-brown silt it carries after a heavy rain.

In the 17th century, British traders developed a taste for the wines from the Douro region. "Op-port-unity" knocked in 1756, when the Marquês de Pombal demarcated the region—establishing it as the only place that port wine could be produced. To this day, port remains the top industry, as well as the top tourist draw, of the Douro Valley. The 50-mile stretch on either side of Pinhão is home to some 4,000 vintners and scores of *quintas*—vineyards that produce port (and often table wine and olive oil). While many *quintas* are private, others offer tours and tastings, and some have accommodations as well.

The Douro hillsides change colors throughout the year, from dusty brown in winter, scrubby green in summer, and glowing gold in fall. The 5,000-foot-high Serra do Marão mountain range guards the region, protecting it from the ocean air and creating a microclimate perfect for growing grapes. The temperature varies from snowy in the winter to arid and 100°F in the summer. Much of the Douro's dra-

matic ambience changed in the 1970s, when a series of dams were built for hydroelectric power, taming the formerly raging river into the gentle giant seen today.

But while the scenery and the port are sublime, the towns along the Douro (Peso da Régua and Pinhão) are fairly dull. If you've got wheels, consider staying at one of the many *quintas* that offer accommodations—ranging from simple rooms on family farms to one of the most breathtaking *pousadas* in Portugal. To many, the Douro Valley will feel low-energy and underwhelming (especially outside of September's harvest time), but some find it relaxing. The valley does have the world's best port and a unique—if subtle—charm.

PLANNING YOUR TIME

This area merits two days (including travel time to and from Porto, with an overnight along the river). Port-wine enthusiasts may well want more time. If you want only a glimpse, you can see the Douro as a day trip from Porto, either on your own (about 2 hours by car or 2 hours by train each way) or with a package tour (see "Getting Around the Douro Valley," later). I find the city of Porto more interesting and would favor it over the Douro Valley when allocating limited vacation time.

Note that since Porto is a business-oriented city, its hotels are often cheaper on weekends. In contrast, the Douro Valley—since it's primarily a tourist zone—is more crowded (and often more expensive) on weekends. Ideally, visit Porto on the weekend and the Douro during the week.

Drivers should make a beeline for the heart of the valley (see "Orientation to the Douro Valley," next), and explore at will. Without a car, you're limited as to where you can stay and which *quintas* you can tour, but you still have enough options to make the trip worthwhile. With a little extra cash for taxis, your choices multiply. To maximize sightseeing thrills, take the slow boat cruise from

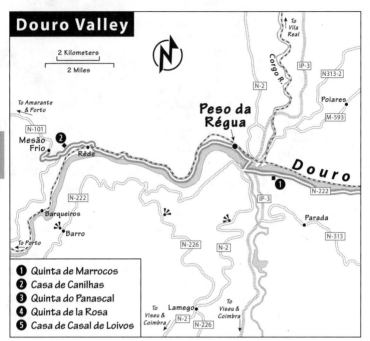

DOURO VALLEY

Douro Valley

2 Kilometers
2 Miles

To Vila Real
To Amarante & Porto
Peso da Régua
Poiares
Mesão Frio
Rêde
Douro
Barqueiros
Barro
To Porto
Parada
Lamego
To Viseu & Coimbra

1 Quinta de Marrocos
2 Casa de Canilhas
3 Quinta do Panascal
4 Quinta de la Rosa
5 Casa de Casal de Loivos

Porto to Peso da Régua. Visit the sights in Peso da Régua, then settle in for the night. In the morning, take the train to Pinhão, hike to Quinta de la Rosa for the 11:00 tour and tasting, or take a taxi to wander through the vineyards at Quinta do Panascal. When you've had enough of the wine and rugged scenery, head back to Porto via train.

Orientation to the Douro Valley

The Douro runs for 350 miles through the northern Portuguese heartland. The most interesting segment—and the heart of the port-wine-growing region—is easily the 17-mile stretch between Peso da Régua and Pinhão.

Coming from Porto, you'll see that the first 55 miles of the Douro are pretty and lush. When you reach the town of **Mesão Frio,** the terrain becomes far more arid and dramatic. The prized, demarcated port-wine-growing region of the Douro technically begins here and stretches all the way to the Spanish border.

Peso da Régua, about seven miles beyond Mesão Frio, is the biggest town of the region and a handy home base. Seventeen miles beyond Peso da Régua is smaller **Pinhão.** Each town has a big, fancy hotel and one or two cheap *residencials*, with *quintas* nearby. Peso da Régua benefits from more striking scenery, but feels urban

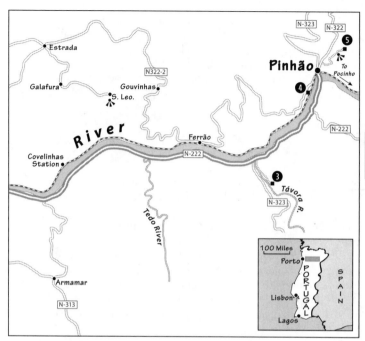

and functional; Pinhão enjoys more of a small-town ambience and has better accommodations. Neither is worth going out of your way to visit.

The Douro Azul company has something of a monopoly in the region, operating the biggest tour boats and running several of the accommodations (including Vintage House Hotel in Pinhão).

I've described the most enjoyable and accessible stretch of the Douro, but there's much more—vineyards stretch all the way to Spain. The train goes as far as Pocinho. Just south of Pocinho, Vila Nova de Foz Côa sits between the Douro and a fine archaeological park with cave paintings.

A big part of your Douro experience will be determined by where you choose to sleep. The most memorable place is the classic Vintage House Hotel in Pinhão. Both the Quinta de la Rosa and Quinta de Marrocos offer you a homey farm experience. All are described later in this chapter.

GETTING AROUND THE DOURO VALLEY

By Boat: Lazy cruise boats float up and down the Douro between Porto, Peso da Régua, and Pinhão. (The feisty Douro was tamed in the 1970s by a series of five dams with locks, including the highest one in Europe, the Barragem do Carrapatelo—which inches boats up and down, like a giant elevator, over 140 feet.)

The boat trip takes about seven hours from Porto to the heart of the Douro, and it comes with lunch and passage through two locks (longer trips include a third lock between Peso da Régua and Pinhão). If you've got the time and don't have a car, this is a slow but scenic way to enjoy the Douro Valley.

Various companies do the trip; generally, several different boats run daily from March through November (no boats Dec-Feb, seniors should ask about discounts, especially on weekdays). Most travelers take a train or bus back to Porto from Peso da Régua on the same day as part of a package deal. But if you want to spend the night on the Douro, it's easy to catch a train back on your own (or buy a two-day package, which includes lodging).

The largest company, **Douro Azul,** has big boats that are popular with tour groups. In Porto, they offer longer journeys from three to eight days with accommodation and meals on board (€300-900/person, tel. 223-402-500, www.douroazul.com). They also have shorter, daily cruises departing from Peso da Régua (see page 327).

Some travelers prefer smaller companies, which can cost a little less and offer a more personal experience. Your best bet is to

comparison-shop the options for the day you want to cruise, with help from the excellent **Porto Tours** office in Porto. Since it's run by the city, this agency offers unbiased advice and charges no commission (daily April-Sept 10:00-19:00, telephone answered daily 9:00-19:00, shorter hours off-season, in medieval watchtower next to cathedral at Calçada Dom Pedro Pitões 15, tel. 222-000-073, www.portotours.com, reservas@portotours.mail.pt).

By Train: A regional train connects Porto's São Bento Station with Peso da Régua (3/day direct, 2 hours; many more with a change in Caide, 2-2.5 hours); some of these trains continue another 30 minutes to Pinhão (5/day). On Saturdays, a historic diesel train choo-choos visitors between Douro towns (July-early Oct; 4-hour round-trip from Peso da Régua to Pinhão and back-€58; 6-hour round-trip from Peso da Régua to Pinhão, Tua, and back-€93; Douro cruises and train/cruise combos available, tel. 259-338-135, www.cenarios.pt).

By Car: The region is easy by car. From Porto, zip on the A-4 expressway to Amarante, then N-101 through the mountains to Mesão Frio (total trip to Peso da Régua around two hours). Once in the heart of the Douro, the riverside road follows the north bank from Mesão Frio to Peso da Régua. From there, you'll cross to the south bank (on the middle of the three bridges) to continue on N-222 into the valley to Pinhão (where you'll cross back to reach the town). The 17-mile stretch of river covered in this chapter is about a 30-minute drive. Everything I've mentioned is no more than a few minutes' side-trip from the river. Note that bridges cross the river at Peso da Régua and at Pinhão, but otherwise are scarce.

When passing through Amarante, it's an easy and logical pit stop to detour into the town center to check out the old Roman bridge and impressive church and convent of São Gonçalo.

If you're driving from Coimbra to the Douro Valley, you'll save time and mileage by coming directly through the mountains (via Viseu and Lamego), rather than taking the expressway up the coast to Porto and then over.

Tours and Tastings in the Douro Valley

QUINTAS

The main attraction of the Douro Valley is touring the *quintas*, the farms that produce port and table wines. It's an informal scene and easy for drivers; simply pull into any *quinta* listed in this chapter (or any marked *rota do vinho do Porto*), and ask for a quick tour and a taste. Even if they have a specific time for tours, you can often get a shorter, less formal tour at other times. Ideally, call ahead and ask when you should show up.

Each *quinta* (KEEN-tah) works differently; most tours and tastings are free. The tours of big companies' *quintas* are slick, but feel like stripped-down versions of the tours you'll do in the port-wine lodges back in Porto (with the happy exception of Quinta do Panascal). The smaller, independent *quintas* are more intimate, and offer a chance to meet the people who have devoted their lives to making the best  wine they can. At *quintas* operated by big companies, it's fine not to buy. But if a family-run place gives you an in-depth tour, it's polite to buy at least a token bottle.

The best *quinta* experiences on this stretch of the Douro are in or near Peso da Régua and Pinhão. For both towns, I've noted the best options for non-drivers.

GROWING—AND STOMPING—GRAPES IN THE DOURO VALLEY

Port wine can technically only be grown in the Douro Valley, which is unique among European river valleys. One glance at those end-

less sculpted rows of terraces—and the harsh, arid terrain that somehow produces something so flavorful—and visitors can't help but wonder: How do they do it?

The heart of the Douro is characterized by microclimates. A few miles can make a tremendous difference in terms of temperature, precipitation, humidity, and farming conditions. Even within the same vineyard, each parcel of land has its own characteristics. These subtle changes infuse the grapes with completely different aromas and flavors. Over the years, vintners have learned to micromanage their grapes, fine-tuning specific qualities to get the very best port for their conditions.

Near Porto, the Douro has moderate temperatures and a fair amount of precipitation. The vineyards you see north of Porto produce not port, but "green wine" (*vinho verde*—Portugal's refreshing and sprightly light white wine). About 55 miles inland, around Mesão Frio, chains of mountains stretch to the north and south. East of here, the climate changes dramatically, becoming very hot and dry in summer, with heavy rainfall and extreme cold in winter.

The terrain around the Douro is dominated by sedimentary rocks that have been buried, heated, and deformed into a metamorphic rock called schist *(xisto)*. Thanks to geological processes, the

easily fractured layers of schist are tilted beneath the soil at an angle, allowing winter rainfall to easily penetrate the earth and build up in underground reserves. The grapevines' roots plunge deep into the ground—up to 30 feet—in order to reach this water through the long, dry summer.

Douro vineyards are terraced, giving the valley an unusually dramatic look. Building and maintaining these terraces *(geios)* is expensive, and grapes planted there must be cultivated by hand. More recently, some of the bigger companies have attempted dif-

Brits on the Douro: The History of Port

Port is actually a British phenomenon. Because Britain isn't suitable for growing grapes, its citizens traditionally imported wine from France. But during wars with France (17th and 18th centuries), Britain boycotted French wine and looked elsewhere. They considered Portugal—but since it was farther away, wine often didn't survive the long sea journey to England.

The port-making process was supposedly invented accidentally by a pair of brothers who fortified the wine with grape brandy to maintain its quality during the long trip to England. The wine picked up the flavor of the oak, and the English grew to like the fortified taste and oaky flavor. The British perfected port production in the succeeding centuries; hence many ports carry British-sounding names (Taylor, Croft, Graham).

In 1703, the Methuen Treaty reduced taxation on Portuguese wines, making port even more popular. In 1756, Portugal's Marquês de Pombal demarcated the Douro region—the first such designation in Europe. From that point on, only true "port wine" came from this region, following specific regulations of production, just as "Champagne" technically refers to wines from a specific region of France. Traditionally, farmers and landowners were Portuguese, while the British bought the wine from them, aged it in Porto, and handled the export business. But that arrangement changed in the late 19th century, when an infestation of an American root insect called phylloxera (which smuggled itself to the Old World in the humid climate of speedy steamboats) devastated the Portuguese—and European—wine industry.

In the Douro Valley, you'll see lasting evidence of the phylloxera infestations in the "dead" terraces, overgrown with weeds and a smattering of olive trees. During the infestations, these particular terraces were treated with harsh chemicals that contaminated the soil, rendering it suitable only for growing olives, but not grapes. Other terraces were left untouched, as Portuguese vintners simply gave up. Unable to produce usable grapes for over a decade, they sold their land to British companies who were willing to wait until a solution could be found. It was, as phylloxera-resistant American rootstock began to be used throughout Europe. Port production resumed, this time on British-owned land.

Today, Porto and the Douro Valley see many British tourists. Though it's largely undiscovered by Americans, this region is a real hot spot among wine-loving Brits.

ferent methods: using bulldozers to create larger terraces (called *patamares*) that can be worked by machines; or smoothing out the hillside and planting the vines in vertical rows. (Purists don't like these new methods, which also have their disadvantages—including fewer plants per parcel.) Within the demarcated region, farmers are not allowed to irrigate, except with special permission.

Because the crops here are worked mostly by hand, it can be hard to find good workers (especially for pruning, a delicate task requiring certain skills). Most young people from the Douro move to the cities on the coast. To encourage them to stay, the government offers subsidies and other incentives.

To make the finest port, many *quintas* along the Douro still stomp grapes by foot—not because of quaint tradition, but because it's the best way. Machines would break the grapes' seeds and stems, releasing a bitter flavor—but soft soles don't. During harvest time (late Sept-early Oct), the grapes are poured into big granite tubs called *lagares*. A team of two dozen stompers line up across from each other, put their arms on each other's shoulders, and march, military-style, to crush the grapes. The stomping can last three or four days, and generally devolves into a party atmosphere—with tourists sometimes paying to join in.

Port traditionally stays in the Douro Valley for one winter after it's made, as the cold temperatures encourage the wine and brandy to marry. Then it's taken to Porto, where the more humid, mild climate is ideal for aging. For centuries, port could technically only be aged, marketed, and sold in Porto. But this was deregulated in 1987, and now any Douro *quinta* that offers tours sells its port directly to visitors.

The vineyards along the Douro are traditionally separated by olive trees, many of which produce fine olive oil. The farming demands of olives fit efficiently with those of grapes. There are also almond, orange, apple, and cherry trees, which locals use to make jam.

Peso da Régua

Peso da Régua (PAY-zoo dah RAY-gwah)—or simply Régua, as it's called by locals—is the administrative capital of the Douro Valley. With 22,000 people, Régua feels urban, with modern five- and six-story apartment blocks and hotels that somehow seem out of place in these starkly beautiful surroundings. While the town itself isn't worth the trip, the views and access into the surrounding countryside make it worth considering as a home base—or at least a transportation hub.

DOURO VALLEY

Orientation to Peso da Régua

Peso da Régua consists of basically two bustling streets that run parallel to the Douro. The main drag (to the right of Hotel Império) is higher up, while the other street dips down to river level. There are three bridges at the east (upriver) end of town. Don't expect much nightlife: Everything in town except the restaurants shuts down at 19:30.

Tourist Information: The town's TI is right next door to the train station (daily 9:30-12:30 & 14:00-18:00; Rua da Ferreirinha, tel. 254-312-846).

Arrival in Peso da Régua: The train station and two recommended hotels are at the eastern edge of the center near the bridges. Buses use a series of stops located directly in front of the train station. The TI is on the opposite end of town to the west—in spite of what the outdated signage at the train station may indicate. The boat dock is more or less in the middle of town (disembark to the right, walk up the hill for train station and hotels).

Tours: A cheesy **tourist train** meets arriving boats in summer and does a one-hour circuit (€10, two stops: mountaintop viewpoint and wine cellar for tasting).

The star of the Douro Valley is the river itself. **Douro Verde cruises** has an info booth at each of the two docks in Régua. The best option for a day on the water is their round-trip excursion to Pinhão (daily at 12:00, €60, includes lunch, return at 17:00 or 18:00). A quicker version without a meal takes passengers on a round-trip from Régua to Vale Abraão with its mega-hotel complex (€10, runs daily, 50-minute trip, tel. 254-322-858, www.douroverde.com).

Various informal **boat trips** take visitors to villages up and down the Douro (ask the reluctant TI for details).

DOURO VALLEY

Rabelo Boats

Up until the 1970s, when the Douro was tamed by dams, boats called *rabelos* navigated the treacherous waters, carrying port

from the hillsides to the cellars of Porto. It was a three-day trip to cover the 50-100 miles. A crew of four loaded the barrels onto the 20-foot boats. For the downstream trip, the captain stood on a platform to spy rocks and shallows ahead, using the long rudder to guide the flat-bottomed boat through whitewater and hairpin turns. It was dangerous work, and the river was once lined with shrines where superstitious sailors prayed.

At Vila Nova de Gaia, they unloaded their cargo—a mere eight barrels, typically—and headed back. For the slow trip upstream, the tall, square sail helped them ride the prevailing westerly winds. Otherwise, they were pulled by ropes up the worst stretches by men or oxen on towpaths that used to line the riverbank.

Nowadays, the Douro is quiet, port is shipped via tanker trucks, and the few remaining *rabelos* are docked by *quintas* for ambience and advertising.

Sights and Tastings in Peso da Régua

Peso da Régua's sights are few, and most worthwhile for people without cars (who can't get into the countryside, where time is better spent). Downtown, you'll find **Casa do Douro,** the grand headquarters of the local port-wine industry (ask to see the pretty stained-glass windows inside, entrance on Rua dos Camilos).

▲Douro Museum (Museu do Douro)

This fine museum—just a block uphill from Casa do Douro—traces the industry and culture of the Douro Valley, with a 3-D relief map of the region, stuffed specimens of local wildlife, models showing the construction of *rabelo* boats, and traditional costumes and musical instruments. Videos allow you to follow each step in wine production as well as view traditional methods that are no longer practiced. A gigantic wall of wine bottles is enough to make any port lover envious. You'll also see items relating to port production: tools, casks, barrels, decanters, port-wine bottles and labels, and advertising posters.

Cost and Hours: €6, April-Oct daily 10:00-18:00; Nov-March Tue-Sun 10:00-18:00, closed Mon; tel. 254-310-190, www.museudodouro.pt.

Tastings: Each afternoon the museum offers four different options for sampling five or six port wines, but a reservation is required at least one day in advance (minimum four people). The price varies based on quality of the wines (€5-15, daily, 15:00-17:00, contact Fernanda Fonseca, tel. 254-310-190, geral@museudodouro.pt). They also have a café and wine bar on the museum terrace where you can sip port wine outside while admiring the vineyards...but with no explanation.

Quinta de São Domingos

This *quinta,* on a hill just above Peso da Régua, produces port for the big company Castelinho. This is the region's giant, impersonal *quinta*—a standard stop for large tour groups. The corporate experience reminds me of some of the port-wine lodges in Vila Nova de Gaia near Porto—not what you came all the way to the rustic Douro Valley for. The only thing good about it is its convenience for those without a car (free 10-minute tour with short movie and two tastes, no reservation necessary, Fri-Wed 9:00-13:00 & 14:00-18:00, closed Thu, restaurant, tel. 254-320-100, www.quintasaodomingos.com). It's just above Régua at the train-station end of town (near the bridges); by foot, walk east (upriver) along the tracks, then cross the tracks through the hard-to-find gate (by the small pink building), and continue uphill to the *quinta* (about 15 minutes total).

Quinta de Marrocos

At the other end of the tasting spectrum is this loose, informal, family-run farm with lodging (see page 330). It's a great place to sample simple ports while chatting with the folks who made them.

Cost and Hours: €4-10, daily 9:00-12:00 & 14:00-18:00, tel. 254-313-012, www.quintademarrocos.com. You could hoof it here from Peso da Régua—it's across the river and about 1.5 miles upstream.

Sleeping in Peso da Régua

You have two basic options for sleeping in Régua: Stay in a basic hotel or *residencial,* or sleep at a picturesque *quinta* in the countryside. The in-town hotels are very handy for those using public transportation, but if you've got a car, the *quintas* offer a better value and a more memorable Douro experience. The fancier places serve meals and have half-board options. If you have a car, get out of town!

Sleep Code

Abbreviations   **(€1 = about $1.40, country code: 351)**
S = Single, **D** = Double/Twin, **T** = Triple, **Q** = Quad, **b** = bathroom, **s** = shower only
Price Rankings
 $$$ **Higher Priced**—Most rooms €100 or more.
 $$ **Moderately Priced**—Most rooms between €50-100.
 $ **Lower Priced**—Most rooms €50 or less.
Unless otherwise noted, credit cards are accepted, breakfast is included, Wi-Fi is generally free, and English is spoken. Prices can change without notice; verify the hotel's current rates online or by email. For the best prices, always book directly with the hotel.

The Douro is extremely crowded during the grape harvest in late September and early October, and good rooms are in short supply to begin with; if visiting during this time, book as far ahead as possible. Simpler places charge the same rates year-round; more expensive hotels charge more for weekends and during the busy season (roughly April-Oct).

$$ Hotel Régua Douro is the only classy option in town. With a top-floor panoramic breakfast room and 77 comfortable rooms—many of them with sweeping river views—it's a fine splurge (Sb-€62-72, Db-€71-90, higher prices are for July-Oct, add about €15-25 for weekends, riverview rooms are often €15 more than cityview rooms, suites available, air-con, elevator, Wi-Fi, pool, Largo da Estação, tel. 254-320-700, www.hotelreguadouro. pt, geral@hotelreguadouro.pt).

$ Império Hotel has a convenient, central location in a stark tower a block from the station and across the street from Hotel Régua Douro. Its 33 spartan but renovated rooms are a little musty and overlook busy streets, but the price is right (Sb-€35-40, Db-€45-50, Tb-€65-75, air-con, Wi-Fi, Rua Vasques Osório 8, tel. 254-320-120, www.imperiohotel.com, info@imperiohotel.com).

NEAR PESO DA RÉGUA

$$ Quinta de Marrocos is a wonderful option if you want to stay on a real-life family farm. The Sequeira family farmhouse operates a simple shop and a family vineyard making good ports and table wines. The four rooms include a rustic yet deluxe living room, where the port's always out. Staying here, with the four dogs and farmhands, is a fun, authentic experience. It's a rare opportunity to spend time with locals who really love what they do (Sb-€50, Db-

€70, 10 percent discount with this book, €20-25 meals with advance notice, on N-222 across the river and about 1.5 miles upstream from Peso da Régua, tel. 254-313-012, www.quintademarrocos. com, info@quintademarrocos.com, Rita and her mother, Maria Elisa). They also rent a private two-bedroom family-friendly house on their property (€120).

BETWEEN RÊDE AND MESÃO FRIO

$$ Casa de Canilhas, located in the countryside about 15 minutes downriver from Peso da Régua, is an old traditional house set among the vines overlooking the river valley (Db-€60-120, Estrada Municipal de Banduja, Mesão Frio, tel. 254-891-181, mobile 917-558-006, www.canilhas.com, info@canilhas.com).

Eating in Peso da Régua

Castas e Pratos, next to the train station, turned an enormous railway storage facility into the hippest restaurant in this otherwise sleepy town. The interior comes with lounge tunes and low lighting. If the weather is nice, dine in an open-air freight car permanently attached to the restaurant. Their mod wine bar has a nice selection of wines for several euros per glass (€20-24 main dishes, high €3 restaurant cover charge includes bread and other treats; restaurant-daily 12:30-15:00 & 19:30-22:30, wine bar-daily 10:30-24:00; Rua José Vasques Osório at train station, mobile 927-200-010, www.castasepratos.com).

A Companhia offers white-tablecloth elegance inside the Douro Museum. Their extensive wine list accompanies their stylish cuisine (€18-20 main dishes, daily 12:30-15:00 & 19:30-22:00, Rua Marquês de Pombal, tel. 254-331-272).

Gato Preto, next door to the Douro Museum, is classy with affordable prices. Try the *arroz do pato* (duck rice) for a local specialty (€8 main dishes, Tue-Sun 12:00-15:00 & 19:00-22:30, closed Mon, Avenida João Franco, tel. 254-313-367).

Pastelaria Nacional serves fantastic pastries but also doubles as a restaurant popular with locals. Paula and her family pride themselves on customer service and on their regional dishes...and her English is fun (€6 bargain *menu* offers choice of 3-4 main dishes, daily 12:00-24:00, Rua dos Camilos 86, tel. 254-336-231).

Pinhão

Pinhão (PEEN-yow)—known locally as
the "heart of the Douro"—feels like a real
workaday small town, where locals go on
with their "im-*port*-ant" business, oblivious to the tourists streaming through
their streets. Inside the big, concrete silos
(balões), the wine spends its first winter
awaiting shipment downstream to Porto.

Orientation to Pinhão

Pinhão has virtually no sights, but it makes for a handy home base.
Even if you don't arrive by train, be sure to check out the **train
station**—adorned with modern tiles illustrating the people and
traditions of the countryside. A few accommodations in and near
Pinhão don't take credit cards; one **ATM** can be found inside the
train station, and the other is in the BPI bank, on the left near the
west end of town (toward Casal de Loivos).

Arrival in Pinhão: The town has a train station along the
main road, and a boat landing down below on the river. The two
*residencial*s are across the street from
the station, and Vintage House Hotel
is just upriver, next to the bridge. If
you're arriving by **boat,** disembark to
the right for Vintage House Hotel; to
reach the *residencial*s or the station,
leave the boat to the left, then loop up
and to the right, around the big concrete wine-storage vats.

Getting Around: Taxi driver **Manuel Anselmo** speaks some
English and is very knowledgeable about local tourism. He can
often be found at the train station if he's not with his clients. A
round-trip visit to the recommended Quinta do Panascal costs
around €25 (mobile 966-192-904, www.taxipinhao.com).

Tours: Vintage House Hotel organizes river trips on traditional *rabelo* boats for guests and non-guests (€10-20 for 1- to
2-hour trips, daily April-Oct at 10:30 and 14:30, schedule depends
on demand and availability, call to reserve, tel. 254-730-230).

Tastings in Pinhão

The region's red wines are some of Portugal's fruity finest.

▲▲Quinta do Panascal

This wonderful *quinta* produces Fonseca—a name familiar to port lovers for its high quality. The affordable, tasty Bin No. 27 is their best-known ruby. It's the only *quinta* that allows you to roam on your own through the terraced vineyards. From the riverside road you'll side-trip up the valley of the Távora River. Venturing up the rough gravel road, you'll feel like you're discovering a special, hidden gem. Yet upon arrival, you'll enjoy the slick efficiency of a corporate producer (Fonseca also owns Taylor, and is a port-wine giant). Because of its delightfully remote location, and because it gets you out among the grapes, it's the best *quinta* tour on the Douro.

The tour is self-guided, so there's no wait once you arrive. You'll be given a 30-minute audioguide and set free to wander through the vineyards and take in the sweeping views (while listening to dry, humorless commentary about the history of port and of the company). Then you'll return to the lodge to watch a 10-minute video—which brings the otherwise still fields to life—while tasting three ports: a white, Bin No. 27, and 10-year-old tawny.

Cost and Hours: €5, April-Oct daily 10:00-18:00; Nov-March Mon-Fri 10:00-18:00, Sat-Sun by reservation only; tel. 254-732-321, www.quintadopanascalvisitorscentre.wordpress.com.

Getting There: This place is only accessible by car; it's well-marked off the Régua-Pinhão road (N-222), up a thrilling little side road that follows the Távora River as it branches off from the Douro (closer to Pinhão). Blind curves make this road dangerous for walking, but a taxi ride (including some wait time) is a good value for those without cars.

▲Quinta de la Rosa

This family-run *quinta* is proud of its wine and eager to show it off on an in-depth, friendly one-hour tour of the facility with a generous finale of four tastings. Three-course meals paired with their wines cost €25 per person; reserve in advance.

Cost and Hours: €3, but credited toward purchase; daily at 11:00; one mile downstream from Pinhão, tel. 254-732-254, www.quintadelarosa.com.

Getting There: This is perhaps the only family *quinta* that is close enough to do without a

car (20-minute hike from Pinhão). For directions and information on their accommodations, see "Sleeping in Pinhão," below.

Vintage House Hotel Wine Academy

The finest ports—for serious wine lovers—are at Vintage House Hotel's Academia do Vinho. These pricey tastings are generally in the afternoon; call to check the schedule and reserve a spot. Since it's right in the center of Pinhão, this place is an easy option for non-drivers.

Cost and Hours: €15-30 tastings, wine shop open daily 10:00-19:00, Lugar da Ponte, tel. 254-730-230, www.cshotelsandresorts.com, see hotel listing in "Sleeping in Pinhão," below.

Sleeping in Pinhão

Your in-town options are a plush splurge hotel or two humble *residencial*s. The *residencial*s are next door to each other, across from the train station. Both operate fine restaurants, and both have riverview rooms that don't cost extra but come with some street noise; neither has owners who speak English, but each sometimes has an English-speaking son available.

$$$ Vintage House Hotel is *the* place if you want to splurge on a fancy, formal hotel on the Douro (as opposed to a hillside manor house). It's all class, with a wonderfully atmospheric bar (under tree-trunk rafters), a good restaurant with an over-the-top formal interior and riverside terrace outdoor seating, and a wine shop featuring expensive tastings for aficionados (see "Tastings in Pinhão," earlier). Each of its 43 rooms has a river view and a terrace or balcony, and elegant tile in the bathroom. The halls are lined with baskets of free local oranges and apples, as well as 19th-century photos of the Douro (Sb-€100-200, Db-€140-225, suites-€175-420, extra bed-€40-60, extra child's bed-€25-30, air-con, elevator, pool, between train station and bridge at Lugar da Ponte, tel. 254-730-230, www.cshotelsandresorts.com, bookings@cshotelsandresorts.com).

$$ Hotel Douro offers 14 basic, clean, and bright rooms, many with cute riverview balconies. A communal terrace also provides a great, lazy-afternoon view of the river (Sb-€37-45, Db-€55-60, breakfast-€3, cash only, air-con, Wi-Fi, Largo da Estação 39, tel. 254-732-404, www.hotel-douro.com, geral@hotel-douro.com, Oliveira family).

$ Residencial Ponto Grande has 17 small, standard rooms—some have views—with lower prices and updated furnishings (Sb-€25, Db-€38, cash only, air-con, Rua António Manuel Saraiva 41A at Largo da Estação, tel. 254-732-456, Vieira family).

NEAR PINHÃO
$$$ Quinta de la Rosa, a mile downstream of Pinhão, is a river-side winery offering 14 comfortable rooms and three suites with light, country-cabana furnishings; all but one overlook the river (Sb/Db-€85-115, a bit less for 3 nights, extra child's bed-€20, ask in advance for the €27.50 three-course dinner including wine and port; tel. 254-732-254, www.quintadelarosa.com, holidays@quintadelarosa.com). They also offer in-depth tours and wine tastings (described earlier) and rent two houses by the week.

Getting There: Drivers leave Pinhão to the west (downriver), cross the concrete bridge, turn left and look for the *quinta* on the left side, up the hill. If walking: From the boat landing, cross the blue pedestrian bridge and continue 20 minutes (or take a €6 taxi from Pinhão station).

ABOVE PINHÃO, IN CASAL DE LOIVOS
$$$ Casa de Casal de Loivos hovers on a lofty perch above Pinhão, with perhaps the most dramatic views in all of the Douro Valley. The warm Sampayo family converted this 17th-century manor house into a six-room hotel with quaintly rustic furnishings and commanding Douro vistas. The family brags that when the BBC filmed a show about the best views in the world, they set up their camera right here (Sb-€80-89, Db-€105-110, discounts for longer stays, fun family-style dinner-€28/person without wine, cash only, swimming pool, closed Dec-Feb, tel. 254-732-149, www.casadecasaldeloivos.com, casadecasaldeloivos@ip.pt).

Getting There: The house is in the village of Casal de Loivos, atop the mountain overlooking Pinhão. Leaving Pinhão to the west (downriver), first follow signs for *Alijó,* then for *Casal de Loivos,* and wind your way up the mountain roads. Once in town, look for the poorly marked villa on your right; if you reach the overlook with the white railing, you've gone a block too far. If you don't have wheels, catch a taxi from Pinhão's train station (about €10).

DOURO VALLEY

PORTUGAL: PAST AND PRESENT

PORTUGUESE CAPSULE HISTORY
2000 B.C.-A.D. 500: Prehistory to Rome

Portugal's indigenous race, the Lusiads, was a mix of peoples from many migrations and invasions—Neolithic stone builders (2000 B.C.), Phoenician traders (1200 B.C.), northern Celts (700 B.C.), Greek colonists (700 B.C.), and Carthaginian conquerors (500 B.C.).

By the time of Julius Caesar (50 B.C.), Rome had conquered rebellious Lusitania (Portugal), establishing major cities at Olissipo (Lisbon), Portus Cale (Porto), and Ebora (Évora). The Romans brought laws, wine, the Latin language, and Christianity. When Rome's empire fell (A.D. 476), Portugal was saved from barbarian attacks by Christian Germanic Visigoths ruling distantly from their capital in Toledo.

711-1400: Muslims vs. Christians, and Nationhood

North African Muslims invaded the Iberian Peninsula, settling in southern Portugal. The Christians retreated to the cold, mountainous north, with central Portugal as a buffer zone. The remnants of these Christian armies became the core of the Reconquista—the retaking of the Iberian Peninsula from the Moors—which lasted for eight centuries. During their long rule, the Moors made Iberia a beacon of enlightenment in Dark Age Europe. But the Christians—who considered them invaders and infidels—drove them out, one territory at a time. Faro was the last Portuguese town to fall, in 1249. Afonso Henriques, a popular Christian noble who conquered much Muslim land, was proclaimed king of Portugal (1139), creating one of Europe's first modern nation-states. John I solidified Portugal's nationhood by repelling a Spanish invasion (1385) and establishing his family (the House of Avis) as kings.

1400-1600: The Age of Discovery...and of Slavery

With royal backing, Portugal built a navy and began exploring the seas using technology the Arabs had left behind, motivated by spice-trade profit and a desire to Christianize Muslim lands in North Africa. Prince Henry the Navigator urged his sailors to go beyond what was then regarded as "the end of the world." Thanks to new maritime inventions—such as the mariner's astrolabe and the caravel—they finally did, slowly making their way down the coast of West Africa. In 1488, Bartolomeu Dias became the first European to sail around the tip of Africa—the Cape of Good Hope. Vasco da Gama followed the same route but continued farther, landing in India in 1498. Suddenly the wealth of all Asia opened up via a fast and cheap sea route. Much to the dismay of Venice, Portugal's new discoveries caused spice prices to drop to one-fifth of their former market value.

Another major event at this time was the European discovery of Brazil by Pedro Cabral (1500). Cabral was on his way to India, following Da Gama's route, but he headed more southwest to bypass rough waters near the Gulf of Guinea. Historians have long debated whether his "discovery" was intentional or accidental, since some Portuguese sailors had previously reported spotting land on the other side of the Atlantic. In any case, Cabral's voyage resulted in the colonization of Brazil—and more riches for Portugal.

Besides trading in spice and silk, the Portuguese also traded in human beings. In fact, the Portuguese were the first Europeans to sail to Africa, capture native people, and bring them back for sale. They built Elmina Castle on the coast of what is now Ghana in 1482, the first of many "slave factories" (slave trading posts) that Europeans established in western Africa. The slave trade soon shifted to the New World, where new sugar plantations created a huge demand for cheap labor. Portuguese settlements sprung up in both Guinea and Angola for slavery purposes. Ships would leave Lisbon for West Africa, pick up slaves, and then sail to Brazil, selling their captives to work on plantations and in mines. The ships would return to Portugal loaded with sugar—creating tremendous wealth for the sea captains, slave traders, and merchants.

The Portuguese had a slave-trade monopoly through the 16th century, but that changed when England and the Netherlands began their own slave trade. Before slavery ended, historians estimate that about four million captives were brought from Africa to Brazil—roughly 40 percent of all the slaves brought to the Americas.

Through trade and conquest, tiny Portugal became one of Europe's wealthiest and most powerful nations, with colonies stretching from Brazil to Africa to India to China. The easy money destroyed the traditional economy.

1600-1900: Slow Fade

The "Spanish Captivity" (1580-1640) drained Portugal. Late in the 16th century, after the young Portuguese king, Sebastian (Dom Sebastião), died in battle without a direct heir, Portugal's throne was up for grabs. After a short reign by Sebastian's great-uncle (who died two years after assuming power), the Portuguese throne passed to another distant relative—the Spanish king, Philip II. Philip wanted the two countries to remain separate, and they did under his rule. But his son and grandson—who ruled after him—cared little about Portuguese autonomy, so they imposed new taxes on the Portuguese and forced Portugal's armies to support the Spanish military agenda. After 60 years, the Portuguese nobility had had enough, and when Spanish troops were tied up in the Thirty Years' War, the nobles launched an uprising. One of the leading nobles, the duke of Braganza, was proclaimed king, becoming King John (João) IV. Although it's been nearly 400 years, Spain and Portugal continue to have a sibling rivalry—with Spain often acting as the arrogant older brother—though the conflicts now happen on the soccer field, not the battlefield.

With a false economy, a rigid class system, and the gradual loss of their profitable colonies, Portugal was no match for the rising powers of Spain, England, Holland, and France. The earthquake of 1755 and Napoleon's invasions during the Peninsular War (1808-1814) were devastating. Portugal was a traditional ally of England, and when Napoleon demanded that Portuguese merchants stop trading with England, they refused. Napoleon sent his army through Spain to invade Portugal, where his troops ravaged the countryside. A French coup then placed Napoleon's brother on the Spanish throne, causing a revolt across the Iberian Peninsula. British troops retook Lisbon and a six-year, back-and-forth struggle eventually ended in Napoleon's defeat.

While the rest of Europe industrialized and democratized, Portugal lingered as an isolated, rural monarchy living off meager wealth from Brazilian gold and sugar. Eventually, the country lost its largest colony in 1822, when Brazil revolted (with the support of the son of the Portuguese king). But Portugal still had a string of colonies across Africa and Asia, including Portuguese Guinea, Angola, Mozambique, Goa, Macau, and Portuguese Timor.

1900s: Dictatorship and Democracy

Republican rebels overthrew the king in 1910, abolishing the monarchy, but democracy was slow to establish itself in Portugal's near-medieval class system. During World War I, Portugal joined the Allies, partly to protect its African colonies from the Germans. The postwar years resulted in political turmoil. A series of military-backed democracies culminated in four decades of António de

Typical Castle Architecture

Castles were fortified residences for medieval nobles. Castles come in all shapes and sizes, but knowing a few general terms will help you understand them.

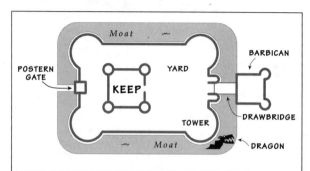

Barbican: A fortified gatehouse, sometimes a stand-alone building located outside the main walls.

Crenellation: A gap-toothed pattern of stones atop the parapet.

Drawbridge: A bridge that could be raised or lowered, using counterweights or a chain-and-winch.

Great Hall: The largest room in the castle, serving as throne room, conference center, and dining hall.

Hoardings (or Gallery or Brattice): Wooden huts built onto the upper parts of the stone walls. They served as watch towers, living quarters, and fighting platforms.

Keep (or Donjon): A high, strong stone tower in the center of the complex; the lord's home and refuge of last resort.

Loopholes (or Embrasures): Narrow wall slits through which soldiers could shoot arrows.

Machicolation: A stone ledge jutting out from the wall, with holes through which soldiers could drop rocks or boiling oil onto wall-scaling enemies below.

Moat: A ditch encircling the wall, sometimes filled with water.

Parapet: Outer railing of the wall walk.

Portcullis: An iron grille that could be lowered across the entrance.

Postern Gate: A small, unfortified side or rear entrance. In wartime, it became a "sally-port" used to launch surprise attacks, or as an escape route.

Towers: Square or round structures with crenellated tops or conical roofs serving as lookouts, chapels, living quarters, or the dungeon.

Turret: A small lookout tower rising from the top of the wall.

Wall Walk (or Allure): A pathway atop the wall where guards could patrol and where soldiers stood to fire at the enemy.

Yard (or Bailey): An open courtyard inside the castle walls.

Typical Church Architecture

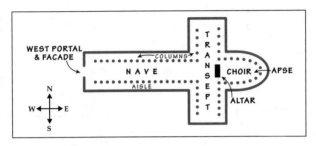

History comes to life when you visit a centuries-old church. Even if you wouldn't know your apse from a hole in the ground, learning a few simple terms will enrich your experience. Note that not every church has every feature, and a "cathedral" isn't a type of church architecture, but rather a designation for a church that's a governing center for a local bishop.

Aisles: The long, generally low-ceilinged arcades that flank the nave.

Altar: The raised area with a ceremonial table (often adorned with candles or a crucifix), where the priest prepares and serves the bread and wine for Communion.

Apse: The space beyond the altar, generally bordered with small chapels.

Barrel Vault: A continuous round-arched ceiling that resembles an extended upside-down U.

Choir: A cozy area, often screened off, located within the church nave and near the high altar, where services are sung in a more intimate setting.

Cloister: Covered hallways bordering a square or rectangular open-air courtyard, traditionally where monks and nuns got fresh air.

Facade: The exterior surface of the church's main (west) entrance, usually highly decorated.

Groin Vault: An arched ceiling formed where two equal barrel vaults meet at right angles. Less common usage: term for a medieval jock strap.

Narthex: The area (portico or foyer) between the main entry and the nave.

Nave: The long, central section of the church (running west to east, from the entrance to the altar) where the congregation sits or stands through the service.

Transept: In a traditional cross-shaped floor plan, the transept is one of the two parts forming the "arms" of the cross. The transepts run north-south, perpendicularly crossing the east-west nave.

West Portal: The main entry to the church (on the west end, opposite the main altar).

Oliveira Salazar's "New State," a right-wing regime benefiting the traditional upper classes. For 36 years the former professor ruled Portugal under an authoritarian regime that banned political parties and independent labor unions. A fascist system of censorship, propaganda, and oppression kept society in order. When opposition arose, the secret police (a.k.a. PIDE—Polícia Internacional e de Defesa do Estado) were used to imprison and torture dissidents.

According to Portuguese historians, Salazar didn't trust Hitler and didn't think the Germans could win World War II. He kept Portugal neutral, even allowing the British to use naval bases in the Azores under an old Anglo-Portuguese treaty. After the war, Portugal was a founding member of NATO—the only dictatorship allowed into the organization at its birth. Salazar wasn't your typical corrupt dictator. As a young man, he considered becoming a priest; as Portugal's leader he continued to be modest, pious, and celibate. Salazar—Europe's longest-serving dictator—ran Portugal until 1968, when he had a stroke and later died.

Salazar's repressive tactics and unpopular wars abroad (trying to hang onto Portugal's colonial empire) sparked the Carnation Revolution of 1974. A little after midnight on April 25, army rebels rolled into Lisbon, and by sunrise the military had taken control from Salazar's successors. They promised to restore citizen's civil liberties and conduct general elections as soon as possible. The coup was nearly bloodless. Residents disobeyed commands to stay in their homes, and instead people flooded the streets in support of the rebels, placing carnations into the barrels of the soldiers' guns as a sign of peace (hence the name "Carnation Revolution"). This new regime worked quickly to free Portugal's colonies. Within a few years, Guinea-Bissau, Mozambique, Cape Verde Islands, São Tomé and Principe, and Angola all became independent. After some initial political and economic chaos, Portugal finally adopted democracy. Eventually Spain became a democracy too, and the two countries joined the EU together in 1986.

PORTUGAL TODAY

The early years of the 21st century were heady days for Portugal. The former backwater was suddenly booming—building super-freeways, planning a bullet train to Madrid, giving out lavish bonuses to workers, and buying fancy consumer goods from the rest of Europe. Scaffolding was everywhere as the Portuguese scampered to finish a number of projects, which were funded in part by the European Union. The buzz was, "This easy money won't be here for long...it's use it or lose it. Quickly!"

The EU has worked to bring relatively poor regions (like much of Portugal) up to par with more-developed parts of Europe through matching grants and cheap construction loans. Since 1986

Portuguese Notables

Viriato (d. 139)—Legendary warrior who (unsuccessfully) resisted the Roman invasion.

Afonso Henriques, the Conqueror (1095-1185)—Renowned Muslim-slayer and first king of a united, Christian nation.

Pedro I, the Just (1320-1367)—King and Father of John I, famous for his devotion to his murdered mistress, Inês de Castro.

John I, the Good (1358-1433)—King who preserved independence from Spain, launched an overseas expansion, fathered Prince Henry the Navigator, and established the House of Avis as the ruling family.

Henry the Navigator (1394-1460)—Devout, intellectual sponsor of naval expeditions during the Age of Discovery.

Bartolomeu Dias (1450-1500)—Navigator who rounded the tip of Africa in 1488, paving the way for Vasco da Gama.

Vasco da Gama (1460-1524)—Explorer who discovered the sea route to India, opening up Asia's wealth.

Pedro Cabral (1467-1520)—Explorer who found the sea route to Brazil (1500).

Ferdinand Magellan (1480-1521)—Voyager who, sailing for Spain, led the first circumnavigation of the globe (1520).

Manuel I, the Fortunate (r. 1495-1521)—Promoter of Vasco da Gama's explorations that made Portugal wealthy. Manueline, the decorative art style of that time, is named for him.

Luís de Camões (1524-1580)—Swashbuckling adventurer and poet who captured the heroism of Vasco da Gama in his epic poem, "The Lusiads."

Marquês de Pombal (1699-1782)—Controversial prime minister who tried to modernize backward Portugal, regulated the port wine industry, and rebuilt Lisbon after the 1755 quake.

José I, the Reformer (r. 1750-1777)—Disinterested king who effectively turned over control of Portugal to the Marquês de Pombal.

Fernando Pessoa (1888-1935)—Foremost Portuguese Modernist poet, immortalized in sculpture outside his favorite Lisbon café.

António de Oliveira Salazar (1889-1970)—"Portugal's Franco," a dictator who led for four decades, slowly modernizing while preserving rule by the traditional upper classes.

this development aid has amounted to about three percent of Portugal's GDP. Another big boost to the economy came from hosting the Euro Cup soccer final in 2004, with new stadiums popping up everywhere. Until very recently, interest rates for these loans were very low. As part of the EU, Portugal was considered a low-risk bet for lenders. But when the banking crisis shook the US in 2008,

Ten Dates That Shaped Portugal

1128 "Portucale" separates from Castile.

1139 Afonso Henriques (Afonso I) is declared the first king of Portugal.

1498 Vasco da Gama sails Portugal into a century of wealth.

1581 King Philip II of Spain inherits the crown of Portugal after King Sebastian dies without an heir.

1640 The Spanish are ousted; the Portuguese gain their independence.

1755 A massive earthquake rocks Lisbon into poverty.

1822 Portugal loses Brazil as a colony.

1910 The monarchy is deposed, democracy fails, and repressive military regimes rule.

1974 A left-wing military coup brings democracy.

1986 Portugal joins the European Community (the forerunner of the European Union), boosting the economy.

things got real. Money became tight worldwide, and lenders began assessing countries on their own merits rather than rolling them in with the EU. The risk of lending to Portugal shot up—and so did interest rates.

Today, a hard reality is hitting Portugal: Much of the money it had spent wildly was not in fact a gift but, rather, a loan. And that loan needs to be paid back with interest at rates that have gone way up since 2008. The interest that Portugal owes on EU loans is crushing the local workforce. Unemployment is around 14 percent, but as high as 35 percent for those under 25 years old. The country produces $240 billion annually—slightly more than the gross domestic product of Louisiana. And that economy is struggling.

In 2012, Portugal's major infrastructure projects stalled. The plans for a high-speed bullet train from Madrid to Lisbon, an extra runway for Lisbon airport, and freeway expansion have all been put on indefinite hold.

A local friend told me, "In pre-euro days—with the *escudo* as our currency rather than the Deutsch Mark in disguise—when there was no money for chocolate milk, we just made do with white milk. Until 1974, when we won our freedom from Salazar, we were on the donkey system. Everything was slow. Then, with freedom we got the fever. And that accelerated with our membership in the European Union. Dazzled by German standards, we were encouraged to have faith in debt. Portugal got drunk on cheap European

Portugal's "Law 30"

Portugal has one of the more progressive drug policies today. In 2000, the government passed "Law 30," which decriminalized the consumption of all drugs. The law recently underwent a 10-year review. Although a conservative government has since replaced the more progressive government that established "Law 30," even former opponents agree that its benefits have far outweighed its harms. "Law 30" will continue to be the law of the land.

Portugal was repressed by a dictatorship until 1974. With freedom, people embraced their liberty, and formerly suppressed activities such as drug use temporarily spiked. In 1999, a group of experts came together to find a solution to the drug-use problem. They realized that the "war on drugs" was actually a "war on people." Similar to the US, only about one percent of Portugal's population (100,000 out of 11 million people) was actually using hard drugs.

The goal of "Law 30" was to establish a legal framework for harm reduction. Drug addicts are considered ill, not criminals. Drug use and possession are still illegal, but no longer punishable with jail time. Instead offenders are given treatment, community service, or fines.

The review studied drug consumption trends from 2001 to 2009. Researchers summed up Portugal's experience this way: "Nothing bad happened." The big negatives some had predicted, including the expected advent of "drug tourism," didn't materialize (young backpackers didn't start converging on Portugal as the new drug mecca).

Statistically, the number of Portuguese people who have tried various drugs did increase a little (possibly because the new law made it more comfortable to admit drug use). But there was no change in actual usage rates. Drug use by young people (ages 15-24) actually fell in the long run; after going up in 2003—immediately after the new law went into effect—rates dropped back down by 2005. The slight increase of consumption in Portugal after "Law 30" was similar to increases in Italy and Spain during the same period—likely a regional trend unrelated to the change.

Other outcomes of "Law 30" are that Portugal now has fewer people with HIV and more people in treatment. The police like the law because it frees up resources to focus on violent crime. The burden on Portugal's prisons and criminal system has been reduced. And the Portuguese government went from being the enemy of its drug-using population to being its advocate.

PAST & PRESENT

loans. And most of what we purchased with those loans was from Germany and France—feeding those economies—now, it seems, at the expense of our own."

In 2011, the EU approved a €78 billion bailout package, but with it came the requirement for strict austerity measures. To enforce these measures, the EU headquarters in Brussels has sent in "The Troika," a trio of managers tasked with helping Portugal get its economy back on a sustainable track. Austerity measures include more tolls on highways, higher deductibles for hospital visits, cutbacks in health care, and new taxes, including a 23 percent tax on all restaurant income. Utilities such as electricity are being privatized. The era of protecting traditional and inefficient industries is over. The retirement age has been raised from 65 to 67. And a worker-friendly scheme from the Carnation Revolution, which took a year's wage and broke it into 14 "months" rather than 12 (to give workers a "bonus" each summer and Christmas), has been rescinded. Now workers making more than €650 a month (about $900) get only 12 months' pay. Because this scheme was never really a "bonus" but rather a forced savings account, the change amounts to about a 15 percent pay cut.

The EU's "Troika" consider the Portuguese to be good, receptive workers willing to take their medicine responsibly (especially when compared with Greece). But Portugal's politicians have few resources and no easy solutions, other than repeatedly raising the VAT (Value-Added Tax)—which both major political parties have done.

The country successfully completed the bailout program in 2014, the second EU nation to break free from Brussels' economic straightjacket (the first was Ireland). The government says it may slowly restore salaries in the public sector that were cut during the crisis, and it is considering lowering taxes. In the meantime, workers face a future where, it's feared, the only certainty is austerity.

PRACTICALITIES

Contents

This chapter covers the practical skills of European travel: how to get tourist information, pay for purchases, sightsee efficiently, find good-value accommodations, eat affordably but well, use technology wisely, and get between destinations smoothly. To study ahead and round out your knowledge, check out "Resources" for a summary of recommended books and films.

Tourist Information

Portugal's **national tourist office** offers practical information, trip-planning ideas, and downloadable brochures on their website (www.visitportugal.com).

In Portugal, your best first stop in any new city is the tourist information office *(posto de turismo)*—abbreviated **TI** in this book. TIs are good places to get a city map and information on public transit (including bus and train schedules), walking tours, special events, and nightlife. Many big-city TIs have information on the entire country or at least the region, so try to pick up maps for destinations you'll be visiting later in your trip. If you're arriving in town after the TI closes, call ahead or pick up a map in a neighboring town.

While TIs are eager to book you a room, use their room-finding service only as a last resort. They are unable to give hard opinions on the relative value of one place over another. The accommodations stakes are too high to go potluck through the TI. Even if there's no "fee," you'll save yourself and your host money by going direct with the listings in this book. Also steer clear of their taxi vouchers (prepaid taxi fares—almost always more expensive than the metered price).

Travel Tips

Emergency and Medical Help: In Portugal, dial 112 for police or medical emergencies. Or ask at your hotel for help—they'll know the nearest medical and emergency services. (If you have a minor ailment, do as the Portuguese do and go to a pharmacist for advice.)

Theft or Loss: To replace a passport, you'll need to go in person to an embassy or consulate (see page 395). If your credit and debit cards disappear, cancel and replace them (see "Damage Control for Lost Cards" on page 352). File a police report either on the spot or within a day or two; you'll need it to submit an insurance claim for lost or stolen rail passes or travel gear, and it can help with replacing your passport or credit and debit cards. For more information, see www.ricksteves.com/help. Precautionary measures can minimize the effects of loss—back up your digital photos and other files frequently.

Avoiding Theft and Scams: Thieves target tourists throughout Portugal, especially in Lisbon. While hotel rooms are generally safe, thieves snatch purses, pick pockets, and break into cars. Keep your passport, credit and debit cards, and cash in a money belt (a pouch with a strap that you buckle around your waist like a belt and wear under your clothes). Be on guard, especially on the Metro and trolleys, and treat any disturbance around you as a smoke screen for theft. Don't believe any "police officers" looking for counterfeit bills. When traveling by train, keep your backpack near you and in sight.

Time Zones: Though Portugal and Spain are neighbors, Portugal sets its clock one hour earlier than Spain and most of continental Europe. (This is always true, even during Daylight Saving Time.) Portugal's time zone is the same as Great Britain's: five/eight hours ahead of the East/West coasts of the US. The exceptions are the beginning and end of Daylight Saving Time: Europe "springs forward" the last Sunday in March (two weeks after most

PRACTICALITIES

of North America) and "falls back" the last Sunday in October (one week before North America). For a handy online time converter, see www.timeanddate.com/worldclock.

Business Hours: In Portugal, some businesses take an afternoon break (about 13:00-15:00). When it's 100 degrees in the shade, you'll understand why. The biggest museums stay open all day. Smaller ones often close for lunch. Banks are generally open Monday through Friday from 8:30 to 15:00. Small shops are usually open on Saturday only in the morning and are closed all day Sunday.

Saturdays are virtually weekdays, though places may close earlier and transportation connections can be less frequent. Sundays have the same pros and cons as they do for travelers in the US: Sightseeing attractions are generally open, and street markets are lively with shoppers, but banks and smaller shops are closed, public transportation is limited, and there's no rush hour. Popular destinations are even busier on weekends.

Watt's Up? Europe's electrical system is 220 volts, instead of North America's 110 volts. Most newer electronics (such as laptops, battery chargers, and hair dryers) convert automatically, so you won't need a converter, but you will need an adapter plug with two round prongs, sold inexpensively at travel stores in the US. Avoid bringing older appliances that don't automatically convert voltage; instead, buy a cheap replacement in Europe.

Discounts: Discounts aren't listed in this book. However, many sights offer discounts for seniors (loosely defined as those who are retired or willing to call themselves a senior), youths (under age 18), and students or teachers with proper identification cards (www.isic.org). Always ask. Some discounts are available only for citizens of the European Union (EU).

Online Translation Tip: You can use Google's Chrome browser (available free at www.google.com/chrome) to instantly translate websites. With one click, the page appears in (very rough) English translation. You can also paste the URL of the site into the translation window at www.google.com/translate.

Money

This section offers advice on how to pay for purchases on your trip (including getting cash from ATMs and paying with plastic), dealing with lost or stolen cards, VAT (sales tax) refunds, and tipping.

WHAT TO BRING

Bring both a credit card and a debit card. You'll use the debit card at cash machines (ATMs) to withdraw local cash for most purchases, and the credit card to pay for larger items. Some travelers

PRACTICALITIES

Exchange Rate

1 euro (€) = about $1.40

To roughly convert prices in euros to dollars, add about 40 percent: €20 = about $28, €50 = about $70. (Check www. oanda.com for the latest exchange rates.) Just like the dollar, one euro (€) is broken down into 100 cents. Coins range from €0.01 to €2, and bills from €5 to €500.

carry a third card, in case one gets demagnetized or eaten by a temperamental machine.

As an emergency reserve, bring several hundred dollars in hard cash in $20 bills. Be aware that most Portuguese banks won't exchange foreign currency; instead you will need to go to a *casa de cambio* (currency-exchange booth). These booths are found throughout large towns, especially near tourist areas, but generally have lousy rates and/or outrageous fees. Smart travelers use their ATM card rather than exchanging currency.

CASH

Cash is just as desirable in Europe as it is at home. Small businesses (such as mom-and-pop cafés, shops, and *quartos*—private rooms) prefer that you pay your bills with cash. Some vendors will charge you extra for using a credit card, and some won't take credit cards at all. Cash is the best—and sometimes only—way to pay for cheap food, bus fare, taxis, and local guides.

Throughout Europe, ATMs are the standard way for travelers to get cash. To withdraw money from an ATM, you'll need a debit card (ideally with a Visa or MasterCard logo for maximum usability), plus a PIN code. Know your PIN code in numbers; there are only numbers—no letters—on European keypads. For increased security, shield the keypad when entering your PIN code, and don't use an ATM if anything on the front of the machine looks loose or damaged (a sign that someone may have attached a "skimming" device to capture account information). Try to withdraw large sums of money to reduce the number of per-transaction bank fees you'll pay.

When possible, use ATMs located outside banks—a thief is less likely to target a cash machine near surveillance cameras, and if your card is munched by a machine, you can go inside for help. Stay away from "independent" ATMs such as Travelex, Euronet, Moneybox, Cardpoint, and Cashzone, which charge huge commissions, have terrible exchange rates, and may try to trick users with "dynamic currency conversion" (described at the end of "Credit and Debit Cards," next).

Although you can use a credit card for an ATM transaction, it only makes sense in an emergency, because it's considered a cash advance (borrowed at a high interest rate) rather than a withdrawal.

Some readers report having difficulty using MasterCard-brand debit cards in Portugal (at hotels, restaurants, and ATMs), even when they've notified their bank ahead of time. For the best chances of accessing money from your US bank account, look for an ATM that uses a network whose logo is on the back of your ATM card (for example, Cirrus or Accel).

While traveling, if you want to monitor your accounts online to detect any unauthorized transactions, be sure to use a secure connection (see page 378).

Pickpockets target tourists; be alert and follow my tips on page 347.

CREDIT AND DEBIT CARDS

For purchases, Visa and MasterCard are more commonly accepted than American Express, though many merchants in Portugal, especially outside the main tourist areas, take only MultiBanco credit cards (issued by a Portuguese bank). Just like at home, credit or debit cards work easily at larger hotels, restaurants, and shops. I typically use my debit card to withdraw cash to pay for most purchases. I use my credit card only in a few specific situations: to book hotel reservations by phone, to cover major expenses (such as car rentals, plane tickets, and hotel stays), and to pay for things near the end of my trip (to avoid another visit to the ATM). While you could use a debit card to make most large purchases, using a credit card offers a greater degree of fraud protection (because debit cards draw funds directly from your account).

Ask Your Credit- or Debit-Card Company: Before your trip, contact the company that issued your debit or credit cards.

• Confirm that your **card will work overseas,** and alert them that you'll be using it in Europe; otherwise, they may deny transactions if they perceive unusual spending patterns.

• Ask for the specifics on transaction **fees.** When you use your credit or debit card—either for purchases or ATM withdrawals—you'll typically be charged additional "international transaction" fees of up to 3 percent (1 percent is normal) plus $5 per transaction. If your card's fees seem high, consider getting a different card just for your trip: Capital One (www.capitalone.com) and most credit unions have low-to-no international fees.

• If you plan to withdraw cash from ATMs, confirm your daily **withdrawal limit,** and if necessary, ask your bank to adjust it. Some travelers prefer a high limit that allows them to take out more cash at each ATM stop (saving on bank fees), while others prefer to set a lower limit in case their card is stolen. Note that in Portugal, the maximum you can withdraw per transaction is €200.

• Get your bank's emergency **phone number** in the US (but not its 800 number, which isn't accessible from overseas) to call collect if you have a problem.

• Ask for your credit card's **PIN** in case you need to make an emergency cash withdrawal or encounter Europe's "chip-and-PIN" system; the bank won't tell you your PIN over the phone, so allow time for it to be mailed to you.

Chip and PIN: Europeans are increasingly using chip-and-PIN cards, which are embedded with an electronic security chip (in addition to the magnetic stripe found on American-style cards). To make a purchase with a chip-and-PIN card, the cardholder inserts the card into a slot in the payment machine, then enters a PIN (like using a debit card in the US) while the card stays in the slot. The chip inside the card authorizes the transaction; the cardholder doesn't sign a receipt.

Your American-style card might not work at payment machines, such as those at train and subway stations, toll roads, park-

ing garages, luggage lockers, bike-rental kiosks, and self-serve gas pumps. If your card doesn't work, here are some suggestions: For either a debit card or a credit card, try entering that card's PIN when prompted. (Note that your credit-card PIN may not be the same as your debit-card PIN; you'll need to ask your bank for your credit-card PIN.) If your card still isn't accepted, look for a machine that takes cash, seek out a clerk who might be able to process the transaction manually, or ask a local if you can pay them cash to run the transaction on their card.

And don't panic. Many travelers who use only magnetic-stripe cards don't run into problems. Still, it pays to carry plenty of euros; remember that you can always use an ATM to withdraw cash with your magnetic-stripe debit card.

If you're still concerned, you can apply for a chip card in the US (though I think it's overkill). One option is the no-annual-fee GlobeTrek Visa, offered by Andrews Federal Credit Union in Maryland (open to all US residents; see www.andrewsfcu.org). In the future, chip cards should become standard issue in the US: Visa and MasterCard have asked US banks and merchants to use chip-based cards by late 2015.

Dynamic Currency Conversion: Although uncommon in Portugal, if merchants offer to convert your purchase price into dollars (called dynamic currency conversion, or DCC), refuse this "service." You'll pay even more in fees for the expensive convenience of seeing your charge in dollars.

"Independent" ATMs (such as Travelex and Moneybox) may try to confuse customers by presenting DCC in misleading terms. If an ATM offers to "lock in" or "guarantee" your conversion rate, choose "proceed without conversion." Other prompts might state, "You can be charged in dollars: Press YES for dollars, NO for euros." Always choose the local currency in these situations.

Damage Control for Lost Cards

If you lose your credit, debit, or ATM card, you can stop people from using it by reporting the loss immediately to the respective global customer-assistance centers. Call these 24-hour US numbers collect: Visa (tel. 303/967-1096), MasterCard (tel. 636/722-7111), and American Express (tel. 336/393-1111). In Portugal, to make a collect call to the US, dial 800-800-128. Press zero or stay on the line for an English-speaking operator. European toll-free numbers (listed by country) can be found at the websites for Visa and MasterCard.

Providing the following information will allow for a quicker cancellation of your missing card: full card number, whether you are the primary or secondary cardholder, the cardholder's name exactly as printed on the card, billing address, home phone number, circumstances of the loss or theft, and identification verification (your birth date, your mother's maiden name, or your Social Security number—memorize this, don't carry a copy). If you are the secondary cardholder, you'll also need to provide the primary cardholder's identification-verification details. You can generally receive a temporary card within two or three business days in Europe (see www.ricksteves.com/help).

If you report your loss within two days, you typically won't be responsible for any unauthorized transactions on your account, although many banks charge a liability fee of $50.

TIPPING

Tipping in Portugal isn't as automatic and generous as it is in the US. For special service, tips are appreciated, but not expected. As in the US, the proper amount depends on your resources, tipping philosophy, and the circumstances, but some general guidelines apply.

Restaurants: Tipping is an issue only at restaurants that have table service. If you order your food at a counter, don't tip.

In most restaurants, service is included—your menu typically will indicate this by noting *serviço incluído*. Still, if you are pleased with the service, it's customary to leave up to 5 percent. If service is not included *(serviço não incluído)*, tip up to 10 percent. Leave the tip on the table. It's best to tip in cash, even if you pay with your credit card. Otherwise, the tip may never reach your server.

Taxis: For a typical ride, round up your fare a bit (for instance, if the fare is €13, pay €14). If the cabbie hauls your bags and zips you to the airport to help you catch your flight, you might want to toss in a little more. But if you feel like you're being driven in circles or otherwise ripped off, skip the tip.

Services: In general, if someone in the service industry does a super job for you, a small tip of a euro or two is appropriate...but not required. If you're not sure whether (or how much) to tip for a service, ask your hotelier or the TI.

GETTING A VAT REFUND

Wrapped into the purchase price of your souvenirs is a Value-Added Tax (VAT, called IVA or *Imposto sobre o Valor Acrescentado* in Portuguese) of about 20 percent. You're entitled to get most of that tax back if you purchase more than €60 (about $85) worth of goods at a store that participates in the VAT-refund scheme. Typically, you must ring up the minimum at a single retailer—you can't add up your purchases from various shops to reach the required amount.

Getting your refund is usually straightforward and, if you buy a substantial amount of souvenirs, well worth the hassle. If you're lucky, the merchant will subtract the tax when you make your purchase. (This is more likely to occur if the store ships the goods to your home.) Otherwise, you'll need to:

Get the paperwork. Have the merchant completely fill out the necessary refund document, called a "cheque." You'll have to present your passport. Get the paperwork done before you leave the store to ensure you'll have everything you need (including your original sales receipt).

Get your stamp at the border or airport. Process your VAT document at your last stop in the European Union (such as at the airport) with the customs agent who deals with VAT refunds. Arrive an additional hour before you need to check in for your flight to allow time to find the local customs office—and to stand in line. It's best to keep your purchases in your carry-on. If they're too large or dangerous to carry on (such as knives), pack them in your checked bags and alert the check-in agent. You'll be sent (with your tagged bag) to a customs desk outside security, where they will examine your bag, stamp your paperwork, and put your bag on the belt. You're not supposed to use your purchased goods before you leave. If you show up at customs wearing your hand-knit Portuguese sweater, officials might look the other way—or deny you a refund.

Collect your refund. You'll need to return your stamped document to the retailer or its representative. Many merchants work with a service, such as Global Blue or Premier Tax Free, that has offices at major airports, ports, or border crossings (either before or after security, probably strategically located near a duty-free shop). These services, which extract a 4 percent fee, can refund your money immediately in cash or credit your card (within two billing cycles). If the retailer handles VAT refunds directly, it's up to you to contact the merchant for your refund. You can mail the documents from home, or more quickly, from your point of departure (using an envelope you've prepared in advance or one that's been provided by the merchant). You'll then have to wait—it can take months.

CUSTOMS FOR AMERICAN SHOPPERS

You are allowed to take home $800 worth of items per person duty-free, once every 30 days. You can take home many processed and packaged foods: vacuum-packed cheeses, dried herbs, jams, baked goods, candy, chocolate, oil, vinegar, mustard, and honey. Fresh fruits and vegetables and most meats are not allowed. However, canned meat is allowed if it doesn't contain any beef, veal, lamb, or mutton.

As for alcohol, you can bring in one liter duty-free (it can be packed securely in your checked luggage, along with any other liquid-containing items). To bring alcohol (or liquid-packed foods) in your carry-on bag on your flight home, buy it at a duty-free shop at the airport. You'll increase your odds of getting it onto a connecting flight if it's packaged in a "STEB"—a secure, tamper-evident bag. But stay away from liquids in opaque, ceramic, or metallic containers, which usually cannot be successfully screened (STEB or no STEB).

To check customs rules and duty rates, visit www.cbp.gov.

Sightseeing

Sightseeing can be hard work. Use these tips to make your visits to Portugal's finest sights meaningful, fun, efficient, and painless.

PLAN AHEAD

Set up an itinerary that allows you to fit in all your must-see sights. For a one-stop look at opening hours in the bigger cities—Lisbon and Porto—see the "At a Glance" sidebars. Most sights keep stable hours, but you can easily confirm the latest by checking with the TI or visiting museum websites.

Don't put off visiting a must-see sight—you never know when a place will close unexpectedly for a holiday, strike, or restoration. Many museums are closed or have reduced hours at least a few days a year, especially on holidays such as Christmas, New Year's, and

Labor Day (May 1). A list of holidays is on page 396; check museum websites for possible closures during your trip. In summer, some sights may stay open late. Off-season, many museums have shorter hours.

Going at the right time helps avoid crowds. This book offers tips on the best times to see specific sights. Try visiting popular sights very early or very late. Evening visits are usually peaceful, with fewer crowds.

Study up. To get the most out of the sight descriptions in this book, read them before you visit.

AT SIGHTS

Here's what you can typically expect:

Entering: Be warned that you may not be allowed to enter if you arrive 30 to 60 minutes before closing time. And guards start ushering people out well before the actual closing time, so don't save the best for last.

Some important sights have a security check, where you must open your bag or send it through a metal detector. Some sights require you to check daypacks and coats. (If you'd rather not check your daypack, try carrying it tucked under your arm like a purse as you enter.)

At churches—which often offer interesting art (usually free) and a cool, welcome seat—a modest dress code (no bare shoulders or shorts) is encouraged though rarely enforced.

Photography: If the museum's photo policy isn't clearly posted, ask a guard. Generally, taking photos without a flash or tripod is allowed. Some sights ban photos altogether.

Temporary Exhibits: Museums may host special exhibits in addition to their permanent collection. Some exhibits are included in the entry price, while others come at an extra cost (which you

may have to pay even if you don't want to see the exhibit).

Expect Changes: Artwork can be on tour, on loan, out sick, or shifted at the whim of the curator. To adapt, pick up a floor plan as you enter, and ask museum staff if you can't find a particular item.

Audioguides: Many sights rent audioguides, which generally offer sometimes dry-but-useful recorded descriptions in English (about €5). If you bring your own earbuds, you can enjoy better sound and avoid holding the device to your ear. To save money, bring a Y-jack and share one audioguide with your travel partner. Increasingly, museums are offering apps (often free) that you can download to your mobile device.

Services: Important sights may have an on-site café or cafeteria (usually a handy place to rejuvenate during a long visit). The WCs at sights are free and generally clean.

Before Leaving: At the gift shop, scan the postcard rack or thumb through a guidebook to be sure that you haven't overlooked something that you'd like to see.

Every sight or museum offers more than what is covered in this book. Use the information in this book as an introduction—not the final word.

Sleeping

Portugal offers some of the best accommodations values in Western Europe. Most places are government-regulated, with posted prices. Especially in resort areas, prices go way up in July and August. Most of the year, prices are soft.

I favor hotels and restaurants that are handy to your sightseeing activities. Rather than list hotels scattered throughout a city, I describe two or three favorite neighborhoods and recommend the best accommodations values in each, from dorm beds to fancy doubles with all of the comforts.

A major feature of this book is its extensive and opinionated listing of good-value rooms. I like places that are clean, central, relatively quiet at night, reasonably priced, friendly, small enough to have a hands-on owner and stable staff, run with a respect for Portuguese traditions, and not listed in other guidebooks. (In Portugal, for me, meeting six out of these eight criteria means it's a keeper.) I'm more impressed by a convenient location and a fun-loving philosophy than flat-screen TVs and a pricey laundry service.

Book your accommodations well in advance, especially if you'll be traveling during busy times. See page 396 for a list of major holidays and festivals in Portugal; for tips on making reservations, see page 360.

Some people make reservations as they travel, calling hotels a few days to a week before their arrival. If you'd rather travel without any reservations at all, you'll have greater success snaring rooms if you arrive at your destination early in the day. If you anticipate crowds (weekends are worst) on the day you want to check in, call hotels at about 9:00 or 10:00, when the receptionist knows who'll be checking out and which rooms will be available. If you encounter a language barrier, ask the fluent receptionist at your current hotel to call for you.

Sleep Code

(€1 = about $1.40, country code: 351)

Price Rankings

To help you easily sort through my listings, I've divided the accommodations into three categories, based on the highest price for a standard double room with bath during high season:

$$$ **Higher Priced**
$$ **Moderately Priced**
$ **Lower Priced**

I always rate hostels as $, whether or not they have double rooms, because they have the cheapest beds in town. Prices can change without notice; verify the hotel's current rates online or by email. For the best prices, always book directly with the hotel.

Abbreviations

To pack maximum information into minimum space, I use the following code to describe accommodations in this book. Prices listed are per room, not per person. When a price range is given for a type of room (such as double rooms listing for "Db-€100-150"), it means the price fluctuates with the season, size of room, or length of stay; expect to pay the upper end for peak-season stays.

S = Single room (or price for one person in a double).

D = Double or twin room. "Double beds" can be two twins sheeted together and are usually big enough for nonromantic couples.

T = Triple (generally a double bed with a single).

Q = Quad (usually two double beds; adding an extra child's bed to a T is usually cheaper).

b = Private bathroom with toilet and shower or tub.

s = Private shower or tub only (the toilet is down the hall).

According to this code, a couple staying at a "Db-€100" hotel would pay a total of €100 (about $140) for a double room with a private bathroom. Unless otherwise noted, breakfast is included, English is spoken, and credit cards are accepted. There's almost always Wi-Fi and/or a guest computer available, either free or for a fee.

PRACTICALITIES

RATES AND DEALS

I've described my recommended accommodations using a Sleep Code (see sidebar on page 357). Prices listed are for one-night stays in peak season, include breakfast, and assume you're booking directly with the hotel (not through an online hotel-booking engine or TI). Booking services extract a commission from the hotel, which logically closes the door on special deals. Book direct.

My recommended hotels each have a website (often with a built-in booking form) and an email address; you can expect a response in English within a day (and often sooner).

If you're on a budget, it's smart to email several hotels to ask for their best price. Comparison-shop and make your choice. This is especially helpful when dealing with the larger hotels that use "dynamic pricing," a computer-generated system that predicts the demand for particular days and sets prices accordingly: High-demand days will often be more than double the price of low-demand days. This makes it impossible for a guidebook to list anything more accurate than a wide range of prices. I regret this trend. While you can assume that hotels listed in this book are good, it's very difficult to say which ones are the better value unless you email to confirm the price.

As you look over the listings, you'll notice that some accommodations promise special prices to Rick Steves readers. To get these rates, you must book direct (that is, not through a booking site like TripAdvisor or Booking.com), mention this book when you reserve, and then show the book upon arrival. Rick Steves discounts apply to readers with ebooks as well as printed books. Note, though, that discounts understandably may not apply to promotional rates.

In general, prices can soften if you do any of the following: offer to pay cash, stay at least three nights, or mention this book. You can also try asking for a cheaper room or a discount, or offer to skip breakfast.

TYPES OF ACCOMMODATIONS

Hotels

Double rooms listed in this book range from $60 (very simple, toilet and shower down the hall) to $400 suites (maximum plumbing and more), with most clustering around $100. Hotel rooms are generally pleasant by American standards. Don't judge hotels by their bleak and dirty entryways. Landlords, stuck with rent control, often stand firmly in the way of hardworking hoteliers who'd like to brighten up their buildings.

All rooms have sinks with hot and cold water. Rooms with private bathrooms are often bigger and renovated, while the cheaper rooms without bathrooms often will be dingier and/or on the top floor. Any room without a bathroom has access to a bathroom in the corridor. Hotel elevators, while becoming more common, can be very small, forcing you to send your bags up separately—pack light.

Prepare for cool evenings if you travel in spring and fall. Summer can be extremely hot. Consider air-conditioning, fans, and street noise (since you'll want your window open), and don't be shy about asking for ice at the fancier hotels. Many rooms come with mini-refrigerators (if it's noisy at night, unplug it).

Most hotel rooms with air conditioners come with TV-remote-like control sticks (these sometimes require a deposit). Symbols are fairly universal: fan icon (adjust wind power); louver icon (choose steady flow or waves); snowflake and sunshine icons (heat or cold); clock ("O" setting: run X hours before turning off; "I" setting: wait X hours to start); and temperature control (20 degrees Celsius is comfortable).

If you're arriving early in the morning, your room probably won't be ready. You can drop your bag safely at the hotel and dive right into sightseeing.

Hoteliers can be a great help and source of advice. Most know their city well, and can assist you with everything from public transit and airport connections to finding a good restaurant, the nearest launderette, or a Wi-Fi hotspot.

Even at the best places, mechanical breakdowns occur: Air-conditioning malfunctions, sinks leak, hot water turns cold, and toilets gurgle and smell. Report your concerns clearly and calmly at the front desk. For more complicated problems, don't expect instant results. Any regulated hotel will have a complaint book *(livro de reclamações)*, which is checked by authorities. A request for this book will generally prompt the hotelier to solve your problem to keep you from writing a complaint.

In Portugal, street noise can be high. If you suspect noise will be a problem (if, for instance, your room is over a nightclub), ask for a quieter room in the back or on an upper floor. You can request a room *com vista* (with a view) or *tranquilo* (quiet), but in most cases, the view comes with street noise.

To guard against theft in your room, keep valuables out of sight. Some hotels have safes at the front desk and some rooms come with a safe. I've never bothered using one.

For environmental reasons, towels are often replaced in hotels only when you leave them on the floor. In private accommodations and some cheap hotels, they aren't replaced at all, so hang them up to dry and reuse.

Checkout can pose problems if surprise charges pop up on your bill. If you settle your bill the afternoon before you leave, you'll have time to discuss and address any points of contention (before 19:00, when the night shift usually arrives).

PRACTICALITIES

Making Hotel Reservations

Reserve your rooms several weeks in advance—or as soon as you've pinned down your travel dates, particularly for Lisbon. Note that some national holidays and religious festivals like the Fátima pilgrimage merit your making reservations far in advance (see page 396).

Requesting a Reservation: It's easiest to book your room through the hotel's website. (For the best rates, always use the hotel's official site and not a booking agency's site.) If there's no reservation form, or for complicated requests, send an email (see below for a sample request). Most recommended hotels take reservations in English.

The hotelier wants to know:
- the number and type of rooms you need
- the number of nights you'll stay
- your date of arrival (use the European style for writing dates: day/month/year)
- your date of departure
- any special needs (such as bathroom in the room or down the hall, cheapest room, twin beds vs. double bed, and so on)

Mention any discounts offered—for Rick Steves readers or otherwise—when you make the reservation.

Confirming a Reservation: Most places will request a credit-card number to hold your room. If they don't have a secure online reservation form—look for the *https*—you can email it (I do), but it's safer to share that confidential info via a phone call or two emails (splitting your number between them).

Canceling a Reservation: If you must cancel, it's courteous—

Above all, keep a positive attitude. Remember, you're on vacation. If your hotel is a disappointment, spend more time out enjoying the city you came to see.

Historic Inns

Portugal has luxurious, government-sponsored historic inns. These *pousadas* are often renovated castles, palaces, or monasteries, many with great views and stately atmo-

spheres. While full of Old World character, they often are run in a very sterile, bureaucratic way. These are pricey ($225-450 doubles), but can be a good deal for younger people (30 and under) and seniors (55 and over), who often get discounted rates; for details, bonus packages, and family deals, see www.pousadas.pt.

From:	rick@ricksteves.com
Sent:	Today
To:	info@hotelcentral.com
Subject:	Reservation request for 19-22 July

Dear Hotel Central,

I would like to reserve a room for 2 people for 3 nights, arriving 19 July and departing 22 July. If possible, I would like a quiet room with a double bed and a bathroom inside the room.

Please let me know if you have a room available and the price.

Thank you!
Rick Steves

PRACTICALITIES

and smart—to do so with as much notice as possible, especially for smaller family-run places. Be warned that cancellation policies can be strict; read the fine print or ask about these before you book. Internet deals may require prepayment, with no refunds for cancellations.

Reconfirming Your Reservation: Always call to reconfirm your room reservation a few days in advance. For smaller hotels, I call again on my day of arrival to tell my host what time I expect to get there (especially important if arriving late—after 17:00).

Phoning: For tips on how to call hotels overseas, see page 369.

Rooms in Private Homes *(Quartos)*

In touristy areas, you'll typically find locals who've opened up a spare room to make a little money on the side. These rooms are usually as private as hotel rooms, often with separate entries. Espe-

cially in resort towns, the rooms might be in small, apartment-type buildings. Ask for a *quarto* (KWAR-too; also known as an *alojamento particular*). *Quartos*, which generally offer a good experience, are less expensive than hotels ($45-75 for a double without breakfast). Given

that the boss changes the sheets, people staying several nights are most desirable; one-night stays sometimes cost extra.

The Good and Bad of Online Reviews

User-generated travel review websites—such as TripAdvisor, Booking.com, and Yelp—have quickly become a huge player in the travel industry. These sites give you access to actual reports—good and bad—from travelers who have experienced the hotel, restaurant, tour, or attraction.

My hotelier friends in Europe are in awe of these sites' influence. Small hoteliers who want to stay in business have no choice but to work with review sites—which often charge fees for good placement or photos, and tack on commissions if users book through the site instead of directly with the hotel.

While these sites work hard to weed out bogus users, my hunch is that a significant percentage of reviews are posted by friends or enemies of the business being reviewed. I've even seen hotels "bribe" guests (for example, offer a free breakfast) in exchange for a positive review. Also, review sites can become an echo chamber, with one or two flashy businesses camped out atop the ratings, while better, more affordable, and more authentic alternatives sit ignored farther down the list. (For example, I find review sites' restaurant recommendations skew to very touristy, obvious options.)

Remember that a user-generated review is based on the experience of one person. That person likely stayed at one hotel and ate at a few restaurants, and doesn't have much of a basis for comparison. A guidebook is the work of a trained researcher who has exhaustively visited many alternatives to assess their relative value. I recently checked out some top-rated TripAdvisor listings in various towns; when stacked up against their competitors, some are gems, while just as many are duds.

Both types of information have their place, and in many ways, they're complementary. If a hotel or restaurant is well-reviewed in a guidebook or two, and also gets good ratings on one of these sites, it's likely a winner.

Hostels and Campgrounds

Portugal has plenty of youth hostels and campgrounds, but considering the great bargains on other accommodations, I don't think they're worth the trouble and barely cover them in this book. Instead, I prefer simple, family-run hotels (listed as a *pensão* or *residencial*); they're easy to find, inexpensive, and, when chosen properly, a fun part of the Portuguese cultural experience. If you're on a starvation budget or just prefer camping or hosteling, plenty of information is available in the *Let's Go Spain & Portugal* guidebook, through the national TI, and at local TIs.

Other Accommodation Options

Whether you're in a city or the countryside, renting an apartment, house, or villa can be a fun and cost-effective way to go local. Websites such as HomeAway and its sister sites VRBO and GreatRentals let you correspond directly with European property owners or managers.

Airbnb and Roomorama make it reasonably easy to find a place to sleep in someone's home. Beds range from air-mattress-in-living-room basic to plush-B&B-suite posh. If you want a place to sleep that's free, Couchsurfing.org is a vagabond's alternative to Airbnb. It lists millions of outgoing members, who host fellow "surfers" in their homes.

Eating

The Portuguese meal schedule is slightly later than in the US. Their breakfast *(pequeno almoço)* is just coffee and a sweet roll. Lunch *(almoço)* is the big meal, served between 12:30 and 14:00, while supper *(jantar)* is from about 19:30 to 21:30. You'll eat well in mom-and-pop restaurants for about €10. All restaurants are smoke-free to meet EU regulations.

Appetizers Aren't Free: One of the most important things to remember when eating in Portugal is that if appetizers (olives, bread, butter, pâtés, and a veritable mini-buffet of other tasty temptations) are brought to your table before you order, they are not free. If you don't want them, push them to the side—you won't be charged for what you don't touch. But taking just one olive means you pay for the whole dish. Simple appetizers usually cost about €1 each, so it won't break the budget—just don't be surprised at extra charges on your bill.

Portions: Many restaurants save their customers money by portioning their dishes for two people. Menus often list prices for entrées in two columns: *dose* and *meia dose*. A *dose* (DOH-zeh) is generally enough to feed two, while a *meia dose* is a half-portion (plenty for one person). Restaurants have absolutely no problem with diners splitting a single *dose*. *Prato do dia* is the daily special.

Paying and Tipping: When you want the bill, say, *"A conta, por favor."* Most mom-and-pop restaurateurs will figure the bill in front of you, so everyone agrees on the final amount to be paid.

As for tipping (as mentioned earlier), the service charge is generally included at restaurants (you'll see *serviço incluído* on menus), but for very good service, add up to 5 percent extra. If the service charge is not included *(serviço não incluído)*, tip up to 10 percent. Leave the tip on the table. (But there's no need to tip if you order food at a counter.)

WHERE AND WHAT TO EAT

When restaurant-hunting, choose a spot filled with locals, not the place with the big neon signs boasting, "We Speak English and

Accept Credit Cards." Venturing even a block or two off the main drag leads to higher-quality food for less than half the price of the tourist-oriented places. Locals eat better at lower-rent locales.

Eat fresh seafood in Portugal (except on Monday, when the fish isn't fresh). *Bacalhau*, dried and salted cod that's served a reputed 365 different ways, is arguably the national dish, but definitely an acquired taste. Fish soup *(sopa de peixe)* and shellfish soup *(sopa de mariscos)* are worth seeking out. *Carne de porco à Alentejana* is an interesting combination of pork and clams—and Portugal's unique contribution to world cuisine.

Non-seafood dishes include *caldo verde* (a popular vegetable soup) and *frango assado* (roast chicken—ask for *piri-piri* sauce if you like it hot and spicy). Potatoes and greens are popular side dishes. Carbs never went out of style in Portugal—it's common to get both potatoes and rice with a meal. As in Spain, garlic and olive oil are big.

For a quick, cheap snack, drop by a bar or café. Bars offer an enticing selection of savory treats on display, such as codfish cakes *(pastel de bacalhau)* in northern Portugal, or deep-fried pastries with flaked cod *(pastéis de bacalhau)* near Lisbon. Sandwiches *(sandes)* are everywhere.

Cafés also offer snacks and are usually cheaper than bars. Many cafés also double as lunch joints, which locals frequent. If you see a menu written on a paper tablecloth and taped in the window, you can be assured of a quick, home-cooked meal. Just don't expect fancy presentation (and be willing to sit at a table with someone—don't worry, it makes for great conversation).

For dessert, a standard, wonderful local pastry is the custard tart, *pastel de nata* (called *pastel de Belém* in Lisbon's fancy suburb of the same name). You'll also find various concoctions made from egg yolk and sugar, such as *barriga de freiras* ("nuns' belly") and *papo de anjo* ("angel's double chin").

Typical Portuguese Foods

Meat and Seafood Dishes

bacalhau	dried and salted cod
carne de porco à Alentejana	diced pork covered with clams
frango assado	roast chicken, commonly served with piri-piri hot sauce
sardinhas grelhadas	fresh sardines, grilled or barbecued

Soups and Stews (*Sopas*)

arroz de mariscos	rice and mixed seafood stew (the "Portuguese paella")
caldeirada de peixe	like *cataplana* (see below), but cooked in a casserole
caldo verde	"green" soup of kale and potato puree
cataplana	seafood and potatoes cooked in a copper clamshell dish
feijoada	pork and beans
sopa Alentejana	garlic soup with a poached egg, cilantro, and bread crumbs
sopa de peixe	fish soup
sopa de mariscos	thick seafood soup

Sandwiches and Snacks

batatas fritas	potato chips
pastéis de bacalhau	deep-fried cod pastries
pastel de bacalhau	fried codfish cakes
prego	steak sandwich
sandes	sandwich
tosta mista	grilled ham and cheese sandwich

Desserts

arroz doce	rice pudding with cinnamon
barriga de freiras ("nuns' belly") / *papo de anjo* ("angel's double chin")	convent sweets made from egg yolk and sugar
pastel de nata	custard tart
pudim	flan
queque	muffin
salame de chocolate	cookies and chocolate pressed together to look like salami when sliced

PORTUGUESE DRINKS

Despite its small size, Portugal is the world's seventh-largest wine producer—150 million gallons in a good year. And Portuguese wines are cheap, decent, and distinctively fruity.

Vinho verde (VEEN-yoo VAIR-day) is light, refreshing, almost always white, and slightly fizzy. This "green wine" is actually golden in color, but "green" (young) in age—picked, made, and drunk within a year. *Alvarinho* grapes, from the northern Minho region, are low-sugar and high-acid. After the initial fermentation, winemakers introduce a second fermentation, whose by-product is carbon dioxide—the light fizz. The wines are somewhat bitter alone, but great with meals, especially seafood. The best are from Monaco Amarante and Aveleda, but the one you'll see on every menu is the perfectly acceptable Casal Garcia. If you like white *vinho verde*, you might enjoy the harder-to-find red version. It's dark in color, like a cabernet, but still fizzy and light in flavor, like a rosé—a unique combination.

The Dão region also produces fine red wines, mostly from the Mondego Valley between Coimbra, Guarda, and Viseu. They should sit for a year or two in the bottle before drinking. The Alentejo region (look for bottles labeled "Borba," a major producer) is known for its high-quality reds, though it's increasingly producing good whites as well.

Madeira, made from grapes grown in volcanic soil in the Madeira Islands, is fortified and blended (as is port), and usually served as a sweet dessert wine. The English and George Washington both liked it ("Have some Madeira, m'dear"), though today's version is drier and less syrupy. A Madeira called *Sercial* is served chilled (like sherry) with almonds. If you find yourself drowning in choices, simply try a glass of the house wine *(vinho da casa)*. Beer *(cerveja)* is also popular—for a small draft beer, ask for *uma imperial*.

If you like port wine, what better place to sample it than its birthplace, Port-ugal? (For a crash course on port wine, see page 300.) *Reserva* on the label means it's the best-quality port (and the most expensive). All bottles of port should have a *selo de garantia* (a seal of guarantee) issued by the Port Wine Institute.

Freshly squeezed orange juice *(sumo de laranja)*, mineral water *(água mineral)*, and soft drinks are widely available. When ordering water, fizzy or not, you will be asked, *"Fresco o natural?"* *Fresco* is chilled, and *natural* is room temperature.

Coffee lovers enjoy a *café*, the very aromatic shot of espresso so

Drinking Terminology

Cold Drinks

água da torneira	tap water
água com/sem gás	water with/without bubbles
água mineral	mineral water
fresco	chilled
leite	milk
natural	room temperature
sumo	juice
sumo de laranja	orange juice

Hot Drinks

café	espresso
café pingado	espresso with a little milk (similar to a macchiato)
chá	tea
galão	1/4 coffee, 3/4 warm milk served in a tall glass (similar to a latte)
meia de leite	coffee with warm milk

Alcoholic Drinks

aguardente	firewater distilled from grape seeds, stems, and skins, with a kick like a mule
cerveja	beer
ginjinha	cherry liqueur, served at special bars in Lisbon and Óbidos
imperial	small draft beer
vinho da casa	house wine
vinho branco	white wine
vinho tinto	red wine
vinho verde	"green" wine (young, fizzy wine, usually white)

popular in Portugal. In Lisbon this is called a *bica*. For an espresso with a little milk (like a *macchiato*), ask for a *café pingado*.

Communicating

"How can I stay connected in Europe?"—by phone and online—may be the most common question I hear from travelers. You have three basic options:

1. "Roam" with your US mobile device. This is the easiest option, but likely the most expensive. It works best for people who won't be making very many calls, and who value the convenience of sticking with what's familiar (and their own phone number). In recent years, as data roaming fees have dropped and free Wi-Fi has become easier to find, the majority of travelers are finding this to be the best all-around option.

2. Use an unlocked mobile phone with European SIM cards. This is a much more affordable option if you'll be making lots of calls, since it gives you 24/7 access to low European rates. Although remarkably cheap, this option does require a bit of shopping around for the right phone and a prepaid SIM card. Savvy travelers who routinely buy European SIM cards swear by this tactic.

3. Use public phones, and get online with your hotel's guest computer and/or at Internet cafés. These options work particularly well for travelers who simply don't want to hassle with the technology, or want to be (mostly) untethered from their home life while on the road.

Each of these options is explained in greater detail in the following pages. Mixing and matching works well. For example, I routinely bring along my smartphone for Internet chores and Skyping on Wi-Fi, but also carry an unlocked phone and buy SIM cards for affordable calls on the go.

For an even more in-depth explanation of this complicated topic, see **www.ricksteves.com/phoning.**

HOW TO DIAL

Many Americans are intimidated by dialing European phone numbers. You needn't be. It's simple, once you break the code.

Dialing Within Portugal

The following instructions apply whether you're dialing from a Portuguese mobile phone or a landline (such as a pay phone or your hotel-room phone). If you're roaming with a US phone number, follow the "Dialing Internationally" directions described later.

Portugal has a direct-dial phone system (no area codes). All phone numbers in Portugal are nine digits that can be dialed direct

Hurdling the Language Barrier

Although many Portuguese people—especially those in the tourist trade and in big cities—speak English, Portugal can surprise English-speaking travelers with one of the biggest language barriers in Western Europe. Locals visibly brighten when you know and use some key Portuguese words (see "Portuguese Survival Phrases" on page 403). Travel with a phrase book, particularly if you want to interact with local people. You'll find that doors open quicker and with more smiles when you can speak a few words of the language.

If you speak intermediate Spanish, you'll be able to stumble through newspapers and read road signs, even if you can't pronounce the words. (Accent marks are keys to pronunciation, but nothing more.)

Surprisingly, English speakers do much better speaking Portuguese than the Spanish do, because we have roughly the same amount of vowel sounds. Spoken Portuguese sounds like a mix of a Slavic language and Spanish. If you want to take a Portuguese language course before your trip here, make sure your professor is Portuguese, not Brazilian—the accents are very distinct.

If you're having trouble communicating in Portuguese, try English, French, and Spanish, in that order (because some locals give Spanish speakers the cold shoulder). The Portuguese do, however, speak more English than their Spanish neighbors, since English is required in school. (Their American movies are also subtitled, while the Spanish get their Hollywood flicks dubbed.)

Considering how fun it is to eat local dishes, the food phrase list in this book is particularly helpful (see "Typical Portuguese Foods" on page 365). Use it, and you'll eat much better than the average tourist.

PRACTICALITIES

throughout the country. For example, the number of one of my recommended Lisbon hotels is 213-219-030. That's the number you dial whether you're calling it from the Algarve or from across the street.

Dialing Internationally to or from Portugal

Always start with the **international access code** (011 if you're calling from the US or Canada, 00 from anywhere in Europe). If you're dialing from a mobile phone, simply insert a + instead (by holding the 0 key).

• Dial the **country code** of the country you're calling (351 for Portugal, or 1 for the US or Canada).

• Then dial the local number. The European calling chart lists specifics per country.

Calling from the US to Portugal: To call the Lisbon hotel from the US, dial 011 (US access code), 351 (Portugal's country code), then 213-219-030.

Calling from any European country to the US: To call my office in Edmonds, Washington, from anywhere in Europe, I dial 00 (Europe's access code), 1 (US country code), 425 (Edmonds' area code), and 771-8303.

More Dialing Tips

The chart on the next page shows how to dial per country. For online instructions, see www.countrycallingcodes.com or www. howtocallabroad.com.

Remember, if you're using a mobile phone, dial as if you're in that phone's country of origin. So, when roaming with your US phone number in Portugal, dial as if you're calling from the US. But if you're using a European SIM card, dial as you would from that European country.

Note that calls to a European mobile phone are substantially more expensive than calls to a fixed line. Off-hour calls are generally cheaper.

For tips on communicating over the phone with someone who speaks another language, see page 369.

USING YOUR SMARTPHONE IN EUROPE

Even in this age of email, texting, and near-universal Internet access, smart travelers still use the telephone. I call TIs to smooth out sightseeing plans, hotels to get driving directions, museums to confirm tour schedules, restaurants to check open hours or to book a table, and so on.

Most people enjoy the convenience of bringing their own smartphone. Horror stories about sky-high roaming fees are dated and exaggerated, and major service providers work hard to avoid surprising you with an exorbitant bill. With a little planning, you can use your phone—for voice calls, messaging, and Internet access—without breaking the bank.

Start by figuring out whether your phone works in Europe. Most phones purchased through AT&T and T-Mobile (which use the same technology as Europe) work abroad, while only some phones from Verizon or Sprint do—check your operating manual (look for "tri-band," "quad-band," or "GSM"). If you're not sure, ask your service provider.

Roaming Costs

"Roaming" with your phone—that is, using it outside its home region, such as in Europe—generally comes with extra charges, whether you are making voice calls, sending texts, or reading your email. The fees listed here are for the three major American providers—Verizon, AT&T, and T-Mobile; Sprint's roaming rates tend to be much higher. But policies change fast, so get the latest details before your trip. For example, as of mid-2014, T-Mobile waived voice, texting, and data roaming fees for some plans.

Voice calls are the most expensive. Most US providers charge from $1.29 to $1.99 per minute to make or receive calls in Europe. (As you cross each border, you'll typically get a text message explaining the rates in the new country.) If you plan to make multiple calls, look into a global calling plan to lower the per-minute cost, or buy a package of minutes at a discounted price (such as 30 minutes for $30). Note that you'll be charged for incoming calls whether or not you answer them; to save money ask your friends to stay in contact by texting, and to call you only in case of an emergency.

Text messaging costs 20 to 50 cents per text. To cut that cost, you could sign up for an international messaging plan (for example, $10 for 100 texts). Or consider apps that let you text for free (iMessage for Apple, Google Hangouts for Android, or WhatsApp for any device); however, these require you to use Wi-Fi or data roaming. Be aware that Europeans use the term "SMS" ("short message service") to describe text messaging.

Data roaming means accessing data services via a cellular network other than your home carrier's. Prices have dropped dramatically in recent years, making this an affordable way for travelers to bridge gaps between Wi-Fi hotspots. You'll pay far less if you set up an international data roaming plan. Most providers charge $25-30 for 100-120 megabytes of data. That's plenty for basic Internet tasks—100 megabytes lets you view 100 websites or send/receive 1,000 text-based emails, but you'll burn through that amount quickly by streaming videos or music. If your data use exceeds your plan amount, most providers will automatically kick in an additional 100- or 120-megabyte block for the same price. (For more, see "Using Wi-Fi and Data Roaming," later.)

Setting Up (or Disabling) International Service

With most service providers, international roaming (voice, text, and data) is disabled on your account unless you activate it. Before your trip, call your provider (or navigate their website), and cover the following topics:

• Confirm that your phone will work in Europe.
• Verify global roaming rates for voice calls, text messaging, and data.

PRACTICALITIES

European Calling Chart

Just smile and dial, using this key:
AC = Area Code, LN = Local Number.

European Country	Calling long distance within ...	Calling from the US or Canada to ...	Calling from a European country to ...
Austria	AC + LN	011 + 43 + AC (without initial zero) + LN	00 + 43 + AC (without initial zero) + LN
Belgium	LN	011 + 32 + LN (without initial zero)	00 + 32 + LN (without initial zero)
Bosnia-Herzegovina	AC + LN	011 + 387 + AC (without initial zero) + LN	00 + 387 + AC (without initial zero) + LN
Croatia	AC + LN	011 + 385 + AC (without initial zero) + LN	00 + 385 + AC (without initial zero) + LN
Czech Republic	LN	011 + 420 + LN	00 + 420 + LN
Denmark	LN	011 + 45 + LN	00 + 45 + LN
Estonia	LN	011 + 372 + LN	00 + 372 + LN
Finland	AC + LN	011 + 358 + AC (without initial zero) + LN	999 (or other 900 number) + 358 + AC (without initial zero) + LN
France	LN	011 + 33 + LN (without initial zero)	00 + 33 + LN (without initial zero)
Germany	AC + LN	011 + 49 + AC (without initial zero) + LN	00 + 49 + AC (without initial zero) + LN
Gibraltar	LN	011 + 350 + LN	00 + 350 + LN
Great Britain & N. Ireland	AC + LN	011 + 44 + AC (without initial zero) + LN	00 + 44 + AC (without initial zero) + LN
Greece	LN	011 + 30 + LN	00 + 30 + LN
Hungary	06 + AC + LN	011 + 36 + AC + LN	00 + 36 + AC + LN
Ireland	AC + LN	011 + 353 + AC (without initial zero) + LN	00 + 353 + AC (without initial zero) + LN
Italy	LN	011 + 39 + LN	00 + 39 + LN

PRACTICALITIES

European Country	Calling long distance within ...	Calling from the US or Canada to ...	Calling from a European country to ...
Latvia	LN	011 + 371 + LN	00 + 371 + LN
Montenegro	AC + LN	011 + 382 + AC (without initial zero) + LN	00 + 382 + AC (without initial zero) + LN
Morocco	LN	011 + 212 + LN (without initial zero)	00 + 212 + LN (without initial zero)
Netherlands	AC + LN	011 + 31 + AC (without initial zero) + LN	00 + 31 + AC (without initial zero) + LN
Norway	LN	011 + 47 + LN	00 + 47 + LN
Poland	LN	011 + 48 + LN	00 + 48 + LN
Portugal	LN	011 + 351 + LN	00 + 351 + LN
Russia	8 + AC + LN	011 + 7 + AC + LN	00 + 7 + AC + LN
Slovakia	AC + LN	011 + 421 + AC (without initial zero) + LN	00 + 421 + AC (without initial zero) + LN
Slovenia	AC + LN	011 + 386 + AC (without initial zero) + LN	00 + 386 + AC (without initial zero) + LN
Spain	LN	011 + 34 + LN	00 + 34 + LN
Sweden	AC + LN	011 + 46 + AC (without initial zero) + LN	00 + 46 + AC (without initial zero) + LN
Switzerland	LN	011 + 41 + LN (without initial zero)	00 + 41 + LN (without initial zero)
Turkey	AC (if there's no initial zero, add one) + LN	011 + 90 + AC (without initial zero) + LN	00 + 90 + AC (without initial zero) + LN

PRACTICALITIES

- The instructions above apply whether you're calling to or from a European landline or mobile phone.

- If calling from any mobile phone, you can replace the international access code with "+" (press and hold 0 to insert it).

- The international access code is 011 if you're calling from the US or Canada.

- To call the US or Canada from Europe, dial 00, then 1 (country code for US and Canada), then the area code and number. In short, 00 + 1 + AC + LN = Hi, Mom!

• Tell them which of those services you'd like to activate.

• Consider add-on plans to bring down the cost of international calls, texts, or data roaming.

When you get home from Europe, be sure to cancel any add-on plans that you activated for your trip.

Some people would rather use their smartphone exclusively on Wi-Fi, and not worry about either voice or data charges. If that's you, call your provider to be sure that international roaming options are deactivated on your account. To be double-sure, put your phone in "airplane mode," then turn Wi-Fi back on.

Using Wi-Fi and Data Roaming

A good approach is to use free Wi-Fi wherever possible, and fill in the gaps with data roaming.

Wi-Fi is readily available throughout Europe. At accommodations, access is usually free, but you may have to pay a fee, especially at expensive hotels. At hotels with thick stone walls, the Wi-Fi signal from the lobby may not reach every room. If Wi-Fi is important to you, ask about it when you book—and be specific ("In the rooms?"). Get the password and network name at the front desk when you check in.

When you're out and about, your best bet for finding free Wi-Fi is often at a café. They'll usually tell you the password if you buy something. Or you can stroll down a café-lined street, smartphone in hand, checking for unsecured networks every few steps until you find one that works. Some towns have free public Wi-Fi in highly trafficked parks, piazzas, or city government buildings. You may have to register before using it, or get a password at the TI.

Data roaming is handy when you can't find Wi-Fi. Because you'll pay by the megabyte (explained earlier), it's best to limit how much data you use. Save bandwidth-gobbling tasks like Skyping, watching videos, or downloading apps or emails with large attachments until you're on Wi-Fi. Switch your phone's email settings from "push" to "fetch." This means that you can choose to "fetch" (download) your messages when you're on Wi-Fi rather than having them continuously "pushed" to your device. And be aware of apps—such as news, weather, and sports tickers—that automatically update. Check your phone's settings to be sure that none of your apps are set to "use cellular data."

I like the safeguard of manually turning off data roaming on my phone whenever I'm not actively using it. To turn off data and voice roaming, look in your phone's settings menu—try checking under "cellular" or "network," or ask your service provider how to do it. If you need to get online but can't find Wi-Fi, simply turn

---

Internet Calling

To make totally free voice and video calls over the Internet, all you need is a smartphone, tablet, or laptop; a strong Wi-Fi signal; and an account with one of the major Internet calling providers: Skype (www.skype.com), FaceTime (preloaded on most Apple devices), or Google+ Hangouts (www.google.com/hangouts). If the Wi-Fi signal isn't strong enough for video, try sticking with an audio-only call. Or...wait for your next hotel. Many Internet calling programs also work for making calls from your computer to telephones worldwide for a very reasonable fee—generally just a few cents per minute (you'll have to buy some credit before you make your first call).

---

on data roaming long enough for the task at hand, then turn it off again.

Figure out how to keep track of how much data you've used (in your phone's menu, look for "cellular data usage"; you may have to reset the counter at the start of your trip). Some companies automatically send you a text message warning if you approach or exceed your limit.

There's yet another option: If you're traveling with an unlocked smartphone (explained later), you can buy a SIM card that also includes data; this can be far cheaper than data roaming through your home provider.

USING EUROPEAN SIM CARDS

While using your American phone in Europe is easy, it's not always cheap. And unreliable Wi-Fi can make keeping in touch frustrating. If you're reasonably technology-savvy, and would like to have the option of making lots of affordable calls, it's worth getting comfortable with European SIM cards.

Here's the basic idea: With an unlocked phone (which works with different carriers; see below), get a SIM card—the microchip that stores data about your phone—once you get to Europe. Slip in the SIM, turn on the phone, and bingo! You've got a European phone number (and access to cheaper European rates).

Getting an Unlocked Phone

Your basic options are getting your existing phone unlocked or buying a phone (either at home or in Europe).

Some phones are electronically "locked" so that you can't switch SIM cards (keeping you loyal to your carrier). But in some circumstances it's possible to unlock your phone—allowing you to replace the original SIM card with one that will work with a European provider. Note that some US carriers are beginning to offer

PRACTICALITIES

phones/tablets whose SIM card can't be swapped out in the US but will accept a European SIM without any unlocking process.

You may already have an old, unused mobile phone in a drawer somewhere. Call your service provider and ask if they'll send you the unlock code. Otherwise, you can buy one: Search an online shopping site for an "unlocked quad-band phone," or buy one at a mobile-phone shop in Europe. Either way, a basic model typically costs $40 or less.

Buying and Using SIM Cards

Once you have an unlocked phone, you'll need to buy a SIM card (note that a smaller variation called "micro-SIM" or "nano-SIM"—

 used in most iPhones—is less widely available).

SIM cards are sold at mobile-phone shops, department-store electronics counters, and newsstands for $5-10, and usually include about that much prepaid calling credit (making the card itself virtually free). Because SIM cards are prepaid, there's no contract and no commitment; I routinely buy one even if I'm in a country for only a few days.

In Portugal, buying a SIM card is as easy as buying a pack of gum (though some European countries require you to register the SIM card with your passport as an antiterrorism measure). Major providers in Portugal include Vodafone, MEO, and NOS; you'll find their shops in every major shopping district and mall.

When using a SIM card in its home country, it's free to receive calls and texts, and it's cheap to make calls—domestic calls average 20 cents per minute. You can also use SIM cards to call the US—sometimes very affordably (Lycamobile, which operates in multiple European countries, lets you call a US number for less than 10 cents a minute). Rates are higher if you're roaming in another country. But if you bought the SIM card within the European Union, roaming fees are capped no matter where you travel throughout the EU (about 25 cents/minute to make calls, 7 cents/minute to receive calls, and 8 cents for a text message).

While you can buy SIM cards just about anywhere, I like to seek out a mobile-phone shop, where an English-speaking clerk can help explain my options, get my SIM card inserted and set up, and show me how to use it. When you buy your SIM card, ask about rates for domestic and international calls and texting, and about roaming fees. Also find out how to check your credit balance (usually you'll key in a few digits and hit "Send"). You can top up your credit at any newsstand, tobacco shop, mobile-phone shop, or many other businesses (look for the SIM card's logo in the window).

To insert your SIM card into the phone, locate the slot, which is usually on the side of the phone or behind the battery. Turning on the phone, you'll be prompted to enter the "SIM PIN" (a code number that came with your card).

If you have an unlocked smartphone, you can look for a European SIM card that covers both voice and data. This is often much cheaper than paying for data roaming through your home provider.

LANDLINE TELEPHONES AND INTERNET CAFÉS
If you prefer to travel without a smartphone or tablet, you can still stay in touch using landline telephones, hotel guest computers, and Internet cafés.

Landline Telephones
Phones in your **hotel room** can be great for local calls and for calls using cheap international phone cards (described in the sidebar). Many hotels charge a fee for local and "toll-free" as well as long-distance or international calls—always ask for the rates before you dial. Since you'll never be charged for receiving calls, it can be more affordable to have someone from the US call you in your room.

While **public pay phones** are on the endangered species list, you'll still see them in post offices and train stations. Pay phones generally come with multilingual instructions. Most public phones work with insertable phone cards (described in the sidebar).

You'll see many cheap **call shops** that advertise low rates to faraway lands, often in train-station neighborhoods. While these target immigrants who want to call home cheaply, tourists can use them, too. Before making your call, be completely clear on the rates.

Internet Cafés and Public Internet Terminals
Finding public Internet terminals in Europe is no problem. Many hotels have a computer in the lobby for guests to use. Otherwise, head for an Internet café, or ask the TI or your hotelier for the nearest place to access the Internet.

European computers typically use non-American keyboards. A few letters are switched around, and command keys are labeled in the local language. Many European keyboards have an "Alt Gr" key (for "Alternate Graphics") to the right of the space bar; press this to insert the extra symbol that appears on some keys. Portuguese keyboards are a little different from ours; to type an @ symbol, press the "Alt Gr" key and 2 at the same time. If you can't locate a special character (such as the @ symbol), simply copy it from a Web page and paste it into your email message.

Types of Telephone Cards

Europe uses two different types of telephone cards. Both types are sold at post offices, newsstands, street kiosks, tobacco shops, and train stations.

Insertable Phone Card: An electronic chip card *(cartão telefónico)* can only be used at a pay phone: Simply take the phone off the hook, insert the card, wait for a dial tone, and dial away. The phone displays your credit ticking down as you talk. While you can use these cards to call anywhere in the world, they're only a good deal for making quick local calls from a phone booth. Each European country has its own insertable phone card—so your Portuguese card won't work in a Spanish phone.

International Phone Card: A prepaid card *(cartão telefónico com código pessoal)* can be used to make inexpensive calls—within Europe, or to the US, for pennies a minute—from nearly any phone, including the one in your hotel room. The cards come with a toll-free number and a scratch-to-reveal PIN code. If the voice prompts aren't in English, experiment: Dial your code, followed by the pound sign (#), then the phone number, then pound again, and so on, until it works.

Ask the clerk which of the various brands has the best rates for calls to America. Buy a lower denomination in case the card is a dud. Before buying a card, make sure the access number you dial is toll-free, not a local number (or else you'll be paying for a local call *and* deducting time from your calling card).

Internet Security

Whether you're accessing the Internet with your own device or at a public terminal, using a shared network or computer comes with the potential for increased security risks. Ask the hotel or café for the specific name of their Wi-Fi network, and make sure you log on to that exact one; hackers sometimes create a bogus hotspot with a similar or vague name (such as "Hotel Europa Free Wi-Fi"). It's better if a network uses a password (especially a hard-to-guess one) rather than being open to the world.

While traveling, you may want to check your online banking or credit-card statements, or to take care of other personal-finance chores, but Internet security experts advise against accessing these sites entirely while traveling. Even if you're using your own computer at a password-protected hotspot, any hacker who's logged on to the same network can see what you're up to. If you need to log on to a banking website, try to do so on a hard-wired connection (i.e., using an Ethernet cable in your hotel room), or if that's not possible, use a secure banking app on a cellular telephone connection.

If using a credit card online, make sure the site is secure. Most browsers display a little padlock icon, and the URL begins with *https* instead of *http*. Never send a credit-card number over a website that doesn't begin with *https*.

If you're not convinced a connection is secure, avoid accessing any sites (such as your bank's) that could be vulnerable to fraud.

MAIL

You can mail one package per day to yourself worth up to $200 duty-free from Europe to the US (mark it "personal purchases"). If you're sending a gift to someone, mark it "unsolicited gift." For details, visit www.cbp.gov and search for "Know Before You Go."

Get stamps at the neighborhood post office, newsstands within fancy hotels, and some mini-marts and card shops. The Portuguese postal service works fine, but for quick transatlantic delivery (in either direction), consider services such as DHL (www.dhl.com).

Transportation

BY CAR OR PUBLIC TRANSPORTATION?

If you're debating between public transportation and car rental, consider these factors: Cars are best for three or more traveling together (especially families with small kids), those packing heavy, and those scouring the countryside. Trains and buses are best for solo travelers, blitz tourists, city-to-city travelers, those with an ambitious multi-country itinerary, and those who don't want to drive in Europe. While a car gives you more freedom, trains and buses zip you effortlessly and scenically from city to city, usually dropping you in the center, often near a TI. Cars are an expensive headache in places like Lisbon.

TRAIN VERSUS BUS

Portugal straggles behind the rest of Europe in train service, but offers excellent bus transportation. Off the main Lisbon-Porto-Coimbra train lines, buses are usually a better bet. In cases where buses and trains serve the same destination, the bus is often more efficient, offering more frequent connections and sometimes a more central station. If schedules are similar, use the maps in this book to determine which station is closest to your hotel.

The best public transportation option is to mix bus and train travel. Always verify bus and train schedules before your departure, and never leave a station without the next day's schedule options in hand. To ask for a schedule at an information window, say, *"Horário para* (fill in names of cities), *faz favor."* (The TI will sometimes have schedules available for you to take or copy.) To study train schedules in advance, see www.cp.pt for all domestic and Spain/France routes (schedules are downloadable PDFs). Another good resource,

PRACTICALITIES

which also has schedules for trains throughout Europe, is German Rail's timetable (www.bahn.com).

Departures and arrivals are *partidas* and *chegadas*, respectively. These key Portuguese "fine print" words may also come in handy in your travels: Both *as* and *aos* mean "on"; *de* means "from," as in "from this date to that date"; *só* means "only," as in "only effective on..."; *não* means "not"; and *feriado* means "holiday." On schedules, exceptions are noted, as in this typical qualifier: *"Não se efectua aos sábados, domingos, e feriados oficiais"* ("Not effective on Saturdays, Sundays, and official holidays").

TRAINS *(COMBOIOS)*

The fastest Alfa Pendular and Intercidades trains serve the main Lisbon-Porto line with an occasional extension to Faro or Braga; these trains require seat reservations. Regional and Interregional "milk-run" trains serve most other routes, making lots of stops. On Portuguese train schedules, *diario* means "daily" and *mudança de comboio* means "change trains."

Rail Passes: Because you'll use a mix of trains and buses on your trip, a Portugal Pass is generally not a good value. If you're traveling beyond Portugal, the Spain-Portugal Pass or Select Eurail pass can make sense, but use the pass wisely, just for your long train trips. These passes are sold only outside of Europe. Even if you have a rail pass, use buses when they're more convenient and direct than the trains. For more information on rail passes, visit  the Trains & Rail Passes section of my website at www.ricksteves.com/rail.

Overnight Trains: If you'll be going from Lisbon to Madrid, book ahead for the pricey overnight Hotel Train (called the "Lusitânia") to ensure you get a berth and/or seat (rail pass accepted if you pay extra sleeper fee). No cheaper rail option exists between these two capital cities. You can save money by taking a bus (Intercentro Lines service using an Alsa bus), or save time by taking a plane (see "Flights," later in this chapter).

BUSES *(AUTOCARROS)*

Portugal has a number of different bus companies, sometimes running buses to the same destinations and using the same transfer points. If you have to transfer, make sure to look for a bus with the same name/logo as the company you bought the ticket from. The largest national company is Rede Expressos (covers buses both north and south of Lisbon, discounts for travelers age 29

Portugal's Public Transportation

Rail
AVE High Speed Rail (Spain)
Bus
Boat
✈ **Airports** (Not All Shown)
○ **Border Towns**

100 Kilometers
100 Miles

Santiago de Compostela
Lugo
To San Sebastián
Vigo
Ourense
Tui
Valença
Braga
Porto
Pinhão
Pocinho
Peso da Régua
To Salamanca
PORTUGAL
Pampilhosa
Guarda
Vilar Formoso
Fuentes de Oñoro
To Salamanca
Figueira da Foz
Coimbra
SPAIN
Atlantic Ocean
Tomar
Nazaré
Valado
Óbidos
Entron-camento
Marvão
Las Casiñas Altas
Cáceres
To Madrid
Sintra
Cascais
Lisbon
Elvas
Badajoz
Mérida
Évora
Beja
Funcheira
Lagos
Tunes
Ayamonte
Salema
Sagres
Faro
Tavira
Vila Real
Huelva
Sevilla
AVE high-speed rail
To Madrid
To Jerez & Cádiz

and under as well as for online booking, www.rede-expressos.pt). EVA Transportes covers some areas south of Lisbon, including the Algarve (www.eva-bus.com), as does RENEX (www.renex. pt). Central Portugal is covered by all major bus companies as well as Rodoviária do Tejo (www.rodotejo.pt) and Citi Express (www. citiexpress.eu). You can pre-plan bus trips between cities online, but you should always confirm the schedule in person.

If the bus station is not central, ask at the TI about travel agencies near your hotel that sell bus tickets. Don't leave a bus station to explore a city without checking your departure options and buying a ticket in advance if necessary (and possible). Bus service on holidays, Saturdays, and especially Sundays can be dismal.

You can (and most likely will be required to) stow your luggage under the bus. For longer rides, give some thought to which side of the bus will get the most sun, and sit on the opposite side. Even if a bus is air-conditioned and has curtains, direct sunlight can still heat up your seat. Long-distance (and most short-distance) buses are non-smoking. Your ride will likely come with a soundtrack: recorded music (usually American pop), a radio, or sometimes videos. If you prefer silence, bring earplugs.

Drivers and station personnel rarely speak English. Buses usually lack WCs but stop every two hours or so for a break (usually 15 minutes, but can be up to 30). Ask the driver, "How many minutes here?" *("Quántos minutos aqui?")*, so you know if you have time to get out. Bus stations have WCs (rarely with toilet paper) and cafés offering quick and cheap food.

Bus schedules in Portugal are clearly posted at each major station. *Directo* is "direct." *Ruta* buses are slower because they make many stops en route. Posted schedules list most, but not all, destinations. If your intended destination isn't listed, check at the ticket/information window for the most complete schedule information. For long trips, your ticket might include an assigned seat.

TAXIS *(TAXIS)*

Most taxis are reliable and cheap. Drivers generally respond kindly to the request, "How much is it to (destination), more or less?" *("Quanto é para* [fill in destination], *mais ou menos?")* Rounding the fare up to the nearest large coin (maximum of 10 percent) is adequate for a tip. City rides cost about $4-8. Keep a map in your hand so the cabbie knows (or thinks) you know where you're going. Big cities have plenty of taxis. In many cases, couples can travel by cab for little more than two bus or subway tickets.

RENTING A CAR

Rental companies require you to be at least 21 years old and to have held your license for one year. Drivers under the age of 25 may incur a young-driver surcharge, and some rental companies do not rent to anyone 75 or older. If you're considered too young or old, look into leasing (covered later), which has less-stringent age restrictions.

Research car rentals before you go. It's cheaper to arrange most car rentals from the US. Call several companies or look online to compare rates.

Most of the major US rental agencies (including Avis, Budget, Hertz, and Thrifty) have offices throughout Europe. Also consider the two major Europe-based agencies, Europcar and Sixt. It can be cheaper to use a consolidator, such as Auto Europe/Kemwel (www.autoeurope.com) or Europe by Car (www.europebycar.com), which compares rates at several companies to get you the best deal. But because you're working with a middleman, it's especially important to ask in advance about add-on fees and restrictions. Big companies have offices in most cities; ask whether they can pick you up at your hotel. Small local rental companies can be cheaper but aren't as flexible.

Regardless of the car-rental company you choose, always read the contract carefully for add-on charges—such as one-way drop-off fees, airport surcharges, or mandatory insurance policies—that aren't included in the "total price." You may need to query rental agents pointedly to find out your actual cost.

For the best rental deal, rent by the week with unlimited mileage. To save money on fuel, ask for a diesel car. I normally rent the smallest, least-expensive model with a stick shift (generally much cheaper than an automatic). Almost all rentals are manual by default, so if you need an automatic, request one in advance; be aware that these cars are usually larger models (not as maneuverable on narrow, winding roads).

Figure on paying roughly $200 for a one-week rental. Allow extra for supplemental insurance, fuel, tolls, and parking. For trips of three weeks or more, look into leasing; you'll save money on insurance and taxes. Be warned that international trips—say, picking up in Porto and dropping off in Madrid—can be expensive (it depends partly on distance).

As a rule, always tell your car-rental company up front exactly which countries you'll be entering. Some companies levy extra insurance fees for trips taken in certain countries with certain types of cars (such as BMWs, Mercedes, and convertibles).

Compare pickup costs (downtown can be less expensive than the airport), and explore drop-off options. Always check the hours of the location you choose: Many rental offices close from midday Saturday until Monday morning and, in smaller towns, at lunchtime.

When selecting a location, don't trust the agency's description of "downtown" or "city center." In some cases, a "downtown" branch can be on the outskirts of the city—a long, costly taxi ride from the center. Before choosing, plug the addresses into a mapping website. You may find that the "train station" location is handier. But returning a car at a big-city train station or downtown agency can be tricky; get precise details on the car drop-off location and hours, and allow ample time to find it.

When you pick up the car, check it thoroughly and make sure any damage is noted on your rental agreement. Find out how your car's lights, turn signals, wipers, radio, and fuel cap function, and know what kind of fuel the car takes (diesel vs. unleaded). When you return the car, make sure the agent verifies its condition with you. Some drivers take pictures of the returned vehicle as proof of its condition.

Navigation Options

When renting a car in Europe, you have several alternatives for your digital navigator: Use your smartphone's online mapping app, download an offline map app, or rent a GPS device with your rental car (or bring your own GPS device from home).

Online mapping apps used to be prohibitively expensive for overseas travelers—but that was before most carriers started offering affordable international data plans. If you're already getting a data plan for your trip, this is probably the way to go (see "Using Your Smartphone in Europe," earlier).

A number of well-designed apps allow you much of the convenience of online maps without any costly demands on your data plan. City Maps 2Go is one of the most popular of these; OffMaps, Google Maps, and Navfree also offer good, zoomable offline maps for much of Europe (some are better for driving, while others are better for navigating cities).

Some drivers prefer using a dedicated GPS unit—not only to avoid the data-roaming fees, but because a stand-alone GPS can be easier to operate (important if you're driving solo). The major downside: It's expensive—around $10-30 per day. Your car's GPS unit may only come loaded with maps for its home country—if you need additional maps, ask. Make sure your device's language is set to English before you drive off. If you have a portable GPS device at home, you can take that instead. Many American GPS devices come loaded with US maps only—you'll need to buy and download European maps before your trip. This option is far less expensive than renting.

Car Insurance Options

When you rent a car, you are liable for a very high deductible, sometimes equal to the entire value of the car. Limit your financial risk by choosing one of these options: Buy Collision Damage Waiver (CDW) coverage from the car-rental company, get coverage through your credit card (free, if your card automatically includes zero-deductible coverage), or get collision insurance as part of a larger travel-insurance policy.

CDW includes a very high deductible (typically $1,000-1,500). Though each rental company has its own variation, basic

Driving in Portugal

Atlantic Ocean

To Santiago de Compostela

100 Kilometers

50 Miles

145m • 3.5h

60m • 1.5h

Porto → Peso da Régua • Pinhão

15m .05h

190m • 4h

Salamanca

75m•1.5h

100m•2h

165m•3h

Coimbra

135m • 2.75h

60m•1h

Ciudad Rodrigo

PORTUGAL

40m•1h

55m•1h

240m•4h

SPAIN

Nazaré

25m•.05h

Fátima

Óbidos

60m • 1.25h

60m•1.25h

80m•1.5h

1.25h

3.5h

Sintra

315m • 5.5h (via Badajoz)

To Madrid

20m•.05h

90m•2.5h

Lisbon

Évora

185m•3h

155m•3h

265m•5h (via Beja)

155m•3h

m = miles
h = hours

Note: Your times may vary based on traffic, construction & road conditions.

13m•.05h

Sagres • Lagos

70m•1h

100m•1.5h

Sevilla

Salema 13m•.05h

Tavira

185m•3h

PRACTICALITIES

CDW costs $10-30 a day (figure roughly 30 percent extra) and reduces your liability, but does not eliminate it. When you pick up the car, you'll be offered the chance to "buy down" the deductible to zero (for an additional $10-30/day; this is sometimes called "super CDW" or "zero-deductible coverage").

If you opt for **credit-card coverage,** there's a catch. You'll technically have to decline all coverage offered by the car-rental company, which means they can place a hold on your card (which can be up to the full value of the car). In case of damage, it can be time-consuming to resolve the charges with your credit-card company. Before you decide on this option, quiz your credit-card company about how it works.

If you're already purchasing a **travel-insurance policy** for your trip, adding collision coverage is an option. For example, Travel

Guard (www.travelguard.com) sells affordable renter's collision insurance as an add-on to its other policies; it's valid everywhere in Europe except the Republic of Ireland, and some Italian car-rental companies refuse to honor it, as it doesn't cover you in case of theft.

For more on car-rental insurance, see www.ricksteves.com/cdw.

Leasing

For trips of three weeks or more, consider leasing (which automatically includes zero-deductible collision and theft insurance). By technically buying and then selling back the car, you save lots of money on tax and insurance. Leasing provides you a brand-new car with unlimited mileage and a 24-hour emergency assistance program. You can lease for as little as 21 days to as long as five and a half months. Car leases must be arranged from the US. One of many companies offering affordable lease packages is Europe by Car (www.europebycar.com/lease).

DRIVING

Drivers in Portugal encounter sparse traffic and very good roads connecting larger cities.

Road Rules: Be aware of typical European road rules. For example, many countries require headlights to be turned on at all times, and it's generally illegal to drive while using your mobile phone without a hands-free headset. You're not allowed to turn right on a red light, unless there is a sign or signal specifically authorizing it, and on expressways it's illegal to pass drivers on the right. Seat belts are required by law in Portugal. Ask your car-rental company about these rules, or check the US State Department website (www.travel.state.gov, search for your country in the "Learn about your destination" box, then click on "Travel and Transportation").

AND LEARN THESE ROAD SIGNS

Speed Limit (km/hr) — Yield — No Passing — End of No Passing Zone — One Way — Intersection — Main Road — Freeway — Danger — No Entry — No Entry for Cars — All Vehicles Prohibited — Parking — No Parking — Customs — Peace

Portugal, statistically one of Europe's most dangerous places to drive, has lots of ambulances on the road. Drive defensively. If you're involved in an accident, expect a monumental headache—you will be blamed. Expect to be stopped for a routine check by the police (be sure your car insurance form is up-to-date). Small towns come with speed traps and corruption. Tickets, especially for foreigners, are issued and paid for on the spot. Insist on a receipt, so the money is less likely to end up in the cop's pocket.

Fuel: Gas and diesel prices are government-controlled and the same everywhere—around $7 a gallon for gas *(gasóleo* or *gasolina)* and less for diesel *(diesel)*. Unleaded pumps are usually green. Note that your US credit and debit cards are unlikely to work at self-service gas pumps, as well as toll bridges and automated parking garages. It might help if you know your credit card's PIN code, but just in case, be sure to carry sufficient cash.

Navigation: On freeways, navigate by direction (*norte* = north, *oeste* = west, *sul* = south, *este* = east). Also, since road numbers can be confusing and inconsistent, navigate by city names. You can pick up a Michelin map in the US or buy one of the good, inexpensive maps available throughout Portugal.

Tolls: Freeways come with inexpensive tolls (about €3-4/hour) and save huge amounts of time. For some toll freeways, you pick up a ticket as you enter, and then pick up tickets at each opportunity along the way (or risk a fine). Don't use the no-stop-necessary speed lane (labeled *Reservada a Aderentes,* reserved for locals with a monthly pass), or you'll pay for a trip across the country in order to exit—a lesson I learned the expensive way.

Rental cars in these areas often come equipped with an electronic sensor, which automatically registers the tolls (you'll pay when you return the car). If you're driving a car without a sensor, you have five days to pay the toll at any post office, some gas stations, and "pay shops" (small stores and kiosks with a red "pay shop" decal).

If you drive into Portugal in a rental car from Spain, France, or another country, you can buy a pass just past the border (e.g., 3-day pass-€20).

Some roads—such as the A-22 along the Algarve—are tolled electronically using cameras, which identify cars by their license plate and charge the appropriate fees via a simple electronic payment system. Each time you drive under a toll camera, a sign tells you the fee (expect to pay about €10 to cross the entire Algarve coast, which covers the width of southern Portugal).

The toll system offers three payment options. To figure out the right option, estimate your total tolls using the calculator at www.portugaltolls.com, or if picking up your car in Portugal, ask for advice from the rental agency. The entire process is slick and easy.

A **TOLLCard** comes in prepaid amounts (€5, €10, €20, or €40) and is valid for one year. To use it, buy the card online (www.portugaltolls.com) or from the postal service (*Correios* or CTT), then activate it by sending a text message from your mobile phone.

PRACTICALITIES

You can check your balance online, plus you'll receive a text message when it runs out (balance is refundable).

TOLL Service is a three-day, €20 prepaid card that includes unlimited travel. It's available online, at post offices, or at the Porto and Faro airports.

With an **EASYToll** card, your credit card will be charged each time you pass a toll. You can buy this card at certain payment points along the border with Spain. To do that, simply pop your credit card into the machine and take your EASYToll card. This covers your car for all toll road use for a month or until you cancel the account. To close your account, go to www.portugaltolls.com, and enter the "identifier number" (located on your EASYToll card) and license plate number. If you don't cancel the account, the next driver can zip around the country on your penny.

Parking: Choose parking places carefully. Parking areas in cities generally have a large white "P" on a blue background. Don't assume it's free—check around for meters or ticketing machines. Keep your valuables in your hotel room or, if you're between destinations, covered in your trunk. Leave nothing worth stealing in the car, especially overnight. If your car's a hatchback, take the trunk cover off at night so thieves can look in without breaking in. Try to make your car look locally owned by hiding the "tourist-owned" rental-company decals and putting a Portuguese newspaper in your front or back window. Ask your hotelier for advice on parking. In cities, you can park safely but expensively in guarded lots. While you should avoid parking lots with twinkly asphalt, thieves break car windows anywhere, even at stoplights.

FLIGHTS

The best comparison search engine for both international and intra-European flights is www.kayak.com. For inexpensive flights within Europe, try www.skyscanner.com or www.hipmunk.com; for inexpensive international flights, try www.vayama.com.

Flying to Europe: Start looking for international flights four to five months before your trip, especially for peak-season travel. Off-season tickets can be purchased a month or so in advance. Depending on your itinerary, it can be efficient to fly into one city and out of another. If your flight requires a connection in Europe, see our hints on navigating Europe's top hub airports at www.ricksteves.com/hub-airports.

Flying Within Europe: If you're considering a train ride that's more than five hours long, a flight may save you both time and money. When comparing your options, factor in the time it takes to get to the airport and how early you'll need to arrive to check in.

For flights within Portugal, the country's national carrier is

TAP (www.flytap.com). For flights between Lisbon and other cities in Europe, also try **Iberia** (www.iberia.com), **Vueling Airlines** (www.vueling.com), **Ryanair** (www.ryanair.com), and **easyJet** (www.easyjet.com).

Be aware of the potential drawbacks of flying on the cheap: nonrefundable and nonchangeable tickets, minimal or nonexistent customer service, treks to airports far outside town, and stingy baggage allowances with steep overage fees. If you're traveling with lots of luggage, a cheap flight can quickly become a bad deal. To avoid unpleasant surprises, read the small print before you book.

Resources

RESOURCES FROM RICK STEVES

Rick Steves Portugal is one of many books in my series on European travel, which includes country guidebooks, city guidebooks (Rome, Florence, Paris, London, etc.), Snapshot guides (excerpted chapters from my country guides), Pocket Guides (full-color little books on big cities), and my budget-travel skills handbook, *Rick*

Steves Europe Through the Back Door. Most of my titles are available as ebooks. My phrase books—for Portuguese, Spanish, German, French, and Italian—are practical and budget-oriented. My other books include *Europe 101* (a crash course on art and history designed for travelers), *Mediterranean Cruise Ports* and *Northern European Cruise Ports* (how to make the most of your time in port), and *Travel as a Political Act* (a travelogue sprinkled with tips for bringing home a global perspective). A more complete list of my titles appears near the end of this book.

Video: My public television series, *Rick Steves' Europe*, covers European destinations in 100 shows, with two episodes on Portugal. To watch full episodes online for free, see www.ricksteves.com/tv. Or to raise your travel I.Q. with video versions of our popular classes, including talks on Portugal and Spain, see www.ricksteves.com/travel-talks.

Audio: My weekly public radio show, *Travel with Rick Steves*, features interviews with travel experts from around the world. All of this audio content is available for free at Rick Steves Audio Europe, an extensive online library orga-

PRACTICALITIES

Begin Your Trip at www.RickSteves.com

My **website** is *the* place to explore Europe. You'll find thousands of fun articles, videos, photos, and radio interviews on European destinations; money-saving tips for planning your dream trip; monthly travel news; my travel talks and travel blog; my latest guidebook updates (www.ricksteves.com/update); and my free Rick Steves Audio Europe app. You can also follow me on Facebook and Twitter.

Our **Travel Forum** is an immense, yet well-groomed collection of message boards, where our travel-savvy community answers questions and shares their personal travel experiences (www.ricksteves.com/forums).

Our online **Travel Store** offers travel bags and accessories that I've designed specifically to help you travel smarter and lighter. These include my popular travel bags (rolling bag and backpack versions), money belts, totes, toiletries kits, adapters, other accessories, and a wide selection of guidebooks, planning maps, and DVDs.

Choosing the right **rail pass** for your trip—amid hundreds of options—can drive you nutty. Our website will help you find the perfect fit for your itinerary and your budget: We offer easy, one-stop shopping for rail passes, seat reservations, and point-to-point tickets.

Want to travel with greater efficiency and less stress? We organize **tours** with more than three dozen itineraries and more than 800 departures reaching the best destinations in this book...and beyond. We offer a 12-day Heart of Portugal tour that hits the highlights of this history-rich country. You'll enjoy great guides, a fun bunch of travel partners (with small groups of 24 to 28 travelers), and plenty of room to spread out in a big, comfy bus when touring between towns. You'll find European adventures to fit every vacation length. For all the details, and to get our Tour Catalog and a free Rick Steves Tour Experience DVD (filmed on location during an actual tour), visit www.ricksteves.com or call us at 425/608-4217.

nized by destination. Choose whatever interests you, and download it via the Rick Steves Audio Europe app, www.ricksteves.com/audioeurope, iTunes, or Google Play.

MAPS

The black-and-white maps in this book are concise and simple, designed to help you locate recommended places and get to local TIs, where you can pick up more in-depth maps of cities and regions (usually free).

Better maps are sold at newsstands and bookstores. Before you buy a map, look at it to make sure it has the level of detail you want.

Train travelers can usually manage fine with the freebies they get at the local tourist offices. But drivers shouldn't skimp on maps—get one good overall road map for Portugal (a 1:400,000 map, such as Michelin's *Spain & Portugal Tourist and Motoring Atlas* or *Portugal Map*, is a fine bet). Good regional driving maps are available throughout Portugal. An up-to-date map is essential—it can mean the difference between choosing an old, slow road or saving an hour by finding the brand-new highway.

RECOMMENDED BOOKS AND MOVIES
To learn more about Portugal past and present, check out a few of these books and films.

Nonfiction
The Book of Disquiet (Fernando Pessoa, 1982). This collection of unpublished poetry and thoughts from the great Portuguese writer, Fernando Pessoa, was compiled after they were found in a trunk following his death.

The First Global Village (Martin Page, 2002). Page explores Portugal's profound influence on the rest of the world.

The History of Portugal (James Anderson, 2000). Anderson provides a concise, readable overview of Portuguese history.

The Last Day: Wrath, Ruin, and Reason in the Great Lisbon Earthquake of 1755 (Nicholas Shrady, 2008). The earthquake that leveled Lisbon not only destroyed one of the leading European cities of the time, but also had a lasting effect on the world at large.

Over the Edge of the World: Magellan's Terrifying Circumnavigation of the Globe (Laurence Bergreen, 2003). Magellan's fascinating tale of circumnavigating the globe is told through firsthand accounts.

Portugal: A Companion History (José Hermano Saraiva, 1997). This easily digestible primer on Portugal is accompanied by maps and illustrations.

The Portuguese: A Modern History (Barry Hatton, 2011). Hatton combines information on the country's history, landscape, and culture with anecdotes from his own experience living in Portugal.

The Portuguese Empire, 1415-1808: A World on the Move (A.J.R. Russell-Wood, 1998). Russell-Wood explores the rise and fall of the Portuguese empire.

Prince Henry the Navigator: A Life (Peter Russell, 2000). This biography reveals the man who helped set in motion the Age of Discovery.

Unknown Seas: How Vasco da Gama Opened the East (Ronald Watkins, 2005). Reconstructing journeys from captain's logs, this book explores the expansion of Portuguese trade routes.

Fiction

Baltasar and Blimunda (José Saramago, 1998). Saramago's love story offers a surrealistic reflection on life in 18th-century Portugal.

The Crime of Father Amaro (Jose Maria Eça De Queirós, 1875). Set in a provincial Portuguese town, this book by the great 19th-century Portuguese novelist highlights the dangers of fanaticism.

Distant Music (Lee Langley, 2003). Catholic Esperança and Jewish Emmanuel have an affair that lasts through six centuries and multiple incarnations; the book also delves into Portugal's maritime empire, Sephardic Jews, and Portuguese immigrants in London.

The Last Kabbalist of Lisbon (Richard Zimler, 1996). The author illuminates the persecution of the Jews in Portugal in the early 1500s.

The Lusiads (Luís de Camões, 1572). Considered a national treasure, Camões' great epic poems of the Renaissance immortalize Portugal's voyages of discovery.

Night Train to Lisbon (Pascal Mercier, 2004). Mercier's international bestseller, turned 2013 film, follows the travels of a Swiss professor as he explores the life of a Portuguese doctor during Salazar's dictatorship.

Pereira Declares: A Testimony (Antonio Tabucchi, 1997). Set in Portugal in 1938 during Salazar's fascist government, *Pereira Declares* is the story of the moral resurrection of a newspaper's cautious editor.

A Small Death in Lisbon (Robert Wilson, 2002). In this award-winning thriller, a contemporary police procedural is woven with an espionage story set during World War II, with Portugal's 20th-century history as a backdrop.

Film and TV

Amália (2008). This film captures the life of Portugal's beloved fado singer, Amália Rodrigues, who rose from poverty to international fame. (If the film is hard to find, listen to a YouTube clip of her lovely singing.)

The Art of Amália (2000). Interviews with the diva are highlighted in this documentary.

Capitães de Abril (2000). The story of the 1974 coup that overthrew the right-wing Portuguese dictatorship is told from the perspective of two young army captains.

Letters from Fontainhas (2010). This trio of short films follows three troubled lives in Lisbon.

Pereira Declares (1996). Marcello Mastroianni plays the namesake in this film inspired by the Tabucchi novel mentioned earlier.

The Strange Case of Angelica (2010). Manoel de Oliveira's film about a photographer haunted by a deceased bride is set against the landscape of the Douro Valley.

APPENDIX

Contents

Useful Contacts

Emergency Needs
Emergency: Tel. 112

Embassies
US Embassy: Tel. 217-273-300, passport services available Mon-Fri 8:00-17:00 (Avenida das Forças Armadas, Lisbon, http://portugal.usembassy.gov)
Canadian Embassy: Tel. 213-164-600, passport services available Mon-Thu 8:30-12:30 & 13:00-17:15, Fri 8:30-13:00 (Avenida da Liberdade 198-200, third floor, Lisbon, www.canadainternational.gc.ca/portugal)

Directory Assistance
Local Directory Assistance: Tel. 118
International Directory Assistance: Tel. 177

Holidays and Festivals

This list includes selected festivals in major cities, plus national holidays observed throughout Portugal. Many sights and banks close on national holidays—keep this in mind when planning your itinerary. Before planning a trip around a festival, verify its dates by checking the festival's website or TI sites (www.visitportugal.com).

Jan 1	New Year's Day
Mardi Gras Carnival	Feb 17 in 2015, Feb 9 in 2016
Holy Week	Week before Easter
Easter	April 5 in 2015, March 27 in 2016
Mid-April	Lisbon Fish & Flavors (*Peixe em Lisboa*, gourmet seafood festival)
April 25	Liberty Day (parades, fireworks, closures)
May 1	Labor Day (closures)
Early-mid May	Queima das Fitas (Burning of Ribbons), Coimbra (end-of-school-year festival)
May 13	Pilgrimage to Fátima
June 10	Portuguese National Day (Camões Day, closures)
June 13	St. Anthony's Day, Lisbon; Pilgrimage to Fátima
June 24	St. João Day, Porto
June 29	St. Peter's Day, Lisbon
June (last 3 weeks)	Festas de Lisboa, Lisbon
Late June-early July	Festival de Sintra (www.festivaldesintra.pt)
July 13	Pilgrimage to Fátima
Aug 13	Pilgrimage to Fátima
Aug 15	Assumption (religious festival, closures)
Aug 19	Pilgrimage to Fátima
Sept 13	Pilgrimage to Fátima
Mid-Sept	Our Lady of Nazaré Festival
Oct 13	Pilgrimage to Fátima
Dec 8	Feast of the Immaculate Conception (closures)
Dec 25	Christmas
Dec 31	New Year's Eve

APPENDIX

Pronunciation of Portuguese Place Names

Alcobaça	ahl-koh-BAH-sah
Batalha	bah-TAHL-yah
Cabo da Roca	KAH-boo dah ROH-kah
Cape Sagres	KAH-peh SAH-gresh
Cascais	kahsh-KAH-eesh
Coimbra	koh-EEM-brah
Douro	DOH-roo
Évora	EH-voh-rah
Fátima	FAH-tee-mah
Lagos	LAH-goosh
Lisboa	leezh-BOH-ah
Nazaré	nah-zah-RAY
Óbidos	OH-bee-doosh
Peso da Régua	PAY-zoo dah RAY-gwah
Pinhão	PEEN-yow
Porto	POR-too
Salema	sah-LAY-mah
Sintra	SEEN-trah
Sítio	SEE-tee-oo
Tavira	tah-VEE-rah

Conversions and Climate

NUMBERS AND STUMBLERS

- Some Europeans write a few of their numbers differently than we do. 1 = 1, 4 = 4, 7 = 7.
- In Europe, dates appear as day/month/year, so Christmas 2016 is 25/12/16.
- Commas are decimal points and decimals commas. A dollar and a half is 1,50, and there are 5.280 feet in a mile.
- When counting with fingers, start with your thumb. If you hold up your first finger to request one item, you'll probably get two.
- What Americans call the second floor of a building is the first floor in Europe.

- On escalators and moving sidewalks, Europeans keep the left "lane" open for passing. Keep to the right.

METRIC CONVERSIONS

A kilogram is 2.2 pounds, and l liter is about a quart, or almost four to a gallon. A kilometer is six-tenths of a mile. I figure kilometers to miles by cutting them in half and adding back 10 percent of the original (120 km: 60 + 12 = 72 miles, 300 km: 150 + 30 = 180 miles).

1 foot = 0.3 meter	1 square yard = 0.8 square meter
1 yard = 0.9 meter	1 square mile = 2.6 square kilometers
1 mile = 1.6 kilometers	1 ounce = 28 grams
1 centimeter = 0.4 inch	1 quart = 0.95 liter
1 meter = 39.4 inches	1 kilogram = 2.2 pounds
1 kilometer = 0.62 mile	32°F = 0°C

CLOTHING SIZES

When shopping for clothing, use these US-to-European comparisons as general guidelines (but note that no conversion is perfect).
- Women's dresses and blouses: Add 30
  (US size 10 = European size 40)
- Men's suits and jackets: Add 10
  (US size 40 regular = European size 50)
- Men's shirts: Multiply by 2 and add about 8
  (US size 15 collar = European size 38)
- Women's shoes: Add about 30
  (US size 8 = European size 38-39)
- Men's shoes: Add 32-34
  (US size 9 = European size 41; US size 11 = European size 45)

PORTUGAL'S CLIMATE

First line, average daily high; second line, average daily low; third line, average days without rain. For more detailed weather statistics for destinations in this book (as well as the rest of the world), check www.wunderground.com.

	J	F	M	A	M	J	J	A	S	O	N	D
Lisbon												
	57°	59°	63°	67°	71°	77°	81°	82°	79°	72°	63°	58°
	46°	47°	50°	53°	55°	60°	63°	63°	62°	58°	52°	47°
	16	16	17	20	21	25	29	29	24	22	17	16
Faro (Algarve)												
	60°	61°	64°	67°	71°	77°	83°	83°	78°	72°	66°	61°
	48°	49°	52°	55°	58°	64°	67°	68°	65°	60°	55°	50°
	22	21	21	24	27	29	31	31	29	25	22	22

FAHRENHEIT AND CELSIUS CONVERSION

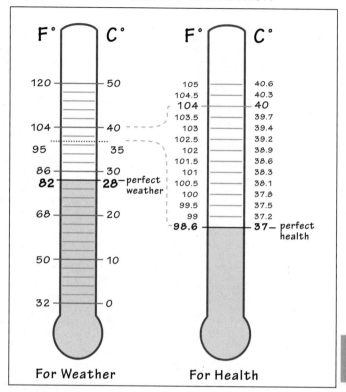

For Weather   For Health

Portugal takes its temperature using the Celsius scale, while we opt for Fahrenheit. For a rough conversion from Celsius to Fahrenheit, double the number and add 30. For weather, remember that 28°C is 82°F— perfect. For health, 37°C is just right. At a launderette, 30°C is cold, 40°C is warm (usually the default setting), 60°C is hot, and 95°C is boiling.

Packing Checklist

Whether you're traveling for five days or five weeks, you won't need more than this. Pack light to enjoy the sweet freedom of true mobility.

Clothing

- ❑ 5 shirts: long- & short-sleeve
- ❑ 2 pairs pants or skirt
- ❑ 1 pair shorts or capris
- ❑ 5 pairs underwear & socks
- ❑ 1 pair walking shoes
- ❑ Sweater or fleece top
- ❑ Rainproof jacket with hood
- ❑ Tie or scarf
- ❑ Swimsuit
- ❑ Sleepwear

Money

- ❑ Debit card
- ❑ Credit card(s)
- ❑ Hard cash ($20 bills)
- ❑ Money belt or neck wallet

Documents & Travel Info

- ❑ Passport
- ❑ Airline reservations
- ❑ Rail pass/train reservations
- ❑ Car-rental voucher
- ❑ Driver's license
- ❑ Student ID, hostel card, etc.
- ❑ Photocopies of all the above
- ❑ Hotel confirmations
- ❑ Insurance details
- ❑ Guidebooks & maps
- ❑ Notepad & pen
- ❑ Journal

Toiletries Kit

- ❑ Toiletries
- ❑ Medicines & vitamins
- ❑ First-aid kit
- ❑ Glasses/contacts/sunglasses (with prescriptions)
- ❑ Earplugs
- ❑ Packet of tissues (for WC)

Miscellaneous

- ❑ Daypack
- ❑ Sealable plastic baggies
- ❑ Laundry soap
- ❑ Spot remover
- ❑ Clothesline
- ❑ Sewing kit
- ❑ Travel alarm/watch

Electronics

- ❑ Smartphone or mobile phone
- ❑ Camera & related gear
- ❑ Tablet/ereader/media player
- ❑ Laptop & flash drive
- ❑ Earbuds or headphones
- ❑ Chargers
- ❑ Plug adapters

Optional Extras

- ❑ Flipflops or slippers
- ❑ Mini-umbrella or poncho
- ❑ Travel hairdryer
- ❑ Belt
- ❑ Hat (for sun or cold)
- ❑ Picnic supplies
- ❑ Water bottle
- ❑ Fold-up tote bag
- ❑ Small flashlight
- ❑ Small binoculars
- ❑ Insect repellent
- ❑ Small towel or washcloth
- ❑ Inflatable pillow
- ❑ Some duct tape (for repairs)
- ❑ Tiny lock
- ❑ Address list (to mail postcards)
- ❑ Postcards/photos from home
- ❑ Extra passport photos
- ❑ Good book

Portuguese Survival Phrases

In the phonetics, nasalized vowels are indicated by an underlined **n** or **w**. As you say the vowel, let its sound come through your nose as well as your mouth.

English	Portuguese	Pronunciation
Good day.	*Bom dia.*	boh<u>n</u> **dee**-ah
Do you speak English?	*Fala inglês?*	**fah**-lah een-**glaysh**
Yes. / No.	*Sim. / Não.*	seeng / no<u>w</u>
I (don't) understand.	*(Não) compreendo.*	(no<u>w</u>) koh<u>n</u>-pree-**ayn**-doo
Please.	*Por favor.*	poor fah-**vor**
Thank you. (said by male)	*Obrigado.*	oo-bree-**gah**-doo
Thank you. (said by female)	*Obrigada.*	oo-bree-**gah**-dah
I'm sorry.	*Desculpe.*	dish-**kool**-peh
Excuse me (to pass).	*Com licença.*	koh<u>n</u> li-**sehn**-sah
(No) problem.	*(Não) há problema.*	(no<u>w</u>) ah proo-**blay**-mah
Good.	*Bom.*	boh<u>n</u>
Goodbye.	*Adeus. / Ciao.*	ah-**deh**-oosh / chow
one / two	*um / dois*	oo<u>n</u> / doysh
three / four	*três / quatro*	traysh / **kwah**-troo
five / six	*cinco / seis*	**seeng**-koo / saysh
seven / eight	*sete / oito*	**seh**-teh / **oy**-too
nine / ten	*nove / dez*	**naw**-veh / dehsh
How much is it?	*Quanto é?*	**kwahn**-too eh
Write it?	*Escreva?*	ish-**kray**-vah
Is it free?	*È gratis?*	eh **grah**-teesh
Is it included?	*Está incluido?*	ish-**tah** een-kloo-**ee**-doo
Where can I find / buy...?	*Onde posso encontrar / comprar...?*	**ohn**-deh **paw**-soo ayn-kohn-**trar** / kohn-**prar**
I'd like / We'd like...	*Gostaria / Gostaríamos...*	goosh-tah-**ree**-ah / goosh-tah-**ree**-ah-moosh
...a room.	*...um quarto.*	oo<u>n</u> **kwar**-too
...a ticket to ___.	*...um bilhete para ___.*	oo<u>n</u> beel-**yeh**-teh **pah**-rah ___
Is it possible?	*È possível?*	eh poo-**see**-vehl
Where is...?	*Onde é que é...?*	**ohn**-deh eh keh eh
...the train station	*...a estação de comboio*	ah ish-tah-**sow** deh kohn-**boy**-yoo
...the bus station	*...a terminal de autocarros*	ah tehr-mee-**nahl** deh ow-too-**kah**-roosh
...the tourist information office	*...a posto de turismo*	ah **poh**-stoo deh too-**reez**-moo
...the toilet	*...a casa de banho*	ah **kah**-zah deh **bahn**-yoo
men	*homens*	**aw**-mayn<u>sh</u>
women	*mulheres*	mool-**yeh**-rish
left / right	*esquerda / direita*	ish-**kehr**-dah / dee-**ray**-tah
straight	*em frente*	ay<u>n</u> **frayn**-teh
What time does this open / close?	*As que horas é que abre / fecha?*	ahsh keh **aw**-rahsh eh keh **ah**-breh / **feh**-shah
At what time?	*As que horas?*	ahsh keh **aw**-rahsh
Just a moment.	*Um momento.*	oo<u>n</u> moo-**mayn**-too
now / soon / later	*agora / em breve / mais tarde*	ah-**goh**-rah / ay<u>n</u> **bray**-veh / maish **tar**-deh
today / tomorrow	*hoje / amanhã*	**oh**-zheh / ah-ming-**yah**

In the Restaurant

English	Portuguese	Pronunciation
I'd like / We'd like...	Gostaria / Gostaríamos...	goosh-tah-**ree**-ah / goosh-tah-**ree**-ah-moosh
...to reserve...	...de reservar...	deh reh-zehr-**var**
...a table for one. / two.	...uma mesa para uma. / duas.	**oo**-mah **may**-zah **pah**-rah **oo**-mah / **doo**-ahsh
Non-smoking.	Não fumar.	no<u>w</u> foo-**mar**
Is this table free?	Esta mesa está livre?	**ehsh**-tah **meh**-zah ish-**tah** lee-vreh
The menu (in English), please.	A ementa (em inglês), por favor.	ah eh-**mayn**-tah (ay<u>n</u> een-**glaysh**) poor fah-vor
service (not) included	serviço (não) incluído	sehr-**vee**-soo (no<u>w</u>) een-kloo-ee-doo
cover charge	coberto	koh-**behr**-too
to go	para fora	**pah**-rah **foh**-rah
with / without	com / sem	koh<u>n</u> / say<u>n</u>
and / or	e / ou	ee / oh
specialty of the house	especialidade da casa	ish-peh-see-ah-lee-**dah**-deh dah **kah**-zah
half portion	meia dose	**may**-ah **doh**-zeh
daily special	prato do dia	**prah**-too doo **dee**-ah
tourist menu	ementa turística	eh-**mayn**-tah too-**reesh**-tee-kah
appetizers	entradas	ay<u>n</u>-**trah**-dahsh
bread / cheese	pão / queijo	pow / **kay**-zhoo
sandwich	sandes	**sahn**-desh
soup / salad	sopa / salada	**soh**-pah / sah-**lah**-dah
meat	carne	**kar**-neh
poultry	aves	**ah**-vish
fish / seafood	peixe / marisco	**pay**-shee / mah-**reesh**-koo
fruit	fruta	**froo**-tah
vegetables	legumes	lay-**goo**-mish
dessert	sobremesa	soo-breh-**may**-zah
tap water	água da torneira	**ah**-gwah dah tor-**nay**-rah
mineral water	água mineral	**ah**-gwah mee-neh-**rahl**
milk	leite	**lay**-teh
(orange) juice	sumo (de laranja)	**soo**-moo (deh lah-**rahn**-zhah)
coffee / tea	café / chá	kah-**feh** / shah
wine	vinho	**veen**-yoo
red / white	tinto / branco	**teen**-too / **brang**-koo
glass / bottle	copo / garrafa	**koh**-poo / gah-**rah**-fah
beer	cerveja	sehr-**vay**-zhah
Cheers!	Saúde!	sah-**oo**-deh
More. / Another.	Mais. / Outro.	maish / **oh**-troo
The same.	O mesmo.	oo **mehsh**-moo
The bill, please.	A conta, por favor.	ah-**kohn**-tah poor fah-**vor**
tip	gorjeta	gor-**zheh**-tah
Delicious!	Delicioso!	deh-lee-see-**oh**-zoo

For many more pages of survival phrases for your trip to Portugal, check out *Rick Steves' Portuguese Phrase Book & Dictionary*.

INDEX

MAP INDEX

Our website enhances this book and turns

Explore Europe

At ricksteves.com you can browse through thousands of articles, videos, photos and radio interviews, plus find a wealth of money-saving travel tips for planning your dream trip. And with our mobile-friendly website, you can easily access all this great travel information anywhere you go.

TV Shows

Preview the places you'll visit by watching entire half-hour episodes of Rick Steves' Europe (choose from all 100 shows) on-demand, for free.

ricksteves.com

your travel dreams into affordable reality

Radio Interviews

Enjoy ready access to Rick's vast library of radio interviews covering travel

tips and cultural insights that relate specifically to your Europe travel plans.

Travel Forums

Learn, ask, share! Our online community of savvy travelers is a great resource

for first-time travelers to Europe, as well as seasoned pros. You'll find forums on each country, plus travel tips and restaurant/hotel reviews. You can even ask one of our well-traveled staff to chime in with an opinion.

Travel News

Subscribe to our free Travel News e-newsletter, and get monthly updates from Rick on what's happening in Europe.

Gear up for your next adventure at rickcsteves.com

Light Luggage

Pack light and right with Rick Steves' affordable, custom-designed rolling carry-on bags, backpacks, day packs and shoulder bags.

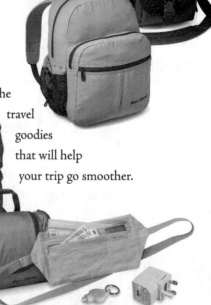

Accessories

From packing cubes to moneybelts and beyond, Rick has personally selected the travel goodies that will help your trip go smoother.

Experience maximum Europe

Save time and energy

This guidebook is your independent-travel toolkit. But for all it delivers, it's still up to you to devote the time and energy it takes to manage the preparation and logistics that are essential for a happy trip. If that's a hassle, there's a solution.

Rick Steves Tours

A Rick Steves tour takes you to Europe's most interesting places with great

with minimum stress

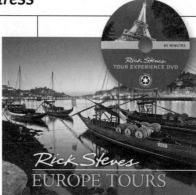

guides and small groups of 28 or less. We follow Rick's favorite itineraries, ride in comfy buses, stay in family-run hotels, and bring you intimately close to the Europe you've traveled so far to see. Most importantly, we take away the logistical headaches so you can focus on the fun.

customers—along with us on 40 different itineraries, from Ireland to Italy to Istanbul. Is a Rick Steves tour the right fit for your travel dreams? Find out at ricksteves.com, where you can also get Rick's latest tour catalog and free Tour Experience DVD.

Join the fun

This year we'll take 18,000 free-spirited travelers— nearly half of them repeat

Europe is best experienced with happy travel partners. We hope you can join us.

See our itineraries at ricksteves.com

Nearly all Rick Steves guides are available as ebooks. Check with your favorite bookseller.

Rick Steves guidebooks are published by Avalon Travel, an imprint of Perseus Books, a Hachette Book Group company.

Maximize your travel skills with a good guidebook.

RickSteves.com 🅕 🅣 @RickSteves

Rick Steves books are available at bookstores
and through online booksellers.

Credits

RESEARCHER

To help update this book, Rick relied on...

Robert Wright

Raised in Memphis, Robert eventually made his home even farther south...in Argentina. He funded his first dream trip to Europe by selling his entire *Star Wars* collection—proof that where there's a will, there's a way. Robert fell in love with Spain and Portugal and has returned every year since. Besides getting a serious food and wine fix, he enjoys exploring architecture and digging into the region's complex, intertwined history.

CONTRIBUTOR
Gene Openshaw

Gene is the co-author of a dozen Rick Steves books. For this book, he wrote material on Europe's art, history, and contemporary culture. When not traveling, Gene enjoys composing music, recovering from his 1973 trip to Europe with Rick, and living everyday life with his daughter.

Acknowledgments

Thanks to Cameron Hewitt for writing the original versions of the Porto and Douro Valley chapters.

Avalon Travel
An imprint of Perseus Books
A Hachette Book Group company
1700 Fourth Street
Berkeley, CA 94710

Text © 2015 by Rick Steves.
Maps © 2015 by Rick Steves' Europe.
Printed in Canada by Friesens. Fourth printing April 2017.

For the latest on Rick Steves' lectures, guidebooks, tours, public radio show, and public
television series, contact Rick Steves' Europe, 130 Fourth Avenue North, Edmonds,
WA 98020, tel. 425/771-8303, www.ricksteves.com, rick@ricksteves.com.

ISBN 978-1-63121-053-2
ISSN 1551-837X

Rick Steves' Europe

Managing Editor: Risa Laib
Editorial & Production Manager: Jennifer Madison Davis
Editors: Glenn Eriksen, Tom Griffin, Cameron Hewitt, Suzanne Kotz, Cathy Lu,
    Carrie Shepherd
Editorial & Production Assistant: Jessica Shaw
Editorial Interns: Stacie Larsen, Mallory Presho-Dunne
Researcher: Robert Wright
Maps & Graphics: David C. Hoerlein, Sandra Hundacker, Lauren Mills, Mary Rostad

Avalon Travel

Senior Editor and Series Manager: Madhu Prasher
Editor: Jamie Andrade
Associate Editor: Maggie Ryan
Copy Editor: Judith Brown
Proofreader: Kelly Lydick
Indexer: Stephen Callahan
Production & Typesetting: Tabitha Lahr, Rue Flaherty
Cover Design: Kimberly Glyder Design
Maps & Graphics: Kat Bennett, Mike Morgenfeld

Photo Credits

Front Cover: The crystal waters of Praia Dona Ana, Lagos © Juampiter/Getty Images
Title Page: Porto © Dominic Bonuccelli
Chapter Openers: p. 1, Salema; p. 17, View from Largo Santa Luzia, Lisbon; p. 121,
    National Palace, Sintra; p. 137, Algarve Beach; p. 179, Roman Temple, Évora; p. 202,
    View of Nazaré from Sítio; p. 240, Coimbra Street Scene; p. 274, Ponte Dom Luís I;
    p. 318, Douro Valley View; p. 336, Monuments to the Discoveries, Lisbon
Additional Photography: Dominic Bonuccelli, Rich Earl, Cameron Hewitt, David C.
    Hoerlein, Carol Ries, Jennifer Schutte, Robyn Stencil, Rick Steves, Ashley Sytsma,
    Robert Wright, Reid Coen, Wikimedia Commons—PD-Art/PD-US (photos are
    used by permission and are the property of the original copyright owners)

ABOUT THE AUTHOR

RICK STEVES

Since 1973, Rick has spent about four months a year exploring Europe. His mission: to empower Americans to have European trips that are fun, affordable, and culturally broadening. Rick produces a best-selling guidebook series, a public television series, and a public radio show, and organizes small-group tours that take over 20,000 travelers to Europe annually. He does all of this with the help of a hardworking, well-traveled staff of 100 at Rick Steves' Europe in Edmonds, Washington, near Seattle. When not on the road, Rick is active in his church and with advocacy groups focused on economic justice, drug policy reform, and ending hunger. To recharge, Rick plays piano, relaxes at his family cabin in the Cascade Mountains, and spends time with his partner Trish, son Andy, and daughter Jackie. Find out more about Rick at www.ricksteves.com and on Facebook.

JIMAO - 8:00
Nº12 Praca da Liberia